Fly-Fishing for Redfish

CHICO FERNÁNDEZ

STACKPOLE
BOOKS

Dedication

To my mom, Angela, who took the first photo of me with a redfish,
and who babied me through her 102 years.
And to my loving wife of 47 years, Marilyn, my soul mate,
from whom I'm still learning so much.

Published by
STACKPOLE BOOKS
5067 Ritter Road
Mechanicsburg, PA 17055
www.stackpolebooks.com

Printed in the United States of America

10 9 8 7 6 5 4 3 2 1

First edition

Cover design by Caroline A. Stover
Photos by the author except where noted

Library of Congress Cataloging-in-Publication Data

Fernández, Chico.
Fly-fishing for redfish / Chico Fernández.
pages cm
Includes bibliographical references and index.
ISBN 978-0-8117-1623-9
1. Red drum fishing. 2. Fly fishing. I. Title.
SH691.C5F47 2015
799.12'4—dc23
2015024108

Contents

Foreword

Fifty-five years ago, I walked into a small fishing tackle shop in south Dade County, Florida. Light-tackle anglers gathered there regularly, most known to one another. I was greeted by the owner and others in the shop and was immediately assimilated into the conversation and the feeling of being with my tribe. Presently, a young man, seeming about my age, passed through the door; no one knew him. He struck up a conversation with the owner, and before long, I was called over to meet the new guy.

As it turned out, though he had just arrived from Cuba, we lived near one another, and we were about the same age. I was captivated by his Cuban accent, although I had failed Spanish in school a number of times. Mostly, as we spoke, I was impressed with the fact that, in Cuba, he had lived in a parallel light-tackle universe: we used the same rods, reels, and lures, and we shared the same philosophy about light-tackle angling. Most amazing of all . . . he was a fly fisher, and I was struggling in that arena myself!

Jesus M. "Chico" Fernández and I began a friendship that day that has lasted, uninterrupted, through all these years. Dating girls, college, real jobs, taking risks, sickness and health, marriage to flight attendants (different ones), and leaving real jobs for the life that called to us both. Through it all, angling has been the glue that held our lives together. That meeting, fifty-five years ago, spawned a friendship that has given way to a brotherhood that is one of the treasures of my life.

"Don Chico," as I call him these days, has always been a perfectionist and a super achiever. He has excelled as a table tennis player, pistol marksman, archer, tennis player, jazz historian, outdoor writer, photographer, cook, canoeist, fly caster, inventor and tier of marvelous flies, and scholar of great literature . . . so it comes as no great surprise that he went and wrote the quintessential book on bonefish and bonefishing in 2004—*Fly-Fishing for Bonefish*. Less a surprise is that in 2015 he has followed up with this masterpiece on redfish and redfishing.

As I read through the manuscript, at his insistence, it was as though I were hearing his voice down through five decades, speaking to me through his writing, the same words that he has shared with me over time. Words, thoughts, science, and wonderful remembrances of a lifetime squinting into the summer and winter sun, looking for redfish tails breaking the greasy glare of shallow water, somewhere in the world of redfish.

Fly-Fishing for Redfish will allow you to eavesdrop on all Chico has shared with me as we came of age together in South Florida. I shall ever see him on the bow of my small skiff . . . silhouetted against the westering sun . . . shooting an impossibly tight 7-weight loop at the last redfish of the day.

Flip Pallot

Preface

The history of fly fishing for redfish goes back, as far as I could find, to the 1800s. In the book *Camping and Cruising in Florida* (1884), by Dr. James A. Henshall, the author mentions that in 1878, while fly-fishing Fort Capron, around the area of Fort Pierce, Florida, he hooked and landed a 5-pound redfish. He also writes about landing jacks to 5 pounds, seatrout to 10 pounds, bluefish to 5 pounds, snook to 6 pounds, ladyfish to 2 pounds, and tarpon to 10 pounds. Anyway, the above is the earliest capture of a redfish on a fly that I could find.

Dr. Henshall's tackle consisted of a 12-foot, 12-ounce ash and lancewood fly rod, which he found rather light for the purpose. He tied his flies on 4/0 and 6/0 hooks using what he called "gay plumaged birds." One fly pattern was tied with a top wing of white egret and lower wing of roseate spoonbill. Another used white and pink ibis. There were many others.

A few years later, in a letter to famous fly tier Mary Orvis Marbury, Dr. George Trowbridge from New York mentioned a fly he was using to fish in Florida, which he called the Cracker, partly because it was "a crackin' good fly," but mostly after the nickname of the Florida natives, "crackers." He said the fly was "too gay and complicated to attempt to describe with clearness." But he added that it was "by far the most killing for Florida fishing that has yet to be tested." Talk about confidence in a fly!

He then tells that while fishing Homosassa River on February 2, 1885, he landed a 6-pound "channel bass" (an old name for redfish) on his homemade fly. He then continued to use the fly and make modifications. By February 1886, having also taken redfish in Mosquito Lagoon, he stopped making changes on the Cracker, feeling it was the right design.

In the next few years, always using the Cracker, Dr. Trowbridge also took jacks, seatrout, bluefish, Spanish mackerel, grouper, mangrove snapper, and even one sheepshead.

Later, he used it to take more tarpon and "channel bass" fishing in the Sarasota area. And on February 23, 1887, he caught a 17-pound redfish on the fly—his biggest so far. But in 1888 he took redfish to 23 pounds 12 ounces in Sarasota, Florida. And later he took a bigger red of 24 pounds 5 ounces.

Dr. Trowbridge's tackle was mostly a light trout rod of 8½ ounces, which in those days was a very light rod indeed. However, several other anglers were also fly-fishing in Florida, and there are accounts of anglers taking seatrout in Corpus Christi, Texas, around the 1870s, so I suspect reds were caught on a fly rod much earlier.

My first encounter with a redfish was during a long stay with my family in Miami in 1952. At that time, we

The Cracker, tied by Robert Buck and invented by Dr. George Trowbridge, who used it to fish for redfish.

resided on a large home by the water, in one of the islands in Miami Beach. My father and mother, my brother Mauro, a couple of aunts and uncles, and I were all staying in this big house. It was quite a party around that house as I remember, especially at breakfast and dinner times.

I remember distinctly that once we were settled in our new house, it wasn't long before my dad, being a fisherman at heart, set up a trip to Everglades City to fish a few days with a well-known guide. Mom, Dad, and I were the only ones interested in going, so it was just the three of us.

We stayed at the Rod and Gun Club, now a historical site, located along the Barron River, right against the Everglades National Park. I remember it being rural, with lots of trees and mangrove shorelines. I was happy there.

The captain's boat, a cabin cruiser, left right out of the Rod and Gun Club, so it was very convenient. We spent several days fishing, going to a different location each day. But one thing was for sure: by the end of first day I was in love with the Everglades, the birds, the animals, and, of course, the fishing. It was there, on the second or third day, that after landing several seatrout and small jacks, that had not fought much, I hooked something solid, that felt heavy against the bent rod.

Now this was a long time ago, but I remember during the fight that the fish would break water, just enough to leave foam all over the surface. I was real excited, especially when the guide, who already knew I wanted to catch a redfish, confirmed that I had a nice red on.

Finally, when the fish was tired enough, the guide reached out for a large net, put it in the water, and had me bring the red to the net. The catch must have been very meaningful because after more than sixty years, my memory of that catch is vivid. Anyway, once I composed myself, I held the redfish in one hand and the bait casting outfit and spoon I was using on the other hand, and posed for my mom's trusty Rolleiflex. The date written on the back of the old photograph is July 15, 1952.

Now let's go back to the present for a moment. While I was writing the above, I decided to send my friend Flip Pallot an email with the old photo of my first red and a brief history of what happened. To my surprise, Flip emailed me back, and told me that he and his dad were also fishing that summer out of the same cabin cruiser and captain, and that he knew the captain well. He said, "Chico, you were fishing with none other than the famous Totch Brown, a native of the Everglades, author, filmmaker, and much more." I couldn't believe the coincidence. I just wish I'd met Flip then.

Anyway, a few months later, my dad and I went back to Cuba. I continued my fishing there, later adding fly fishing to my arsenal of tackle around 1956. But of course, Cuba is too far south to hold redfish, or seatrout, so I was fly-fishing then for bonefish, snook, and tarpon in the salt, and black bass and panfish in the many ponds and rivers around the island. So I didn't have a chance to fish for redfish again for many years.

In 1959, unexpectedly, my family came to Miami to live—permanently as it turned out. My parents didn't want to come, my brother was too young to care, but I . . . well . . . I was thinking of the Everglades. Indeed, I had managed to bring with me most of my tackle: spinning and bait casting equipment, and my prized possession at the time, an Orvis Battenkill 9½ foot bamboo fly rod for an 8-weight line, more or less. It's a rod I still own and often cast, just for fun and to remind me that the basics never change.

Within a week of moving to Miami, I met Bill Curtis at the local tackle shop, The Tackle Box. He wasn't a famous bonefish captain yet, but he fly-fished and that was all I needed to know. And only a few weeks later, also in The Tackle Box, I met Flip Pallot (later of *Walker's Cay Chronicles* fame), Norman Duncan (who invented the Duncan Loop and created the Outside Fly), and John Emery (who became one of the great fly-fishing guides in South Florida).

The author's first redfish, caught in the Everglades in 1952.
ANGELA FERNÁNDEZ

Bill was older than the rest of us, so he had a job and a family, but the rest of us were dating a lot, sometimes studying, but mainly fishing. We were always together, like the Four Musketeers.

Around 1960 or so, I joined the Tropical Anglers Club, which was mainly a light-tackle club, but which had a fly-fishing division. And for a while, I could win the fly division easy, but soon another angler started to give me competition, Al Pflueger Jr. We became friends and soon started to fish the Everglades, mostly using Al's new 13-foot Boston Whaler with a 20-horsepower engine. For a push pole, we used a fiberglass pole normally used to handle hot or live wires by workers of Florida Power & Light. They were heavy, about five to seven pounds or so, but we were lucky: we didn't know the difference.

It was while poling those flats in Flamingo, in a place that's very popular today, Snake Bight, that I caught my first redfish on a fly. It was great fun, exciting but easy. Al and I would take dozens of reds sight-casting in a decent day, and on a good day, we'd catch more.

Later, Norman had a skiff modified to pole the flats, and soon the Four Musketeers were fishing the flats all over South Florida. It's a wonder we had time to study.

We used a variety of big flies, much bigger than we use today, for reds, snook, and other game in the flats. But one of the flies we used most was Pflueger's Redfish Fly, which consisted of white bucktail with a big stripe of tinsel on each side and a big red hackle up front, often on a 3/0 hook and over 4 inches long. Norman also had a favorite fly he tied which consisted of a white chenille body, yellow bucktail for wings with gold tinsel, and a red hackle, which he eventually tied inverted to make it more weedless. And I eventually started to tie my Seaducer with tinsel on each side, in white and red, yellow and red, and the old popular combination—white, yellow, and grizzly mix—which the old timers call the shrimp color. And I used wire weedguard when needed. Still do.

But fly patterns weren't as important then as they are today. In those days, reds seemed to take basically all the flies we offered them. You'd think they came in the flats looking for flies.

We didn't have much money then, so when we fished areas a few hours from Miami, the Four Musketeers would rough it. After all, we were young and thought we were bulletproof. So when fishing the beaches at Marco for a few days to sight-cast to snook and reds along the beach at dawn, we would camp right on the beach.

Then, camping for us generally meant sleeping on the sand, which by the way, is as hard as concrete to sleep on. As if the tough accommodations were not enough, we were not alone. Often swarms of mosquitos or no-see-ums flew around us, while other unwanted guests crawled around us.

On the early trips, the evening's menu often consisted of peanut butter and grape jelly on white bread, and since the bait knife was the easiest to get to, the sandwich had a faint taste of mullet. But this was totally uncivilized, so I eventually rebelled and started bringing large submarine or Cuban sandwiches that were precut in three sections. No knife needed.

I still have great memories of sipping iced tea at the beach after the evening meal, while seated on the blanket that would be my bed that night, and slowly looking around, trying to absorb it all.

As my eyes adjusted to the low light, I could see out for miles into the water or look up and see millions of stars.

There wouldn't be another soul in the beach in those days, and my thoughts and dreams generally turned to what I anticipated the next day's fishing would be. Those were the days, my friends, those were the days. But as more anglers became aware of inshore and flats fishing, more skiffs, kayaks, canoes, and paddleboards have come into the flats. And today there is more pressure on Mr. Redfish than there has ever been.

Fortunately, the redfish's range is huge, so fishing pressure is well spread out in most places. And any angler today who is willing to pole slowly and cover ground is likely to find a red—maybe lots of reds.

This book will help you catch reds and other gamefish that also come into brackish water shallows by teaching you about the redfish's behavior, its habitat, and the tackle you need and how to use it. But before we go into what this redfish book is about, there is someone else who frequently comes into the redfish's flats that I feel you should get to know: the fishing guide. When you hire a good fishing guide, a dedicated one, you'll share a skiff with someone who has accumulated a huge wealth of knowledge. You'll not only learn about the red's ways and the environment it lives in, but you'll also learn the proper way to release fish, how to run a skiff in shallow water, boat safety, and more. And if you bring your son or daughter, imagine what a great education and influence this can have in their lives. So when fishing with a guide, take advantage of the opportunity, ask questions, and learn from the day's experience.

I have great respect for good fishing guides. As a matter of fact, many of my old friends are guides, as you'll see when you read this book.

This book is about fly-fishing for a wonderful gamefish, *Sciaenops ocellatus*, better known by its many common names: redfish, red drum, channel bass, and others. The red is a truly remarkable gamefish for the fly fisherman, yet in many fly-fishing circles, they do not get the credit they deserve. After all, people often say that reds don't jump like a tarpon or make the blistering long runs of a bonefish. They call redfish dumb and dull. But you'll soon learn this isn't true. As a matter of fact, after a lifetime of fly-fishing for them, I've come to the conclusion that they are one of the most exciting fish you can pursue with a fly rod and that they're often difficult to fool, especially in shallow water. I'm hooked on reds.

If you still have doubts, just look at the redfish's qualifications and tell me what other gamefish can match them. You can sight-cast to reds in shallow water, from a couple of pounds to well over 30 pounds, depending on location and time of year. They'll grow to over 100 pounds, and I've seen them in the flats to well over 50 pounds.

And what a beautiful range of coloration they can show us! From light silvery tones, generally in light bottoms, to a deep bronze in darker waters or bottoms, and sometimes a very bright red coloration that I love. Every redfish angler loves to see the occasional showing of a blue tail on a smaller fish. And every fish has a single spot or several of them, varying from one individual to another. Frankly, redfish are beautiful.

Their range is well over 2,500 miles of coastline. I've caught them in the flats of North Carolina, in the thick spartina grasses in Georgia, all the coastline of Florida (including the Everglades), and even some areas of the Florida Keys, the shallow marshes in Louisiana, and to the end of Texas. And they extend well over a hundred miles into Mexico. That's a lot of different ecosystems, and a lot of places where you can fish for reds.

And the range of temperature they'll tolerate is immense. I've taken them in temperatures from the lower 30s, where I was freezing, to temperatures in the low 90s, where I was melting.

And I've sight-cast to them in water so shallow that their backs were out of the water, too shallow for them to tail. Other times I've cast to them, on the surface, in 30 feet of water.

Many times I've taken them in pure fresh water in the Tamiami Trail canal that crosses the Everglades east to west, and in pure salt water in beaches and oceanside flats. They'll go anywhere to feed.

And since they can feed anywhere within the whole water column, you may find reds pinning crabs right against the bottom while showing their tails above water, or crashing finger mullet or shrimp on the surface. And they can do this in clear water where I often could not get within casting range, to water so muddy it looked like Cuban *café con leche*, where a red may come within a rod's length of the boat. Frankly, I can't think of another gamefish that can be fished in so many different conditions.

Then, there is the redfish's character, different than other gamefish, as far as I'm concerned, and so full of contradictions. In the right areas and conditions, a red may be fairly easy to catch. And you often hear that redfish are a good beginner's fish. But in other conditions, like shallow, clear waters with heavy fishing pressure, they can be almost impossible, even for experts. I can love them, but they can really test my patience!

Reds have great personality, but their mood seems to change in some areas from day to day. And often in the same conditions as yesterday's great fishing, today they won't take flies very well. And once hooked, they may make a powerful run, or they may run toward the boat and even hide under it. Every fish is different.

Another great attraction for me is that often turbid waters or low-light conditions won't let you see the fish until the last seconds before it spooks, and this makes for a very close and personal encounter. All of a sudden, the fish is right there. You can see it well and you have very few seconds to make a fast short cast and pass the fly by its lips. And that often is difficult. But if you get a red to take the fly that close, you see it all. The red's reaction to the fly, the opening of the mouth, inhaling the fly . . . I just love that.

So, inspired by Mr. Redfish, and wanting to show you how I feel he is different from other gamefish, I wrote a poem. It's short, so it's okay.

Ode to a Country Gentleman.
If Mr. Tarpon is the acrobat of the flats,
with lots of somersaults and pirouettes,
and Dr. Bonefish the PhD,
showing off his smarts and sophistication,
then Mr. Redfish is the country gentleman,
with lots of savvy and bulldog power.
A sip of whiskey for him, please,
But do skip the caviar.

But that's not all. I find that besides all the excitement and charm of the redfish and his ways, there is another aspect to a redfish trip that is also wonderful. And that is, fishing in the redfish's neighborhood. The mostly brackish backwaters a redfish inhabits are an unusual environment that has always been exciting to me. The water tinted by mangrove roots or other grasses, trees and lush vegetation on the shorelines, wading birds on the shallows, birds of prey flying above, maybe an alligator here and there, a great variety of other fish—from black drum and seatrout, to snook, sharks, and rays—all of it constantly giving you a clue that this is a different world.

At times, this world gets so quiet, I can easily hear the subtle sounds of the skiff or canoe being poled. And I feel peace and tranquility that I know is good for me, good for my soul. It's a great part of why I go fishing for redfish.

I tell you all of this because I am hoping that this book, far beyond teaching you how to catch reds, will also encourage you to enjoy their world so much that you'll join me in the fight to preserve it.

PART I

The Redfish's World

Chapter 1

The Redfish in Its World

Red drum (*Sciaenops ocellatus*) are members of the family Sciaenidae (drums), of which there are twenty-two species in the western Atlantic, Gulf of Mexico, and Caribbean. Most of the drum species are able to produce sound (drumming) for communication using special muscles along the wall of the swim bladder. Spotted seatrout (*Cynoscion nebulosus*), weakfish (*Cynoscion regalis*), and black drum (*Pogonias cromis*) are three of the other drum species that fly anglers frequently pursue in shallow coastal habitats.

Red drum are popular sport and food fish throughout their range, so they have many colloquial names, including redfish, spottail bass, puppy drum (juveniles), bull reds (large adults), and channel bass. Redfish is by far the most widespread common name, and that's how red drum will be referred to from now on. Although they have been captured as far north as New England, their typical range is warm-temperate and subtropical climates—from southern Virginia through Florida and the Gulf of Mexico.

Redfish are adaptable—they tolerate a wide temperature range, use a variety of habitats, and have a wide-ranging diet. Fortunately, redfish require shallow inshore habitats during their early years, and so are readily accessible to fly anglers. And for those anglers in the know, even large adult redfish can be found in the shallows and caught on the fly.

Salinity and Temperature

Redfish tolerate a wide range of salinity (fresh water to full salt water) and temperature (36 to 100°F), so fly anglers can catch them in much of their range throughout the year. However, within these temperature and salinity tolerances, redfish have preferences, and knowing these preferences is the first step for an angler figuring out how to catch redfish on the fly.

In general, redfish fare better when salinity changes are gradual. Redfish are able to regulate the salt content of their blood and tissues—in fresh water they are able to retain higher salt concentrations than their surroundings, whereas in salt water they maintain lower bodily salt concentrations than their surroundings. It takes time, however, for fish to adapt to new salinity conditions. This is why you might notice redfish disappear from an area at the start of a freshet (a large and sudden pulse of fresh water into an estuary), only to return days later—although the salinity conditions haven't changed, the redfish have adapted to the new conditions, and so return to their normal patterns. This also explains how redfish can move from coastal areas into upper reaches of estuaries and back in a matter of a few days. Their ability to live in most salinity conditions makes them perfectly suited for estuarine and coastal waters.

Like most other fish, redfish are cold-blooded, so they are unable to regulate their body temperature. All of their body processes, such as swimming and digesting, are influenced by temperature, and it takes some time for them to adjust to temperature changes. Rapid changes in temperature can be physiologically stressful, and can put redfish into the doldrums until things stabilize. And on occasion, sudden and extreme changes in temperature can cause large kills of redfish, as happened in the northern Gulf of Mexico in 1983 (estimated more than 10,000 killed) and 1989 (more than 50,000 killed) when water temperature dropped precipitously.

Because they are cold-blooded, redfish often gear their movements toward remaining in water of acceptable or preferred temperature. By "acceptable," I mean within their range of temperature tolerance and without sudden changes. "Preferred" means those temperatures where redfish are most comfortable, and their physiology most efficient given the season and their life stage (for example, juvenile vs. adult). During summer, for instance, redfish

A redfish looking for food in a brackish water grass flat.

are adapted to warm water temperatures, so you can even find feeding redfish in shallows that feel like bathwater.

To cold-blooded animals, temperature is key to all aspects of physiology—including their ability to feed, digest, and avoid predators. During cold winter months, I have numerous times watched redfish feed aggressively for forty-five minutes or so, then change behavior completely. They stop tailing and rest, almost comatose, on patches of dark bottom. The fish I have caught in this resting phase have all had full stomachs. My guess is that in the cold water, these fish feed, then find a dark spot of bottom to warm up in the sunlit shallows and speed the digestive process. It can sometimes take five or six casts to get the attention of these resting fish, and only occasionally do they show interest in eating the fly. But after an hour or so, they usually start moving and slowly get back into feeding mode.

Redfish will even change their behavior as water temperature changes during the day. On one of my favorite flats, I have measured the water temperature on a winter morning at 53 degrees, and seen almost no movement by redfish. On calm sunny days, as the rising tide brings warmer water and the sun heats the shallows, the temperature can rise to 58 or even 60 degrees by midday. Redfish feeding and tailing increases dramatically as the water warms, so targeting the late morning and early afternoon hours will likely bring you the best results.

So what is the preferred temperature range for redfish? It's generally between 50 and 80 degrees, but this varies a little bit with latitude. A redfish in the northern Gulf of Mexico, for example, is more likely to be active in water temperatures in the low 50s than is a redfish in the southern Gulf. And when the water is well above or below their preferred range, redfish can alter their behavior considerably—often by inhabiting deeper water where the temperature tends to be more stable than the shallow waters of the flats. So on days when the flats seem to be absent of redfish, temperature may be the culprit, especially if water temperature is near the upper or lower end of the redfish's range.

As you can see, temperature is a major factor that influences redfish movement, behavior, and location. Understanding the influence of temperature on redfish will greatly increase your chances of catching more fish under

An aerial view of a redfish's world in the southernmost part of the Everglades. Notice the copper color produced by tannic acid.
PAT FORD

a variety of conditions. During winter, for example, the sun will warm the water faster on a dark-colored flat protected from wind than deeper surrounding water, so these places will likely hold redfish. And as the warm water drains off the flat in the afternoon, the edges of this flat are likely places to find redfish taking advantage of the warm water and flow of prey being washed off the flat. In contrast, in this same location during the hot sultry days of summer, redfish may wait until a rising tide moves cooler water onto the flat before moving into the shallows, or may only become active during the cooler early and late parts of the day.

We'll get to more discussion on how redfish use temperature and habitat to their advantage, but a good understanding of the habitats is necessary first.

Habitats

One of the reasons redfish are such a popular gamefish is that they are able to use most of the habitats available to them in coastal areas. Habitats used by redfish include seagrass beds, mangroves, marshes, oyster bars, mud and sand flats, and beaches. Each habitat provides a different mix of advantages and disadvantages. Redfish know these tradeoffs inherently. Anglers have to educate themselves about redfish habitats to put themselves in the right place at the right time.

Many factors influence patterns of habitat use by redfish, and high on the list is fish age. Juvenile redfish, for example, are generally found in different habitats than subadults and adults—low salinity and open bottoms seem best for small juveniles, which eventually use a wider array of habitats as they grow. This habitat pattern may be to avoid being eaten and because of age-specific food preferences. This makes sense, since different types of prey are present in different habitats. This also helps explain why redfish of different sizes tend to prefer different habitats, and why particular flies are best suited for different sizes of fish. The size redfish we generally target (18 to 36 inches) represent the ages that most often use the shallow coastal habitats we fish—seagrass, oyster bars, mud flats, and marshes. On average, larger fish use open coastal habitats most of the time (there are exceptions, of course). In late summer and fall, large redfish can be found in shallower habitats, when they migrate to near shore waters for spawning. More on this in chapter 2.

The presence of large predators is also a strong factor influencing when and where redfish can be found. In general, shallow water will keep redfish safer from large predators, such as dolphins and sharks, than deep water. But I've seen dolphins chasing redfish in water so shallow that if the dolphins didn't keep moving, they'd get stuck, so no habitat is perfectly safe. In addition, osprey will take small redfish from shallow flats. Because they're keeping an eye out for danger from above, redfish in clear water often spook if a false cast sends a fly line into the fish's field of view.

Food also affects when and where redfish can be found. Many of the prey eaten by redfish also change their behavior and location according to tide, season, and time of day, and redfish must be clued in to this to find enough to eat. In each habitat redfish encounter a different suite of prey, which suits their opportunistic nature. As I will discuss in chapter 4, redfish eat a wide variety of prey, including crabs, shrimp, worms, brittle stars, and many species of fish—from mullet to menhaden to killifish to gobies. However, as any angler with redfish fly-fishing experience can attest, redfish can focus on a particular prey species to the exclusion of all others. Learning how redfish use different habitats, and the prey available to them in those habitats, is an important component of successfully finding the right fly for the right habitat.

Understanding redfish comes from seeing the habitats from the redfish's perspective, and the following descriptions of habitats is the first step. These habitat descriptions also lay the groundwork for the following three chapters which describe how redfish use these habitats, and, of course, for the chapters that explain how anglers can use this information to catch more redfish with a fly rod.

SEAGRASS

Anglers pursuing redfish may encounter four species of seagrass. Each species has ecological requirements that differ slightly from the other species, and anglers can use this knowledge to better understand how redfish perceive these habitats. Seagrass provides habitat and food for many small organisms that are either eaten directly by redfish or eaten by larger organisms that are then eaten by redfish. Seagrass also provides redfish shelter from predators—burrowing into thick seagrass is a common predator-evasion tactic of redfish, as well as seatrout.

In the subtropics and the northern Gulf of Mexico, anglers are most likely to encounter two or three species of seagrass—turtle grass, shoal grass, and in limited situations, widgeon grass.

Turtle grass (*Thalassia testudinum*) has wide, flat, often very long blades (I've measured blades to 36 inches during summer) that provide great habitat for an abundance of redfish prey. It is the most common seagrass in the subtropics and in some portions of warm-temperate regions. The warm-temperate Big Bend area of Florida, for example, has vast expanses of seagrass beds dominated by turtle grass. Turtle grass is a marine seagrass that can tolerate estuarine salinities, but not full fresh water. It tolerates salinities from 3 to 60 ppt (but grows best between 24 to 35 ppt), and if salinity drops below 15 ppt for more than a couple weeks, the grass will die. (The abbreviation ppt means parts per thousand, which is how salt content of water is measured. Fresh water is 0 ppt, full ocean seawater is around 35 to 40 ppt.) Since turtle grass doesn't spread quickly like some other seagrasses, it can take an area a long time to recover from the loss of turtle grass, which is becoming an increasingly important conservation issue.

Turtle grass is also unable to tolerate exposure to air on a regular basis. So a flat that gets exposed to air during an average low tide (on a regular basis throughout the year) will not support turtle grass. Areas of turtle grass that are exposed to air during extreme low tides are evident by the "burned" look of the remaining stubs of grass blades. Turtle grass is also unable to tolerate a lot of wave action, so areas that are consistently exposed to waves usually do not support turtle grass.

Turtle grass is primarily a tropical and subtropical species, so it is also susceptible to cold temperatures. In the northern parts of its range, turtle grass grows actively only during summer and becomes dormant during winter. Thus, during winter, as grass blades break off or die, they are not replaced, resulting in relatively barren bottoms. As the water warms and day length increases in spring, the plants start growing again, restoring the lush grass bed. So if you are exploring an area during winter, don't write it off as barren—check it out again in summer. You may be surprised. Also, don't discount areas with seagrass beds that die back in winter—many of the bottom-dwelling organisms that live in the seagrass during summer are still there during winter, and they are more easily accessible by the redfish.

Shoal grass (*Halodule wrightii*) blades are narrow, flat, and generally not as long as turtle grass blades. It is also present throughout subtropical and warm-temperate regions. It has similar salinity tolerances (12 to 50 ppt) to turtle grass, and is similarly unable to handle long-term exposure to fresh water. However, shoal grass has some advantages over turtle grass that an angler can use to his or her advantage. First, shoal grass can tolerate relatively frequent exposure to air, so it can persist in shallow areas not inhabitable by turtle grass. These are areas that are often exposed at low tide during spring tides. Second,

The author and Captain John Bottko wading a flooded spartina grass flat, looking for tailing redfish and sheepshead.

WOODY HUBAND

shoal grass tolerates wave energy better than turtle grass. So true to its name, shoal grass is a good indicator of areas that are especially shallow at low tide. The importance of this will be evident momentarily. Third, shoal grass can tolerate colder temperatures than turtle grass, so seagrass beds dominated by shoal grass tend to remain fuller during winter than beds of turtle grass.

(An exception to the typical salinity ranges listed above for turtle grass and shoal grass is worth noting here. Both species can be found in the hypersaline lagoons of Texas, such as Laguna Madre, where these grasses do relatively well in salinities higher than 50 ppt. This is fortunate for anglers because the presence of these seagrasses supports a prey base that feeds the large populations of redfish and spotted seatrout found in these lagoons.)

Anglers fishing for redfish in the subtropics and portions of the northern Gulf of Mexico can use their knowledge of the ecological requirements of turtle grass and shoal grass to pinpoint where on a grass flat to concentrate their first efforts on looking for tailing redfish. On many grass flats, shoal grass dominates the areas closest to shore, or shallow bars, while turtle grass dominates deeper areas. In many cases, there is a relatively distinct area where the dominant grass transitions from shoal grass to turtle grass. In such cases, this transition zone marks a difference in depth—the shallower area is likely exposed to air during low tide on a relatively consistent basis, while the deeper area remains submerged. This transition zone is where you will often find tailing redfish on an early rising tide. This can even be true on a smaller scale—a flat stretched across undulating bottom might have turtle grass in the troughs and shoal grass on the ridges. Near low tide, look for redfish to be holding in the turtle grass areas, and for them to begin their foraging from these areas on the rising tide.

Many anglers ask why, if they can see the differences in depth, do they need to know about seagrasses. The reason is that the difference in depth between turtle grass and shoal grass areas is often a matter of only a few inches—an almost imperceptible difference to anglers, but one that makes a big difference to redfish. This slight difference in depth is especially true in the Gulf of Mexico, where tidal range is relatively minor and flats can cover large expanses of bottom. In such scenarios, concentrating on the transition zone between turtle grass and shoal grass can greatly increase an angler's focus on the best areas for tailing redfish.

One disadvantage to fishing in shoal grass beds is that the grass blades can grow in such thick stands that it's too difficult for redfish to dig into the bottom in search of prey. Such dense seagrass will also quickly swallow a fly, and the redfish will never see it. So in these areas, concentrate your searching for tailing fish on edges where shoal grass and turtle grass meet, or where there is a patch of open bottom. In contrast, although turtle grass blades can also grow in dense concentrations, I have not yet seen a location where redfish are unable to feed along the bottom. Dense turtle grass can be difficult to fish with a fly, but this is a challenge that can be overcome and is addressed on page 170.

There is something very special about fishing the backwaters with a variety of seagrasses. Here you often see the fish close to you, requiring fast and accurate cast. And when you hook up, the fight is close and personal. This is one of my favorite places to fish reds, snook, and baby tarpon. GEORGE CONTORAKES

Eel grass (*Zostera marina*) is the only species of seagrass found in warm-temperate and temperate regions along the Atlantic Coast (it does not occur in the Gulf of Mexico), and can tolerate salinities from 10 to 35 ppt. It has wide, flat, long blades, similar to turtle grass, and provides valuable habitat to redfish and their prey. In the Atlantic, eel grass is generally confined to shallow, protected areas because it cannot tolerate much wave energy—primarily in estuaries from North Carolina northward. The most extensive eel grass beds can be found on the leeward sides of the barrier islands of the Outer Banks, in shallow, clear areas protected by marsh islands, and in the shallows (especially protected embayments) of the Chesapeake Bay. Although susceptible to wave disturbance, eel grass does thrive in areas with moderate currents or water exchange, which is a good thing for anglers pursuing redfish because water exchange generally equates to an abundance of prey. The depth at which eel grass grows is limited by the need for sufficient sunlight for growth, and since estuarine waters are often turbid, eel grass is usually limited to shallow waters.

Widgeon grass (*Ruppia maritima*) is a fast-growing grass that is thin-bladed, but since it is highly branched, it provides complex habitat for many small fishes and shrimps. Its branching structure forms thick clumps that provide habitat for the many species of mudminnows (killifishes, mollies, mosquitofishes) that live in backcountry areas. It's found in subtropical and warm-temperate regions, and is tolerant of a wide range of salinities (2 to 70 ppt). In higher salinity waters, turtle and shoal grass outcompete it, so it's most often found in areas that experience low salinities that inhibit growth of the other grasses. Note that low salinities do not have to occur throughout the year, but only for periods long enough to eliminate turtle grass and shoal grass from the area. Thus, widgeon grass is most common in backcountry areas of the Gulf of Mexico that receive strong freshwater flows during the wet times of year, but have enough salt water to keep freshwater plants from growing. In the southern Gulf of Mexico, backcountry areas with widgeon grass are good places to find redfish during cooler months. In the northern Gulf, areas with widgeon grass tend to be good fishing spots in summer.

DRIFT ALGAE

Drift algae (usually a mixture of red and brown algae species) is the tumbleweed of the sea, sometimes attached to grass blades, but often carried by tidal and wind-driven currents and deposited in areas where the current slows. Drift algae is most abundant during winter, and in areas where seagrass goes dormant, it can provide shelter for small organisms, and thus a feeding habitat for redfish. Countless times, I've watched redfish tail with their noses stuck so far into a clump of drift algae that I've been able to sneak up and grab their tail with my hand. As the drift algae grows through the winter and is

Seeing a stingray gliding over a grassy flat, even when it's not mudding and attracting redfish, is still a good sign. It reveals life in the flats. Besides, I always enjoy seeing how smoothly they glide over a few inches of water.

moved around by currents, it often collects in depressions and along windward shorelines. Sometimes it even carpets the bottom and can be more than 2 feet deep. In general, I've found that areas with such thick accumulations of drift algae don't hold much prey and don't make for the best fishing compared to areas with a mixture of seagrass and drift algae, or areas of sparse algae.

MANGROVES

Although sixty-five mangrove species exist worldwide, I'll only cover two species that are considered fish habitat—red mangrove (*Rhizophora mangle*) and black mangrove (*Avicennia germinans*). Both species of mangroves are can tolerate sea water due to a variety of special physiological and physical adaptations (particularly their ability to exclude or excrete salt, which would otherwise kill the plants), and these mangroves are essential components of coastal ecosystems. Not only do they provide habitat for gamefish and their prey, mangroves help hold our coasts together and buffer coastal areas from storms and waves. They also help collect land-based sediments that would otherwise smother coastal habitats, such as seagrass and oyster bars.

Both species of mangroves are found along low-energy shorelines. Shorelines that are consistently buffeted by high energy from waves and strong currents are not suitable for these plants. In the subtropics, mangroves are the dominant wetland vegetation, but they are replaced by salt marsh plants in warm-temperate areas. A series of warm winters will allow mangroves to encroach northward, but a winter freeze will quickly wipe out the mangroves and the salt marsh plants will once again dominate.

Mangroves are an important part of the food web in coastal environments. The combination of sediments trapped by the mangrove prop roots, the continual dropping of leaves from the mangrove trees, and byproducts of organisms within the mangroves forms the detritus that is the center of the food web in mangrove habitats. Bacteria and fungi, and even some fishes, such as mojarras, feed on the detritus. An extensive community of algae, sponges, barnacles, oysters, clams, mussels, and other organisms (often referred to as the "fouling community" because they grow on "foul"—the mangrove roots) grows directly on the prop roots. In turn, small organisms, such as shrimp, crabs, worms, and fish feed on the detritus and on organisms in the fouling community, and are then preyed upon by larger organisms. The often turbid water, the structure of the mangrove prop roots, and the abundant food combine to make these great habitats for small fish and invertebrates, which in turn attracts redfish.

When fishing for redfish, anglers most often encounter the red mangrove. One of the most important adaptations of red mangroves is the support structures, called prop roots, that elevate the plants above the water. Because the prop roots support most of the plant above the water, red mangroves take advantage of submerged areas that other land-based plants can't. And since many of these areas are exposed at low tides, they aren't suitable areas for seagrass to grow, so mangroves are the only source of shelter and food for gamefish in these areas. From an angler's point of view, the most important feature of red mangroves is that prop roots create a complex labyrinth of habitat for redfish and their prey.

Red mangroves provide shade during the warm days of summer, and redfish often take advantage of this cool shade. During winter, redfish will often rest on the open bottom that is adjacent to red mangroves, warming in the sun, but with the shelter of the mangrove prop roots close at hand. Mangroves in shallow or intertidal areas are accessible to redfish only during deeper water events, whereas mangroves along deeper shorelines provide shelter and feeding opportunities at all times.

Black mangroves are limited to areas closer to the high tide line than red mangroves. Instead of relying on prop roots, the black mangrove trunk grows directly from the soil, and the plants have pencil-size aerial roots (pneumatophores) that stick up vertically from the mud bottom. The pneumatophores allow the plant to obtain oxygen from the air to supply the roots. This strategy allows the black mangrove to live in sediment that is

Any time you see red mangrove trees or oysters, sooner or later you are going to see redfish. Lots of food lives and hides around mangrove roots or oyster bars. AARON ADAMS

naturally anoxic (contains no oxygen) and full of sulfur (the rotten egg smell of marsh muds). You can recognize black mangroves because they have tens or hundreds of these stick-like pneumatophores surrounding the area around the base of the tree.

Although pneumatophores are successful adaptations that allow black mangroves to thrive in tough environments, they can't tolerate continuous coverage by water because they need air exposure to get oxygen to the roots. So black mangroves grow in areas where the pneumatophores can be exposed to air for at least some of the tidal cycle, or in areas where they are near the high water mark with little tidal range. Black mangroves are most often found in two types of locations: inland of red mangroves in shallower water closer to the high tide line; and along shallow, often muddy shorelines, such as the protected, murky backwaters and creeks of an estuary or lagoon. Both of these types of locations are frequented by redfish.

Because black mangroves don't have large prop roots like red mangroves, they provide a different type of habitat than red mangrove prop roots. Black mangrove roots rarely have anything growing on them, but instead are often surrounded by bottom-dwelling organisms. In areas with a notable tidal range, the activity of these organisms revolves around the tide. Key among these organisms, at least from the perspective of redfish, are fiddler crabs, marsh crabs, mud crabs, and small fishes (mostly killifishes) that feed on the bottom detritus.

Since the pneumatophores are near the high tide line and often are only submerged for part of the tidal cycle, they provide only limited shelter to the small fishes found along these shorelines. The areas adjacent to black mangroves are usually open mud or sand, which don't provide much shelter for prey. This is one reason redfish can frequently be found along these shorelines, especially around low tide, where they can corral small baitfish against the shoreline.

Areas with black mangroves growing behind (landward of) red mangroves can offer interesting fishing opportunities. During especially high tides, redfish will swim past the red mangroves and into the flooded black mangrove forest. These redfish will feed on crabs, safe in the shade of the mangrove forest. While inaccessible to anglers during these times, as the tide falls the redfish will move out of the black mangroves and can be targeted by anglers set up at ambush points—breaks in the line of red mangroves that expose the edge of the black mangrove forest, where redfish can be intercepted as they leave the black mangroves with the falling tide.

SALT MARSH

Salt marshes fill the same ecological role in temperate regions that mangroves do in the tropics and subtropics. Salt marshes are the dominant type of coastal wetland from mid-Florida northward. In the Gulf of Mexico, salt marsh habitats are dominant north of Cedar Key, Florida, on the east and Port Isabel, Texas, on the west. On the Atlantic coast, salt marshes dominate north of Cape Canaveral. The border between salt marsh and mangroves is not static, but fluctuates with long-term changes in temperature.

Salt marshes are limited to the intertidal zone because salt marsh plants can't tolerate being submerged all the time. Because geography and tidal range differ between the Gulf of Mexico and the Atlantic coast, salt marshes have different characteristics in these regions. In the Atlantic, tidal range is large (4 to 6 feet), and the slope of the coast is steep relative to the Gulf of Mexico, so the amount of area suitable for salt marshes is rather narrow in the Atlantic. In contrast, the combination of the Gulf's shallow slope and the small tidal range (less than 3 feet, with microtides in some locations) means that large areas of coast are intertidal, and thus exposed to salt or brackish water—suitable for salt marsh plants. Thus, Gulf Coast marshes tend to be rather extensive in aerial coverage.

In general, the salt marshes of the Gulf of Mexico can be divided into four types that correspond to four geographic zones. The three types from the Mississippi Delta eastward are dominated by sand, mud, and silt from the Mississippi River. Type one occurs from northern Florida to Mississippi, where much of the coast is fringed by salt marshes. These marshes are protected by low-lying barrier islands or by extensive shallows that break up much of the wave energy long before it reaches shore. Type two marshes occur in the Mississippi Delta, and extend from the Gulf of Mexico to far inland. These marshes are relatively well protected by extensive mud shallows on their seaward edge, but the outer edges of these marshes are subject to forces of erosion during storms. The extent of these marshes has been reduced considerably in recent years. Type three marshes occur on the western side of the Mississippi Delta. These marshes are located on and behind low-lying, relatively stable, sandy islands called chenier islands. The fourth type of Gulf of Mexico salt marsh occurs in Texas, where extensive barrier islands create expansive and shallow lagoons, much of which are ringed by salt marshes. In many areas, the landward sides of these lagoons are covered by extensive salt marshes and backcountry lakes that are great places to find redfish and spotted seatrout, especially during the warmer months.

I often use a classic double-ended canoe and a push pole to reach supershallow waters. This is my Merrimack canoe in the backwaters of the Big Bend area in Florida. A beautiful, quiet, and peaceful area to fly-fish. STEPHEN FERNÁNDEZ

Salt marshes are divided into low marsh and high marsh zones, with each zone dominated by different species of marsh grass. Tide, rainfall, and salinity are major structuring forces of a salt marsh, and combine to create high and low marsh zones. The portion of the salt marsh that abuts land is called the high marsh and is exposed to salt water only during strong spring high tides. Although tides generally don't bring enough salt water into the high marsh for redfish, recognizing where areas of high marsh occur will help you find fish in the low marsh. This is because a healthy high marsh generally indicates sources of fresh water, which is also important to low marsh plants.

The low marsh is fully intertidal, and occupies the area between mean sea level and the mean high water mark. The low marsh is subject to daily incursions of the tides, so is an area of high salinity and the sediments remain wet. Plants in the low marsh must have special adaptations enabling them to tolerate salt water—they are able to exclude salt water from their tissues and excrete salt from the water they do take in.

Sediments of the low marsh tend to be oxygen-poor. This would kill most plants because the roots need oxygen to survive. Salt marsh plants are able to transport to their roots some of the oxygen they bring in through their leaves, so they can remain firmly rooted in the anoxic (no oxygen) sediments. Healthy roots, in turn, help stabilize the sediments of the marsh.

Smooth cordgrass (*Spartina alterniflora*) is often the overwhelmingly dominant plant species in low marshes with high salinity. In areas of brackish water and low tidal range, like much of the northern Gulf of Mexico, black needlerush (*Juncus roemerianus*) can be the dominant marsh grass. These grasses are good indicators of where in the salt marsh you will most likely find gamefish.

Like seagrasses and mangroves, low marsh plants have particular growing requirements. First among them is tidal flushing. Sediments in areas of the low marsh that are frequently flushed by tides have a greater percolation rate, which bathes marsh grass roots with new water each tidal cycle. This means the sediments are better aerated, so have a higher oxygen content, which results in better

The author casting for reds on a very rough Jacksonville, Florida, beach. This is a very different world than the usual backwaters, often requiring a long cast. I loved it.

WOODY HUBAND

plant growth. Although smooth cordgrass and black needlerush can tolerate sediments with low oxygen, they grow best in aerated sediments.

Sediment type is also important. Fine-grained sediments are more densely packed and have higher nutrient levels than sandy soils, which results in better growth. Tides help deposit fine-grained sediments in the low marsh, so once again areas with frequent tidal flushing are best. Finally, smooth cordgrass grows best in medium salinity, and black needlerush in medium to low salinity, which relates back to the importance of freshwater input to a healthy salt marsh.

Put all this together, and you will see why grasses in the low marsh grow best (and are tallest) along the edges of creeks that receive frequent tidal flushing and perhaps some fresh water as well, and in the most seaward portions of marsh that benefit from daily incursions of tides. On marshes that are alternatively flooded and drained at high and low tides, tall marsh grass can indicate the locations of troughs. The troughs receive water on the incoming tide first, and retain water longest on the outgoing tide, and so they attract redfish foraying onto the march from deeper adjacent waters. These troughs might be only a few inches deeper than the surrounding bottom, but that is all a redfish needs.

Finding creeks and troughs is also important because, since they drain the salt marsh on ebbing tides and fill the marsh on flooding tides, there is often current associated with them. The creeks with the strongest flows will usually have a deep hole at their mouth. Redfish will often hold in these holes during low tide and move into the creeks with the rising tide. Creeks with especially strong tidal flows may even have undercut banks at creek bends and hard or oyster shell bottom. This is because the currents are strong enough to sweep away fine-grained marsh sediments. Spots where shells have been swept into a pile are favorite places for redfish and spotted seatrout to wait for a meal to be delivered by currents.

Outer portions of the low marsh that abut deeper water provide safe holding places for redfish to wait out low tide, and then quick access to the marsh on the rising tide. These deeper spots also provide cool water temperatures during summer and warm water during winter, but still provide easy access to the marshes when conditions are right.

OYSTER BARS

In areas with abundant seagrass or mangrove habitats, oyster bars are just one of three major habitats where gamefish find prey and shelter. But in areas with no mangroves and little or no seagrass, oyster bars are very important habitats because, in addition to salt marshes, they provide the best habitat for redfish prey. Oyster reefs can be entirely subtidal (always submerged, even at low tide) or intertidal (exposed at low tide and submerged at high tide). Intertidal and shallow subtidal reefs are the most important to fly anglers.

Just as with seagrasses, anglers can use the ecological requirements of oysters to get closer to the redfish's perspective of oyster bar habitats. First, oysters are filter feeders (they filter plankton and particles out of the water they pump through their gills), so they need a constant supply of new water to bring them food. This is why oyster bars grow in areas where new water arrives with each rising tide or where tidal currents or flow from creeks and rivers continually bring new food for the filter-feeding oysters. Oyster bars tend to grow across the prevailing currents, with a higher mound forming in the middle and the reef tapering at each end, often into deeper water. In less than perfect growing conditions, scattered oyster clumps or patchy bars form instead.

Second, oyster growth and survival is related to salinity. Oysters can't tolerate fresh water for more than a couple weeks. And although oysters grow best in high salinity water, so do their predators, parasites, and diseases, so oyster survival isn't very high. So in general, oysters grow best in medium salinity areas. And since oyster bars composed of live oysters harbor more prey than oyster bars of just shell, you might expect more redfish around live bars than shell mounds.

Oyster bars can be generally categorized into three types. A *point bar* begins at the shoreline (often a point on the edge of a marsh), and extends outward over open bottom into current-swept waters. An *isolated bar* grows on sandy or muddy bottom without any association to land or marsh habitats. A *fringing bar* grows parallel to a shoreline or marsh fringe (bounded by land, marsh, or mangroves), with seagrass or open bottom on the outer edge.

Because they are solid structures rising off the bottom, all oyster bars that are exposed to currents will influence those currents. Depending on their size and orientation, oyster bars might produce small eddies, concentrate water flow through narrow channels, or completely deflect currents onto a different path. When large point bars block currents, they often create an area of slow water on the upcurrent side of the bar. Upcurrent stillwaters are usually areas of slow, swirling water, and baitfish drifting downstream often get confused by these slowly whirling currents and collect in these eddies.

More common, and easier to fish than upcurrent stillwaters, are downcurrent eddies. Large point bars can deflect currents so that most water passes over the outer end of the bar, leaving only a very slow, downcurrent eddy near shore. The slow currents at the shoreline end of the bar bring little food, so these areas often have few live oysters, and tend to hold fewer prey for gamefish. However, these backwaters can be good habitats for resident baitfish like killifishes.

Moderate currents passing over fringing bars (often the edges of creeks) create turbulence near the bar that can dislodge small prey, and can create small eddies where baitfish may try to hold in the current. Both occurrences are good situations for fishing with a fly rod—a crab or shrimp pattern (to imitate dislodged prey) or a small baitfish pattern (to imitate fish holding in the eddies) are good in these situations.

In areas with slow currents, redfish will tend to feed along edges of oyster bars on a rising tide and rest in the deeper holes next to, between, and behind oyster bars at low tide. During spring high tides, they will often take advantage of higher water to feed along oyster bars that are not normally accessible.

The holes between oyster bars and the deep water behind bars are especially good places to find redfish near Louisiana and South Carolina. In these murky water areas, flies that can be heard or detected by a gamefish's lateral line system can be effective. Crab and shrimp patterns with small rattles tied into their bodies are good for bouncing over open bottom. In holes that might have snags on the bottom, a fly that pulsates and sends out vibrations, but stays in midwater, such as a Seaducer, is a good bet. Redfish often forage in deeper holes adjacent to and between isolated oyster bars, and fall for these tactics.

Redfish tend to feed on the edges of oyster bars, rather than directly on them. Oyster reefs tend to be crowded, so many organisms must venture away from the reef in search of food. When small fish, shrimp, and crabs venture from the shelter of oyster bars onto open bottom in search of food, they are easier targets for waiting redfish. Remember this when fishing oyster bars—concentrate on the edges to maximize chances of success.

Finally, oyster bars show similarities in seasonality of prey. In warm-temperate areas, for example, juvenile fish that might be eaten by redfish are most abundant from late spring to summer, peaking in June to July. Timing is similar in the subtropics, but juveniles of some species (such as pinfish and croaker) arrive in late winter, and juveniles of other species (such as some mojarras, mullet, and ladyfish) arrive in fall and winter. In the Carolinas and northern Gulf of Mexico, peak abundance of juvenile fishes occurs in late summer to early fall, with medium abundances in late spring and late fall. As you might expect, lowest abundances occur in winter when water temperatures are lowest, and this is when redfish rely on year-round resident prey species, such as killifishes.

MUD FLATS, SAND FLATS, AND BEACHES

Mud flats don't typically experience strong currents or wave action. If they did, the fine sediments that make up the mud would have been carried elsewhere. In contrast, sand flats are usually located in areas exposed to more current or wave energy than mud flats, often on the leeward sides of barrier islands. Ripples or ridges on the sand bottom are indicative of frequent exposure to currents or waves.

These open bottom habitats feature little in the way of habitat structure, but numerous burrowing organisms, crabs, and small fishes use these habitats. Most often, however, it is the adjacent habitats (salt marsh, mangroves, seagrass) that determine which prey are available, and the astute angler will take this into consideration when choosing flies for these habitats. Fiddler crabs, for example, are high on the prey list of redfish feeding on tidal flats adjacent to black mangrove shorelines and low marshes. The fiddler crabs sometimes venture from their burrows near the high tide, and are easy for a redfish to spot on the open bottom. Otherwise, mobile prey tend to dominate tidal flats—they move across the flat with the tide, often in the shallowest areas. Killifishes and mollies, for example, are often abundant on mud flats adjacent to red mangrove shorelines or salt marsh creeks. And blue crabs and lady crabs, always on the move, roam these tidal flats in search of a meal. On subtidal mud and sandy-mud flats, ghost shrimp and other burrowing organisms are common.

Redfish can be found along beaches throughout the year, but are most common in this habitat from fall into winter in the subtropics, as well as early spring and fall in the northern Gulf of Mexico. Schools of small redfish are often found along the beaches of the Chandeleur Islands in March and April. Elsewhere in Louisiana, redfish that roamed the backcountry lakes in spring will move to the cooler water along beaches in midsummer if the shallow backcountry gets too warm.

When using beach habitats, redfish tend to feed upon mobile and seasonal prey. Various species of swimming crabs and mole crabs are examples of resident mobile prey. And large schools of migratory fishes are seasonally present along many beaches. The barrier island beaches of Texas, for example, yield their best beach fishing of the year each fall, as redfish (and other gamefish) are attracted by large schools of baitfish readying for fall migrations, including mullet, anchovies, and menhaden and other herrings.

Notes on Seasonal Use of Habitats

In late fall and winter, the shallow waters of backcountry areas can quickly drop in temperature when a strong cold

I've always said that you can't just live for the moment of the strike. You should enjoy all that's around you while on your trip. Absorb the world of the redfish, its neighborhood. And so, here is an osprey with not one, but two meals, as it heads for a place to enjoy them. PAT FORD

front passes through, which can spell trouble for gamefish. Thus, during winter, marshes that are adjacent to deeper water or have deep holes where gamefish can wait out the cold periods will hold the most gamefish. During winter, shallow, dark marsh bottom is warmed by the sun, so temperatures in the shallows can rise quickly during the day, causing a surge in activity. You will find that redfish will move onto the shallows to warm up in these shallow, sun-heated waters. Mid to late afternoons are the best times to fish these areas because it often takes a few hours of sun to raise the water temperature. On shallow, subtropical flats of southwest Florida, I have recorded an increase in water temperature of 6 degrees from morning to midday.

Redfish will also take advantage of the warming effect of the sun on the shallows without venturing onto the flats. After a day of warming in the sun, an ebbing tide will carry warm water off the flat, and redfish will wait along the edges and feed on prey that is swept off flats. In South Carolina, the dark bottoms surrounding oyster bars are good places to find large schools of redfish in winter. Because of the low number of prey species that remain through the winter, flies that imitate resident fishes, such as the mummichog are productive.

A somewhat different pattern takes shape during the heat of summer. The summer sun may warm the flats beyond the comfort zone of redfish. When this happens, redfish search out cooler waters, found in deeper holes or along drop-offs. As a rising tide moves the cooler water from deeper areas into the shallows, redfish often follow the cooler water to feed on the flat. During summer in the subtropics, redfish will use the shade of mangrove shorelines to keep cool during the day. As tides drop and water cools late in the day, these fish often emerge into adjacent seagrass and open bottom habitats. Thus, fishing during the day might require casting flies under overhanging mangrove branches, while evening fishing efforts should focus on the flats.

Changes in patterns of tailing redfish provide a good illustration of how seasonality influences best fishing times. The sight of redfish tailing in grass beds is most common during midday in winter, and early and late in the day in summer. In winter, redfish will enter the shallows to feed as the water warms, and as the tide floods the flat. When the water is especially cool, you might have to wait an hour or two into the rising tide before the redfish become active. In summer, the water is coolest at dusk or dawn, and redfish can be especially active during a rising tide when the cool water from deeper areas floods the flat. Similarly during summer, a rising tide early and late in the day is great for fishing for redfish in the marshes of South Carolina and Georgia.

Some regional nuances also bear mentioning. For example, in central eastern Florida, the abundance of redfish in creeks tends to increase as water temperature drops. In other words, redfish use deep estuarine creeks as overwintering areas or refuges during cold snaps. In Texas, abundance of redfish in shallow bays and rivers declines in winter because fish move to warmer, deeper waters near the mouths of estuaries or offshore. In North Carolina, large redfish are most abundant along the beaches in spring (April–May) and fall (October–November). In backcountry salt marsh habitats of the northern Gulf of Mexico, you'll generally find the greatest numbers of redfish beginning when water temperatures warm in spring and ending when temperatures start to drop in the fall. The exception is shallow areas that become too warm in the heat of summer. These shallower locations are best fished in spring through early summer and later summer to fall. During midsummer, many of the larger fish may move to deeper coastal habitats, such as beaches.

Chapter 2

The Red Drum's Life

Most anglers don't realize that the majority of redfish fly anglers target are juveniles and subadults. This is because, in general, redfish spend their juvenile and subadult years in estuarine habitats, then move into deeper ocean and Gulf of Mexico waters once they mature. This is one reason we must be conscious of fishery regulations—we must make sure enough younger fish survive to become adults and reproduce for future generations. However, large adults occasionally move into shallow coastal and estuarine habitats, and you can learn how to target them. Understanding how redfish are adapted to shallow estuarine habitats and when they use these habitats will help you find and catch more redfish on fly. The first step toward this understanding is to learn about the redfish's life cycle.

Life Cycle

Redfish spawn in groups around the full moon during the late summer and fall. The spawning season and spawning locations vary somewhat by region: from mid-August through October near passes and inlets in Texas; mid-August through late November in lower portions of estuaries, passes, inlets, and nearshore coastal areas in Florida; and August through early October in estuaries, nearshore ocean waters, and barrier island inlets in North Carolina.

Near dusk, male redfish begin calling females by drumming (females are unable to make the drumming sound). Spawning occurs by broadcast spawning—groups of fish eject eggs and sperm into the open water, where fertilization occurs. Female redfish can lay from 20,000 to 2 million eggs per spawn, with larger females generally producing more eggs. Redfish have to spawn in or near the ocean because the optimum salinity for eggs is 30 ppt, and the salinity within the upper reaches of estuaries will be too low. The optimum temperature for eggs is 77 degrees. The fertilized eggs hatch in approximately 24 hours, and the larvae (which look nothing like adult redfish) live as plankton in the open waters of the coast and estuaries for approximately three weeks before metamorphosing into juveniles (miniature versions of adults).

Immediately after metamorphosis, early juvenile redfish prefer the complex habitats provided by seagrass or salt marsh. Juveniles then move to shallow, protected, generally open (sand or mud) bottoms of estuaries and marshes, and can tolerate salinities of 0 (fresh water) to 50 ppt. Juveniles grow rapidly in their first year, averaging 11 to 12 inches at one year old. Juveniles often migrate toward lower salinity water as they grow through their first year, and then move to the shallow estuarine habitats frequented by anglers, who generally catch redfish aged one to four years old.

Redfish grow rapidly during their first five years, then their growth rate slows considerably. For example, data from Texas indicate that redfish reach 13 inches at one year old, 20 inches at two, 23 inches at three, 34 inches by six, and 39 inches by eight. As you can see in the table on page 21, however, growth rate varies considerably among locations.

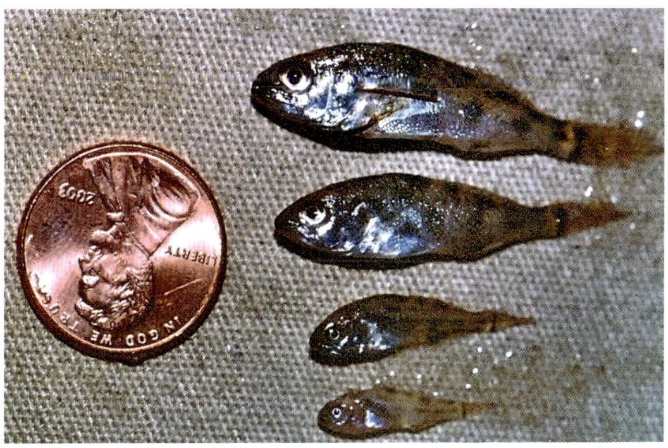

Postlarval red drum next to a penny to show its diminutive size at this stage of life. AARON ADAMS

A juvenile redfish in hand. At just a few inches, this little guy is a target to a great variety of predators, including snook, tarpon, sharks, and more. AARON ADAMS

On average, redfish mature at around three to four years of age (30 to 36 inches), spending these first years in estuarine habitats, but their age and size at maturity, and how long they remain in estuarine habitats, varies slightly by region. In general, although males can mature as early as one year old, they usually reach maturity at around three years old. Females (which tend to be larger than males) mature at three to six years of age (most commonly near three years old). In North Carolina, for example, 50 percent of male redfish are mature at two years old (~25 inches), and 100 percent of males are mature by age three, whereas 50 percent of female redfish are mature at three years old (~32 inches), with 100 percent mature by four years old. Other estimates based on Texas fishes report:

Older juvenile redfish can be found in seagrass, marsh cordgrass, and tidal creek habitats, and are often near oyster bars, depending upon the location and the types of habitats available. In South Carolina, North Carolina, and northern Florida, for example, one-year-olds are often associated with oyster bars, whereas two- and three-year-olds are common on flats (seagrass, mud, sand, and flooded marsh at high tide). As they grow, redfish widen their use of habitats, and large juveniles and adults can be found in just about any habitat with appropriate food. Overall, they tend to favor habitats with little to moderate current and soft bottom (mud, muddy sand). In areas with current, they tend to favor embayments or coves out of the current, or areas behind protective points or oyster bars.

Until they reach maturity and move to deeper adult habitats, redfish tend to remain in relatively small areas. In Florida, for example, tagging studies revealed that juvenile redfish remained within a 3- to 6-mile radius of where they were tagged. In other locations redfish appear to be more mobile, but still tend to remain within a single estuary or lagoon.

After they mature, adult redfish spend most of their time in deeper habitats in the Gulf of Mexico and Atlantic Ocean. In some areas, however, redfish remain associated with estuarine and shallow nearshore habitats for the first few years of adulthood. In Texas, for example, redfish tend to remain in or near estuarine habitats until six years old, and will inhabit nearshore coastal waters in summer and offshore waters in winter as adults.

Throughout their range, large adult redfish are most accessible to fly anglers during the fall, when they enter nearshore waters to spawn. Between spawning events, anglers can find large redfish—in large schools or as singles—along beaches and on estuarine flats near deep water. Spawning requires a lot of energy, so redfish take advantage of the abundant prey found in nearshore and estuarine waters during fall.

A notable exception to these general patterns of movement is the mostly enclosed lagoon system of east central Florida (Mosquito Lagoon, Indian River Lagoon, Banana River). In this area, most of the redfish seem to remain within the lagoons their entire lives (even spawning in the lagoons), rather than migrating offshore as adults. Thus, fly anglers can pursue large adult redfish on a regular basis in these locations. Given their proximity to large urban areas, and their many years of experience with anglers, however, these large redfish can be difficult to catch.

For unknown reasons, Gulf Coast redfish are heavier for their length than are Atlantic Coast redfish, and differences in length-to-weight relationships can also vary among specific locations. These differences in growth are

This little "three spotted" redfish took a small shrimp fly against a sawgrass shoreline.

I took this big red on the surface in 30 feet of water. The fish fought hard and deep before I could bring it to the boat and release it. CORBETT DAVIS

likely due to a combination of diet, temperature, and habitats. Thus, the table showing weight-to-length relationships includes information for numerous locations. Of course, the table provides average length-to-weight relationships—weight varies with diet, spawning, and time of year—so should be used as a guide, not a steadfast rule. In addition, females generally grow faster and get larger than males.

The difference in growth rates and age at maturity between males and females is likely due to different energy requirements for reproduction. It takes more energy for a female to produce eggs than for males to produce sperm. In addition, the larger the female, the more eggs she can produce, so it pays for females to be larger. The tables below provide examples of regional differences in growth rates and length-weight relationships. Remember that length-weight relationships will change depending upon season—fish will tend to be heavier during spawning season.

The maximum size recorded for redfish is approximately 95 pounds, but most redfish never reach that size. Maximum age recorded varies among locations, but tends to be around forty years. In the northern Gulf of Mexico, redfish live to a maximum of thirty-seven to forty years, while in North Carolina, the oldest redfish recorded thus far was fifty-six years old.

Although adult redfish have been recorded to move from tens to hundreds of miles, recent genetic analysis indicates that Atlantic and Gulf populations are genetically distinct. That means there is little, if any, migration between the Gulf and Atlantic. Even within a region, redfish are most closely related to other redfish within 400 to 550 miles, and less closely related to redfish farther away. Thus, there is genetic distinctiveness between Florida East Coast and Gulf Coast populations, and between Florida Gulf Coast and northern and western Gulf populations. This is because most adults tend to spawn near the estuary where they lived as juveniles, and ocean

Average Estimated Weight (pounds)

Fish Fork Length (inches)	South Carolina	Florida Atlantic	Florida Gulf	Northern Gulf of Mexico
15	1	1.3	1.3	1.3
16	1.5	1.6	1.6	1.6
17	1.75	2.0	2.0	2.0
18	2	2.3	2.4	2.3
19	2.5	2.8	2.8	2.8
20	3	3.2	3.3	3.3
21	3.5	3.7	3.8	3.9
22	4	4.3	4.4	4.5
23	4.7	4.9	5.1	5.2
24	5.3	5.6	5.8	5.9
25	5.9	6.3	6.6	6.8
26	6.4	7.1	7.4	7.7
27	7.7	8.0	8.3	8.7
28	8.6	8.9	9.3	9.7
29	9.5	9.9	10.4	10.9
30	10	11.0	11.5	12.2
31	11.3	12.1	12.8	13.5
32	12.4	13.4	14.1	15.0
33	14	14.7	15.5	16.5
34	14.9	16.1	17.0	18.2
35	15.8	17.5	18.6	20.0
36	17	19.1	20.3	21.9
37	18.7	20.8	22.1	23.9
38	20.6	22.5	24.0	26.0
39	22.4	24.3	26.0	28.3
40	23.1	26.3	28.2	30.7

Calculated from Beckman et al. 1988; Wenner 1992; Ross and Stevens 1995; Murphy and Taylor 1990.

Fish Length (inches)					
Estimated Age (years)	North Carolina	South Carolina	Florida Atlantic	Florida Gulf	Northern Gulf of Mexico
1	18	14.3	14.7	13.3	20.8
2	25.2	19.9	22.9	21.9	24.6
3	30.4	27.3	28.3	27.4	27.6
4	34.8	31.8	31.8	30.9	28.7
5	34.8	34.4	34.1	33.1	29.5
6	35.6	35.4	35.6	34.4	30.3
7	36.2	37.1	36.7	35.3	31.3
8	36.9	37.9	37.3	35.9	31.9
9	37.4	38.6	37.8	36.2	32.4
10	38	39	38.0	36.4	32.9

Calculated from Beckman et al. 1988; Murphy and Taylor 1990; Wenner 1992; Ross and Stevens 1995.

currents probably keep the larvae close to where the adults spawn.

Morphology

Morphology is the study of shape and form. Knowing the advantages and limitations of a gamefish's form is helpful to anglers devising a fishing strategy.

Like many fish species, redfish have a fusiform shape—a body that is tapered on both ends. But unlike another flats species pursued by anglers—bonefish—redfish are not built for speed. Bonefish have a forked tail, which is hydrodynamically efficient and results in a fast fish. In contrast, the redfish's tail is fan shaped, which is good for short bursts of speed but creates too much drag to allow long sustained runs. Thus, whereas the bonefish is a greyhound during the fight, the redfish is a bulldog.

Redfish have a subterminal mouth (the mouth is located on the underside of the head), which indicates that they focus on bottom-associated prey. The classic tailing posture is the result of the fish pursuing prey, with its snout in the bottom. Crabs, snapping shrimp, worms, and bottom-dwelling fish, such as blennies and gobies, are generally their focus when in this posture.

The bony crusher-plates in the front of a redfish's throat allows it to eat prey that has a shell. When they slurp in a crab, shrimp, or other tough prey, they use the plates to crush it so it can be digested. If you ever check the stomach contents of a redfish, you'll notice that all of the crabs in the stomach have crushed shells. This allows the stomach juices to digest the soft tissue. In the intestines, you'll notice that much of the shell remains undigested, and is eventually passed.

But just because redfish rely heavily on bottom-dwelling prey like crabs and shrimp doesn't mean that is all they eat. They also eat large numbers of fish. In fact, as redfish age, fish become a more important part of the their diet, especially as adults. The subterminal mouth doesn't seem to inhibit redfish in pursuing surface-dwelling mullet, for example, and they can attack poppers and other surface flies ferociously.

Like many fish, redfish have a good sense of smell. (Most fish have a sense of smell that is nearly a million times better than humans.) Their sense of smell is especially useful for finding bottom-associated prey that burrow into the bottom or hide in thick seagrass or marsh grass. Filter-feeding bottom organisms, like tube worms, are constantly passing water through their bodies to filter out plankton for food. Redfish are probably able to detect the outflows from tubeworms and slurp the worms from the bottom. Some days, it seems that redfish feed exclusively on these worms. Even prey that moves will

Often a redfish will exhibit a bright blue tint on the tail. It's really beautiful, and often easy to see in the water. I have mostly seen this coloration on medium to small fish, and generally in clear water.

give off a scent that can probably be detected by redfish. Since marine organisms have to pass water over gills to obtain oxygen from the water, they leave a scent trail in the water that leaves the gills. Redfish can use this scent trail to track down potential prey.

Sound travels almost five times faster in water than in air, and it travels farther too. Low frequency sounds travel farther than high frequency sounds. And like most fish, redfish have a well-developed system for detecting sound and movement. Thus, that thud from dropping something in the boat surely alerts nearby redfish to your presence. In basic terms, sound and vibrations (such as from a moving fish) travel through the water the same way—as waves. Redfish have two organs for detecting these waves. The first organ is the lateral line, which consists of a row of cells running the length of the body and is best for detecting low-frequency sounds, generally at close range. The lateral line cells have small cilia that extend out from the cell, and passing sound or motion waves create changes in pressure that cause the cilia to

Diana Rudolph and Captain Dale Perez with a light-colored redfish that blended well in the environment of the light sandy bottom of a flat in the southernmost part of the Everglades where it was taken.

Sandy Moret and Captain Steve Huff with a bandana on, holding a dark-colored red that blended well in the dark color waters of the backcountry. SUE MORET

Angler Mike Wilson holding a red with a single spot, and Captain Chuck Naiser holding one of the few without spots.

bend. The movement of the cilia creates a nerve impulse that is sent to the brain.

Redfish also have an inner ear system that can pick up waves from nearby and far off sources, and is best suited for detecting high-frequency sounds. The inner ear system is made up of three pairs of small chambers, each containing a small "earstone" (otolith). When sound or motion waves move from the water to the solid otoliths, the shape of the wave changes, which causes the otoliths to vibrate. These vibrations are detected by cilia that line the inner walls of the ear chambers, and a nerve impulse is sent to the brain.

How well redfish can see is an open debate. Some days it seems they're blind and can't see a fly just inches from their nose. Other days they charge a fly from dozens of feet away. They are certainly able to see a fly line that is false-cast over their heads. Most likely, redfish rely on sight at close range. In general, visibility is not great in the shallow coastal waters where redfish live, so they likely can't see prey at long distances. They use sound and motion waves and smell to detect prey from longer distances, then rely on sight as they close in on the prey. Redfish can

While most redfish have a single spot by the tail, it is not uncommon for them to show more than one spot. This one has seven spots. And I've seen some with twenty spots and more. Cool.

also see a wide range of colors, especially the blue, green, and yellow portions of the light spectrum.

Redfish are able to change color, though not to the extent of many other fish species. Some fish, such as

Brooke Denkert Black releasing a nice red that took a shrimp pattern.

flounder, can change color instantaneously as they move from one bottom color to another. Redfish lack this ability for quick color change, but they are able to take on the general color theme of their surroundings. In tannin-stained waters and over dark bottom, for example, redfish are often dark—from a red to dark copper hue. In clearer coastal waters or open sandy bottoms, they can be silver. This a good strategy for hiding from predators, but this can make also it more difficult for sight-fishing anglers to spot redfish.

Redfish are highly tuned to their environment, and take advantage of the habitats and prey around them. The angler who understands how redfish use their surroundings is more likely to be in the right place at the right time, and more likely to choose the appropriate fly for the occasion.

Chapter 3

Tides

Tides are the result of gravity and inertia. The gravitational pull of the moon creates a bulge of water on the side of the earth facing the moon. The inertia of the water on the side of the earth opposite the moon caused by moving water in response to the moon's pull creates a second bulge of water that is kept from leaving the earth all together by the gravitational pull of the earth. These two bulges of water, one on the side of the earth closest to the moon, the other on the opposite side of the earth, correspond to high tides. Halfway between the bulges of water are areas of extra-low water, on opposite sides of the earth from one another, which correspond to low tides. As the moon revolves around the earth, the bulges of water remain aligned with the moon,

An aerial view of a redfish flat at low tide. Notice many parts are completely out of water. Yet in a couple of hours the tide will be coming in, and redfish, snook, and the whole gang will move in with the tide, feeding on crustaceans and fishes. A low incoming tide is probably my favorite tide stage. PAT FORD

so the areas of high and low water rotate around the earth (and the earth is spinning on its axis too). The changes in water height that correspond with the passing of the areas of high and low water are called tides.

Because it takes slightly longer than a 24-hour day for the moon to complete a full revolution around the earth, a tidal "day" takes 24 hours and 50 minutes. This is why the timing of high and low tides changes daily—each tide approximately 50 minutes later than the day before—and follows a lunar cycle that takes slightly less than a month to complete (a full lunar cycle is 29.53 days).

The sun has about half the influence on tides as does the moon. But the sun's influence is sufficient to enhance or dampen the moon's effect on tides. When the sun and moon are aligned (either both are on the same side of the earth or on exact opposite sides of the earth) they exert their combined gravitational pull so that the bulges of water are larger than when the sun and moon are not aligned. And when the bulges of water are larger, the amount of water between the bulges is less, which translates to higher than normal high tides and lower than normal low tides. These extreme tides are called spring tides, and are associated with new and full moons. And as if that wasn't enough, the pull of the moon and sun vary depending on how close they are to the earth, so the severity of the spring tides can vary.

When the moon and sun are at right angles to one another, they partially negate each other's gravitational influence, resulting in a more even distribution of water over the earth's surface, and a less-than-normal tidal range. These less-than-normal tides occur at the times of quarter moons and are called neap tides. So within the monthly tidal cycle, every two weeks spring tides will occur, and on the alternating weeks, neap tides.

Because the earth is round, you might expect all locations on earth to get two high and two low tides per day, but this is not the case. Differences occur due to the topography of the oceans and continents and the inclination of the moon's rotation relative to the earth. Some locations get two high and two low tides of approximately equal height per day (called semidiurnal tides), others get only a single high and low tide a day (diurnal tides), and some locations get two high and two low tides of unequal height per day (mixed tides).

In addition, the moon's inclination and ocean basin topography influence tidal range, resulting in extreme tidal ranges in some areas (a 50-foot spring tide range in the Bay of Fundy, for example) and minor tidal range in others (a 2- to 3-foot spring tide range in most of the Gulf of Mexico). The tidal range during spring tides in the part of the world inhabited by redfish is highly variable—more than 6 feet in South Carolina, less than 2 feet in the northern Gulf of Mexico, and "microtides" in the semienclosed lagoons of Texas.

As the local height of the ocean changes with the tides, currents are created. Rising water travels around and over obstacles via currents, filling coastal bays and flats. As the tidal bulge passes, water level drops, and the ebbing tide drains the shallows. Since the amount of time between high and low tides for any given area is always approximately the same, regardless of the tidal range (e.g., six hours between high and low for semidiurnal tides), the strength of tidal currents varies between spring and neap tides. During spring tides, when tidal range is greatest, the greater volume of moving water creates stronger currents, whereas the weak neap tides cause the weakest tidal currents. Redfish behavior changes in response to the different currents and water movements, so understanding the tides is an important component to finding the fish.

Spring Tides

When spring high tides flood the shallows at the new and full moons, redfish take advantage of the higher water to forage in areas they normally can't access or that is too shallow under neap tide conditions for them to feel comfortable. Shallow sand and grass flats, shorelines, shallow mangroves, and especially salt marsh habitats hold many prey that are only accessible for a few days every couple of weeks during spring tides. High spring tides are also the best times to fish for redfish along the ridges of oyster bars and flats that don't have mangroves or shallow shorelines. And it is usually during spring tides that you find redfish feeding and resting in the skinniest water. Spring tides are my favorite for searching for redfish along shallow muddy shorelines lined by black mangroves.

During spring tides, the fishing can be fantastic, but often just for short blocks of time. The amount of time between high and low tide is always the same, regardless of whether it is a spring or neap tide, so the drop in water level is very fast during spring tides. Redfish have to avoid becoming stranded too far from deep-water refuge as the tide ebbs. As the tide rises, redfish wait along the edges of salt marshes for the water to enter the marsh grass. As soon as the water is deep enough, redfish will move onto the low marsh flat, first through creeks and troughs, then out into the flooded marsh grass. They are searching mostly for crabs—fiddler crabs and portunid (swimming) crabs—and to a lesser extent for the juvenile shrimp and small fish that also rise into the marsh with the tide. Fiddler crabs and even some swimming crabs will hang on to a smooth cordgrass stalk, just above the water line—a safer place than in the water where they might become a

A flood tide often makes it hard to find fish. Partly because the high water makes it hard to see them, but also because with so much water the fish are spread out in a much larger area. Still, it does give you the opportunity, in some areas, to explore places that are usually too shallow to be accessible. AARON ADAMS

redfish's dinner. As redfish move through the cordgrass, they often have to push their way through the thickly packed stalks. On a calm day, you can often track a redfish's movement through a salt marsh by watching the cordgrass stalks shudder when bumped by a passing fish. Unlucky crabs are knocked from their safety perch high on the grass, and passing redfish quickly investigate their plop into the water. Similarly, as the tide rises into black mangrove stands, redfish first prowl the edge in search of food, then continue to push inward looking for fiddler crabs that were a bit too greedy and didn't make it back into their burrows as the tide approached.

In areas with large tidal ranges, the latter half of the flooding tide and first half of the ebb can be difficult fishing in the marsh. As the tide continues to rise, the redfish often move even higher into the marsh or forage throughout the extensive flooded low marsh. When the tide is near full flood, it can be deep enough in the flooded salt marsh that the fish remain hidden, and the amount of area to cover in search of fish is overwhelming. The same is true of other habitats. High water during spring tides can make normally shallow grass and mud flats too deep for tailers and for sight-fishing, and can allow redfish to access flooded mangrove forests where anglers can't reach

It's a high rising tide, almost flooding, and I'm taking the opportunity to putt-putt slowly on my skiff, deep into mangrove infested backwaters, looking for openings that may have reds and snook. I just love exploring areas like these.

JUAN BALLOVERAS

them. As the tide continues to ebb, however, the fish slowly move out of the flooded areas, usually using the same types of avenues they used to access the shallows on the flooding tide. And don't give up too early in the ebbing tide—you'll be amazed at how late in the ebbing tide redfish will wait before leaving the marsh for deeper water. The water is often so shallow that their backs are out of the water as they leave the flat.

Neap Tides

During neap tides (which coincide with the quarter moons), tidal range is at its minimum for the monthly tidal cycle. The skinny water where you found schools of tailing fish at high tide just the week before might not even be deep enough to hold fish during a high neap tide. Many salt marshes and black mangrove stands will not have enough water on them to cover a redfish. Redfish are still feeding, and keyed to the tides, but often feed less aggressively or feed in different areas.

During the slow currents of neap tides, redfish will sometimes cruise in search of prey or try to ambush prey in potholes in seagrass beds. Troughs next to oyster bars and along red mangrove shorelines are also good places to find redfish during these tides—cruising in search of food or just resting on the bottom ("laid up," as anglers say). And they may be actively feeding in deeper areas, such as over deep grass beds, along channel edges, and in depressions and troughs between flats, providing fishing opportunities throughout the tidal cycle.

More on Barometric Pressure and Wind

Since tides are caused by movements of such massive areas of high and low water, you might think tides are impervious to influence from any other force, but this is not the case. Both barometric pressure and wind can greatly influence tides on a local scale, and significantly change tidal heights from the predictions of a tide chart. This is especially true in shallow embayments and lagoons, as well as in the shallow Gulf of Mexico. And while the wind- or pressure-induced differences in tide may sometimes seem minor to us, they can strongly influence redfish behavior.

During periods of low pressure, the atmosphere exerts less pressure down on the water, so tides can rise higher. Low barometric pressure is most often associated with either a warm or cold front, so a region may experience a weather change in association with a change in barometric pressure. When barometric pressure is high, tides are suppressed, so they may not rise as high as predicted. High pressure is usually associated with fair weather.

Wind can also have a dramatic effect on tides. For example, strong, onshore winds can make high tides higher than predicted and in extreme conditions can even prevent low tides from occurring—in effect creating a ghost tide. Offshore winds will have the opposite effect—both high and low tides will be lower than predicted. In many cases, a strong wind won't prevent tides from occurring, but will delay the onset of the ebb or flood. For example, a strong onshore wind may lengthen the duration of high slack tide, but eventually the force of the ebbing tide is too much and the water level drops quickly in the short amount of time remaining before low slack tide.

The degree of influence from wind depends on water depth and the shape of the basin. For example, tides in an enclosed bay will be more impacted by wind than tides on a flat with no surrounding land or shallows to restrict water flow. For enclosed basins, depending on how long and strong the winds blow and the size of the area affected, it may take a day or two for tides to return to normal once the wind subsides. And when wind and tide travel in the same direction, stronger tidal currents can result, piling up water against flats.

High pressure and strong offshore winds will tend to dampen a high tide and enhance the corresponding low tide, while low pressure and onshore winds will enhance the high tide and dampen the corresponding low tide. In areas with a small tidal range, such as the Gulf of Mexico, the changes in barometric pressure and wind can have a greater effect on water level than a normal tide, and can influence the behavior of redfish much the same as spring and neap tides. First, a strong offshore wind (or strong high pressure) might completely offset the high water expected from a spring tide, which will prevent redfish from accessing the shallows as they normally would, or confine them to potholes or deep locations on or near the flats. The extreme low spring tide will then be even lower than expected, perhaps forcing redfish off the flats altogether. If the same wind blows during a neap tide, the minor high tide that was predicted might not happen, so it will seem like low tide throughout the tidal cycle. In either case (spring or neap tides), during strong offshore winds the edges of flats, deeper holes and troughs between flats, deeper grass beds and sand basins, and the deeper water near marsh edges may provide redfish the best feeding opportunities.

In contrast, a strong onshore wind (and an approaching strong low pressure) may give redfish an extended stay at the shallow-water buffet. A strong onshore wind can push a spring high tide even further into the shallows and mangrove flats, can delay the onset of the ebbing tide, and can keep the water level from becoming as low as predicted at low tide. In a sense, the predicted

It's dead low tide, practically no water in the flat, and only the birds can dine now. But soon the tide will rise, and redfish and other gamefish will join them. Then, finding birds feeding in a few inches of water could easily signify the presence of redfish. I always look for birds actively feeding on a flat. PAT FORD

tide heights shift up a notch. The extra water gives redfish a wider selection of locations and, potentially, a longer time to forage.

The tides of the Gulf of Mexico are also more notably influenced by weather (atmospheric pressure and wind) than their Atlantic coast counterparts. The shallow continental shelf, shallow coastal bays and marshes, and small tidal range allow wind and atmospheric pressure to have a greater influence than they do in areas with deeper water and greater tidal range. The shallow lagoonal marshes of Texas are especially vulnerable to influences of weather. They are so shallow and experience such a minor tide that portions of these lagoons can become unfishable in windy conditions. Winter winds out of the north are especially bad because they push much of the water out of the marshes and pile it on the backsides of the barrier islands. So it pays to keep an eye on the weather when fishing the salt marshes and lagoons of Texas.

The small tides of the northern Gulf of Mexico mean that many of the inland ponds and lakes of Gulf Coast marshes, and the creeks that connect them to the Gulf, hold fish throughout the tidal cycle. There just isn't enough tide relative to water depth to influence the behavior of fish. This is great news for anglers because these waters provide vast protected areas that are perfect for fly fishing. You'll often hear reliable reports of dozens of redfish on the fly in a day of fishing in these backcountry lakes. In contrast, anglers fishing in backcountry in northeastern Florida and South Carolina have to be especially wary of tides to avoid being stuck in the marsh until the next high tide.

Anglers can take advantage of typical weather patterns to plan the best times to fish different areas. For example, typical weather patterns combine with the spring and fall equinox to create periods of highest water levels of the year in April and May and again in September and October, with the best chance for low water from December through February. This is because typical onshore winds of spring, summer, and fall combine with the spring tides to push water well into the shallow marshes and bays. During winter, strong offshore winds combine with the lowest tides of the year to drain many shallow marshes and bays, which may concentrate gamefish in deeper holes and sloughs. As you might expect, redfish

This low tide exposes several patches of oyster bars. When the incoming tide covers them, redfish love to feed around them. Not only will I look for reds around oyster bars, but I also will make a few blind casts around them when visibility is poor.

are keyed in to weather and tides and can change their behavior and location to take advantage of these periods.

In addition to affecting tide heights, wind can have a dramatic influence on tidal currents. A strong wind pushing against the tide can slow the current and dampen the effect of the tide. In contrast, a wind blowing with the tide can increase the current's speed and enhance the tide. It pays to note the interaction of wind and tide and their joint effects on currents.

Currents

Currents, whether completely tidal or a combination of tide and wind, constantly refresh the water in redfish habitats. Habitats closer to deeper water have stronger currents than backwaters far removed from deep edges, and are more thoroughly flushed by the tides. The new water delivered by currents supplies food to filter-feeding organisms like clams and some worms, which in turn feed crabs, shrimp, and other small carnivores. Redfish feed on all of the above, so by being in tune with the tides they are also in tune with their prey.

Currents during spring tides are also stronger, so areas that are not inviting to redfish because they experience only minor tidal currents during neap tides may receive enough water exchange during spring tides to attract redfish. In some instances, the effect of tidal currents and tidal height is so great that some flats are only productive during spring tides and others only on neap tides. This has to do not only with depth of the tides but also with the amount of water exchange a flat will experience due to tidal currents. These extremes are especially apparent in locations with high tidal range, like the Carolinas, where fishing for tailing redfish in flooded marshes occurs almost exclusively during spring tides in summer and fall.

Tides and Habitat from the Redfish's Perspective

Even if you have a tide chart, the direction, strength, and duration of wind, as well as changes in barometric pressure, can have significant effects on water level that result in higher or lower water than predicted by the tide charts. If you are very familiar with an area, you will know what the "normal" tide levels should be and can adjust your fishing strategy according to wind effects. However, if you are new to or visiting an area, if you left the tide charts on the kitchen table back home, or if you aren't quite sure of the effect of wind on the local tides, you can examine the mangrove and marsh habitats to determine what the normal water levels should be, and then adjust your strategy if necessary.

Black mangroves grow near or slightly above the high tide line, and the adjacent bottom is often open mud or sand. Thus, the distance of the waterline from the black mangrove pneumatophores will give you a ballpark estimate of where the tide is relative to typical high tide. If you are in an area that has seagrass, the water line relative to the shallow edge of the seagrass will give you an idea of where the tide is relative to typical low tide.

Red mangrove prop roots host a diverse group of organisms that grow on the roots (which you may remember are called a fouling community). The different species of the fouling community grow at different locations on the prop roots based on their need to be covered by water all or only part of the time. This results in a transition in species from the top to the bottom of the mangrove prop root. You can use this knowledge to estimate tidal height relative to normal. The upper end of the oyster clusters growing on prop roots, for example, will be at the upper portion of the intertidal range. Oysters can tolerate exposure to air (they close their shells and wait for water to cover them again before opening), but need to be in water for much of the tidal cycle, so will grow only as high on the prop roots as most midlevel tides will cover. The upper limits of oyster growth will tell you the height of the typical midtide. Barnacles have similar requirements, but can usually tolerate more air exposure, so can grow higher on the prop roots than oysters. Sponges and tunicates need to be covered by water almost all the time, so they are good indicators of the low tide line. In contrast, mangrove leaves can't tolerate being submerged in salt water on a regular basis. With some observation, you'll note the lower edge of mangrove leaves will hang parallel to the water surface, so the water will reach the lowest mangrove branches only on strong high tides. This lower edge of mangrove leaves is a good indicator of typical high tide levels.

The differences in requirements of oysters and mangrove leaves results in a gap between the uppermost oysters and the lowest mangrove branches. When water fills the gap between the oysters and mangrove branches, or is as high as the mangrove branches, you know you are experiencing an especially high tide. A typical high tide will cover the uppermost oysters. A typical low tide will expose the upper two-thirds of an oyster-encrusted prop root. You can use the water depth in relation to the oyster growth on prop roots and the height of mangrove branches as a rough guide to water level, and how the water levels you observe on a particular day might relate to what is typical for that area.

In salt marshes and mangrove swamps, creeks are the avenues redfish use to enter and exit these areas with the tides. On rising tides, redfish that have been waiting out the low tide in the creek mouth or in deeper water nearby pass through the creek mouth on their way into the marsh. As the tide rises, redfish will ride the tide up creeks that disappear into the low marsh. On falling tides, redfish often lay in wait at the creek mouths to pick off prey that is swept out of the creeks. Each creek will have its own variation on exact timing (because of depth, width, length, etc.), but in general, early in the rising tide and late in the dropping tide are good bets for intercepting redfish at these locations.

Redfish use of marsh edges is a bit different. In the typical situation, redfish will gather along edges of the low marsh during low tide. Often, you can cast to these fish in the hours around low tide, just as you would to fish holding in holes between oyster bars. Blind casting to steep edges of the marsh, whether an outer marsh edge or the edge of a wide creek, especially edges lined with oysters, can be an effective way to fish during the hours around low tide. Many fish, shrimp, and other gamefish prey that reside in the low marsh in high water find themselves evicted from the marsh for the hour or two around low tide. These prey collect along the edges waiting for the rising tide to allow them back into the marsh. As the tide begins to rise, the prey that have been waiting along the edges will be the first to head into the shelter of the marsh grass or across the shallows of the mud flats. During spring tides, redfish will ride the tide into the marsh grass in search of crabs and shrimp. If the tide is weak, you may find gamefish mostly restricted to marsh edges and creek beds.

Because of differences in tidal range, marsh slope, number of creeks, and other factors, each salt marsh will have optimum feeding times and zones for fish. Salt marshes with wide-reaching low marsh but no creeks may only see redfish venture a short distance into the marsh, since they don't want to get too far from the safety of deeper water. Plus, since the abundance of prey tends to decrease with distance from a marsh or creek edge, there's not much incentive for redfish to venture too far into the marsh. A similar-looking marsh, but with numerous creeks or shallow sloughs, may provide avenues for redfish to venture farther onto the flats in the same amount of time.

Redfish use the high water associated with spring high tides in summer in subtropical locations to gain access to black mangrove root habitat to feed on fiddler crabs and other crabs. (Fiddler crab burrows are usually scattered among the black mangrove pneumatophores.) Although fiddler crabs are usually most active at low tide, when they can be found feeding on detritus and debris left by the previous high tide, some will venture outside the safety of their burrows during high water, and are fed upon by redfish. More on this in the next chapter.

Chapter 4

Red Drum Foods

Fly anglers who pursue redfish are simultaneously blessed and cursed because a redfish's diet is so varied. They are blessed because they can choose any number of flies that, with the correct presentation, may elicit interest from a redfish. They are cursed because redfish will sometimes eat one prey item exclusively, and with such a large variety of potential prey (and corresponding flies) to choose from, an angler can go home frustrated and fishless. Knowing about the redfish diet helps fly anglers narrow the choices of flies on those tough days.

Because they have had commercial value in the past, redfish are well studied. And this abundance of data includes information on diet. This is why we are able to discuss regional and seasonal differences in diet that should be helpful to redfish anglers throughout the redfish's range.

General Patterns in Redfish Diets

An examination of scientific diet research reveals that redfish eat sixty or more species of prey. With their subterminal mouths, their diet is heavy on bottom-dwelling organisms, such as swimming crabs, mud crabs, common shrimp, snapping shrimp, blennies, gobies, and pinfish. But redfish also feed on fishes that live throughout the water column, including species in the mullet, killifish, and herring families. Their diet can vary somewhat by location, but the general patterns are true throughout their range, with most changes due to replacement of one species with another similar-looking species.

JUVENILE DIET

The diet of the smallest juvenile redfish remains similar among locations. For example, juveniles less than 2 inches eat mysids (very small shrimp-like crustaceans), juveniles 2 to 3 inches eat mysids and small fish, and juveniles 3 to 7 inches eat crustaceans such as crabs and shrimp, and small fish (often juveniles of other fish species). Conservation-minded anglers should take notice: a healthy fishery needs healthy juvenile habitats and bountiful prey, so protecting these habitats is important.

A few tiny grass shrimp in the palm of the hand. Juvenile redfish, especially, love to feed on them. STEPHEN FERNÁNDEZ

A juvenile blue crab. Redfish love to feed on this guy. And a good crab pattern will imitate him really well. AARON ADAMS

Once juveniles pass 7 inches in length, their diet still focuses on crabs and shrimp, with some more fish, until they reach approximately 30 inches. Over 30 inches, they will still eat crabs and shrimp, but fish become even more important in their diet, especially during winter and spring. Although there is a slight increase of prey size as redfish grow, the difference is so minor it is inconsequential. On average, redfish eat prey in proportion to prey availability—they eat more common prey more often. This reflects their opportunistic nature. Thus, in habitats with more prey species, the redfish diet is more varied.

HABITAT AND SEASON

At first look, the redfish diet can be overwhelming—so many species in so many habitats, in so many locations, and each prey species changing abundance by season. Knowing that redfish can consume sixty prey species is interesting, but a little overwhelming. Do you really need sixty different fly patterns to go fly-fishing for redfish? Of course not. You need to simplify things. The first step is to determine which prey species are most abundant and most common in the habitats you are fishing. There may be times when a rare prey is all they will eat, and you will need a specific fly for these occasions, but for the most part, sticking with imitating the dominant prey is the best bet.

With few exceptions, habitats that are more complex (more structure, more hiding places for prey) harbor more species of prey. Seagrass beds contain more species of potential prey than mud flats, for example, so the suite of potentially successful flies for redfish feeding in seagrass beds is larger than that for mud flats. You can look at this a couple ways. One is that in a seagrass bed, redfish have so many things to choose from that any number of flies should work. Another perspective is that at any particular time they may be focused on one or two prey types, and it can be overwhelming with so many flies to choose from. This underscores the importance of presentation—for a fish that has such a varied diet, how a fly is presented is probably as important as what prey the fly represents.

Oyster bars are also complex habitats that support a large variety of prey, as are salt marshes. Although prey will live throughout the oyster bar, the oyster bar edges—where the bar meets surrounding habitats of mud or seagrass—tend to hold the greatest types and numbers of prey. For salt marshes, prey abundance and number of different prey species is higher along the edges of marshes, creeks, and troughs.

In contrast, I see the short list of prey available on a mud flat as a positive. Only a handful of prey that a redfish is looking for will be on a mud flat, so options on flies are greatly reduced. In fact, when fishing for redfish on shoreline mud flats, I use only two flies, and one of those patterns (a fiddler crab imitation) I use 90 percent of the time.

Familiarity with habitat-associated differences in prey can mean the difference between a good or bad fishing day. I've examined the stomach contents of redfish feeding in areas with drift algae, for example, which is most common during winter. Items found, in order from most to least abundant, were mud crabs (often the common mud crab, *Panopeus herbstii*), snapping shrimp (*Alpheus* spp.), and small gobies and blennies. In contrast, I found that redfish feeding on mud flats adjacent to black mangrove shorelines ate mostly fiddler crabs and juvenile blue crabs. And in North Carolina, redfish feeding on or near oyster reefs ate mostly crabs and shrimp, but redfish feeding in nearby non–oyster reef habitats ate mostly fish.

In addition to habitat-associated differences, redfish diet also varies seasonally. Reasons for the diet seasonality are many. Some prey are available only during particular seasons, such as large schools of anchovies along Gulf Coast beaches in the fall. Some prey are present year-round, but only become major diet items during times of year when other prey is not as available. Sometimes a prey species is available year-round, but redfish only eat the prey in a particular season. This is often the case for prey species that grow too large as adults to be eaten by redfish, so redfish eat mostly juveniles. This seems to be the case for blue crabs and their relatives—adults are occasionally eaten by large redfish, but most of these swimming crabs that end up in redfish stomachs are juveniles and subadults. Mullet is another example of this pattern—juveniles (finger mullet) are high on the prey list in fall, when they are most abundant, but adults are usually too large to be eaten.

Depending on the location, an angler might cast to redfish in seagrass, mangrove, open bottom, marsh, salt marsh, or beach habitats. Much of this depends upon region—a subtropical angler won't be fishing salt marshes, and a warm-temperate angler won't be fishing mangroves, for example. Seagrass beds are major habitats for redfish in parts of the Gulf of Mexico, but seagrass is largely absent from Georgia, South Carolina, and much of North Carolina. In these latter areas, mud flats, oyster bars, and marshes are the important redfish habitats. These habitats harbor different numbers and species of prey. Some prey species are present throughout the redfish's range (blue crabs, for example), but many are limited to portions of the range, usually along temperature lines. The combination of seasonality and habitat are probably the most important aspects of redfish ecology from an angler's perspective.

Redfish in the northern Gulf of Mexico tend to eat more fish in winter, while in southwest Florida crustaceans are high on the list during winter. This is mostly due to prey availability. Crabs and shrimp are available year-round in southern Florida, but are absent, in low abundance, or dormant (buried in the mud) during the cold of winter in the northern Gulf. Redfish off the coast of Louisiana gorge on menhaden in the fall, whereas redfish in south Florida have no such feeding opportunity. Whether these types of differences should influence an angler's choice of flies is debatable, but as many anglers know, subtleties often make the difference between catching fish or not. This doesn't mean anglers need a completely different fly box for each location they fish, but rather a good selection of flies that represent the major groups of prey eaten by redfish.

To some extent, focusing on regional differences in redfish diet can seem like splitting hairs. After all, just because northern Gulf redfish eat more fish in winter doesn't mean they won't slurp up a crab fly. It's also important to consider the methods used in the studies that examined redfish diets. These studies generally don't take habitat effects into account, so they are estimates of the total diet of regional populations of redfish. The diet reflects the overall stomach contents of redfish captured in multiple habitats. So these studies provide good frameworks for choosing the most appropriate flies, but a prudent angler will also take habitat into consideration. For example, in contrast to the study that showed that redfish on Florida's Gulf of Mexico coast preferred baitfish in winter, I found that redfish feeding in estuarine seagrass beds in winter feed primarily on crabs and shrimp. This difference was probably because my study occurred exclusively in seagrass beds, whereas the large-scale study captured redfish from deeper, more open water habitats.

In general, adult redfish feed primarily on fish (menhaden, anchovies, mullet, killifish), shrimp, and crabs. Broken down seasonally for the Gulf of Mexico, fish (mostly menhaden and anchovies) are most common in winter, while crabs and shrimp are the most common prey eaten in summer and fall. In the Atlantic, fish tend to be even more important in the adult redfish diet. In addition, fish are important prey during fall more in the northern than the southern Gulf of Mexico. To a great extent, this is because redfish in the northern Gulf eat a lot of menhaden in the fall, when large schools of menhaden migrate along the coast. It appears that this mostly a chance occurrence rather than a purposeful behavior. When redfish encounter a school of menhaden, they will eat menhaden and ignore everything else. But when they're in habitats where menhaden aren't present, they'll readily eat other prey. These are just a few examples of

This is the actual stomach content of a 7-pound redfish. It had about half a dozen small shrimp and two large crabs, but still took a fish pattern fly with no hesitation.

local variations in redfish diet resulting from regional differences in habitats, degree of seasonality, and species of prey. Following is a more detailed description of seasonal variation in diet by region.

REDFISH DIET BY REGION

In Texas, studies indicate that the overall seasonal diet reflected the seasonal changes in the availability of the prey. Blue crabs are important prey items in all seasons, whereas white shrimp and menhaden are eaten mostly in fall and spring, respectively. In fall, crustaceans (crabs and shrimp) were present in 83% of redfish stomachs. Most white shrimp were eaten by redfish less than 17 inches, whereas larger fish showed less preference for any one prey. In addition to white shrimp and blue crab, other crustaceans in the fall diet included (in order): lesser blue crab, brown shrimp, mud crabs, grass shrimp, porcelain crabs, and snapping shrimp. Fish were also present in 40% of stomachs, including (in order): blackcheek tonguefish, shrimp eels, Gulf menhaden, bay anchovy, hardhead catfish, mullet, least pufferfish, midshipman, and sea robin.

In spring, fish were by far the dominant prey, making up more than 80% of the diet, including (in order): Gulf menhaden, mullet, black-cheek tonguefish, shrimp eels, southern flounder, pinfish, Gulf toadfish, and rough silverside. Crustaceans occurred in only 45% of redfish stomachs: blue crab, lesser blue crab, mud crabs, grass shrimp, and river shrimp. Although brown shrimp are abundant in estuarine habitats in spring, redfish apparently don't eat them since relatively few end up in redfish stomachs.

In Louisiana, the general groups of prey (fish and crustaceans) were similar in all seasons, but the dominant prey and a few of the prey species, changed seasonally. In winter, fish (primarily menhaden) were present in 80% of redfish stomachs, followed by crustaceans (primarily blue crabs, 50%). In spring, redfish ate fish (primarily anchovies, 83%) and crustaceans (primarily blue crabs, 55%). In summer, redfish ate fish (86%, with lizardfish a strong contributor), and crustaceans (primarily shrimp, 89%). But in fall, crustaceans (primarily shrimp, 81%) were more common than fish (primarily anchovies, 65%).

In Mississippi and Alabama, the seasonal diet is less clear, with somewhat different findings in two studies. One study showed that the diet of redfish up to 31 inches, for all seasons combined, was dominated by common shrimp (present in 40% of stomachs), swimming crabs (54%), and various species of fish (43%). When broken down by season, the most common prey were: (winter) common shrimp, in 53% of the stomachs; (spring) swimming crabs 71%; (summer) swimming crabs 65%; (fall) various fish species 50%. Another study found that fish were most important as prey in winter and spring, blue crabs in spring and summer, and shrimp in fall. Polychaetes (marine worms) were also found in the redfish stomachs. In this second study, the overall proportions of redfish prey were: blue crabs (present in 54.8% of stomachs), common shrimp (40.4%), and various species of fish (43.3%). So despite some seasonal differences in diet, both studies were similar in the most important prey.

Redfish diet from North Carolina through northern Florida is similar. In South Carolina, for example, redfish size has a strong effect on diet. The diet of fish less than 21 inches is dominated by fiddler crabs (52% of the prey items), with other groups far behind: various species of fishes (7%), blue crabs and closely related species (7%), mud crabs (11%), and grass shrimp (19%). The diet for redfish greater than 21 inches shifts dramatically toward fishes (46%, including mullet, menhaden, killifish, and croakers), with lesser numbers of blue crabs and relatives (21%), fiddler crabs (19%), and mud crabs (4%). This suite of prey reflects the importance of salt marshes to redfish in South Carolina.

Similarly in Georgia, redfish less than 12 inches ate mostly crustaceans, with white shrimp, grass shrimp, and mud crabs (primarily the common mud crab, *Panopeus herbstii*) at the top of the list. For redfish between 12 and 31 inches in length, crustaceans are still dominant, but fish (with mummichogs, Atlantic menhaden, and striped mullet the most common species) also appear in the diet. Redfish diets are similar in North Carolina and northeast Florida, where diet is generally related to habitat—more crabs and shrimp on oyster bars and in marshes, and more fish on open bottom habitats.

Seasonal variation in redfish diet in Southeastern states is similar to that found in the northern Gulf of Mexico. In winter, the diet is varied, and given the lower abundance of most prey, redfish are probably the most opportunistic during this season. Mummichogs, Atlantic menhaden, and striped mullet are high on the list, as are grass shrimp and snapping shrimp. During spring, crabs and fish are most common. Redfish take advantage of the high abundance of juvenile white shrimp during summer and fall, but also eat mud crabs and fiddler crabs: in summer, white shrimp are most common in redfish stomachs, followed by fiddler crabs and mud crabs; in fall, mud crabs top the list, followed by white shrimp and fiddler crabs.

Redfish peak feeding appears to occur in spring and fall. Some of the seasonal differences are due to availability of prey, but redfish temperature preferences probably also play a role. This may be reflected in a Georgia study: 80 percent of the redfish captured in water greater than 69 degrees had food in their stomachs, but only 67 percent of redfish from water less than 68 degrees had food in their stomachs. I guess being cold-blooded has its drawbacks.

Red Drum Prey

Before we get into specifics on the different types of prey, it's worth thinking about how many fly patterns you really need to imitate the dominant prey in each habitat. Scientific studies of fish diet break the prey into small categories—if possible, they identify the prey by species. For prey that are more difficult to identify (because they are more digested), the studies identify the genus or family. While species identification is important for fish ecology studies, in many cases anglers don't need that much detail—many prey species are similar enough in appearance that one or two fly patterns is sufficient to imitate the whole group. For example, although there are three species of common shrimp, as juveniles (when they are most eaten by redfish) all three species are nearly identical in appearance. This is something to keep in mind as you read the rest of this chapter.

CRUSTACEANS

Crabs

Although the number and types of species may vary among locations, crabs are present in all redfish habitats. However, some species are most common in certain habitats, some species are present throughout the redfish's range, and some species are found in only limited locations. We can use this information to narrow the list of probable crabs we might find in each habitat.

A challenge to fly anglers is choosing flies appropriate for the situation at hand, but doing so from a reasonably sized fly box. A first step toward keeping a well stocked, but reasonably sized, fly box is to focus on the similarities in prey characteristics and to design or choose flies that best represent these characteristics. For example, a characteristic of crabs is that although the species may vary, within each group the general colorations and behaviors are similar among species.

Swimming crabs (family Portunidae), mud crabs (family Xanthidae), and spider crabs (family Majidae) are the most common crabs in shallow estuarine and coastal habitats. By far, the crab most commonly eaten by redfish is the blue crab and its close relatives. Blue crabs and their relatives can be found in virtually all coastal and estuarine habitats. And although mud crabs and spider crabs generally don't make the top five on the list of prey items in large-scale diet studies, redfish certainly eat plenty of them in shallow habitats. Mud crabs are favorites in seagrass beds and around oyster bars, and spider crabs in seagrass beds and on mud flats. No fly angler pursuing redfish should be without a few mud crab or spider crab patterns.

Like most prey, crabs will be colored to match their surroundings, and this can mean that members of the same family, or even species, that are in different habitats may have different coloration. The many species of mud crabs you'll find on oyster bars, for example, will be varying shades of brown, whereas most mud crabs found in seagrass beds will be green or tan. In addition, redfish

An adult blue crab usually takes a defensive pose when it cannot escape by swimming away. A big redfish would love to find this crab in the open. STEPHEN FERNÁNDEZ

tend to eat the juveniles of many prey species that grow large as adults, such as blue crabs and spider crabs. And fortunately for fly anglers, these juvenile blue and spider crabs are similar in size to many of the mud crabs found in the same habitats. So an olive crab fly cast into a grass bed or a tan or brown crab fly cast along the edge of an oyster bar should be a decent imitation of many of the crabs found in these habitats. At this point, the presentation of the fly will give it the characteristics of different species.

How you present your fly should vary with the type of crab. Swimming crabs are voracious predators and scavengers, and always seems to be on the move. They can be found along the bottom of grass beds, clinging onto grass blades, swimming near the surface, digging small holes in patches of open bottom as they excavate a clam dinner, along sandy beaches, and climbing among mangrove prop roots and marsh grasses. When pursued by a redfish, however, they usually try to bury in the bottom or hide. They may try to swim away before the redfish sees them, but quickly dive for cover when pursued. And only as a last resort do they try to swim away because their chances of out-swimming a redfish are slim. Give blue crab imitation flies action until the redfish sees your fly, then let it dive for the bottom.

When tying or buying your crab flies, consider how they move through the water. Swimming crabs, for example, swim through the water sideways and are oval in shape, with pointy ends. So a primary consideration for choosing a fly pattern to imitate a swimming crab is orientation of its parts (legs, claws, eyes) and shape of the fly. For a swimming crab imitation, you'll need a fly that appears to swim sideways when stripped, and drop to the bottom when needed. In contrast, mud crabs are generally round, and walk or scurry along the bottom. So a fly to imitate mud crabs should be round and you would strip it slowly, if at all, along the bottom.

Redfish have small teeth that rim their jaws, which are good for grabbing prey, especially fish. But they also have crusher plates at the front of their throat that they use to crush crabs and shrimp before swallowing them. Keep this in mind when you are fishing for redfish—give the fish enough time to slurp in the fly, but not too long, or it will realize the fly is not a meal when it tries to crush it, likely spitting it out. You must pay attention to the body language of the fish to know when it's taken the fly. You'll know the fly has been chewed and spit out if you retrieve the fly and find its shape has been flattened.

The most common swimming crabs eaten by redfish are blue crab (*Callinectes sapidus*), lesser blue crab (*Callinectes similis*), lady crab (*Ovalipes ocellatus*), and speckled crab (*Arenaeus cribrarius*). Juvenile swimming crabs are most abundant in spring through summer, somewhat earlier farther south, and are a favorite of redfish.

Mud crabs and spider crabs are both walking crabs. They lack the rear paddle-like leg that allows swimming crabs to actively swim through the water, so they tend to be slow movers. They also maintain a close association with hiding places on the bottom. Mud crabs and spider crabs are round or tear-shaped, and generally move backwards or try to hide if threatened. They can be found in seagrass, oyster bars, and mangrove shorelines. They are present throughout the year, so they can be particularly good patterns during winter when many seasonally abundant prey species are absent. Never give mud crab and spider crab flies much action. A good pattern is round and gets to the bottom quickly. A good presentation, very close to the fish, is a must for these flies.

Mud crabs typically feed along the bottom, and hide at the base of grass blades, burrow into the soft bottom, or scurry under a shell when chased. As their name implies, they are most often associated with soft bottoms, including seagrass, mangrove swamps, salt marshes, and open muddy bottom near seagrass and oyster bars. I have examined the stomach contents of many redfish caught while they were tailing in seagrass beds, and most were dominated by mud crabs. However, some species of mud crabs are common on oyster bars, so this can also be a good habitat to use flies that imitate mud crabs. Mud crabs on oyster bars, like mud crabs in seagrass beds, tend to hide during the day and venture out at night to feed. However, the habitats—oyster bar vs. seagrass—force a different feeding behavior by redfish in search of a mud crab meal. In seagrass a redfish can move slowly with its snout in the bottom. As the redfish finds mud crabs hiding at the bottom of the grass blades, it can easily push aside the grass blades and capture some of the mud crabs. It would be a tough way to find food to have to root around in oyster piles, which is another reason for redfish to concentrate their feeding efforts around the edges of the bars rather than on the bars. Mud crabs seem most abundant in winter and early spring, which is also when many other species are less abundant.

The most common species of mud crabs that occur in areas frequented by redfish include common mud crab (*Panopeus herbstii*), Say's mud crab (*Neopanope sayi*), Texas mud crab (*Neopanope texana*), depressed mud crab (*Eurypanopeus depressus*), and spotted mud crab (*Eurypanopeus abbreviatus*). All of these mud crabs live subtidally—that is, below the low tide line. The spider crabs redfish eat are the southern spider crab (*Libinia dubia*) and the common spider crab (*Libinia emarginata*).

When tying or choosing flies to imitate mud crabs, don't go large. Typical mud crab size ranges from 1/2 inch to 1 3/4 inches across, with a fly 3/4 to 1 inches across being a good choice. And although spider crabs grow considerably larger as adults (body to 4 inches, legs to 12 inches), the size eaten by redfish is typically around 1 to 2 inches in body size.

When choosing a fly to imitate mud and spider crabs, your choice of color can be simplified to the basics—dark green, brown, or tan, depending upon the species and location. For example, the Florida mud crab has a yellowish to tan carapace and brown legs, and often red or brown spots. In contrast, the common mud crab is brownish green, while Say's mud crab ranges from medium green to brown. As mentioned above, a safe bet is to use flies that are similar to the color of the habitat or bottom.

Now it's time to highlight a group of prey that is not abundant in many diet studies, and is overlooked by many anglers, but should be one of the top flies for anglers fishing salt marshes and black mangrove shorelines—fiddler crabs (family Ocypodidae). The reason fiddler crabs often don't show up in scientific diet studies ("Red Drum: Natural History and Fishing Techniques in South Carolina" by Dr. Charles Wenner is an exception) is that most diet studies don't collect redfish from shallow habitats. Instead, fish come from deeper habitats where fiddler crabs are absent. The few studies that have been conducted in salt marsh and black mangrove habitats show that, when available, redfish love to eat fiddler crabs. For example, fiddler crabs comprise 52% of the diet of South Carolina redfish less than 21 inches (grass shrimp are 19%, mud crabs are 11%), and 19% for larger

Fiddler crabs mostly feed on the low tide stages when Mr. Red cannot reach them and hide during high tide. However, those crabs that stay to feed a little longer may encounter a big redfish. So during high tides against shorelines, a crab pattern is very effective. STEPHEN FERNÁNDEZ

fish. In my own examinations of redfish stomachs from black mangrove shorelines in southwest Florida, fiddler crabs are also a common prey item.

Fiddler crabs dig burrows in soft ground in the intertidal zone or just above the high tide line, mostly in areas protected from waves and strong currents. Black mangrove shorelines and salt marshes are great places to look for fiddler crabs. In the subtropics, fiddler crabs are most common among black mangrove pneumatophores or above the high tide line of a red mangrove stand. In warm-temperate salt marshes, fiddler crabs are common in low marshes that are routinely flooded at high tide, and along the banks of tidal creeks that crisscross the low marsh. Fiddler crabs usually are out of their burrows feeding during low tide, and retreat into their burrows during high tide. But the burrows may be shallow enough or some fiddler crabs may remain active enough at high tide to be found and eaten by redfish. A walk through the marsh at low tide will tell you where the biggest groups of fiddler crabs are located. You will likely hear them as they skitter across the marsh mud, and will see the crabs retreating to their burrows as you approach. Sometimes fiddler crabs will climb the stalks of the marsh grass during high tide, and I've heard some theorize that redfish purposefully bang into the grass blades hoping to knock fiddler crabs into the water. I have seen fiddler crabs clinging to smooth cordgrass just above the water line. I have also seen these crabs knocked off the grass when the grass is bumped by a passing redfish, so the theory may have some merit. In this situation, a good "plop" in front of a redfish feeding in a flooded marsh is part of a good presentation.

Although the enlarged claw is the most notable characteristic of fiddler crabs, it is not a necessary component of a fiddler crab fly. Only the males have this appendage associated with territorial and courtship displays. Females do not have an oversized claw. So when tying flies to imitate fiddler crabs, it makes the job a lot easier if you just ignore the large claw.

You may encounter five or more species of fiddler crabs in redfish territory, all in the genus *Uca*. Ive's fiddler crab (*Uca speciosa*) is the most common in south Florida. Other species include mud fiddler (*Uca pugnax*), Burger's fiddler (*Uca burgersi*), sand fiddler (*Uca pugilator*), and panacea sand fiddler (*Uca panacea*). Each species prefers particular habitat characteristics (such as sediment type, type of vegetation, near the high or low tide line), but fiddler crabs are similar enough in appearance that you don't have to be able to tell the difference between the species, or even know the types of sediments they prefer, to choose a fly. Instead, if you know fiddler crabs live in the intertidal zone then you will know what types of

Here is a close-up of a fiddler crab. While coloration varies with the different species of fiddlers, shape stays pretty much the same. STEPHEN FERNÁNDEZ

Often as the tide rises, fiddler crabs stop feeding and hide in their borrows to escape the reds that will come with the tide looking for them. But a few will try climbing up the grass. This is not a good choice. A red can easily push the grass down with its nose until the crab hits the water, and then it's all over. AARON ADAMS

areas to look for and what locations are likely best for using fiddler crab flies. And they have similar body shape (squarish) and coloration (typically olive, brown, mottled brown, tan, and orange-brown), although there are exceptions. Often, the male's claw is more brightly colored than the body, which may be a good characteristic to incorporate into a fly pattern if you choose. Typical body size for fiddler crabs is half an inch to an inch.

Finally, when along the beach, redfish will encounter mole crabs (family Hippidae), also known as sand crabs, and a couple species of swimming crabs (primarily lady crab (*Ovalipes ocellatus*) and speckled crab (*Arenaeus cribrarius*). Beaches with some wave energy will support the most mole crabs. They are oval in shape; generally tan, brown and white, or gray; and they grow up to 1 inch long. These crabs ride the current created by waves to move into and off the beach and along the shoreline. Between forays into the surf, they burrow into the sand. Lady crabs and speckled crabs live on sandy bottoms offshore of sandy beaches and sometimes can be found on sand flats on the back sides of barrier islands.

This is a juvenile common shrimp, which redfish often find in the flats. Its coloration can vary depending on the environment and water color. A great variety of shrimp patterns, even those with a little chartreuse or orange color to act as an attractor, will make a good imitation. STEPHEN FERNÁNDEZ

Shrimp

Redfish eat a lot of shrimp. In some locations, during some seasons, shrimp are at the top of the menu. While common shrimp (family Penaeidae) top the list, other types of shrimp are also eaten by redfish, including snapping shrimp (family Alpheidae), and to a lesser extent grass shrimp (Family Palaemonidae) and mantis shrimp (family Squillidae). Depending upon the species and the habitat, in order to escape from predators the shrimp may burrow into the sediments, scurry under oysters rocks or into burrows, hide among the bases of the grass blades, or grab onto seagrass blades and try to become "part of the seagrass."

Common shrimp are what we usually think of when we think of shrimp, and they are the species we eat in restaurants. There are three species in the redfish's geographical range—pink shrimp, white shrimp, and brown shrimp—with each being more abundant in different areas. Pink shrimp can be found in subtropical estuaries throughout the year, but are most abundant in summer and fall. In warm-temperate regions, juvenile pink and white shrimp are mostly found in spring and fall. Brown shrimp dominate in the northwestern Gulf of Mexico. Fortunately for fly anglers, the species are similar in appearance, and all use seagrass beds with soft sediments or mangroves and marshes as juveniles before migrating to deeper water as adults. The color of juveniles varies slightly among the species, generally reflecting habitat type, and includes clear and translucent shades of green, gray, and brown.

Redfish also eat pink shrimp—the same ones we eat in restaurants—except they usually find shrimp in the juvenile stage. AARON ADAMS

Mantis shrimp in the redfish's geographic range live in burrows in sand-bottomed seagrass beds, and are similar in appearance to the praying mantis (thus the name). The most common species encountered by redfish is the green mantis shrimp (*Pseudosquilla ciliata*), which is good at blending in with the color of its surroundings. Since it is often found in seagrass and mud bottoms, the shimp is generally tan to green in color. It reaches 2 to 3 inches in length. Mantis shrimp usually don't venture far from their burrows and are most active at night. When chased, its defense posture is to turn and face its adversary while retreating backward toward its burrow.

Snapping shrimp live in burrows in areas of mixed seagrass and open bottom, in seagrass beds, or on oyster bars. When living in seagrass beds, they are usually olive green, and can be a shade toward brown when living on

As redfish grow larger, they start to eat more fish. Top and bottom are species of killifish, and in the center a pinfish.
STEPHEN FERNÁNDEZ

oyster bars. They move slowly along the bottom or over oysters, and retreat into shelter when they see a predator approaching. The species most encountered by redfish is the common snapping shrimp (*Alpheus heterochaelis*), with sand snapping shrimp (*Alpheus floridanus*) and green snapping shrimp (*Alpheus normanni*) less common.

Grass shrimp (family Palaemonidae) are common in seagrass beds and on oyster bars, and can be common in some salt marshes. They are small (less than 2 inches long) and mostly clear. Despite their size, they can be common in redfish stomachs, especially during winter and early spring, when they are at their greatest abundance and other prey are less abundant. Some days in winter and early spring, redfish will ignore larger shrimp flies in favor of small flies that imitate grass shrimp (the same can be said for spotted seatrout). Most often, the redfish focus on the common grass shrimp (*Paelomonetes pugio*) and several related species that are indistinguishable by all but experts.

BONY FISHES

Despite their obvious dependence upon crustaceans for much of their diet, redfish eat a lot of fish. Fish are present in redfish diets in all regions and in all seasons, but the relative importance of fish as prey changes seasonally, and the types of fish most often eaten change with location. For example, juvenile mullet are abundant in the fall, and are very high on the menu during this season, especially in the subtropics. A small, white surface fly fished over a grass bed will grab the interest of any redfish within hearing distance during this time of year. By contrast, in the northern Gulf of Mexico, menhaden are the fish prey of choice in the fall. Other species of fish are present year-round, but are less reported in diet studies because they occur in habitats generally not sampled during these studies. This group of fish includes blennies, gobies, killifishes, and pinfish. The challenge to anglers is to figure out which species of prey fish are most abundant in their region in each season, and focus on flies imitating these prey fish. Since redfish have such varied tastes, I'll focus on the prey fish that occur most frequently in their diet.

Mullet, Pinfish, Spot, Croaker, and Mojarras

An angler might encounter three species of mullet in the redfish's geographic range, and redfish will eat any of these species at the right time and place. These are white

Big redfish love a good mouthful, and mullet fill the bill. It's exciting to watch a big red popping mullet on the surface. Often the mullet will be sent flying a couple of feet in the air. Here is the place for a surface fly like a big popper or deer head streamer. STEPHEN FERNÁNDEZ

mullet (*Mugil curema*), fantail mullet (*Mugil gyrans*), and striped mullet (*Mugil cephalus*). Fortunately, these species of mullet are similar enough in appearance that a couple fly patterns should suffice. Of greater importance is fly size. Redfish mostly feed on juvenile mullet. At this size, they are popularly referred to as finger mullet, are 3 to 6 inches long, and are most abundant at this size in late summer and fall. It's quite a treat to watch redfish bust through a school of finger mullet, sending mullet airborne. Even when the feeding is not so obvious, however, during fall redfish usually have an eye out for finger mullet. Many times while fishing to tailing redfish in the fall, I have had redfish stop tailing and chase down a mullet fly.

Pinfish are also present throughout the year in all locations inhabited by redfish, but they are most common in redfish stomachs during fall, when they've reached 4 to 6 inches in length. Pinfish larvae come into estuaries during late winter and early spring, and many migrate offshore in the fall. Fortunately for redfish, this seasonal migration out of estuaries coincides with redfish spawning season, which places redfish near the mouths of estuaries—right in the migration pathway of pinfish. I've also seen redfish herd pinfish across a grass flat, so it's a good idea to have pinfish imitations in your fly box.

Redfish have no problem eating other species in the drum family. The most common members of the drum family that end up in redfish stomachs are spot (*Leiostomus xanthurus*) and croaker (*Micropogonias undulatus*), both of which are bottom dwellers with silver bodies.

Mojarras are abundant in shallow, soft-bottom, coastal and lagoon habitats, including mangroves, salt marsh, seagrass, and open bottom. Most mojarras have a relatively high body profile and all are silver in color, some with mottled sides. Redfish typically eat mojarras less than 5 inches in length. Common species are silver jenny (*Eucinostomus gula*), tidewater mojarra (*Eucinostomus harengulus*), striped mojarra (*Diapterus plumieri*), spotfin mojarra (*Eucinostomus argenteus*), and mottled mojarra (*Eucinostomus lefroyi*). All but striped mojarra are similar in size and shape. The striped mojarra has a higher body profile and grows larger, so it is generally only eaten when small. Small mojarras can be present throughout the year, but are most common in spring.

Baitfishes

Numerous species of what are commonly referred to as "baitfish" are seasonally important to redfish. Protected beaches will often have schools of baitfish moving back and forth along the shoreline. Often, smaller species (like silversides) will be closer to shore and larger species (like herring) will be farther off the beach. However, this pattern may change depending upon how active predators have been—feeding gamefish will push herring up against the beach, and sometimes herring will even jump onto the beach to escape. Finding these schools of baitfish is not always easy because they blend in with their surroundings, are often on the move, and may be well below the surface and somewhat scattered if they are not being actively pursued by predators.

In the northern Gulf of Mexico, and to a lesser extent along the North Carolina coast, menhaden is highest on this list of baitfish during fall and spring. On the Atlantic coast, adult Atlantic menhaden (*Brevoortia tyrannus*) spawn offshore of North Carolina during winter and

Especially in the northern range, menhaden are a good food source for redfish. AARON ADAMS

A bay anchovy. Redfish love to find a school of these anchovies. AARON ADAMS

move inshore in spring. Juveniles begin congregating in dense schools in estuaries as they leave shallow areas and migrate out of estuaries in the fall (typical size is 4 inches). Some juveniles and adults are found in sounds and bays along the South Atlantic Region during mild winters. Gulf menhaden (*Brevoortia patronus*) spawn in nearshore coastal waters from fall through spring. Juveniles migrate out of estuaries after about one year, with peak migration during fall through early winter. Adults then migrate back inshore in early spring. These migration patterns explain the seasonal occurrence of menhaden in redfish stomachs, and should start you thinking about when and where you can take advantage of these patterns. Other species, including finescale menhaden (*Brevoortia gunteri*) and yellowfin menhaden (*Brevoortia smithi*), are difficult to distinguish but are also important redfish prey.

Anchovies—including dusky anchovy (*Anchoa lyolepis*), bay anchovy (*Anchoa mitchilli*), and striped anchovy (*Anchoa hepsetus*)—are most abundant in late summer and fall and can be found in open waters (they generally don't occur in seagrass beds) from estuaries to beaches. The schools are usually easy to identify—keep an eye out for schools of fish that look brown from above. Usually the best place to find redfish feeding on these anchovies is along coastal beaches.

Bottom-Dwelling Fishes

Bottom-oriented fishes are present throughout the year in coastal habitats and are eaten frequently by redfish, but they usually don't show up in diet studies. This is because, as mentioned earlier, these species live in shallow habitats generally not sampled during diet studies. These habitats are, however, frequented by both redfish and fly anglers. Important families of fish in this group include toadfish (family Batrachoididae), gobies (family Gobiidae), killifish (family Cyprinodontidae), and mojarras (family Gerreidae).

Toadfish are present in just about every habitat you will find redfish. The Gulf toadfish (*Opsanus beta*) is common in the Gulf of Mexico, and the oyster toadfish (*Opsanus tau*) lives along the Atlantic coast. Both species can grow quite large (12 inches or more), but redfish will eat smaller juveniles of a few inches in length.

Gobies and blennies are similar in shape and color to toadfish, so you can imitate them with similar patterns. Overall, I've found gobies and blennies to be more common in redfish stomachs than toadfish. Gobies occur in seagrass beds, open bottom, and oyster bars, where they rest on their pectoral fins and dart about to feed or to chase off competitors. They generally don't move great distances and hide from, rather than swim from, feeding redfish. The gobies eaten by redfish range from brown to dark green and are typically around 2 to 3 inches in length. They are round like a pencil, with a larger head tapering to a more narrow tail. Species likely eaten by redfish include frillfin goby (*Bathygobius soporator*), code goby (*Gobiosoma robustum*), clown goby (*Microgobius gulosus*), and naked goby (*Gobiosoma bosci*).

Like gobies, blennies are territorial, bottom-associated, and don't move great distances. Their color ranges from mostly mottled tan to brown to green, and they have a large head tapering to a slender tail. They are taller than they are wide, so from the side, they provide a high profile. They are typically from 2 to 4 inches in length. Blennies are common on oyster bars, and to a lesser extent in seagrass beds. Common species encountered by

The goby, a bottom-dweller, is another redfish favorite. AARON ADAMS

redfish include striped blenny (*Chasmodes bosquianus*), Florida blenny (*Chasmodes saburrae*), crested blenny (*Hypleurochilus geminatus*), feather blenny (*Hypsoblennius hentzi*), and freckled blenny (*Hypsoblennius ionthas*).

Killifishes and Friends

Killifishes (aka mudminnows) live in shallow seagrass, mud, oyster bar, mangrove, and marsh habitats. In other words, they run into redfish a lot. Killifish are small (from 1 inch up to 7 inches long) and have earth-toned coloration. During spring and early summer mating seasons, the males can have some relatively bright coloration. Among the most common killifishes associated with redfish habitats are mummichog (*Fundulus heteroclitus*), Gulf killifish (*Fundulus grandis*), sheepshead minnow (*Cyprinodon variegatus*), longnose killifish (*Fundulus similis*), striped killifish (*Fundulus majalis*), bayou killifish (*Fundulus pulvereus*), and marsh killifish (*Fundulus confluentus*), with the species varying by location and habitat type. The sailfin molly (*Poecilia latipinna*, family Poeciliidae) is similar in size and coloration and is common in backwater habitats. Fortunately, killifish and mollies are similar in size, shape, and color, so the same flies should work throughout the redfish's range.

Another common food for redfish in the backwaters is the Gulf killifish. This one is pale in coloration. A great variety of fish pattern flies will match killifish. AARON ADAMS

WORMS AND SUCH

Redfish also eat numerous species of Echinoderms and Polychaetes, but only some of the Polychaetes (worms) can be imitated with a fly. Polychaetes are segmented worms that come in many body shapes, but for our purposes we will divide the many species into two general categories: tube dwellers and free moving. Among the most recognizable tube dwellers are the numerous filter-feeding species with large, bushy crowns that extend from the worm's tube or burrow. The crowns quickly retract into the tube if the worm senses danger. The second group of Polychaetes searches for food along the bottom, and either lives in a tube, burrows into the sediment when seeking shelter, or simply lives on the bottom, and are shaped similar to earthworm. Some species of Polychaetes grow up to about three or four inches, and these species are of most interest to redfish.

PART II

Tackle and Equipment

Chapter 5

Flies for Reds

As you've learned by now, a redfish is an exciting gamefish for the fly fisher. Depending on where you are fishing, you could get a shot at a 3-pounder or a 30-pounder. You can sight-fish them in a great variety of environments, from an oceanside flat in Georgia, to a soft-bottom flat in the southern part of the Everglades, to a marsh in Louisiana. And they can be feeding anywhere within the water column, on an endless variety of different species, so one could come up to the surface and produce an explosive strike that you'll long remember.

But all these factors that make the redfish so exciting also make choosing a good fly for the time and place you're fishing, well, a bit challenging. Now before we try to select a fly judging from all the different factors mentioned above, let me tell you first about the different redfish flies.

Types of Flies

The flies below are classified as crab flies, shrimp flies, fish flies, and so on, and that's what we think they imitate, based on the input of many anglers. But really, we don't know what the redfish thinks. Maybe it sees a fly moving away from it and wonders what the silly thing is, moving so strangely, but the fish is hungry, so it eats the fly anyway. Who knows? Yet I have to think that a crab fly dropping down to the bottom cannot look to a redfish like a minnow. And a long white and yellow Seaducer darting just under the surface must surely look to him like a minnow or at least a shrimp. Anyway, this school of thought has caught a lot a fish for me, so I'm sticking with it.

CRABS

The first crab fly imitations were tied for permit, since they seldom even looked at early fly offerings. When the designs evolved to a point where the fly patterns were finally successful, thanks mainly to Captain Steve Huff and angler Del Brown, anglers could finally take permit on the fly consistently.

And from there, it didn't take long before saltwater anglers started to tie smaller versions of the permit crab flies for bonefish and eventually for redfish too with equal success. And now we use a variety of crab flies for all kinds of other species. I've taken a large rainbow runner while chumming behind a boat when they wouldn't take any other fly I had. And I've landed many tripletails with a heavily weighed crab fly. A crab fly is also a great pattern for enticing a difficult black drum. And most of the sheepshead I've taken in the flats have been fooled with a dark-colored crab fly.

Let's face it: a great variety of gamefish, especially in the flats, feed on crabs. And the redfish is certainly no exception here. As a matter of fact, sometimes they are only feeding on crabs.

For me, the ideal situation to fish a crab pattern is in fairly clear water, when a fish is still or not moving much. A tailing red or a redfish laid up is ideal. Another good situation is when casting in shallow water, say well under a foot, where you can drop a lightly weighted crab without spooking the red.

Open bottoms and sandy bottoms are good conditions for a crab, because a red can easily see the crab fly dropping and laying on the bottom. In heavy grass, your small crab fly may get lost in between blades of grass and be hard for even a nearby red to see. Remember, your fly may look just like a mud crab or a swimming crab, but it does not have odor, so the fish must see it. For this reason, you shouldn't use a little crab fly for very muddy water, where it will likely not be seen, or for covering ground with a faster retrieve, like blind casting or working a shoreline. Swimming crabs move slowly, and walking crabs move even slower. So work or retrieve a crab fly very slow, or not at all.

Here's an assortment of good redfish crab patterns. From left to right, all in size 2 hooks: Merkin tan and light green with lead eyes; Merkin light salmon with bead chain eyes; Tim Borski's Critter Crab; Pat Dorsy's Red Slappa' with bead chain eyes; and Vince Maggio's Redfish Candy in tan, green, and grizzly feather. The first three were tied by Chris Dean.

Generally, I lead a fish very little when using a crab fly. I place it close enough to get the redfish's attention right away—unless I'm casting to a very spooky fish that is traveling. In that case, I'll try to anticipate where the red is going, lead it by a few feet and drop the crab, and then hope I can draw its attention, either when the fish sees the fly on the bottom or when I move it to intercept it. Anyway, when the fly plops on the water, if I see or feel that I have a red's attention, I may want to let it drop and stay. If the fly landed out of the fish's area of awareness, I will try and slide it into place with a slow, even pull, and when close enough, I let it drop. If my cast was way off, I pick it up and try again to drop it in the right place. Often they'll see it dropping, think it's a crab trying to run for cover or to bury himself under the sand or mud, and rush and grab it before it reaches bottom. I love to see that.

Once in the right place, if I decide to give the fly some action, it will be very slow. Some anglers like to drag it on the bottom, some don't. If you move it, do it gently—no hard or jerky motion. You are not jigging the fly. It's often not so much the action as it is moving it just enough to get a fish's attention.

Jazz pianist Vince Maggio, also an expert in shallow water redfishing, puts it well: "When it comes to retrieving a crab fly, less is always more."

Yet as effective as these crab patterns can be at the right time and place, many of my fly-fishing friends, some of them great anglers, do not want to fish crab patterns. And I think it is perhaps because they need to be fished so differently than other flies. You fish them so slow, even dead on the bottom, that it almost feels like you are fishing bait. Well, one such friend of many years is David Olson, a great angler and tournament caster. During a short interview for this book, he told me: "You know, I just don't like fishing crab flies." But then, thinking about it some more, he added: "But I have to admit, there are times that the crab fly is all they'll take." And there was a bit of resignation on the tone of his voice. He is right: there are times and places where you've got to have a crab fly.

And if I know I am going to use a crab pattern, I may use a fluorocarbon tippet, to let the more dense material help me sink the crab faster. And once the fly is on the bottom, the fluorocarbon will help me keep it close to the bottom too.

These are some of my favorite shrimp pattern for reds. Top row, from left to right: Jorge Martinez's small Copper Shrimp on size 4 hook; Puglisi Spawning Shrimp in tan on size 4 hook; and Puglisi Spawning Shrimp in copper brown on size 2 hook. Bottom row, from left to right: Oblak's Never Miss Marabou Shrimp on size 6 hook; Tim Borski's Chernobyl Crab variation in orange on size 2 hook and bead chain eyes (tied by Chris Dean); Tim Borski's Mackerel shrimp fly (tied by Chris Dean)—Tim may catch lots of mackerel with it, but I've taken innumerable amounts of reds, snook, and seatrout with this fly; and Pat Dorsy's Kwam in tan and light chartreuse—a great fly in many color combinations.

By the way, you could also use a "crabby like" imitation like the Red Slappa', a variation of the Kwam, by Pat Dorsy, which is also a good redfish producer. "Crabby like" flies are a blend between a crab and a shrimp pattern, longer, slimmer, and with a tail, so they can be fished faster.

SHRIMPS

Redfish consume a great variety of shrimp in the entire water column while feeding in the flats. Shrimp can be crawling on the bottom, holding on to a blade of seagrass, or hopping on the surface, and they usually occur in great abundance in the flats. This is probably why shrimp patterns are by far the most popular of all the redfish fly patterns.

The average size of the shrimp a redfish consumes in the flats is about an inch to three inches in length and the color is usually a translucent shade of green, gray, or brown. You can use a shrimp pattern lightly weighted to keep it close to the surface or one weighted with a big lead eye to fish the fly right on the bottom, or to let it drop on a pothole where they often lay. And the pattern can be hopped up and down like a shrimp trying to flee a predator, or it can be retrieved slow and steady like a shrimp just swimming. Depending on the circumstances, I've been successful fishing shrimp flies fast, slow, on the surface, right on the bottom, and anywhere in between. You can't go wrong with them.

And when it comes to covering ground while blind casting or fishing a shoreline, a shrimp pattern is a good choice, as is a fish pattern. Every fish in the flats will eat it. From reds and bones, to snook, tripletail, and tarpon. If I had to pick the most versatile redfish fly pattern, it would be a shrimp pattern. "Everybody eats a shrimp pattern," Captain Dave Denkert often tells me when we go fishing, and he is right.

Just keep in mind that there can be a great variety of shapes and colors on shrimp fly patterns. Flies like a Spawning Shrimp, any of the Borski shrimps like his Mackerel, Dorsy's Kwam, Denkert's Shrimp, and my Seaducer or River Shrimp, all are supposed to look like a shrimp to the redfish and other gamefish, but I tell you, they sure look different from each other! But since they are all very effective on reds, I carry them in my fly boxes.

Here, I'm holding a Borski's Mackerel shrimp pattern, one of the best flies for backwaters, from redfish to baby tarpon. Notice a little bit of chartreuse up front as an added attractor color. PAT FORD

One great fly mentioned above, the Kwam, by a top angler from Miami, Pat Dorsy, has a long craft fur tail behind a crab shape body, and makes a good crab or shrimp imitation. It probably looks more like a shrimp than a crab to redfish in my opinion. And it's one of the best all-around flies for both redfish and bonefish. When I go red fishing, I don't always have fly patterns to simulate every food the redfish eats, but I always have shrimp patterns.

FISHES

While reds consume a large quantity of crabs and shrimp, as they grow, they pursuing bigger meals, and the percentage of fishes in their diet increases. They'll feed on mullet, pinfish, mojarras, menhaden, anchovies, and more, which are generally fast-swimming food, and therefore you can work a fly imitating them much faster and cover more water if you need to. The reds also feed on many bottom-dwelling fish, like toadfish, gobies, and more. Flies imitating them are usually darker in color, and you fish them slow and close to the bottom. A variety of different shades of brown patterns with a deer hair head and lead or big bead chain eyes can be deadly when you work them close to the bottom.

But in the upper half of the water column and all the way to the surface, flies imitating fish do well when tied with big eyes, in white or light colors and with some

Several fish imitations. Top row, left to right: Chico's Glass Minnow, Vince Maggio's Redgetter using a rabbit strip and light mono eyes on size 4, Jorge Martinez's White Muddler variation on short-shank size 2 hook. Bottom row, left to right: Jorge Martinez's Weightless Fish pattern—to ride just under the surface; Puglisi Baitfish patterns in size 2 hook in black and dark purple (great for muddy waters), Everglades Special, and a white with tan back—I use these often.

flash along the sides to sparkle like a baitfish, maybe with a darker back and not weighted or lightly weighted. And in larger sizes, say three to five inches, this is a good pattern to entice a big red too. Also a fish pattern streamer is a great fly for covering water or working a shoreline. And if fishing in off-color or muddy water where visibility is a problem, a big-fish imitating streamer in black or chartreuse is a good choice.

Some of my favorites are Enrico Puglisi's many baitfish patterns, with doll eyes, translucent artificial hair, and some flash on the sides. White and yellow have proven good, but in murky waters, dark colors like black and purple are great. And in clear water or on beaches, when the reds are feeding on glass minnows and other small fishes, I use my Glass Minnow imitation with a heavy mono body and painted eyes. But any slim, white streamer with some flash will also work.

OTHER TYPES OF FLIES

But not all patterns can be classified into a particular redfish food. Some flies, depending on how full or sparse they're tied, whether they're weighted or not, or how they're retrieved, can look like different species of food. They may have the ability to hop like a fleeing shrimp, or dart like a fish. Yet other flies, often highly successful, not only don't look like anything in the flats, but often have colors or color combinations that rival a carnival in Rio. Yet they catch lots of red.

So following, in no particular order, are some unclassified but important fly patterns.

Chernobyl Crab

Somewhere between a shrimp and a fish imitation is the famous Chernobyl Crab, tied by one of the great saltwater fly tiers, artist Tim Borski. It is also Borski's favorite fly to fish. Here is what he had to say about it:

> Yes I called it a crab, but I fish this fly more like a shrimp pattern. That is, much faster than I'd fish a regular crab fly. And the fact that it's tied inverted (hook up) and also has a double mono weedguard, makes it very weedless around structure or grass. For me it has been very effective on reds. Actually, I could fly-fish the world, except

Miscellaneous flies with their own category. Top: an interesting red or often red and orange eel-type pattern that both Flip Pallot and Captain Rob Fordyce often use on redfish in clear water, and even on bonefish. I've taken a few reds with it, but haven't used it enough yet. Bottom, left to right: a Clouser in white and orange on a size 1 hook—in any color, one of the best all-around flies you can use. And Tim Borski's Chernobyl Crab—which Tim uses in many colors and sizes for anything from bonefish to blue-water fish, and yes, even redfish. I love it for reds in an all orange color.

This big, fat seatrout took an orange Chernobyl with bead chain eyes on a size 1 hook. STEPHEN FERNÁNDEZ

> blue water, with a box full of Chernobyl Crabs, in different weights. I've taken reds, steelhead, big bass, bonefish, you name it, with this fly.

And since Tim loves fishing redfish in muddy waters, where he only sees the dark fish's backs, his redfish flies are necessarily big, bulky, and dark.

The Clouser

Tied by Bob Clouser around 1987, the Clouser Deep Minnow was originally designed for smallmouth bass. But since then, almost every gamefish I can think of, in fresh and salt water, has taken this fly, tied in one of its multiple variations.

Tie the Clouser on a size 4 hook in a light color like white or white and yellow, lightly weighted, and you can cast it easily with a 6- or 7-weight line in less than a foot of water to tailing redfish, and dart it around without getting caught on the bottom. But tie it on a 1/0 hook in white and chartreuse or red and white with lots of flash, and use heavy lead eyes, and then you can blind cast a deep shoreline for big snook. And with the same fly and a sinking line, I've taken many grouper and snapper in the reef. Yet an all-black pattern with heavy bead chain or lead eyes is great for black drum and even sheepshead. Indeed, depending on how it's tied and worked, it can look like a shrimp or a baitfish. Called the Clouser for short, this fly is incredibly versatile.

The Magic of Marabou Flies

No material moves in the water quite like marabou. It's so soft that the slightest movement brings the fly to life. You have to see it to understand. Just strip it straight and steady, and it will swim and breathe like it's alive, slithering through the water. Let it lay still, and it continues to move. Now touch it. Just one small strip, and the marabou wings of the fly undulate beautifully, seductively. Go ahead and strip it with lots of action, and it goes crazy, wiggling all over the place. There is nothing like marabou.

And because of its ability to have so much action when hardly being moved forward, you often can keep a marabou fly in the strike zone longer, while keeping it moving and looking very much alive. That is, you can keep it close to a mangrove shoreline, in a pothole, or close to a laid up red, right on the fish's nose, until it can't resist anymore. In fact, I've seen reds, and bones, pick up a marabou fly right off the bottom when it was laying still. But I knew the fly was constantly moving, perhaps by the slightest of currents, as it rested on the bottom.

Marabou flies are popular for big tarpon, but not many anglers use them for the rest of the saltwater fish. Bonefish, permit, snook, redfish—they all love marabou. My first permit on a fly, in the 60s, was taken with an Optic white marabou fly with big eyes painted on the single brass bead. Believe me, fish love marabou, and that includes Mr. Red.

I remember around 1960 or so that some of the old-timers in South Florida would talk to me about marabou flies. They had one favorite way to fish them, and it was by hardly moving the fly. They called it "fishing it soaked." They would tell me: "Just fish it soaked in front of him, and he'll take it. Won't be able to resist it." And you know, still today, after so many years, there are times when I find myself fishing a marabou fly very slowly, soaked, and my mind goes back and fondly remembers those old-timers.

Also, because marabou is so light and skinny when wet, it's easy to false-cast and make a good presentation. And that too is a great advantage.

Usually, marabou flies are at their best in clear water, but in the last couple of years, I've found that, dressed fuller, a marabou fly will also work well in off-color and murky waters. You just have to make sure that the marabou is full soaked in order for the fly to work properly, because a mid- to full-dressed marabou fly is pretty dense and takes a while to absorb water all the way through. You see, if a marabou fly is dry inside, even though it's wet on the outside, you won't get that full marabou performance. So I recommend you slap the fly on the water and work it for a few feet, then repeat the process a couple more times. After that, grab the fly between your index and thumb and squeeze all the water out of it, and finally slap it again and work the fly for a few feet. By now, you should see the fly do its marabou dance. You are ready to fish.

Having said that, this reminds me of something that I do at home with all my marabou flies, especially those that are dressed more fully, before I put them in my fly box. I fill my sink with water and thoroughly soak the flies. Then I take them out, dripping, and using my index finger and thumb, I squeeze the water out. The flies are still wet, of course, and very stiff and skinny too. Now I hook them on a board or foam, facing up, while they drip from the tail end. Then I let them dry for a few hours or overnight. Once dried, you'll find the wings of the marabou are a bit more contained, and easier to put in the fly box. And once on the water, your "presoaked" marabou fly will quickly begin breathing and swimming naturally. It's an old habit of mine that works well and takes little time. You may want to give it a try.

Of course, if you are fishing muddy water, with low visibility, then you need the bulk that comes from deer heads and bucktail, for example, to cast a large and bulky profile. Because Ms. Marabou is about lively action and undulation, not bulk.

CHICO'S MARABOU MADNESS

For years, I've been playing with a large fly, 4 inches or longer, tied only with marabou, with a bit of flash on the side, and large, heavy lead eyes. The idea was to fish the fly deep, with a fast-sinking line, for grouper, snapper, and other large reef fish. I would let the fly sink until it was close to the bottom, and then, because marabou has so much action, I could practically leave it there, hardly moving it, staying in the strike zone, for much longer. The fly worked great. I landed lots of fish with it and lost lots of flies to big fish on the bottom. Great fun.

A few years later, I started to fish slow-sinking clear lines in brackish water with these "all-marabou" flies, and taking snook, reds, tarpon, seatrout, and such, in channels, canals, and mouths of rivers and creeks, keeping the fly close to the bottom. The working name of the fly was Marabou Seaducer, but with time, because some friends told me I was mad about marabou, the name Marabou Madness stuck.

I don't know what took me so long, but in the last few years I've been using the fly in the flats to sight-cast to snook, baby tarpon, seatrout, and of course, redfish. And

Marabou flies wiggle and breathe, even when not being moved, an action that drives fish mad. Top, left to right: four Marabou Madness on size 2 hooks with wire weedguard. The first one is without weight, and the rest come with bead chain eyes. Bottom, left to right: two large Marabou Madness in 3/0 hooks for big redfish and snook, in all chartreuse and in black and dark purple. The flies were tied by Chris Dean.

This big 17-pound snook took a large black Marabou Madness for Stephen Fernández, while Captain Steve Huff made the quiet approach.

it has worked so well that it has become one of my favorite flies in the backcountry.

In clear water, a sparsely tied Marabou Madness is deadly. I hardly have to add any action to it for it to wiggle convincingly. And a little action will get it to pulsate and entice. I often just drag it through the water, and let it swim. Other times I let it sit there, and fish take it.

I know that most of you reading this, if you've been a fly fisher for a while, know all about marabou, but I bet you probably aren't using any marabou for your redfish flies. Please start immediately.

This year, on a recent trip to the Ten Thousand Islands, fishing with my old friend Captain Steve Huff, my son, Stephen, took a 17-pound snook with a 4-inch black Marabou Madness. The snook was sitting still just under the surface, and when the fly landed 3 feet from it, the fish came up to the fly and crashed it so hard and fast that the snook's head and pectoral fins came out of the water on the strike. We'll all remember that strike for a long time.

And tying a Marabou Madness is easy. The wings are all marabou. On the larger flies, I like a whole marabou feather, stem and everything. Add a bit of flash on each side, then a bump of chenille to raise and add bulk to the hackle of marabou that's coming. Then wrap marabou around the shank for a hackle. Then weight the fly a little with a bead chain. I seldom use lead eyes on this fly on the flats. Also, I always use wire for a weedguard, not mono. Wire works much better than mono, helping stabilize the fly so it rides straight even when retied fast. This is also true with my Seaducer, where I always use wire weedguards.

Flashers: The Mylar Treatment

In 1968 I was trying to design a fly for mackerel that had lots of flash, but would be more durable against the mackerel's teeth than my all feather Seaducer or bucktail patterns. So I picked up the toughest material I had in my tying bench, a big spool of silver Mylar, and grabbing a few dozen strands, I tied the wings and then added a hackle up front also made completely out of Mylar. And since I was tying commercially those days, I gave it a name: the Mylar Special.

The fly worked well for mackerel, small kings, and other species, but through all those early years, it never occurred to me to tie it with gold Mylar and try it on reds; it may have been a good fly in those days. Rats!

Today, we have several successful patterns for redfish that are made mostly or entirely out of some type of Mylar. And when you retrieve these flies, whether in clear or muddy waters, they sparkle like a broken mirror. These flies often have many times more sparkle than any natural bait. They are really an attractor pattern. But the reds, and other fish, love them.

A few years ago I visited Captain Scott Wagner, of Savannah, Georgia, to fish for redfish on the clear, oceanside flats of that area. On the first morning, I got some refusals with an all white baitfish pattern, and later got some follows with a tan shrimp pattern. Both were favorite patterns, but I couldn't get a bite.

Then Scott suggested I try his Gold Flash, an attractor pattern he uses for reds all the time. He said it worked great, and handed me one. The fly was a bit over three inches long, and was mostly gold Mylar with a short head of cactus flashy chenille and unweighted. I looked at the fly and knew one thing for sure—the reds were not going to miss seeing it. And one look at Scott, and I knew he had full confidence in it. I tied it to my tippet.

By lunchtime I had taken four reds. And the biggest, about 13 pounds, ran me well into the backing and put up quite a fight. The next two day's fishing was a repeat of the first day. We took lots of reds, all on the Gold Flash. It worked great.

Many miles south of those ocean flats in Georgia, Captain Mark Krowka, winner of just about every fly tournament run in the Florida Keys, also uses a flashy fly for reds, one he calls the Glitterus. Mark ties this fly with the usual Mylar tail, but what makes his version different is that he ties what he calls a "cross beam" of Mylar across the white yarn body, instead of rubber legs or other material. And it sure looks different in your hand! Having Mylar sticking out of the body, like flashy legs, and a tail of Mylar behind gives the fly more movement, while the extra bulk pushes more water. The tail, Mark warns, should not be tied too long, or you'll miss strikes. And he prefers light dumbbell eyes so he can fish reds in deeper water, but still fish the tailing reds with the same fly.

The Glitterus uses a double mono weedguard of 16-pound-test stiff mono but tied to angle forward. This way when the red takes the fly, the weedguard folds forward and the red does not feel a pinch. Mark believes this is vital to get the maximum percentage of hookups.

Mark uses the Glitterus almost exclusively for reds, even in tournaments, with great results. And he tells me that it's not unusual to let the fly sink to the bottom and have a red come up to it and pick it up. That's always neat.

On the other hand, not all flasher-type flies flash excessively. The Starling, designed by Tim Borski, has lots of flash material, but the copper and dark brown colors produce a more subtle effect that in the off-color waters, where Tim prefers to fish for reds, is deadly. The fly is meant to ride inverted, with the hook up, which helps make the fly a bit more weedless. But Tim also adds a double weedguard, and this helps keep the weeds away even more.

One advantage of using a flashy fly is that it is often more visible to the angler when retrieving it if worked close to the surface, and therefore easier to see the relationship between fly and fish. This way, you know whether the fly is in the right place or not. And if it isn't, then you know to pick it up and try again. In many cases, being able to see the fly in the water is a huge advantage—believe me.

But what about Tim's dark Starling? Will we be able to see it in the water? Remember, in the off-color or muddy waters Tim likes to fish, a dark or black fly stripped close to the surface shows up like a neon sign. So you will still know where your fly is in relation to the fish you are casting and know if you need to keep stripping or pick up and try again. You'll find that in dark waters, low light, and nighttime blind casting, dark is good. Real good.

Spoons

When it comes to spoon flies, the saltwater fly-fishing community is firmly divided into two schools of thought. One school believes that any artificial that is not tied in a

Flashers for redfish. Top, left to right: a copy of the brass spoon used by Jim Corbett in India and made by my friend Corbett Davis, Captain Jon Cave's Wobbler spoon, Jim and A. J. Dupre's Dupre Spoon. Bottom, left to right: Captain Scott Wagner's Gold Flash fly, Captain Mark Krowka's Glitterus, and Tim Borski's dark, flashing Starling.

conventional fashion with natural or artificial material, such as a spoon, is not a fly. And the other school believes that if a spoon is light enough to cast in a conventional manner, it is a fly.

As a fly fisher of many years, I've always thought that the fact that a spoon fly can be made light enough to cast is not enough to call it a real fly. After all, I've seen small plugs with two sets of treble hooks light enough to be cast easily with an 8-weight fly rod, and they certainly are not a fly. And so, neither was a spoon fly.

Then, about a dozen or more years ago, I changed my mind in the most unusual way. I read a book called *Man-Eaters of Kumaon* by Jim Corbett. Corbett was a legendary hunter, outdoorsman, author, and conservationist who wrote several books about his adventures of finding and killing man-eating tigers in India on foot during the early part of the twentieth century. I loved these books, and have read them several times.

Corbett mentions in his book that after one morning's hunt he decided to take the afternoon off to catch some dinner for the whole crew by fishing from one of India's famous rivers. His target was the mahseer—a powerful fish that lives in strong river currents and can grow to over a hundred pounds.

Armed with an 11-foot tournament bamboo trout rod, a reel with 50 yards of "casting line" and 200 yards of fine silk backing, a gut leader, and a "one inch homemade brass spoon," he headed for the river. After walking over half a mile looking for the right pool to find a fish for dinner, he finally discovered just the right place. Then he positioned himself where he could cast, and started by making a short cast, dropping the spoon in the current and starting to strip line off the reel to make a longer cast. But just then, a fish took the spoon. With so much line stripped off the reel, Corbett felt lucky that he was able to clear the line all the way to the reel, and then he says the fish took all 50 yards of casting line (fly line) and 100 yards of silk backing as it headed downstream.

After a very long fight, which he describes in detail, Corbett landed what he estimated as a 50-pound Mahseer. So big indeed was the fish that he could not carry it by himself to the camp, several miles away. The story goes on, but I'm telling you the story so you understand that it was the adventure of it all, and the fact that I consider Mr. Corbett a true sportsman, that led me to want to fish a spoon with my fly rod. And soon after, it became clear to me that the redfish was the perfect fish for me to live this adventure.

Now a few years had gone by since I first read Mr. Corbett's book and one day while fishing with friend Corbett Davis, a well-known jeweler and fly fisherman in Florida, I mention the story and my desire to catch a redfish on a homemade spoon. My friend Corbett mentioned casually that they'd be easy to make in his shop, but said no more. Two weeks later the UPS truck brought me a few 1-inch spoons. Some made of brass and some of copper. A short note said, "Go get 'em, Chico." That's Corbett for you.

And so, on my next trip to the Everglades, armed with a 7-weight fly rod and a homemade 1-inch spoon, I got to cast to a redfish cruising slowly in about a foot of water. The light spoon was easy to cast, and as I retrieved the spoon by the fish, all I could think about was Jim Corbett. The spoon flashed by the red, it lunged forward and took the spoon, just like a mahseer would have—well, I'd like to think. When I lifted the fish off the water, the brass spoon was right on the corner of its mouth. So it's this story—the adventure—that brought me back to the spoon. What can I say, I'm a romantic; I'm just funny that way.

A spoon-type fly is incredibly effective, whether casting to tailing reds or just blind casting on an overcast day. A good spoon is a great attractor fly because it not only flashes like a broken mirror, but it also pulsates and pushes water at the same time. And it can be almost 100 percent weedless. So you can retrieve it through spartina grass, pencil reeds, oyster bars, and all kinds of structure, no problem. Yet it still retains a pretty good hook-up ratio. And even in poor visibility, you can usually see the spoon flashing in the water, so you know if your fly is in the right place or if you need to pick it up and try another placement.

The better spoon flies today are light enough that you can cast them easily with a 7-weight rod on a calm or light wind day. However, when the wind picks up, they become harder to cast and more erratic, which makes accuracy a bit more difficult. You can still fish them, but it's just not as easy as casting other flies. So on a windier day, say blind casting, I'd use an 8- or 9-weight outfit and do just fine. Also, some spoons ride higher in the water column than you may want. An easy solution is to use a fluorocarbon tippet or full leader that will get it down. Or use a clear sinking wet tip or if only blind casting, a clear full sink line. That will do it for sure.

The most popular color spoon is gold, which redfish love. But copper, chartreuse, and silver are also popular. And dark colors are also good, not just for reds, but for sheepshead and black drum.

Then, there is the twist. Because of its design, a spoon fly may twist your leader. Some spoons do this more than others. I find that using a heavier tippet, say going from 12-pound tippet to 16 pounds, will help you. And using the stiffer fluorocarbon for tippets or full leaders also helps.

Some anglers use a swivel that is light enough, and they tell me it solves the problem. The problem is, I wouldn't be caught dead with a swivel on my fly rod. It is just not fly fishing to me.

The two most popular spoons flies I know are the Wobbler and the Spoonfly. Spoon flies have been around for a long time. But the first guy to popularize them in modern times that I know of was Jon Cave, an excellent fly fisher and fly-casting instructor. Jon spent a lot of time testing and retesting his creation, the Wobbler, made of woven Mylar tubing and with a double weedguard. It's a great fly and very popular. But a few years later, Jim and his father, A. J. Dupre, created another design, the Spoonfly, made from a flat sheet of Mylar precut to shape. It's also a great spoon fly and very weedless.

To my mind, both flies take a different approach to a spoon fly. The Dupre is lighter and rides higher in the water column, and because it's wider, it'll probably push more water. The Wobbler is a tad heavier and rides deeper in the water column. And because the blade is thinner, it's going to spin and twist less, if at all. You may or you may not want to fish them, but they can be deadly on reds.

Top fly fisher David Olson has fished for reds most of his life. The spoon is not his first choice of fly, but still he had this to say about them: "Reds will find a spoon fly more readily than any other fly. And if reds are ignoring my fly, the spoon is the fly I'll try next." I agree.

Rabbit Strip Flies

I've caught tarpon, steelhead, black bass, snook, redfish, and many other species with flies tied with rabbit strips. This rabbit strip has two different actions going at the same time. One is from the leather itself, which can undulate, especially if it's long. And at the same time, another action comes from the many hair fibers attached to the strip. It's not like marabou, bucktail, or feathers; it's rabbit strip action—it's unique. And it's very attractive to predators, including Mr. Redfish.

First try working a rabbit strip more or less straight or with a little action, and you get that classic undulation that is so alive in the water—often snakelike if the strip is long enough. Then you change to a more erratic short strip and stop, strip and stop, and you get a pulsating movement that you see in almost no other fly. And even when moved slow, or just laying on the bottom, the many hairs on the strip will be constantly moving. Fish just love that.

But a rabbit strip that is too long or cut too wide can be heavy to cast when wet. And that is one reason many anglers shy away from these flies. However, the perfect rabbit strip fly to entice most redfish is mostly less than three inches long. Often the rabbit strip itself is less than two inches. So these flies are not really hard to cast, even when weighted, as they generally should be with bead chain or lead eyes. And I find longer ones are not too hard to cast at all with an 8- or 9-weight rod. There are lots of pattern variations for redfish using rabbit strips. You may want to give them a try.

Seaducer

I started tying my Seaducer in the early 1960s to fish snook, baby tarpon, and redfish in the flats and shallow mangrove and sawgrass shorelines. The fly, like many other patterns, is a variation of the hackle fly, a fly that has been around since the 1800s, maybe longer.

The main reason I started tying the Seaducer was that the hackles that are wrapped around hackle flies to make the head of the fly were tied only with the stiff portion of the feather. This often produced a fly where the wings and the head of the fly did not blend as one. The wings would end, then the hackles—the head of the fly—would start. So I tied the hackle head using the whole feather, including the bottom of the feather, with its soft marabou-like fibers. This produced a fly with a much better profile. Now the wings and head blended into one, and the whole fly had a better, more realistic profile, looking more like a shrimp or fish. And as I recall, somewhere during the time I was perfecting the pattern, the name Seaducer came up, and stayed. Eventually, I wrote about it in the Winter 1979 issue of *The Fisherman* magazine.

Another advantage to adding the bulkier bottom of the feather is that it formed a better head for the fly and added more buoyancy. Now the fly really stayed suspended, unlike the hackle fly, which sank much faster. And the bottom pin fibers of the feather, being like marabou, added motion as the fly was retrieved.

With three large feathers for a hackle, even a large fly would stay suspended or sink very slowly. So I could cast to a big red or snook in a foot of water with a big fly and still keep the fly inches under the water, even when retrieving slowly. And today, this fly is still one of my favorites in the backcountry, and one of the patterns I most often use to fish shorelines for snook, redfish, and baby tarpon.

Finally, I may add that not every tier or fly shop has a Seaducer the way it should be, which is why I have photos for you to see. It really is a simple fly to tie correctly.

Crystal Shrimp

Around 1990 I took a trip to Alaska, in which I landed several different species of salmon, plus rainbows and char, using the standard Woolly Bugger pattern with

Chico's Seaducers and Chico and Stephen's Crystal Shrimp are some of my most often-used flies in the brackish backwaters. Top, left to right: a slim Seaducer on a size 4 hook, a style often used in Texas for shallow water reds; a small Seaducer in all black with double weedguard; and a standard Seaducer in classic white, grizzly, and red. Middle, left to right: a large Seaducer in the "old shrimp colors" of white, yellow and grizzly on a size 2/0 hook; a 5-inch Seaducer I often use for big reds in Louisiana on a 3/0 hook; and a large Seaducer in orange and red, this one with big lead eyes and wire weedguard to fish deep, often on a sinking line. Bottom, left to right: a Crystal Shrimp in orange and white; an all black Crystal Shrimp—one of my favorite colors for this pattern; and a Crystal Shrimp in the "old shrimp colors" of white, yellow, and grizzly, all of them on 1/0 hooks.

marabou tail. Coming back to Miami, I started to think again about making some sort of a saltwater Woolly Bugger mainly for snook, reds, and baby tarpon. But my idea was to use feathers instead of marabou, more like my Seaducer, but faster sinking so it could fish deeper flats and shorelines—a fly I would often use weighted.

At the time, my thirteen-year-old-son Stephen, who was already deep into saltwater fly fishing, was my official fly tier when I didn't have the time to tie them myself; indeed for many years he tied all of my Alaska flies, including the Woolly Buggers. So, since I was way behind on my article deadlines, I simply handed him a few of the regular Woolly Buggers, some of the Seaducers we already used for snook and reds, and let him figure out how to blend them in to a saltwater fly.

A few days later, after some trial and error, we were fishing the new fly in Flamingo, Everglades. Over the next few months, the fly went through a few more minor changes, but we were already having great results. The fly sparkled, breathed well in the water, and sank faster than the Seaducer.

Then one day, Stephen tied a half dozen of them, all white on a size 2 hook, and came to my office in the house to show them to me. And as he held them in the palm of his hand while we looked at them, all white, sparkling, and translucent, he said that they looked like

This nice redfish went for a black Crystal Shrimp fly in about a foot of water. Fooled him! STEPHEN FERNÁNDEZ

they were made out of crystal. One of us said, Crystal Shrimp, and we loved the name immediately. And I don't mind telling you that today, unless I am fishing very shallow for reds, I'm more apt to use the Crystal Shrimp than almost any other fly.

Surface Flies

By design, saltwater surface flies are often heavier or more wind resistant than regular streamers, making casting a bit harder. Add the fact that a redfish's mouth placement is better suited to feed at its level or below, and a beginner fly fisher will wonder: *Why in the world would you try a surface fly on reds?* It's about the strike, man, the strike.

A surface fly at rest floats high, its back getting a sun tan. Then when you retrieve it, the fly is still mostly on top of the water. So when a redfish rises to the surface and inhales it, whether the fish sips it slowly or crashes it violently, it is going to have to expose part or all of its body for you to see. You'll remember the strike, believe me.

Just watch a skiff where the angler is working a surface fly, and you'll notice that, the angler, his friend, the guide, everyone, has their eye glued to the fly. Why? Because no one wants to miss the moment of the strike. And it is, for me, the most exciting way to take a redfish on a fly. I don't want it any better!

Redfish, having such a broad palate for all kinds of foods in the flats, will feed on the surface at one time or another. But as you know, reds are mostly looking down when looking for food, so to get them to come up for a surface fly, you need to find the right conditions.

If redfish are feeding on the surface, either popping shrimp or chasing bait, this is a great time. Also if you see reds riding high in the water column of a flat or at least off the bottom, this could be a good time too. But if a red is right against the bottom hunting, you'd better get a weighted fly. Also, in many areas a tailing red will take a small surface fly that does not pop too loud, and often not popped at all.

Other times, when the body language shows that a red is aware of the surface, looking up, I go and try a surface fly. I've seen reds feeding in such shallow water that their backs were occasionally showing, and they came up for a small popper or a foam pattern like the Hot Lips, and sipped it gently. Too cool.

Bigger reds, say over 15 pounds, are often likely to take a fly on top, because by then they are feeding more on fish like mullet. I've taken big reds on poppers and sliders in Louisiana, in 30 feet of water in Pensacola, and in the Indian River in mid-Florida. And what a strike!

The size of surface fly I like for the average redfish in the flats, say three to twelve pounds or so, is not too big, around two to three inches or so. But I also like Brooks Bouldin's small popper, and they are usually under two inches. In terms of colors, since a surface fly is mostly going to be seen from the bottom up, as a silhouette against the sky, color is generally not that important.

Still, even knowing this, I have white, yellow, and even brown colored surface flies that I have a preference for, and I believe they are better. But who knows what a redfish thinks when it sees a fly from below!

If you're blind casting, you mostly need to find the fish deep enough for the red to rise to the fly but not so deep that the fish wouldn't be hunting on the surface. I think that depth ranges from over a foot to thirty inches or so—just a rough guess to give you some guidelines.

Finally, I don't recommend fluorocarbon when fishing surface flies. Fluorocarbon is very dense and will often sink a fly faster, which can be an advantage on many underwater streamers and crab patterns, but it's a disadvantage on a surface fly, often affecting the fly's action, even to the point of sinking it. Stick to mono here.

Now, let's look first at the hard heads: the poppers and sliders. And then soft heads: the deer hair heads and foam heads.

Poppers

A popper is just a simple streamer with a head in front made out of a material that will float, such as balsa wood, cork, packed deer hair, or even foam. And the front of the head is either flat or concave, so when you retrieve, it will pop lightly or loudly depending on how fast and sharp you retrieve. You can even strip it in with minimum action, and let it pop slightly like a shrimp on the surface. This "pop gurgle" type of noise can attract a fish

Surface flies for reds. Top row, left to right: Brooks Bouldin's small red popper, Dean's popper, and a larger Joe Brooks's old style popper where the thread is hidden under the popper's head. Second row, left to right: three sliders on a size 2 hook in yellow, black, and the old style colors of Florida crackers in the 50s and early 60s: varnished cork, red hackle, and grizzly wing feathers—I've caught a ton of reds, snook, and baby tarpon with this old color combo—brings out memories. Bottom row, from left to right: Steve Huff's Hot Lips made with a foam head, and one of the most successful surface saltwater flies around, Olson's Deer Hair Slider—this one rides high on the water column, and it's one of my favorites. And my old River Shrimp, tied with a deer hair head, partially trimmed but some hairs left uncut—this one will ride just under the surface, and in that brown color it's been very effective.

from quite a distance and entice them to show themselves. It is really the dinner bell fly.

The wings can be made of many materials, including Mylar, for some flash added to the noise. But I prefer feather wings that breathe well and add life, or bucktail for its extra buoyancy. It depends what I need at the time.

You can also paint big beautiful eyes to make it look good to your fellow fly fishers. The reds won't know the difference, but it can't hurt. The hook's ring eye can come out of the middle of the body or on the bottom. I feel generally that when the eye is in the middle, it is easier to pick the popper off the water and to cast, because it tends to fly fairly straight. And this is my preference, by far. On the other hand, a popper with a ring eye on the bottom will pop louder with less effort and tend to leave a larger gap on the hook, which could help hookups. But a bottom placed ring eye will often come off the water spinning, making it harder to pick up off the water.

Many tiers use an extra long shank on a popper to increase the gap. But doing so adds to the weight of the popper considerably, which makes it harder to cast, and once on the water it won't float as high or move as lively. That's why, whenever possible, I much prefer a popper that is made with a standard or slightly long shank length, like that on a Mustad 34007.

One of the times I love a popper is during conditions of poor visibility, such as high water or heavy overcast days, for example. Then, instead of blind casting with an underwater fly, which is boring since you can't see anything, it is often best to cast a "dinner bell." A popper. It is fun to fish, you are entertained by the casting and placement of the popper and by watching it work . . . and of course you have the anticipation of the strike. As a matter of fact, the whole crew in the skiff will be watching, as the popper makes its dance back to the boat.

And then, there are rare times when even not getting the strike with a popper can be exciting. I remember fishing for the big reds in Louisiana one winter, with Captain Lance Ledet and a friend during one of my hosted trips. We had taken a few fish that day already, so we decided to fish a big popper, just for fun. Besides, visibility had diminished as rain clouds approached.

After taking a couple of smaller reds, our friend cast the big yellow and red popper against a grassy shoreline and started the retrieve back. We all watched the popper. Halfway to the boat, a big wake approached the popper, got right behind it, and then disappeared. He kept working the popper. But a couple of seconds later the big redfish rose and slowly put its nose right on the popper. The fish just stayed there, looking at the popper intensely. We, of course, were dead quiet, not moving a muscle, not wanting the boat to rock even a little. Then the red moved its head a little, perhaps to change the angle of its eye on the popper, decided to refuse it, and slowly sank out of sight. We, on the other hand, all had a meltdown. And that evening, during cocktail hour in the camp, that's all we could talk about. The rest of the anglers in the group had heard enough about the submarine red, but I bet you I'll never forget him.

Sliders

Sliders, which were very popular in the 40s, 50s, and 60s, not only in brackish waters for snook, redfish, seatrout, and baby tarpon, but also as a black bass fly, are not in vogue anymore. And that's a shame because this unsung hero of the surface flies is really a great pattern, but only if tied with a light enough hook and used in the right conditions.

When I came to Miami in 1959, the old fly fishers, who used the slider a lot in the backwaters of the Everglades, use to call it the "water walker." I like that name, and even today, when I work one lightly on a calm surface, I think of it as a water walker. But today, no one seems to know what to do with them.

If you want to cover lots of water, especially if it's calm, a slider is a great choice. In conditions of good visibility, but shallow water, where you don't want the noise of a popper, but you still want the thrill of a surface strike, a slider is again a great choice. After all, an angler using a casting or spinning rod who wants to cover lots of ground on a calm day is often going to choose a cigar-shaped plug, and "walk the dog." Get it? (Walking the dog is a type of action on a surface plug where it moves across the water shaking its head side to side, almost zig-zagging.)

So first, the slider has to be well designed. If you use too big a hook, select a hook with a long shank, or apply too many coats of paint on the body, your fly will be too heavy. And then it will be harder to cast, and worse yet, a heavy slider will sit low and dead on the water, without the liveliness that comes from a buoyant surface fly. Make sure that, like the popper, you make it with a hook of standard length shank. A long shank hook, mainly because of its extra weight, will often kill a slider's delicate action. As a matter of fact, in the old days, sometimes we even used freshwater bronze hooks on sliders that were going to be used in brackish water for reds, seatrout, baby tarpon, and snook, even though we knew that they would eventually rust, just to keep it light. And the action was always much better.

Don't use bucktail for wings. Use saddle hackles for that delicate breathing action on the surface. It won't make a difference to a 5-pound jack, but a nice snook, or a good size redfish will see the difference. As to the best colors, again, most people say it doesn't matter, and maybe they're right. However, when being retrieved, a slider sometimes, for a moment here and there, will submerge, and any fish following will see color, I think. Anyway, I have had good luck with all white, white with red hackle, all yellow, yellow with a red hackle, and all black. Also, I like the old Florida classic color for the water walker: a natural cork with clear finish, red hackle, grizzly tail, and a pair of big eyes in white with black pupils. It's an old color that has worked for me on sliders, and whether it matters or not, it brings back memories, and that too is part of the fly-fishing experience.

To start, make sure you use a loop knot to keep the slider free to move. Then use a steady retrieve with a little action when covering water. If close to a fish or shoreline, use small twitches. A tease. And often, if a fish follows but cannot make up its mind, then use a series of small erratic, short pulls.

And if you find reds chasing bait, then a slider, perhaps in white with some flash added to the wing, works great. And in this case, I'll work the slider faster to imitate the fleeing baitfish.

Now, allow me another story:

Not too long ago, my son, Stephen, and I went fishing with my old friend, Captain Steve Huff, out of Everglades City in the Ten Thousand Islands. By early afternoon we were having a good day, with a few snook and a couple of redfish being landed and released. So with a few fish under our belly, so to speak, Stephen decided to fish a bright yellow slider to see the strike.

We had only travelled the flat a hundred feet when Huff spotted a big red just laying on the surface in two feet of water. Stephen place the slider a couple of feet in front of him and the big red exploded on the fly, but missed it completely. Fortunately, Stephen contained himself and did not strike the fish, so the slider was still there floating on the surface, and going up and down with the waves after the big strike. For a few seconds, the slider laid on the surface, bright and yellow, very visible, at least to us, against the brown tannic water. But unknown to us, there were two other reds we had not seen that must have been under the bigger fish; they simply hadn't had a chance to rise to the occasion. But now, before the big fish could return and take the slider, they both came up and tried to outrun each other in an attempt to eat that slider. Stephen, who was already retrieving, simply increased the speed, as if trying to get away. And for a few seconds the two reds tried to push each other to the side, until one of them made that extra effort, launched forward, and with its body out of the water, the slider disappeared in its mouth, only 20 feet from the skiff by now. Boy what a strike! We all saw it clearly. Then, after a good scrap, Huff took some photos of us, and we put the fish back. It looked to be 30 inches or so.

And today, if you ask any one of us if we remember the red that took the yellow slider, we can tell you the story in detail. So, do get some good sliders.

Chewables

The loud "dinner bell" popper, and its cousin, the slippery and mostly quiet slider, are great surface flies, but they are hard heads. There are other ways to keep a fly on the surface, even make some noise, while using a head with a much softer, more natural feel to a red when the fish takes it in its mouth. And part of the bonus of using these "soft heads" is that the fish keep them in their mouth longer, and so hook-up percentages tend to increase. Timing is definitely more forgiving with soft bodies.

The great artist and fly fisherman Dave Whitlock told me years ago that he called flies with soft heads "chewables," and I've never forgotten that term. You can make soft head floating flies using many materials, but two of the most common are closed-cell foam and the hollow hair from the belly of deer, antelope, or elk.

FOAM HEADS

Closed-cell foam can be used to make flies that pop, slide, and then dive when retrieved. And foam head flies are usually easy to cast because they are so light. Also, they land with a nice splat that is almost natural, I think, because more often than not it attracts a fish but seldom spooks them. I use them all the time on reds.

By far one of the best foam heads I've used is the Hot Lips, designed by Captain Steve Huff. This is a fly in which the foam around the head of the fly ends at the hook's eye ring, forming two lips. Indeed Steve paints the inside of the lips red, like a mouth. The fly usually has a combination of feathers and hair for a tail.

But what makes it so special is that the two lips, when retrieved properly, make a very natural, subtle noise. It's a fishy pop-gurgle, perhaps like a shrimp or small baitfish swimming on the surface. And whether fished with small fast pops or a light pop and wait retrieve, the fly is deadly. I always have some in my backcountry fly boxes.

The Hot Lips can be tied with a weedguards, but most are not. The two lips up front also act as kind of a built-in weedguard. It's amazing how often I'll be fishing a shoreline with a Hot Lips, misjudge my cast and land in the mangroves, and still, if I pull slowly and let the line jump the branches, I am able to get it free. Angler Sandy Moret, winner of many fly-fishing tournaments in the Keys, is the best I've ever seen at getting a Hot Lips off the mangroves.

I think he often does it on purpose to tease me! He can land on the mangroves, then slowly dance the fly, limb to limb, until it lands inches from the shoreline. Then he'll start retrieving the fly back, as if nothing had happened. I get a kick out of that.

DEER HAIR FLIES

A well-trimmed hair head fly cannot only ride on the surface, but also push a lot of water, which is a great fish attractor. Here then is a more quiet dinner bell than poppers. These soft, chewable offerings tend to ride lower on the surface than a head made of cork, balsa, or cell foam—especially after it's been fished for a while and is a bit waterlogged. However, riding a bit low and pushing a wake, this can be one of the most deadly flies you ever use on the surface. There's something about pushing a wake that fish find very real. Don't underestimate this. On the other hand, if you want to make noise on the surface, then this fly is not the best choice for you. I have seen hard-packed hair heads that pop well, for a while, but there are better materials to make noises on the surface.

My favorite deer hair head pattern for redfish and snook on top is the Olson's Slider, designed by fly fisherman and tournament caster David Olson. The fly was designed with a cone head shape made of deer hair and trimmed to size, and a single hackle up front like the prop of a single-engine plane. The tail is usually a combo of hair and grizzly feathers. And my preferred color for this pattern is the tan and grizzly with a bright orange hackle for a propeller.

Around the mid-90s, Flip Pallot invited me to do one of his *Walker's Cay Chronicles* shows, to take place around Indian River and Mosquito Lagoon in mid-Florida. The plan was that Flip was going to pole all day, and I was going to fish. I liked the plan. When it came time to choose a fly that first morning, Flip told me he'd prefer if I chose a surface fly so they could record the fly on the water while being retrieved and because of the exciting strikes it would produce. I chose a large Olson Slider in tan and orange.

A detailed story of all that happened during those two wonderful days would make a long article. But suffice it to say that with that one single fly, riding on the surface or pushing a wake, we landed snook, baby tarpon, a big seatrout, and redfish to over 35 pounds. All surface strikes. The fish would take the fly and keep it in their mouths. I could strike late, no problem, and the fly was still in the fish's mouth. Hook-up percentages were very high. Anyway, what a two-day experience! The loud strike of the snook, and the slow slurp of the biggest redfish are still engraved in my memory.

At the end of the second day, when we were through filming, the whole filming crew went out to dinner to celebrate what they anticipated would be a good show. Everyone was happy. Then, somewhere between drinks, Flip ask me to show him again the fly that had single-handedly taken all the fish. I put the beat-up Olson Slider in the palm of his hand. He looked at it closely, its brown colors now very pale, orange hackle gone—it was a mess. After a long inspection, he smiled and said: "You can retire this one Chico, but do get David to tie 'us' a few more." I did.

So you see, fishing reds on the surface, with any one of the patterns mentioned above, is a wonderful and exciting experience. I recommend it. However, while there are times to fish on top, there are also many times, and places, where it would be futile to persist. In those times, which are often the majority, I just go to a weighted streamer. And that's a lot of fun too.

Selecting a Fly

The challenge of selecting a good fly for redfish in the area you are fishing on a given day is that there are so many variables to consider. A redfish's flats range alone is 2,500 miles of coastline. From warm, temperate flats in North Carolina to the thick spartina grasses in Georgia, the subtropical flats of the Everglades, north to the marshes in Louisiana, and to the end of Texas and over a hundred miles into Mexico. That's a lot of different ecosystems. Then redfish consume many different species of crab, shrimp, fish, and more—all of which have inspired thousands of different fly patterns to choose from. So to select a fly, you must juggle many factors, like the fly's sink rate, pattern imitation, size and bulk, color, and more.

Then consider the redfish themselves. By the time they are big enough to target in the flats, they are already eating lots of crabs and shrimp. And as they grow, they add fish to their diet. You'll find they are opportunistic in nature. So if lots of grass shrimp are in the area, for example, that's probably what you'll find them eating.

But when it's all said and done, it is mostly a game of selecting a fly that when retrieved is swimming at the right height in the water column so it can get the red's attention, without spooking it, and look good to eat, while giving the impression that it's trying to escape. Or, if all else fails, ask your guide.

SINK RATE

The most important factor in fly selection is usually the sink rate of your fly. When I look around the area I'm about to fish, instinctively I start my fly selection with sink rate. That is, I decide where in the water column I want my fly to ride for the given conditions I'm looking at. You need a fly that is going to swim at the depth level where redfish will see it. After all, pattern, size, and color don't mean anything if the redfish doesn't see the fly because it's swimming too high or too low.

So if you see reds tailing in a foot of water or more, you may want a fly with lead eyes or at least big bead chain eyes so that your fly will sink quickly to the bottom and stay there while you retrieve. And if you see reds swimming right against the bottom, that is also a good time for a heavy fly. On the other hand, if you cast a weighted fly to tailing reds in heavy grass, more often than not, the fly will be buried in the grass and the red won't see it. Then I'll try a surface fly, such as a small popper or a Hot Lips and make very light noise to draw a fish's attention. Or I'll wait until the reds stop tailing in a place, and when they start to move to another spot, I'll cast a slow-sinking fly, such as a Seaducer or unweighted Crystal Shrimp and try passing it by a red's area of awareness, which in thick grass is probably 18 inches, or less if the water isn't clear.

Other times reds will be moving around the middle of the water column, often above thick turtle grass, for example. And then a fly with a midsize bead chain or brass eyes may be ideal for those conditions. And if the reds are feeding on grass shrimp or baitfish on the surface, or are cruising close to the surface or pushing a wake, then any of the many flies that travel just under the surface are a good choice. And so are sliders and other surface flies that you can work fast.

I feel that many refusals are really a failure to show the redfish your fly. And the most common mistake is that the fly is not going deep enough. I can't tell you how often I've seen an angler make several good, accurate casts to a tailing redfish without getting a response. Then I watch him change flies again and again, only to still be ignored. Finally, at the last resort, he chooses to listen to me or the guide and changes to a fly with a faster sink rate. Surprise: he hooks up. Conclusion? The redfish didn't see any of the flies he was offering, because the flies hadn't gone down enough to reach the redfish's area of awareness.

Also, a tailing red is often best fished with a fly that gets to the bottom fast. Often, redfish pick the fly up right off the bottom. But not always. Captain John Turcot, fishing shallow water for tailing reds in the Mosquito Lagoon, in mid-Florida, uses a white size 4 Clouser Minnow, fully dressed, with tiny 1/80-ounce lead eyes. This fly will sink extremely slow. Plus, it will land softly on flat, calm days and swim back with a straight minnow imitating retrieve—that is, not hopping up and down, but darting forward. So it's not always lead-eyed flies for tailing reds. Also, I've taken many tailers in Louisiana, Texas, and the west side of Florida fishing on the surface with a small Hot Lips or popper, and I've experienced some very exciting strikes.

But in most situations, it's about going down. Captain Dave Denkert, who when it comes to redfish in the Everglades and Florida Bay is one of the best, often poles for tailing reds in much deeper water than Captain Turcot, and therefore he usually prefers a weighted fly that lands with a "plop" so the reds can hear it. He said they will rush to the sound, and take it. He wants the fly working right on the bottom. And you know what? They both do extremely well catching reds. I know: I've fished with both of them. The main difference here is that even though these captains are both fishing the flats, they're fishing in different depths. Casting to a red in less than a foot of water, or in 2 feet of water makes a big difference. In under a foot of clear water, a loud pop of a weighted fly will spook most reds. But in 2 feet of water, that same pop may very well attract him and produce a strike. And in terms of weight to the fly, while tiny 1/80-ounce eyes worked for Turcot in that super shallow water, Dave needed heavy lead eyes to get down to the redfish level in the deeper flat. In the high stages of the tide, and later in the low stages of an outgoing tide, even the same flat contains two different worlds.

Fishing for big reds in marshes, like those in Louisiana, you'll often be sight-casting in 3 feet of water to fish that are cruising right against the bottom and looking down. So you have a situation where most of the reds you'll see will be when they are fairly close to the skiff. Now to make a quick presentation, you not only need to cast quickly, but you also need for the fly to get the bottom *pronto*, so the red can see it before he sees the you or the skiff. Here, a fly heavily weighted with lead eyes is of the essence. And yes, a fluorocarbon tippet or full leader may help you a bit too, but it's no substitute for lead eyes.

PATTERN

Now that we know where we want the fly to travel in the water column and have selected the right weight or buoyancy, let's talk about selecting a pattern. Here you must decide whether to use a fly that imitates a crab, a shrimp, a fish, or perhaps just a big, loud attractor pattern that doesn't look like anything living in the flats, but is easy to see and different, and the reds often eat it too.

I choose specific patterns for several reasons. The first one is, of course, to imitate a food source in the flat that I know the redfish eats in that area. That could be an imitation of a fiddler crab while fishing in high tide or a shrimp imitation over a grass flat. Or it could be a larger fish pattern, blind casting or sight-casting, in a good open or grass bottom or even on beaches.

In areas with bigger reds, I know they'll often be looking for a bigger mouthful, and that's usually baitfish. A bigger red will feed on juvenile mullet, mojarras, menhaden, anchovies, and more, as long as the prey doesn't get too big. Around six inches seems to be the limit. So fishing a big fish imitation around three to five inches in length may get you a big redfish in the right areas. And if they are chasing baitfish on the surface, a large popper or slider retrieved fast may be just the ticket.

Second, I may choose a pattern for its ability to be fished fast, slow, or even dead on the bottom. If I'm blind casting an area, or fishing a shoreline, I need a fly that is big enough to see at a distance, if the water is fairly clear, and can be moved fast enough to cover lots of ground. Here, a baitfish pattern, maybe imitating a pinfish or small mullet, is great. It can be fairly big, say three inches, and I can retrieve it at mid to fast speed, because that's natural for a fleeing fish. A crab pattern, on the other hand, would be terrible to cover water.

But if I am fishing for tailing redfish which are usually not moving much, or a fish laid up, then I want a fly that will slowly pass by a redfish's lip while wiggling, undulating, and looking alive, giving the fish plenty of time to decide. So here, a shrimp pattern or a marabou fly, with the right weight to reach the fish's level of awareness, are good choices. Another way to go on a tailing red or a red just laying in shallow water, especially in open flats or areas with not too much grass, is to use a crab pattern. Just cast it, maybe slide it a bit to place it right in front of the red, and let it drop. The red may take it on the drop, or inspect it and then pick it up right off the bottom. Or you may need to move it very slow, on or near the bottom.

Some days, a red won't pay attention to even your best flies. You feel as if you've never fished for them before. Nothing you try works. You are being ignored. I hate when they do that to me. This could be for no apparent reason at all. Or it could be because the reds are feeding on large quantities of shrimp or bait and your perfect imitation gets lost among thousands of others. What to do?

Well, here an attractor pattern may be the answer. It certainly could be a spoon fly, which flashes a lot and pushes water. Or you may consider a larger than usual fly pattern, like a shrimp or fish pattern tied on a size 1 or 1/0 and 50 percent larger than you usually use. It's worked for me before.

SIZE AND BULK

As a whole, reds feed in the flats on juvenile species, mostly from one to three inches long. And bigger reds eat bigger prey to about six inches, or so. But the size of the prey does not keep getting bigger as they keep growing.

Most crabs the reds eat in shallower waters have a carapace about an inch long. Dr. Aaron Adams, whose work is in the first pages of this book, often uses a fiddler crab pattern just over an inch long tied on a size 4 hook. He takes lots of reds with this pattern. Also, you'll find that the shrimp and fish they feed on are usually less than three inches in length.

The two main factors that dictate the best size, and bulk of a redfish fly in the flats, other than when you are matching a food they are eating, are water clarity and depth. And, to some extent, light level and size of the redfish will be factors, too. Everything being equal, I feel that water clarity has the biggest effect on the size and bulk of the fly you should use.

When I started fly-fishing the Everglades for redfish in 1959, there were no flats boat per se, so we fished a variety of open skiffs. The poling platform had not been invented yet. And we often poled with a wooden dowel bought from a local lumber store. My favorite fly rod was a bamboo Orvis Battenkill, and I mostly fished without polarized glasses. Yes, I know it was pretty basic equipment, but you know what? The redfish were easy. Real easy.

It was not unusual to take several dozen reds sight-casting, and many just a few feet from the boat. As a matter of fact, we used large bulky flies, often tied on 2/0 and 3/0 hook size, to make sure the reds could spot them easily. Because if they saw the fly, they'd take it. This was even in clear waters. Those were the days, eh?

Anyway, times have changed. Typical of any fishery that sees pressure, the fish get smarter, needing longer leaders and longer casts. And the flies get smaller, dressed more sparsely and often more subdued in color. And that is exactly what has happened to a great part of the redfish fishery. I have fished in areas with clear waters, where you needed a 12-foot leader or longer and a 6-weight line, with inch-long flies tied on size 6 hooks. It can be fun, but challenging. I wouldn't have believed it fifty years ago.

When fishing reds in clear water, they are more aware of a skiff's proximity, your movements while casting, or a line being false-cast over them. They can see a lot more of their surroundings, and so they are spookier. And they are also sensitive to a large fly dropping from the sky, meaning it's best to use a smaller fly, sparsely dressed, often with more subdued colors. This way the red is less likely to spook from your presentation and yet, in the clear water, sure to see it.

However, some well-known redfish areas, like South Florida, also have snook and tarpon in the mix. So you may be poling the flats and be just as likely to see a snook, or a tarpon, as you are a tailing redfish. This is great. And it's certainly one of the many reasons I love fly-fishing the Everglades, but it presents a problem. Tarpon, and to a greater extent snook, have lots of small teeth that will easily cut through the average 10- to 16-pound tippet. So I always use a 30- or 40-pound-test "shock" or "bite" tipper, about 10 inches long, just to overcome the abrasion that often results during the fight. And it works great, unless you need to use a small fly, say less than two inches long tied on a size 4 hook.

In this case, the heavy mono or fluorocarbon bite tippet does not let the small delicate fly swim properly, and you won't get many hits. So you have to compromise. Either tie the small fly directly to your tippet and hope you don't hook a snook, or just use a very light bite tippet of 20 pounds and hope the snook doesn't abrade much. Or use a bit bigger fly, say 2½-inch fly on a 2-inch hook and 30-pound bite tippet. Personally, I think it's a gamble on the probabilities of hooking a large snook judging from the conditions. Your call. Or the guide's call.

The selection of flies in off-color waters, or even murky waters, is a different matter. Here visibility is very low, so redfish use their sensory lines to track prey until they get close enough to see it. In this case, it is best to use a larger, bulkier fly pattern that pushes a lot of water as it's being retrieved, making it easier for the red to track it down from a distance, even when it cannot see the fly yet. Bulk really makes a difference in these cases. And when a red does get close enough, the bigger fly silhouette will make it easier for the fish to see. Remember that spoon flies and poppers also push water as you retrieve, and help the red find your fly. In other conditions of low visibility, like heavy overcast skies and early morning or late afternoon, all the flies mentioned above for muddy waters would be good choices.

As redfish get larger, most of them eventually move to deeper waters. But in some areas, like Louisiana, mid-Florida, and the Carolinas, big reds also frequent shallow water, giving the fly fisher an opportunity to sight-cast for them. And I can tell you that, for an angler who has fly-fished for reds in the usual places, to then hunt reds that are well over a yard long is, well, emotional. Get ready to see your backing.

The big red drum usually prefer a bigger offering, but not as big as you would think judging from their size. A good size fly for Louisiana, for example, is 3 to 5 inches long. I've also done well with a 4 inch baitfish pattern with big eyes and a dark back. Remember they love fishes when they get big.

Also, just for fun, I've tried a big crab pattern, a bit bigger than a large permit crab, with lead eyes, on big reds that are not moving much or tailing, and they took the crab real well. Also, when I see them swimming off the bottom, in the middle to upper section of the water column, I love to use a surface fly like a popper, a bushy Seaducer, or a large Olson Slider on a 3/0 hook or so. The strike, as they break the surface and slurp the fly, is unforgettable. I highly recommend it.

In situations of low visibility, like a heavily overcast day, I often fish a big, bright fly that I can see as I retrieve it to better judge the relationship between fish and fly. Or if the water is murky, then try a large and bulky black fly that will show up well in low visibility. Remember, you want that fly to pass very close to the redfish. But if the red doesn't take the fly and you know it passed close enough that the fish could see, it was a refusal. From there, you can change flies, confident that the one you just tried is not of the fish's liking today. But the big reds are an exception. In general, food consumed by reds is under three inches and mostly one to two inches long, or so. The crabs are even smaller in most cases.

COLOR

In essence, you want to match the color of the food the redfish may be feed on as close as possible. Swimming or walking crabs are generally tan, tan and green, olive green, or tan with spots. Mud crabs tend to be darker, like a reddish gray, brown, dark green with spots, and black. Grass shrimp are clear, sand, or greenish in color. Snapping shrimp are olive green to brown, and the common shrimp tends to be translucent with shades of brown or green. Ghost shrimp are white.

Bottom dwellers like gobies and blennies are generally brown. But pinfish and several other baitfish have white and sometimes yellow colors and flash. A white and yellow streamer with some Mylar would work well, and they are the favorite colors of several well-known guides.

The above should give you some idea of the colors to match redfish food. But another guideline is the color of the bottom. To live in its environment, the prey, crustaceans or baitfish, needs to stay as invisible as possible, both to be able to sneak up on the prey they are feeding on and to hide from the predators, like redfish, who are constantly hunting for them.

And since they can't outrun a red or snook, the best defense is to match the color of the bottom they are inhabiting at the moment. So on a light sandy bottom, a tan fly may be my first choice, but on a dark grassy bottom, I may choose a darker color green or brown.

Also, I've found that adding a little bright color to a subdued pattern works very well. For example, a tan and brown shrimp pattern is often enhanced if you add a little chartreuse or bright orange at the front end. A fluorescent color even better, but just a little. It has worked for

me in many places, from the Everglades to the Louisiana marshes and Texas flats.

Muddy Waters

You can have lots of good fishing by sight-casting for reds in muddy or just off-color waters.

Visibility is poor in these conditions, so by the time you see the fish, it's generally very close. It's a game that needs short and accurate casting if you are to succeed. The advantage is that the reds also have low visibility, so they'll often be very close to the skiff and still won't know you are there. Chances are you'll have time to make a good accurate cast and pass the fly by his nose.

And in this situation, the right fly is usually big, bulky, and dark. I often use dark colors or black in muddy waters because they cast a silhouette that is visible to the fish. Another way to go is to use a dark fly with lots of flash added to the sides, like a dark brown with gold flash, or black with purple flash. And you could also use a fly made only or mostly of Mylar for lots of flash. Just make sure it's bulky enough to also push water. Finally, when choosing a baitfish pattern, besides adding some large eyes, it's often good to copy the way a fish's camouflage shading is distributed. Something called "countershading." This gradual shading from dark on top to light on the belly is a great way for baitfish to conceal themselves.

When a predator from above, maybe a bird of prey, is looking for its next meal in the flats, it sees the dark backs of bait against a usually darker bottom, so the lack of contrast makes it hard to see the prey. And a predator in the water, maybe a redfish, is hunting close to the bottom and looks up on a bright day, it sees the light white bellies of baitfish against a bright sky, which also makes them hard to distinguish. Countershading is a great camouflage. So if you are trying to imitate a particular fish with a fly, make sure you have a darker back on a light belly. Maybe match the color of the back to the baitfish you are trying to imitate, like a dark green or even close to black in some species. But in a light bottom sandy beach, the bait will have a light color back, matching the beach's light bottom. So this fly imitation may be white, with some flash and a light gray or pale green back. But if you are trying to make sure a red sees your fly, then a dark or black fly makes an easy-to-see silhouette against most backgrounds—even at night

Favorite Colors

Just for fun, I thought I'd mention the favorite color combinations for redfish of some of my guide friends I frequently fish with. So in no particular order:

Captain Steve Huff is partial to a mostly all-chartreuse fly, which may have a grizzly feather and some flash added, in murky water or clear water. He's fooled several snook over 20 pounds with this fly color.

Captain Dave Denkert loves his almost plain tan shrimp fly with a few dark bars. It's a simple and plain fly, but very successful in the Everglades.

Artist Tim Borski loves his Chernobyl in brown and fishes it almost exclusively in the dark muddy waters where he loves to hunt for reds.

Captain Mark Krowka likes mostly all gold flash for his redfish fly, even under the pressure of tournaments.

Top angler David Olson said, "Give me a boring tan with a little orange hackle."

Captain Steve Huff, Captain Rob Fordyce, and Dr. Aaron Adams—to name a few—are all fans of imitating a mojarra, pinfish, or other baitfish using a plain yellow and white streamer and a little flash.

Marine artist Jorge Martinez is partial to an all-tan body fly for reds, with a little pink accent in the head, to imitate most crustaceans.

My all-time favorite redfish and snook fly color, which I often tie on my Seaducer pattern, is the classic shrimp colors of white, yellow, and grizzly feather mix. The blend of these three colors produces in the water a light yellow barred image that can often pass for a shrimp or a baitfish. I've caught thousands of reds and snook with it over the years. And I'll continue to do so.

Attractor Patterns for Strikes

Let's say you arrive at one of your favorite redfish spots to find grass shrimp all over the place, and the reds and other gamefish feeding on them. So you tie your favorite imitation of a grass shrimp and start casting. You expect a strike on every cast but after a few dozen casts you realize the shrimp fly is lost among thousands of other lookalike shrimp. You are being ignored. Or let's say instead, you find reds on a grass flat, just laid up, not doing much. But after a few casts, you have no takers. The reds seem to have "an attitude" this morning. You are being ignored, again. So what to do in either case to get their attention? I'd change to an attractor pattern.

An attractor pattern is usually a bright, loudly colored fly, with some or lots of flash added, and often on the big side. The attractor can be a combination of colors or a single color often not seen in the flats, like orange or chartreuse. In situations that don't call for you to "match the hatch"—to look like the next shrimp or baitfish—you need to cast a fly with an appearance that sets it apart from everything else, a fly that is a sharp contrast with its surroundings. And this is what an attractor pattern does. You are trying to get a reaction from the red. And an attractor does that very well. My two favorite attractor colors are a mostly orange fly or a mostly chartreuse fly, always with some flash on the sides or middle. A spoon can be a good attractor fly.

ANGLER VISIBILITY

Regardless of all the other considerations, there are times when I'll choose a redfish fly only for its ability to be seen while retrieving. If I find redfish in light or bottom conditions where I see the fish, but I can't see the fly at all, and I'm having trouble maneuvering the fly past the redfish's lips, then I go looking for a fly will be visible while I retrieve it. This could be a bright or flashy fly, a surface fly, a spoon fly—anything I can see well. And I find in these situations that any fly color, shape, or size that helps me place the offering by a red's lips is a good fly.

WEEDGUARDS

The world redfish live and feed in has plenty of grass, shorelines, structure, and other places a hook can get snag or pick up grass, so most redfish flies have some type of weedguard to allow the fly to swim as snag free as possible. A good weedguard will deflect grass or help the fly bounce off heavy structures, letting the fly cover plenty of water while swimming naturally. You can tie several types of weedguards on your fly, and they all work, to some degree. But you should know that none are 100 percent snag-free. Sometimes, even the best weedguard will not prevent your fly from hooking a mangrove root, or picking a blade of grass. And, to some extent, you will also miss more strikes with a weedguard than if you did not have one on your fly. I know good anglers who will not use them at all. But personally, when I fish the redfish world, I almost always fish with a weedguard. I feel I get more strikes than I lose because my weedguards have helped me stay snag-free or grass-free.

Single Strand Mono

The most popular mono weedguard is probably the single strand mono, tied just behind the hook's eye and angled either perpendicular to the shaft of the hook, like 90 degrees to the shank, or angled back toward the point of the hook about 45 degrees. This method works very well whether the fly is riding upright or inverted. Most of my smaller redfish flies have single strand mono guards.

Double Strand Mono

In areas with more structure or grass or lots of thick cover, you may want to use a weedguard that is stiffer, and here a double mono weedguard is a good idea. Just like the single strand above the double mono strand, forming an inverted V shape, can be tied straight down and angled back to the point of the hook about 45 degrees. They work very well.

But another method is to tie the two shafts of mono angled forward, about 45 degrees, from the eye of the hook. If you've never seen a fly with this type of weedguard, it'll look funny to you, but I'm telling you, it works great. Some flies, like crab patterns, are a natural for this design.

And one proponent of the forward-angled weedguard, Captain Mark Krowka, uses it exclusively on his famous Glitterus fly. Mark uses two 16-pound hard mono shafts angled way forward on his fly. This system has proven very effective in pushing grass and structure out of the way. Also, Mark feels it is a huge help in hookups, because when a red takes the Glitterus, the mono shafts fold forward and the red eats it with confidence. He said his hook-up percentage has increased dramatically. If Mark's results in tournaments are any indication, this is a weedguard design to try on you favorite fly.

Spring Loop Weedguard

This method can be tied with either single or double mono. Tie the mono first at the end of the bend of the hook, and then bring it forward to secure it just behind the eye. You can use this method on both upright and inverted riding flies. It's quite effective.

Occasionally I've found that the fly would bounce off, mostly on seatrout and snook. This isn't noticeable with redfish, who seem to keep the fly in their mouths longer. I've used this method with good success on the big reds in Louisiana and on smaller reds on Clouser flies.

Inverted Flies

Another way to avoid getting snagged is to use an inverted fly—that is, one tied so that the hook always rides with the point up. That way it is more difficult for the fly to catch grass or stick to branches or underwater structures. Yet the fly will still hook a red that takes it.

One popular inverted fly is the Bend-Back, which is tied to ride with the hook up and the shank of the hook slightly bent back, hence the name. I've fished this fly a lot since my friend Nick Curcione introduced me to its charms around 1975 on a trip to Belize. But even as good as the Bend-Back is at avoiding grass and snags, I almost always fish reds and other fish in the backcountry with a stiff single shaft of 30-pound mono as a weedguard and don't seem to have any problem with hookups.

Mono Materials

Monofilament is the most popular material for weedguard construction. It's translucent, fairly stiff, and easy to purchase and work with. Mason hard mono is a popular choice.

However, I feel that many anglers and fly tiers should look to try fluorocarbon. It is stiffer, denser, doesn't cause glare, and is thinner and more translucent than mono. The few flies I've used with fluorocarbon have worked really well. I don't see the downside.

Top fly fisher, jazz pianist, and fly tier Vince Maggio has been using fluorocarbon on his redfish flies for years with great success, and he often uses mono as stiff as 50-pound-test when sight-casting in heavy grass flats.

Wire Material

Mono if fine for most fly patterns, especially smaller and midsize flies. But when it comes to preventing a big and bulky fly from snagging on structure, give me wire.

A single shaft of wire, tied just behind the eye of the hook and brought down at an angle to end just ahead of the point of the hook, makes a formidable weedguard for large flies. And if you want more stiffness and "spring," you could use a double shaft of wire. Flip Pallot and I have used wire weedguards since the 1960s. And we continue to do so.

Certain flies just swim better and more naturally when they have a wire weedguard. My Seaducer is one of them. Not only does the springy wire deflect grass and help a 1/0 hook bounce off structure, but the weight of the wire acts as a keel on the bushy buoyant Seaducer, keeping it riding straight. It's my favorite weedguard material for this pattern.

Size Matters

The bigger the fly, the stiffer a weedguard material you need to use to deflect objects. While a size 4 shrimp pattern does not need much stiffness to bounce off heavy grass or structure, a 1/0-weighted fly, with its bigger gap, needs a stiffer weedguard. Captain Rob Fordyce put is well when I interviewed him in the Florida Keys: "You are not trying to drive the fly through the weeds; instead you just want the fly to bounce off the structure or grass. So a light fly will bounce easily with lighter mono, but the heavier flies will need a heavier weedguard." No argument here.

Sharpen Your Hook

Now that you have selected a fly that you have confidence in, it's time to examine the hook for sharpness and barb size. The point of the hook is probably its most important part. How sharp a hook is will often dictate whether or not it will penetrate the fish's mouth deep enough to pass the barb and hold it. So to make sure this happens, the first thing I do is take the point of the hook and touch it lightly on the nail of my thumb to see if it sticks. If it's sharp, it will stick and will not move. If it's not, it will slide down the nail, and I'll know it's time to sharpen the hook. So I'll take out my file and, stroking it toward the point, I'll sharpen it on three sides, forming a triangular shape on the point. Some anglers do it on four sides making a diamond shape, and that's fine too.

If you have a chemically sharpened hook, you probably do not have to sharpen it yourself. However, I will still check the point against my thumb just in case. And if it happens to feel dull, I'll touch it up with my file or stone.

Some anglers go to the extreme of reducing the point's length while sharpening. This way, the distance from the point to the barb is much shorter, and the barb will go into the flesh much sooner. It's a subtlety, but when looking for a big fish or when competing in a tournament, it could make a difference. Personally, I only do this if I see that the point on a particular hook model is extra long. Then I'll file it down.

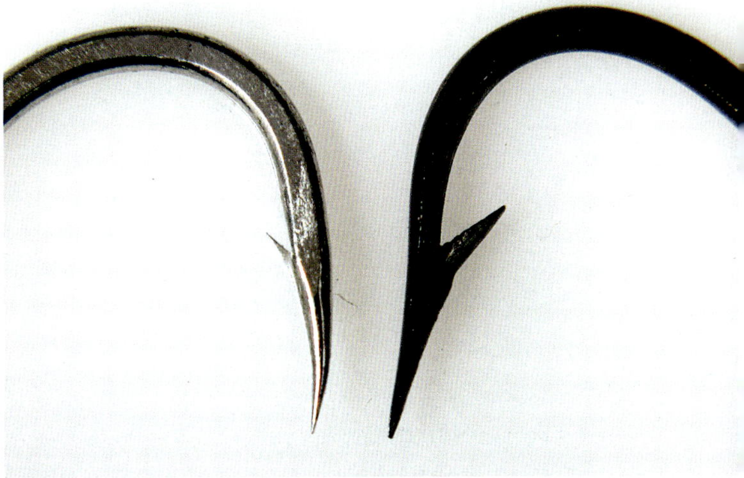

A Gamakatsu SL12S on the left, with what is often called a "micro barb," and a Mustad 34007 on the right, with its standard barb. You can see the huge difference between them. Penetration with the smaller barb is infinitely easier, and the small barb holds the fish just as well for most practical purposes.

BARBLESS

When you set a hook on a fish deep enough to penetrate the barb, the chances of the fish dislodging the hook during the fight are greatly reduced. That's why you want a hook with a barb that is low enough to allow the barb to penetrate flesh easily, but still high enough to "stick."

Over the years, I've found that you don't need a big barb on a hook to hold a fish. The now-popular "micro barbs" hold a fish just as well, often making it difficult to remove the hook on a fish. So for me, a low barb, reducing a large barb with a file or a large barb that has been lowered by flattening it with a pair of pliers, are all good methods to facilitate penetration.

A low barb or flattened barb offers many advantages. First, when you set a hook on a fish, the low barb takes considerably less effort to penetrate a fish's mouth. Remember, a barb only works if it penetrates completely into the flesh; otherwise, you have a better chance of losing the fish.

And a hook with a low barb or plastered barb takes less time to remove, tears little tissue if any on a fish's mouth, is less harmful to the fish, and greatly improves the odds of a healthy release. Also, if you happen to get hooked for any reason, you'll appreciate the extra ease of removing a low barb—I guarantee it. On the other hand, going completely barbless, that is, filing the barb off completely to a perfectly smooth wire, has not worked for me. I tend to lose too many fish. I'll stay with very low barbs or flattened barbs. I am glad to say that many fishing camps I've visited in the last ten years are asking their anglers to flatten the barbs or use ultra-low barbs. Bravo for them.

Here are two of the Mustad 34007, an often-used stainless steel hook, with a plastered barb on the left and as it comes from the factory on the right. You can easily see that the plastered barb will offer less resistance to penetration. And it still holds a fish well. I always plaster the barb or file the barb down when using hooks with such big barbs.

When to Change a Fly

Selecting a fly from so many choices takes some thinking. But even if you have chosen a fly that worked early in the day, it may not be working after lunch. And sooner or later, you'll think of trying a different fly.

If you keep getting refusals and you suspect your fly is not getting down fast or deep enough, what should you do? The first thing I do is test the fly. I bring the fly in

Redfish Flies and Bonefish Flies

What's the difference? You may have seen some of the redfish flies in this book elsewhere as bonefish flies. And even in my bonefish book *Fly-Fishing for Bonefish*, some of the patterns, often in different sizes, are really the same.

Well, it turns out that in the same type of flat, same conditions, and same food, a fly that works for a tailing red will often work for a tailing bone and vice versa. Indeed some flats in Florida Bay and Miami, for example, have both redfish and bonefish, and the same fly may work for both. The exceptions of course, is the surface flies, which are best to keep for reds. ■

and drop it on the water at my feet. I look at the fly going down and try to judge how many seconds it took to go down. The next fish I cast to, I make sure I'm letting it go long enough to reach where I want to fish the fly. If in a couple of other tries I see that I can't get down fast enough before the fish has moved, I change to a heavier fly. Easy enough. On the other hand, if I am dragging bottom and find myself stripping too fast just to keep the fly from tangling on the bottom, it's time for a lighter weight, or an unweighted fly. *No problema*, man.

However, if the presentation is good, and I see the fish notice the fly, maybe start to go for it and stop, or move out of the fly's way, then I know the red has seen the fly and refused it. I may give the fly a couple of other chances, but then it's time to change. What to change to?

My usual change is to a different pattern. So if a tailing fish refused a crab pattern, I'll change to a shrimp pattern, or a dark-colored fish pattern. Marine artist Jorge Martinez is a great fly tier and a top fly fisher, especially when it comes to sight-casting. His advice on changing flies after a refusal has often help me find a solution. Jorge told me: "It's about extremes, Chico. When I get refusals, I never make a subtle change. I go from a small fly to a very large fly, from a dark color to a light one. And this really works for me." Actually, it has also worked for me. Give this philosophy a try.

Advice from Guides

No one knows the redfish flats better than a good seasoned redfish guide. No one. They fish the area day in and day out. And on days they are not booked, they often go out themselves to keep exploring and learning. I have fished the southern part of the Everglades, Flamingo, for over fifty years. But my favorite guides in that area constantly find reds when I can't, in the same places I know so well!

I know three different guides that fish the same areas in Flamingo, and use completely different flies successfully. Often they're fishing within a few hundred yards of each other. How come? It looks like the guides disagree on which is the best fly, but that is often not true. The difference in fly selection has more to do with where and when they are fishing these flats.

One guide fishes in the deeper parts of a flat because he can approach the reds closer and it's easier for a beginner client to make the shorter cast. So he uses a heavily weighted fly to reach the bottom fast. The next guide likes finding tailing reds and fishes the lower stages of the tide in super shallow water and uses a small fly with little or no weight. And then another loves fishing areas that are muddy and have off-color water so he can get right up to the red, and make a real short cast passing the fly right by the fish's lips, and his fly is, of course, big, bulky, and dark.

This is why a guide may want you to tie a particular fly for your day out fishing with him, instead of a fly you have had luck catching reds in the past. He knows where he is going to fish that morning and the fly you need. He probably was there yesterday.

Chapter 6

Fly Lines for Reds

When it comes to tackle, the first question I usually get in a school or seminar is: What rod should I buy? When the question should really be about what size and weight flies will be needed. With that information, you'll know what size fly line to get. And then, and only then, will you know what weight rod to get.

For example, if you are going to fish for permit, it usually requires that you cast a heavy crab fly in windy situations. These crab flies require a mid to heavy fly line to carry the weight, so at least a 9-weight but usually a 10-weight is the perfect size. Once you know you need a 10-weight line, then, and only then, you can start to choose what 10-weight rod you need for permit.

Well, in the case of redfish, most flies are sizes 6 to 2, often weighted and under 3 inches. In this case, a 7- or an 8-weight fly line will cast these flies well. So the corresponding 7- or 8-weight rod is usually perfect for most redfishing.

And if you go to Louisiana for the real big red drum, the flies are much larger, often over 4 inches and heavily weighted, so then a 9- or 10-weight fly line is perfect to cast these bigger flies. The corresponding 9- or 10-weight rod will be able to land these big reds in a reasonable time.

You see, heavy or light, the weight of the fly does not help your casting. It's only the weight of the fly line that counts. It's the weight of the fly line that will carry the fly to its destination. Actually, in spite of the great amount of tackle and other paraphernalia that exist today in fly fishing, I still feel that no single item is as important, especially in sight-casting, as owning the right fly line, with a well-designed leader. These are followed closely by a good fly rod.

Anatomy of a Fly Line

A fly line consist of two parts: the core and the coating. The core is a braided or single strand material that resides along the center of the fly line, and it is mainly there to give the line its strength. It can also be used to control the degree of stiffness of the fly line. Covering the core is the coating, often made of PVC, which serves to give the line mostly its weight, taper, density, and color. Most fly lines used for redfish are about 100 feet long.

In selecting a fly line for redfish, or any other fish, you need to consider several factors: the weight of the line, to properly match the rod; the taper or shape of the line, which will determine how far or how fast you can deliver a fly; the density, which will determine whether you want the line to float or sink and how fast; and if you have a choice, the color or lack of color.

Weight

In the fly-fishing world, when we are talking about fly line weight, we are talking specifically about the weight of the first 30 feet of the fly line. And while this may sound strange to a beginner, it actually makes sense since that is the portion of the line you will mostly be casting; give or take a few feet.

Years ago, the American Fishing Tackle Manufacturers Association (AFTMA) adopted a method to differentiate fly lines by the weight of their first 30 feet, measured in grains. And today, all fly line manufacturers have adopted and follow these guidelines. Below are the designation and weight in grains of the range of lines used for redfish.

To give you some guidance, the most often-used line weight for reds are the 7, 8, and 9. Not counting extreme conditions, they can do it all. And if I had to have one rod for redfish, something I refuse to do, it would probably be an 8-weight, or maybe a 7-weight. You get the picture.

From left to right: a white long head "bonefish type" fly line, for more delicate presentation; a dark gray fast-sinking head to get a fly down to the bottom; a blue short head "redfish type" fly line, good for short fast casts or heavy flies; a clear floating line with a with a "redfish type" short head, great for spooky fish or blind casting in relatively shallow waters; and a bright orange "bonefish taper" type line, good for accuracy because you can see the line so well in the air—just don't let Mr. Red see it in the air, too.

5-weight	140 grains	plus or minus 6 grains	134–146
6-weight	160 grains	plus or minus 8 grains	152–168
7-weight	185 grains	plus or minus 8 grains	177–193
8-weight	210 grains	plus or minus 8 grains	202–218
9-weight	240 grains	plus or minus 10 grains	230–250
10-weight	280 grains	plus or minus 10 grains	270–290

As you probably can imagine, there are some pluses and minuses in choosing a heavier or lighter line. A lighter line generally requires less effort to cast, lands more softly on the water, and the complete matching outfit, that is, rod, reel, and line, is lighter on the hand. But a size or two heavier in weight will help carry a bigger or bulkier fly with ease, will push through the wind easier, but can be more tiring to cast and will land with more disturbance on the water.

The truth is that when fishing reds, I usually carry at least a couple of rods, fully rigged to the fly. For example, I may have a 7-weight rigged with a light size 4 fly and 12-foot leader for shallow water, tailing fish, or very clear water. Then maybe I'll have an 8- or 9-weight with a shorter 9- or 10-foot leader and a bigger size 2 or larger fly, perhaps heavily weighted, for deeper flats, muddy waters, and such. And as I fish the day, from flat to flat, I may change outfits. I may even have a rod with a sinking line, rigged with a heavy fly for deep potholes, channels, canals, and other promising locations. More about that later. In terms of fishing ultra light for reds, my lightest rod is a 6-weight. I find it fun to cast, and the line still has enough weight to easily cast a size 4 fly, even weighted.

Now, there are more and more saltwater 5-weight rods and lines, mostly to fish the small bones of the Bahamas, Belize, Yucatan, and other places. But they can also be used to fish for little tarpon, small reds, and dozens of other small saltwater species. They can be great fun, but you have to pay your dues to use a 5-weight. First, you have to be a very good fly caster to be able to cast in the wind with accuracy. But, perhaps more importantly, you have to understand fighting large fish in shallow water. Redfish, like any fish in the flats, and especially in the warm summer days, can get exceedingly tired during a long fight, often dying at the end or being eaten by a predator after release. You need to fight a big red on a light rod as you would a big tarpon on an 11-weight rod—that is, right of the butt of the rod and with all the fish-to-line angles that will tire a fish quickly. If you don't know how to do this, stay with the standard weights.

I can fish a 5-weight and have done so in the past, but still prefer a 6-weight. I have good friends who fish the 5-weight and love it, but they have paid their dues learning for many years. Going any lighter is simply not practical. Your choice.

As far as 10-weights, the only time I've fished them on reds have been in Louisiana for really big reds and while using extra big flies in muddy waters. Still, my heavy rod for those big reds is mostly the 9-weight, which is much lighter in my hand and can subdue a red over 30 pounds and much bigger in a relatively short time.

Now, what about over-lining? That is, using a 7-weight rod and putting a heavier 8-weight line. As a rule, I don't recommend this. However, if you're going to fish

Going Ultra Light, angler David Olson took this nice red by making a quiet presentation with a 5-weight line. Captain John Turcut is holding the redfish.

in conditions where all the casts are going to be short, and you will be false-casting with very little line in the air, then the heavier line will help you. Also, as you'll see in the taper section below, short taper lines, like many so-called "redfish tapers" are often build heavier anyway. So be careful over-lining with a redfish taper or you may end up with a line two sizes heavier. This varies with manufacturers.

Taper

Now that you have chosen the weight, probably a 7- or 8-weight line, let's talk about the shape of the fly line, that is, the taper. There are basically three types of tapers for single-handed rods. The level line (L), the double taper line (DT), and the weight-forward line (WF). The line you want, and the most popular line taper by far, is the weight-forward.

A weight-forward taper has most of its weight, and line thickness, in the first 25 to 50 feet or so, which is the portion you'll mostly be using to cast your fly. The rest of the line has a thin level taper. There are four main components to a weight-forward line: a front taper, a belly, a rear taper, and a running line. There's also one very important measurement: the head.

The front taper section is the presentation section. Depending on how long it is and how fast or slow it tapers, the front taper can present a fly very delicately or have the power to turn over a very heavy fly, even in a strong wind. It is usually about 4 to 8 feet in length. The belly section is the fattest section of the fly line and therefore the heaviest. This is the section that is most responsible for carrying the fly during the cast. The longer it is, the further you can cast. But the shorter it is, the faster you can load the rod and make a quick cast. As always, there is a compromise. The rear taper helps stabilize the line in the air, helping make the cast smoother. You don't want the belly to drop in diameter too quickly. I usually like fly lines with a medium to long rear taper. A rear taper is often longer than the front taper.

The running line will help you get distance, by "shooting" line through the guides, at the end of a cast. You can cast further with a thinner running line, but you lose control, and therefore accuracy. You can have more control and pick up more line off the water with a thicker running line, but you lose distance. Another compromise.

Finally, the combination of the front taper, the belly, and the rear taper (every component but the running line) is called the head of the fly line. I feel that matching the length of the head to the fishing conditions is probably the most important factor in fly line selection.

In good hands, a fly line with a 50-foot head is capable of making a long and smooth cast easily. But making a short fast cast with this line can be difficult. However, if the caster is using a shorter 30- or 35-foot head, making an accurate medium to short cast is much easier. And I feel that making a fairly long cast is still not too hard. Since presentation will not be as delicate as the long head line, the short head lines are a better compromise for most sight-casting for reds and other fish in the off-color waters of the redfish world. This is especially true for beginners and intermediate casters.

So if you need to make a long presentation to a tailing bonefish, or redfish, in shallow water, a fly line with a long head is great, because you are going to have lots of line out of the tip of the rod when making these long casts. And the longer more delicate front taper will help you land the fly on the water like a rose petal. And many top casters prefer this line.

But if you're fishing in off-color waters for redfish, where casts are going to be mostly medium to short distance, a short head line will load the rod faster, with a minimum of false-casting, and you'll get the fly to the fish fast, before it spooks.

Personally, I have many fly lines, including long head and short head lines, because I do it all, in salt water and fresh water, from bluegill to bonefish to billfish. But as a whole, when I fish the backwaters for redfish, whether Louisiana or South Florida, I prefer a shorter head in most cases. Only on spooky fish and shallow, clear water do I go to the longer heads.

Let's do the math. Most short heads by most manufacturers are about 30 to 35 feet or so. Most leaders for the backcountry are about 10 feet, so by the time you have the full weight of the line out of the tip of the rod, you have over 40 feet of line out. Now I propose to you that many of the reds you'll catch in the flats, you'll take under that distance. And if the red is another few feet further, say 50 feet away, you can easily shoot some line and reach him.

And when you find yourself fishing in low-visibility situations, either because of water clarity or overcast conditions, and every red you see is 10 to 25 feet away, the heavy short head line will load your rod sooner, making that quick short cast much easier. Please don't take the above words lightly. Consistently making quick, short casts, with accuracy is one of the hardest things to do

A nice red taken while tailing on a flat, calm day, using a "bonefish taper" and a 12-foot leader for the most delicate presentation.

PAT FORD

A fly line with a short head is ideal for these close quarters—and a short rod is also essential here. I'm casting to baby tarpon in a narrow creek.

when you are sight-casting. And those who can do it well take lots of reds.

On the other hand, a long head line is slower to get in motion, slower to cast. In great hands, a caster will make them work on short casts, and make some beautiful and delicate long casts, but the bread-and-butter short to mid casts are going to be harder to do. And if it's windy, they'll be even harder.

Most lines labeled bonefish tapers tend to have the longer heads, about 45 feet or longer. Most lines labeled redfish taper tend to have about a 30- to 35-foot head or so. But other lines, with different names, may be a short or long head. So take the time to look on the back of the fly line box to see the head length. You may have to look at the diagram, and actually add the measurements of the front taper, the belly, and the rear taper to get the head length.

By the way, some of these shorter heads may be a bit heavier in the front 30 feet than the weight of the line should be. That is, an 8-weight, which should be about 210 grains, may be closer to 230 grains in the first 30 feet, for example. It's more like an $8^1/2$-weight, but you'll still be happy with them. And if you need more info on a line, every manufacturer gives you lots of up-to-date info on its Website. Do take the time to check them out.

Another way to get more weight in the first 30 feet or so to get a good load on the rod is simply to "over-line" the rod. That is, put a 9-weight line on an 8-weight rod. It works fine, sometimes, but I usually don't recommend it. And here is why: if you over-line with a short head, which usually runs a bit heavier, you are going to be over-lined by much more than one line size, and this may be too much. And if you do this with a long head line, maybe a bonefish taper line, and you try to cast to a red further away, the long head will be several sizes too heavy for the rod.

So if you happen to have a heavy line already from another outfit, and you want to try it on your lighter rod, for short casts, fine, try it. It may work for you. But I wouldn't buy new heavy line, and instead I'd buy the short head line, such as a redfish taper line.

There are, of course, exceptions to every rule. If you fish for reds in areas where the water is usually shallow and clear, then a light long head fly line, such as a 6- or

7-weight and a long leader, is an ideal outfit. And the fact that the longer heads married to a long leader is slow to get going is not a disadvantage here, because you often see a tailing or cruising red in those shallow waters at long enough distance that you are likely to have enough time to make a delicate cast. It's technical fishing for reds, and it's lots of fun too.

Density

COLORED FLOATING LINE

Your first line, and probably your most often-used line while fishing for reds, should be a colored floating line. The name of the game when sight-casting for reds, or any other fish, is control. You must be able to make accurate casts to a fish, and if you miss, be able to pick up the fly line off the water and cast to the fish again, without spooking it. This can only be done well, and consistently, with a floating fly line.

A floating line, because it has air all along the line, is fatter in diameter, and travels much slower in the air. This is actually an advantage because it's easier for the angler who is false-casting to a fish to see where the fly line is going, so the angler can correct for direction and for distance to be more accurate. If you miss (and we all miss a lot), the high floating fly line is easier to pick up off the water with a minimum of disturbance. A good floating line is vital for sight-casting in the flats. Floating line is also a must for working a shoreline, where you need to constantly cast as close as you can to the shore or to structure, and you also need to repeatedly pick up off the water.

Finally, you can fish a line better if you can see it. So a color you can see is easier to cast accurately, whether to a fish or a shoreline. And when you present to a fish, and the fly drops on the water and disappears, the only way you have of knowing, roughly, where the fly is in relation to the fish is to look at the end of you floating fly line and mentally calculate another 9 or 10 feet of leader. With this information in your mind, you or your guide will make a decision whether to strip the fly and try to entice the fish or to pick the line up and make another presentation.

So you want a weight-forward, floating, colored line for your first line. And by the way, if the line you chose happens to come in two tones—that is, the head is one color and the running line is another—this is a good thing. That way you can easily tell where the head of the line, which has most of the weight, is at any given time. Believe me, you'll find this useful throughout a day's fishing.

Make no mistake, if you are a beginner or you are going to have only one fly line for reds, or bones, this is the line to have. The rest, below, is specialty stuff—great, but only for certain situations.

CLEAR FLOATING LINE

A colored floating line is not perfect, of course. If you false-cast the fly line over a fish, especially in shallow water, the fish will often see the fly line against the sky and spook. And if your line lands over the fish or too near, which is called "lining a fish," it will also spook. You can improve your chances of keeping the fly line away from the fish's eye by using a longer leader, say 12 feet or longer. But still, with the increased pressure on fish in every flat, some areas have become harder to fish. I know anglers, trying for maximum stealth, who use 14-foot leaders with good success in clear shallow water. In muddy waters, this isn't a problem.

Now if you want maximum stealth, and you are both a good caster and a good angler, there is a solution: a totally clear floating fly line. It's like casting a long fat leader, but with the weight to load the rod. Although I've been using clear sink lines of one type or another for almost fifty years, when the floating clear lines appeared in the market, I resisted their call. But eventually I gave in a few years ago. Now, I have no doubt that they spook significantly less fish. In the right conditions, and in the hands of a good angler, they are deadly.

I find that either the fish don't see the line or they don't mind the line, because often I'll think I've spooked a red for sure, yet a few seconds later, I'm hooked up! Fishing a school of reds in a deep flat, where the school ends up running under the fly line seldom spooks the school and often gets a hookup. And sometimes, even when the line actually landed over some of the reds, I'd still get a hookup. Also, when blind casting in a flat in low visibility, I don't spook nearly as many fish—often none. I can't count the days I've taken a dozen reds, and snook, blind casting shallow in a flat, where if I had fished a colored line, I may not have taken but one or two fish, maybe none. Really.

But, as always, there is no magic. Except for blind casting situations, it takes a good caster, and angler, to fish clear lines effectively. First of all, you don't see the line in the air very well, so it will tend to throw off your casting timing. When trying to cast accurately to a cruising fish or a shoreline, you don't get any help from the visual of the unrolling fly line because you can't see the line well enough to make a judgment. And when the fly lands on the water and sinks, you don't see the fly or the fly line on the water. You only see your rod. So you better remember where the fly landed to relate it to the fish you are trying to entice into a strike. It's tough. It's like casting a light jig with 6-pound monofilament: once the jig lands on the water and the splash dissipates, nothing will tell you where the jig is located. It's the same with a clear fly line.

However, if you are casting a big fly, it is a bit easier to see in the air, so you'll be more accurate casting to a fish or shoreline. But with a small fly, accuracy is difficult. A good angler will do well with these clear lines, and a few tournament winners in the Keys and the Everglades are using clear floaters in most or all of their fishing, but it takes lots of practice and many days on the water to fish them well.

CLEAR TIPS

A good compromise between an all-colored floating line and an all-clear floating line, so you can still see the line but have some of the advantages of a clear line, is a clear wet tip line, either with a floating clear tip or a sinking clear tip.

These are regular weight-forward floating color lines in which the last 6 to 12 feet or so are totally clear. This way, you can see most of the line in the air, for accuracy and to help while false-casting, but the front portion of the fly line, which is closest to the fish, is clear. Say you're using a wet tip with a 10-foot clear tip and a 10-foot leader; then you would have 20 feet of clear line up front. This design has a lot of stealth. And if you need the fly to sink a little more, say fishing deep flats or deep shorelines, you can get the same line but with a clear sinking-tip. And an extra bonus is that the higher density of the sinking-tip also helps turn the fly over easier in the wind or while using a heavy fly.

Also, because you already have a few feet of clear line, you can easily fish these lines with a short leader, say an 8-foot leader, which would be easy to turn over, even in a stiff wind. So that 8-foot leader with a 10-foot sink- or float-tip would give you 18 feet of clear line before you reach the color part of the line.

Both these lines have a valid design, and I have several friends who use them successfully for spooky redfish in shallow overfished waters, big seatrout, or snook.

And while wading for redfish in the surf of Jacksonville, I learned that friend and veteran angler John Bottko does well with a clear sinking wet tip. I watch him fish the surf on a windy day and cast with ease. The floating running line would come off the water easily when he shot line, while the clear sinking wet tip up front helped sink his weighted flies to the redfish's level. He was the only one who took redfish that day. I didn't argue with him on line selection.

Clear Sinking Neutral Density Lines

In the early 1960s, Flip Pallot, Norman Duncan, John Emery, and I used 150-pound mono to make clear sink fly lines for our 9-weight rods. These were, as far as Flip and I know, the first clear sinking fly lines made.

In those days, we would drive down to the Keys in the evening, and fly-fish all night for the big tarpon that were laid up in the shadow of the bridges, waiting for bait to come to them with the tide. Standing on the bridge, we would cast big streamers upcurrent and worked the fly back toward the tarpon. The fly would come into the light of the bridge, and then as it approached the shadows, a big tarpon would come up and crash it on the surface. We would hook the fish from above, and the tarpon would usually make a short run into the open, make a couple of jumps, and then run back with the tide under the bridge, usually breaking us at the backing. There wasn't a chance in a million we were going to land any tarpon this way, and we knew this. It was just done for the thrill.

However, fly lines were expensive, about eight dollars in those days, so losing one was no thriller. I could go on a date with eight dollars in those days. Yet we weren't going to stop fishing for those big tarpon. So we decided to make our own fly lines. We would stretch the heavy mono between two posts on a clothesline and then laboriously sand it into the shape of a weight-forward fly line. Yes, I know, it was insane. We had no fingerprints. But this way we could afford to lose many fly lines, because they cost us pennies. We obviously did not consider our time. And it has been pointed out by some that by not having fingerprints, we could have gone into more profitable businesses. But, no, we were fly fishermen, and were not changing our profession. Still haven't.

These fly lines, made out of super stiff 150-pound mono, could not be wound into a fly reel or the memory would be so bad you would have never been able to cast them. So we stored them in big 2-foot loops and secured them with pipe cleaners. Yes, we were pipe smokers those days too.

We would arrive at the bridge with fly rod in hand and a few of these "homemade" fly lines on the other hand. Then, when we lost a fly line to a big tarpon, we simply would rig another line and cast again. We went through fly lines pretty quick on a good night. And we could still afford to date. Anyway, fifty years later, manufacturers are now making clear sinking lines that cast like a dream, and Flip and I have our fingerprints back.

A neutral density sinking line has no air inside, so for the same weight designation, it's smaller in diameter than its floating counterpart. This means it cuts through the air more easily, and casts better and further than a floating line, especially in the wind. Also, skilled casters can take a quality clear sinking line, apply a good dressing to it, and cast the whole hundred feet. It's quite a tool. Many guides and anglers use a clear sinking line as

A seatrout taken while blind casting in shallow, clear water, with a clear weight-forward fly line. With a colored line, I would have spooked lots of fish. CORBETT DAVIS

their second or third fly line while fishing for reds because it is effective in a great variety of situations.

I love fishing deep flats, say two to five feet deep, for schooling reds, but often it's not easy to cast a fly to them. A school of redfish in deep flats will move all over the place. So you need to cast long, and quickly. A slick clear sinking line can make those fast, long casts if you are a good caster. And when you do make a mistake and the school of reds runs under you fly line, they seldom spook from it. It's an ideal line for this situation. Also, dredging deep with a weighted fly over big potholes or a shallow channel, you can hit bottom and the line will not usually spook fish. And finally, when you need to blind cast an area for reds, whether a deep flat, or a beach, a full sinking clear line is usually my first choice. If I'm wading the surf, because the whole line sinks, I'll have to use a shooting basket, of course.

FAST-SINKING LINES

Not many redfish anglers use fast-sinking lines—their minds are mostly on the flats and tailing reds. And I don't blame them. But still, when the reds are not in the flats, because of weather conditions or water levels too low for the flats, I don't mind heading for deeper waters from time to time. You can have a great thrill fishing a fly deep in a channel or mouth of a river or creek and hooking a large fish that takes you to the backing, not knowing how big the fish is, or even what species you have on.

Just like you can buy lines that float with air inside, or lines with neutral density that sink slowly, you can buy lines in which the manufacturer has added powdered tungsten to the coating mix, and depending on how much tungsten has been added, these lines can sink really fast. They are usually a dark color, extremely thin for their weight and able to cast into a strong wind like nothing you've ever seen. They come in a variety of sink rates, rated in "ips," or inches per second.

To get a line that can fish deep in the redfish's world, often keeping the fly right on the bottom, you may want to try a sink rate of about three to six inches per second. The lines I am talking about are weight-forward lines, and they come in two configurations: full-sinking lines, and hybrid lines where it's the first 30 feet or so, the head, that has all the tungsten. These hybrids usually have a bright colored running line and a dark colored 30-foot sinking head. It's these hybrids I recommend you buy. The fast full-sinking lines are all dark in color and sink much deeper, actually deeper than you need for redfish, so they are not practical for most backwater fishing. I use them in the ocean to go really deep, often past 50 feet.

These fast-sinking lines where the first 30 feet or so only sink are often called wet tips, even though they are really "wet heads." They run usually, at least, a line size heavier than your rod calls for, but with these fast-sinking lines, they cast great.

However, be aware that manufacturers use a designation for these lines based on their weight in grains, and not the numbers system all other type of lines use. The info in the box will actually give you the actual weight of the line in grains—200 grains, 450 grains, 800 grains. To give you an idea of what to buy, a 7-weight outfit will probably cast well with 250 grains, and an 8-weight with around 275 grains, and a 9-weight with around 300 grains. And again, each manufacturer has lots of information on the Internet about matching their lines to a particular rod weight.

Fly Line Designation

When I started fly-fishing in the 1950s, line weight designation on the fly line box looked something like this: GAF or GBF. This meant a weight-forward line with the running line marked as a thin G, the A or B a fat belly, and then the F the front taper, as well as I can remember. Anyway, the system was not very accurate, but it was all we had.

Today, fly line sizes have a more accurate designation, using a "3 part code." Here is how it works: a weight-forward (WF), 8-weight (8), floating line (F) will be marked on the fly line box as WF-8-F. If it's a sinking line, it may be marked WF-8-S. If it is a fast-sinking line with 350 grains, for example, it may be marked WF 350 S. Or if that same line has a floating running line and the first 30 feet sinks, it may be marked WF-350-F/S. Pretty easy.

What I Take Fishing

Depending on where I am going to fish for reds and the time of year, I may bring with me two or three outfits, which, by the time I board the skiff, are rigged and ready. Now keep in mind that I have dozens of fly rods and over a hundred fly lines; after all, this is my business. So I don't mean to imply you need to have all the outfits I mention. I just want to give you an idea of what I usually take with me and my thinking behind it.

The first thing I think of is what flies I'll need, considering what I know of the place I'm going to fish, or what the fishing guide and local friends tell me of the area and present conditions.

So let's say I know we are going to fish for tailing and cruising fish first thing in the morning with a rising tide. After lunch, with a higher tide and the wind probably picking up a bit, we'll be fishing deeper flats for mudding redfish and a few blind casts to potholes. In this case, for the early morning tailing fish, I'd probably want to cast a small size 4 crab pattern or a lightly weighted shrimp pattern in size 4 or 2. So to fish these and other light flies, I'd probably bring a 6- or 7-weight line. If I want to bring the 7-weight, maybe the more delicate bonefish taper line, but more likely the 6-weight with the shorter head redfish taper. My leader here would probably be 11 or 12 feet long. Either line will land softly in the shallow clear flats. In other words, a light rod with a long leader. To fish the deeper waters in the middle of the day, I'd use a weighed shrimp or baitfish pattern on a size 2 hook or so. An 8-weight with the heavier redfish taper will turn over any fly I'd need in this case.

In case of low visibility, due to muddy waters or heavy overcast days, for example, I now always carry a clear floating or a clear sinking line, depending on the area I'm fishing. In the above conditions, it's deadly. And because I often blind cast with larger flies, especially in deeper waters, my clear lines are mostly 8- and 9-weights. I mostly use a 9-foot leader with these clear lines since that's all you usually need.

Now in areas where I know I'll encounter deep channels, rivers, and creek mouths, if I'm in the mood, I will occasionally bring a fast-sinking line for my 9-weight, so around 300 grains or so, often with a short leader from 7 to 9 feet, depending on water clarity. With this rig, I've not only taken big redfish, snook, seatrout, and tarpon, but also mangrove snapper, grouper, tripletail, and more. On more than one occasion, it has made my day. I find the idea of hooking a variety of other species exciting. Try it, you may like it.

Now somewhere between the colored floating lines and the clear sinking lines, there's a place for a good clear floating or clear sinking-tip line. And several anglers I know fish them successfully. But for me, it seems that when I leave the visual security of a colored line, I want a full clear, invisible line. So I don't use the clear tip lines right now.

Finally, if you have one outfit, say an 8-weight, you can do all of the above fishing by just using a long 12-foot leader for the tailing fish I mentioned in the morning. Shorten the leader to 9 feet and use a heavier, larger fly for midwater depth. And blind cast later in the day with a larger fly. It will work fine. It's just that if you know what you need, and have the inclination to spend the time and money to bring two or three outfits rigged, chances are you'll do better. But there's nothing wrong with staying minimal; I can dig that too.

CARING FOR YOUR FLY LINE

A new fly line casts like a dream. It slides through the guides with a minimum of effort as you double-haul, shoots like you are casting downwind, and floats like a cork, so it's easy to pick off the water for the next cast. It has all the great qualities you dream of in a line. You're happy the first time you cast it. But as you continue to use the line, these wonderful qualities that were helping you cast so well slowly diminish. You start to realize that the line is not what it used to be. What happened?

During the course of fishing and also practice casting, your fly line is exposed to a variety of harmful elements. The remains in your hands of solvents found in insect repellents such as DEET and sunscreen, algae in the water, exposure to high heat such as leaving the line in a hot car, casting in grass (let alone on the street), dirt and scum from backcountry waters, casting from shore and stripping line on the ground, contact with aerosols, and much more. That's what happened.

Now I understand that many of the elements and conditions mentioned above can't be avoided if you're going to practice and fish with your line. It's just that a line needs a couple of minutes of care from time to time. At this stage of the life of your line, it mostly needs lubricating with line dressing and cleaning from time to time..

Most fly lines today are hydrophobic, meaning they repel water, so just keeping the line clean is often enough to restore the line to good casting conditions. Also, most PVC line coating has a silicone lubricant for starters. So often just wiping the line clean with a cloth, and then applying a silicone-based line dressing will do. Simply pour line dressing into an applicator box or a piece of cloth, then run it through the fly line, and you're done.

As for the make of line dressing, most of them are silicone-based, no magic there. Feel free to try different makes if you want, but frankly, you can't go wrong using the line dressing recommended by the manufacturer of the line you are using. If dissatisfied, then experiment with others. That's what I do. And by the way, fly line dressing dramatically increases the life of your fly line too, so it's a win-win proposition.

Another solution that also works well, especially if the line is starting to get dirty, is to use one of the many cleaning pads also made by manufacturers of fly lines. These pads look and feel smooth, but in reality they are actually of a fine abrasive nature. They'll clean light dirt without damaging the line. The few pads I've tried have worked well for me.

However, I do not recommend using products outside the fly-fishing world to clean you line, such as automobile products. Some may work for you, but I've found that most have a variety of additives and solvents that can be harmful to your fly line. Remember, solvents have odor, silicone is odorless. In the end, I'd say: let's keep our money with the fly fishers; the car companies are doing quite well without our help.

Now, once you have your line clean and lubricated, you should get in the habit of dressing the line at frequent intervals, depending on how often and where you fish. For me, I dress my lines the night before I go fishing, usually the whole line. Then when I'm fishing the next day, depending on conditions, I may apply dressing once or several times a day. But this time I only apply it to the portion of the line I'm using. Also, during hot and humid days, it seems I need to dress the line more frequently throughout the day. Yet in cool, dry conditions, I may not think about it all day.

Also, make sure that you have not put too much line dressing on your fly line—you don't need much. A fly line with excess dressing will feel slippery of course, but the extra lubricant has more friction when going through the guides, and it will pick up debris, dirt, and more with ease. So, if you suspect that you have applied too much, just take a dry rag or paper towel and pass it through the whole line. You'll easily see the excess when it comes off.

Keeping the line dressed and in top shape is so important that I always make sure to keep the line dressing applicator or a cloth in my pocket while I'm fishing. This way, if I'm being poled along a flat and I start to become aware that my line is not slick enough, it's not shooting well or the front taper is sinking a bit, I don't have to put my rod down and walk to the back of the skiff to get dressing from my tackle bag, while rocking the skiff and sending wakes across the water. Instead, I reach in my pocket, pull out the dressing, run it along the fly line all the way to the front of the line (even including a foot or two of the leader), and I'm done in no time.

And by the way, the reason I always run the fly line dressing past the end of the fly line and into the leader is mostly so I get some of the slick silicone lubricant on the nail knot or whatever other connection is holding the leader to the fly line. This way, when I fight a fish to the boat, and part of the leader comes into the rod, maybe past two or three guides, the knot will slide in easily. And if the fish makes a sudden dash for freedom and the knot has to fly out of the guides in a rush, the knot is likely to slide out of the guides without snagging on one of the guides, which would break the tippet for sure.

But no matter how often you clean your fly line, sooner or later, the many harmful elements we discussed above will get to it in such a way that just adding your silicone dressing will not help. By now the line may be dirty, and if you look closely, you can see the dirt. Well, it's time for a deep cleaning to restore it.

You can wash your new car on your driveway, dry it off, and it will look like it just came out of the showroom. But a few years later, when some of the paint has oxidized and dirt and grime stick to the paint here and there, washing isn't enough. And waxing on top of the oxidized dirty finish will only preserve that ugly finish. So it's time to polish the car, then wax it so it will look good again when you wash it. Well, the fly line is the same. You cannot put line dressing on top of a line that has accumulated dirt over many fishing trips. You'll only be preserving the dirt below the dressing. The line will not perform well and may even start to sink in some areas. So roll up your sleeves and get the soap and water out. Get a large container that will hold a fly line in loose coils, or use the sink in your kitchen. Fill the container or sink with enough warm water to cover a whole fly line. Now add a few drops of "mild" dish soap. Not strong detergent!

Strip the line off the reel and into the warm soapy water in loose big coils, so it has the minimum of memory. Now let the line soak for a few minutes. Close to the soaking fly line, spread a large towel. This could be on the floor or a table you move by the fly line. Now take a clean, moist rag or paper towel, and run the fly line from the sink through it, applying only mild pressure. Just enough to strip the dirt off the line. And as you strip, deposit the loops of fly line on the towel, so the line stays clean.

Then allow the line to dry for a few minutes, and then apply dressing as you always have. And as always, if you feel you have too much dressing, take a dry clean rag or paper towel, and gently run it through the whole line, if it was too much, you'll see excess dressing in the rag or paper towel. And don't worry about taking off too much dressing off the fly line—the properties of silicone are such that there will always be enough dressing left to do the job. Next, go fishing.

Finally, to reduce the amount of times you'll have to clean your line, always wash the palms of your hands with water and a rag or towel to make sure you don't transfer bug repellent, sunscreen, or mustard from your sandwich. It really makes a big difference.

STORING YOUR FLY LINE

The fly lines I used in the 1950s required a lot of babying to perform at their best, and their best wasn't much. Today, a good fly line is light-years ahead of those old lines, both in performance, and in durability. Still, even today, you should still take care of your fly lines when storing them for a prolonged period of time.

Ideally, strip the line off your reel, and wipe it clean with a dry cloth or rag. If the line shows memory, stretch it. The best way to do this is to "stretch and hold" each section for a few seconds. The "hold" part is important. The line is now in ideal condition to go fishing with.

Now, find a dry, dark, cool place to store the line, certainly away from UV light, and lay the line in loose coils. This should prevent it from developing any memory during its storage time. Or you can store the lines in their respective reels: just be prepared to take some time stretching them out before they are ready to be used.

THE PASSING OF A FLY LINE

You took care of her. You apply dressing frequently, and gave her a complete cleaning with mild soap when needed. But with time, dirt stuck to her more frequently, you notice cracks in her finish, she didn't shoot the same, and parts of her did not float any more. It was inevitable, it was time for a new line.

But don't be sad. I've long come to the conclusion that having to buy a new line is cause for a celebration. Bring confetti and serpentine. It means you have overcome many of life's obstacles, like work and bills, and you have fished enough to wear out a fly line. Congratulations, it's time to buy yourself a brand new fly line. Besides, a surprise awaits you. I bet that when you take that new fly line out in the flats and cast it for the first time, I can guess what you'll say: "I should have bought it sooner." Yes, casting a new line is wonderful.

Now, a word of warning.

While the present fly line "weight system" has worked fairly well for many years, things are changing. Many manufacturers have gotten in the habit of making lines that are heavier than the weight stated. That is, an 8-weight that should weigh close to 210 grains, often weighs 230 or much more. Making this line more like an 8½- or a 9-weight.

This may help a beginner start to load the rod, but he or she is better off taking a few lessons and learning how to cast. In the meantime, you may buy an 8-weight that is heavier than stated to use on a medium or soft 8-weight rod, and find out the line is much too heavy to cast medium and long cast properly. This is why I prefer that when you test a rod you are thinking of buying, you do it with the line you are going to fish with. More info on how to do this in the next chapter.

Chapter 7

Fly Rods for Reds

Bonefish and permit live and feed in clear water. That is one of the reasons they are hard to approach in the flats within casting range before they spook. And knowing this, I am usually rigged with the proper rod action to cast between 30 feet to 65 feet or so, occasionally farther.

But redfish live in a brackish water world, and this makes a big difference. A backcountry flat may have clear water one day, when the reds are impossible to approach any closer than 50 feet, and the next day, have heavy wind, lots of rain, or a strong tide that changes the clear water into a Cuban *café con leche.* On those days, visibility is low, and when you do see a red, it's 20 feet from the skiff, or much closer. Now short, fast, and accurate casts are the order of the day. Any redfish angler with some experience has watched a redfish in murky water swim just a couple of feet from the skiff., where your rod tip is further from the skiff than the red. Try and make that cast!

Because of situations like this, sight-casting for reds requires the angler to handle a much wider distance range than when bonefishing, from a leader length cast to 60 feet and more. And considering that I've seen reds tail a couple of feet from the bow of my Whipray skiff, I've always said the redfish range was 0 to 60, a take-off from the old racing days.

So now you know what you need. You're trying to choose a rod with the right properties to make mostly short and medium casts, quickly and accurately. It can be challenging, but never boring. Before we talk about what rod to get, you should first learn about the different qualities of a rod, like length, taper, stiffness, and more. Then we'll talk about buying a rod, using your existing rod, or adding a specialized rod.

Rod Casting Weight

Here we are talking, not of the actual weight of the rod, which is a few ounces, but of the weight of fly line a particular rod was designed to handle best. As you saw in the line chapter, the most often-used line weight for reds is probably the 8-weight with a matching 8-weight rod, followed closely by the 7-weight, and then the 9-weight. You'll see that there are good reasons to choose rods for redfish between 7- and 9-weight, with a 5- and 6-weight on the extreme light side, and a 10-weight on the extreme heavy side. It mostly depends on the size of the flies you need to cast and the size of the redfish.

THE KING—8-WEIGHT RODS

When it comes to fly-fishing for redfish, the 8-weight rod is the king; it does it all. The 8-weight line is heavy enough to cast almost any fly you use for reds and the rod is powerful enough to land practically any size redfish. I've taken reds close to 30 pounds with an 8-weight, no problem. When I go to Louisiana for the big winter reds, the 8-weight outfit is my usual light rod. With a 9-weight being my main rod, I keep the 10 ready for when conditions require it.

But there are other reasons for having the power of an 8-weight when fighting a redfish, besides the big Louisiana reds, such as when you encounter reds around heavy grass, like some areas in Rockport, Texas, or backwaters of the Glades, for example. In those cases, any decent size red will get in the grass if you don't have some muscle to keep it out. And once inside the grass the fight is over. You have to pole or wade to the fish, and try and find it, usually laying still by now, in a big ball of grass. And that's not fun. But if you have the power of an 8-weight, you get the thrill of seeing the strike, enjoy a short hectic fight as you try to muscle the fish away from the grass, and you release the red in good health. Done.

An 8-weight rod, bent under the pull of a nice redfish.

Any lighter weight of rod won't be able to keep a nice-size red out of the grass, and anything heavier, like a 9- or a 10-weight, may not be fun to cast all day. And in conditions where you need a heavily weighted fly, say with lead eyes, an 8-weight has the power to cast them. It's just a great all-around rod for reds, and for the backwater.

THE QUEEN—7-WEIGHT RODS

The 7-weight is the sweetheart of the redfish world—the queen. It has most of the power of the 8, lands softer, feels lighter in the hand, and can cast to most everything an 8 can, plus it lands softer in the flats. You could even argue that it's the best all-around redfish rod. My son, Stephen, and my friend Flip Pallot are both 7-weight fans, and I can't blame them.

On calm days, in shallow waters, and with spooky fish, it has the edge over the 8-weight. And while we're at it, a 7 is probably the best all around rod for bonefishing the Bahamas, Belize, Yucatan, and other places, while an 8 would be better to cast the big bonefish flies in the Florida Keys. Just a thought.

The 7 does have a bit less power than the 8 when casting in a strong wind. And it will not cast flies as big as an 8 can, such as larger poppers, deer hair flies, or a heavily weighted Clouser, for example. But it should cast most of the flies one usually uses for reds.

GOING LIGHT ON REDS—6-WEIGHT RODS

It's a low incoming tide, the weather is warm, and it's almost flat calm. Conditions look good. I'm holding my trusty 8-weight rod with a 9- or 10-foot leader and a fly with no weight added. Only a few minutes pass before the first tail appears at the edge of the flat. We start to pole to the fish, but before we can get within casting range, another fish appears further to the left, splashing water as it tails. Soon other reds appear. Some are tailing and others just pushing a wake, looking for prey.

Meanwhile, I make sure we don't pole too close in this shallow water, so we stop about 50 feet from the red. I make a couple of false casts, then one last false cast as I concentrate on accuracy, and as I'm ready to shoot a few feet and make my presentation . . . the fish spooks. It saw the line in the air. This happens one more time before I add almost 3 more feet to my leader, and now I have a 12-foot leader. That should do it.

This time, a tad over 50 feet away, I make my false cast no problem, shoot a little line, and as soon as the fly line hits the water, the fish spooks. The fish moves from 50 to 100 feet and starts to tail again. I try again a couple of more times, with the same results. It's obvious that I'm not going to be able to present a fly to these fish. And I didn't bring a lighter outfit this day.

So I climb up on the poling platform and let my friend try his luck. Well, he didn't need luck because he had brought, just in case, a 6-weight rod, rigged with a long belly bonefish taper, a 12-foot leader, and a size 4 unweighted shrimp pattern. Guess what? The fly lands on the water like a rose petal, a couple of feet from another tailing red. The fish continues feeding. And as soon as it noticed the fly, the red dashed over and grabbed it. My friend lands the fish, soon lands another one, and then he let me give it a try. Because in these conditions, he who has the light rods wins, every time. And we both knew it.

This scenario has happened to me many times. Sometimes I'm the one who brought the light rod, and sometimes I'm the one that has to borrow it. It's amazing how many times I've had to learn this lesson. The fact is that if you think you may encounter reds in shallow, clear water, and especially if it's calm, you need a lighter rod to land softly or at least a leader 12 feet long.

The above conditions often happen in places with heavy fishing pressure, areas know for clear shallow water, or simply days when the reds are more sensitive in their behavior. Then you need a delicate, quiet presentation. Here, maybe a 7-weight with a 12- to 14-foot leader will do, but frankly, a 6-weight is often significantly better.

There are several advantages to using a lighter rod, such as a 6-weight, when fishing for redfish. A lighter fly rod, and therefore a lighter line, lands on the water significantly softer and with less splash, than a line that's one, let alone two, sizes larger. Also, the light lines are less visible in the air when you are false-casting, and that too is a great advantage when fish are spooky. Although no matter what size line you're using, you shouldn't false-cast right over a fish.

A modern 6-weight is super light on the hand, fun to cast in the right conditions, and fun for fighting even the smallest redfish. I love my 6-weights. And yes, I have a couple. The only way to be more stealthy is to use the light rod with a clear floater, instead of a colored line. But as I mention in the line chapter, a clear, light, thin-diameter line is difficult to cast with accuracy because you can't see the line in the air, and must concentrate only on the flight of the small fly for accuracy. There are also times to put the light rod down. Heavy winds or big flies require a heavier line. Don't think about it: go back to your trusty 8-weight.

When and if you reach a point that you'd like to have a 6-weight outfit for redfish, just remember that you want a saltwater 6-weight. These are much stiffer and usually faster action that the slower trout action 6-weight. You need the power to cast into the wind flies that are often weighted and tied on hooks as large as size 2. And also, you need the backbone to fight a good-size red and subdue it in a reasonable amount of time.

But buying the light outfit is not enough, as I suspect you know. Casting a light rod and line in the flats, 40 to 60 feet to a tailing or cruising redfish, even on a calm day, requires a good caster—period. Don't try to get around it. Practice, take lessons, and practice again.I've been casting for fifty-five years now, and I still practice. I'll always practice. Which is fine because I love casting. There's more about how to practice casting on pages 146–47.

But casting and accuracy are not enough when using light rods in the salt. You also need to be good at fighting fish. You can't just bend the rod on a hooked fish and take your time until it comes to the skiff practically dead tired. Two ways to become good at subduing fish with light tackle are to take a saltwater fly-fishing school from someone who knows their stuff or to fish with a good saltwater flats guide. I've taught for over twenty-five years in the Florida Keys Fly Fishing School, my own schools in Miami, and many places in the United States and abroad, I can tell you the average angler does not know how to apply pressure on a fish. Take the time to learn. It will help you, not only with super-light rods, but also with your big tarpon and billfish rods. Fighting a fish in the flats too long, especially on hot summer days, can kill the fish, sometimes even when you see it swim away after a release. It is the responsibility of every angler to learn proper fighting techniques.

Then, there are 5-weight saltwater outfits. They were originally designed with small bonefish in mind, such as you find in the Bahamas, Belize, Yucatan, and many other places. They, of course, can be used on small redfish, small snook, baby tarpon, and many other small saltwater species. However, all the requirements and warnings I mentioned above for the 6-weight apply to the 5-weight in a much larger degree. The guys and gals that I've met and fished that use a 5-weight are very good casters and fight fish with these light rods right off the butt. Using the down-and-dirty methods, as tarpon anglers often call them in the Keys. Don't go to the 5 until you can use the 6 well.

Personally, I've taken reds and baby tarpon with 5-weight and even 4-weight rods, but my lightest rods for the salt today are 6-weights. This could change as technology advances, so stay tuned . . .

THE HEAVY WEIGHTS

Redfish grow bigger than bonefish and even bigger than permit, and it's partly because of their size that there are times and conditions were a heavier fly rod and fly line make sense. Some of those conditions are heavy winds, big flies, targeting big reds, or using heavy fast-sinking lines, but mostly a combination of two or more of the above.

I found that fishing for reds in the beaches of Jacksonville, with Captain John Bottko, I often had to fight strong winds while casting big heavy flies to fish close to the bottom. Here a 9- or 10-weight is essential, as is a clear sinking line.

Fishing for reds in 40-degree temperatures in Hilton Head, South Carolina, with my friends Corbett Davis and Fuzzy Davis, I found the conditions challenging those two days. We fished in 18 inches to 3 feet of water, mostly casting to schools of reds pushing wakes. They would be moving all the time, and we couldn't get any closer than 60 feet, so often we needed to make 80-foot casts. I soon found out that these conditions, using a big weighted fly, really called for a 9-weight. But I had an 8-weight and floating lines. We took a few reds, and it was lots of fun, but a 9-weight with a sinking clear line would have more than doubled the amount of reds we landed.

I have fished several times in Louisiana, mostly with Captain Lance Ledet. As you probably know, the fish are big and take flies very well. But you have to cast a 4-inch fly, weighted, often to a midrange or short quick cast. Many fish are over 20 pounds and a few over 30. Here, I mostly fished a 9-weight, but occasionally a medium action 10-weight. I also brought a 6- or 7-weight, mostly to cast to the tailing sheepshead. Although I did hook and land a couple of 20-pound reds with the light stick by "mistake."

Another time, in Pensacola, Florida, I fished again with Corbett Davis for the schools of big reds that cruise on the surface in 30 feet of water. You have to run the boat in front of the school, make a long cast with a big fly, and if you hook up, in 30 feet of water, they're going to go down to the bottom and fight hard all the way. Well, we landed a few of them that weighed up to about 30 pounds, and they fought ultra hard. Here my preference is a 10-weight rod that is stiff and fast action to make the extra-long cast and to fight the big reds in deep water. Corbett, on the other hand, went with an 11-weight and had no problem casting or landing the big reds

One of the most exciting fishing trips I've ever experienced was in the spring of 1981, when I traveled from my home in Miami to the small island of Mateo, in the Outer Banks of North Carolina, to meet my friend Joel Arrington and Captain Vernon Barrington. The motivation was a call from Joel a few days earlier, telling me he had a captain friend who could find giant red drum (that's big redfish in North Carolina talk) in the flats. Some were well over 50 pounds, he said. The world record in those days on a fly was 16 pounds or so.

The morning after I arrived, Joel and I met Captain Vernon Barrington, who was very experienced on the big reds. However, I wasn't too thrilled about his big 23-foot boat without a push pole or an electric boat motor, which meant there was no way to make a good approach for a fly caster. And Vernon, on the other hand, wasn't too thrilled about a fly fisherman.

So we stood by the dock for a few minutes engaging in idle talk, but really, not saying much. Suddenly, Vernon seem to make a decision. "Follow me," he said and started a fast walk. We soon arrived at a local restaurant that offered breakfast. As we came through the door, it was obvious everyone knew our captain and said hello. But Vernon was all business, and without looking at the menu, he simply ordered three of the special five egg omelets, the Vernon Omelet, named after him, of course. Then we sat down.

When they arrived, the giant omelets and the trimmings just barely fit on the big oval trays. Vernon started right away, and I followed. He ate every bit, and so did I. I could tell he was a little surprised. He was pleased when I congratulated him on his choice of breakfast. Well, somehow I must have passed the test, because a few minutes later, we were on plane, on a 23-foot boat, headed for the flats.

When we arrived, Vernon took time to look around, even used binoculars, while the engine just idled. Joel and I looked for fish too. The water was about 3 feet deep and the wind was blowing well over 15 miles per hour, which Vernon called a light breeze. But I thought it was blowing like hell.

It didn't take long before Vernon found fish. He pointed them out, a few hundred feet away, pushing wakes against the tide and wind. He engaged the engine in gear, and we started to putt-putt toward the fish. He said this was a quiet approach, the fish won't even know we were there. "Get ready," he advised. I was suspicious of the effectiveness of this approach, but we had no other way. So with a slow-action 11-weight rod, a floating line, and an 8-inch white and dark back sailfish fly, I was as ready . . . Or so I thought. I had little confidence in getting within range, which, considering the strong wind and large fly, wasn't going to be 100 feet.

Here I'm holding a world record redfish on 12-pound-test line, which tipped the scale at 42 pounds 5 ounces. JOEL ARRINGTON

At about 300 feet away, we could easily see the school of big reds, maybe fifty of them moving at a good clip. I stood ready. Now they were 250 feet away, and they looked real big. I waited. Then they were about 200 feet from us, and we were no longer upwind. Vernon announced that this is as close as we'd get, and with a good encouraging pat in the back, he cut the engine off and said, "Get 'em."

I was surprised. Vernon was too, and he expected me to make a cast. Then I explained that this was fly fishing. I could not make a cast that far, even on a flat calm day. No one could, I explained. Joel supported me on this.

So with all the patience he could muster, Vernon asked me to show him my cast. I gave it all I had, which in the present conditions, was 75 feet or so. Vernon wasn't pleased. But one thing was sure: he knew those big reds and their habits as well as anybody.

The next few approaches we got well under 100 feet and mostly downwind. But the big fly and the big fat floating line were too much for me. I told Vernon to give me a few minutes, and I changed the Fin-Nor No. 3 with the floating line for my Seamaster S handle with a mid-sinking line. I knew the sinking line would cast much better in the wind, especially with that big fly.

This time we were able to stay and drift with the school for a minute or two, well inside of 80 feet. I could easily see each individual fish in the school. They were huge. On average, the fish ran from the high 20s to well over 50 pounds. My heart was pounding, my throat was dry, my hands were sweaty, and I fought hard as I false-cast to keep a decent-size loop in the wind.

My first cast landed at the edge of the school. I let it settle with the help of the sinking line, and when the big fly had disappeared from sight, I started a retrieve. Several fish parted from the school but one kept following the fly for 20 feet. Finally, it lost interest and went back to the school. Vernon said the fish was well over 50, which did not help my next cast.

Finally, we made another approach, and I again got the fly at the edge of the school. This time, three reds parted from the school and followed the fly with interest. The spirit of competition was helping me here. One fish was really big and the other two were about average to large in size. They followed the fly for a long time, while I died on every strip. Finally, one of the midsize fish took the fly.

I cleared the fly line I had on the deck by now, the line hit the reel, and the red made a long run deep into the backing. Then it started to bulldog its way, until we finally brought the fish to the boat. This red tipped the scale at 42 pounds 5 ounces and was the largest one taken on a fly. Today, it's still an IGFA world record on 12-pound-test tippet. And, I don't mind telling you, it was one of the most exciting moments of my fly-fishing career.

The next day, with the wind down a bit, I took a 26-pounder that became the IGFA world record on 16-pound tippet. And Joel also took a red in the mid-20s. I don't remember seeing as many big fish that second day. As you can see, to make a long cast with a big bulky fly, it took a heavy fly line. So more often than not, it's not the size of the fish that dictates the choice of fly line and rod, but the size of the fly you need to cast.

By the way, when writing this passage, I thought of Vernon. I had thought of him many times but we had not talked in thirty years. So I tracked him down online and gave him a call. We had the most wonderful talk. He is retired now, living deep in the mountains of North Carolina, doing a lot of brown and rainbow trout fishing these days. He invited me to come up some time and wet a line. And I just might do that when I'm up that way.

"We lived a great adventure that day, Chico," were Vernon's parting words. And the memories of that day came to me, as clear as if it had happened last week. I can see Joel leaning on the gunwale of the big boat taking photos of me, while I struggled to hold the big red in one hand, rod on the other.

Rod Length

In terms of rod length, on the average, the popular 9-foot length used for bones, permit, and most saltwater species is the best choice. It's simply a great all-around size that does so many things well. It can cast long and medium distances well, and with a good degree of accuracy. And when you miss that first cast to a tailing red, the 9-footer can pick up a lot of line off the water to make that second cast smooth and easy.

Besides, you may also want to go bonefishing, or fish a beach for snook, reds, or even stripers up north. The 9-footer is the best length for all that.

However, I don't recommend you get a rod any longer than 9 feet. A 9½-foot rod may cast a little further sometimes, but it's cumbersome to maneuver, much less accurate, and less effective in fighting fish, especially at the end of the fight. Don't do it.

A SHORTER ROD

I may as well tell you that my favorite rods for reds are usually short rods, under 9 feet. So if you already have a 9-foot rod and you want to start doing more flats and shoreline fishing in the backwaters for reds and snook and black drum and the like . . . then I'd consider a shorter rod if I were you.

Short rods for the backcountry aren't new to me. Back in 1960, while fishing the Tamiami Trail with Captain Bill Curtis, I was lucky enough to meet the famous Rocky Weinstein. At the time, Rocky was an Everglades fishing guide, both for fly fishermen and bait fishermen. Rocky hated bottom fishing and tried hard to get more and more fly fishermen to take up snook and red fishing. He also tried hard to sell his one piece, 7-foot fiberglass fly rod to every customer, while on the water. He sold me one the first day I met him.

Standing on the shores of the Tamiami Trail canal, Rocky asked me to cast to the opposite shoreline and place the fly just under the branches of a big mangrove tree. "That's where a big snook would be, you know, just under those shadows." And I knew he was right.

With my $9^1/_2$-foot Orvis Battenkill bamboo rod, I could easily reach the 50 feet to the shoreline, but the big loop the soft, long rod produced did not allow me to get under the branches. As a matter of fact, I ended up tangled on them.

Well, this is what Rocky did. He then stepped up, and with the short rod produced some needle-sharp loops that easily squeezed under the branches. I was sold. And Bill couldn't stop laughing: "He can do that to you every time." I use the rod for years, built others similar myself, and took lots of reds and snook with them in the backwaters. Somehow, I stopped using them, but as I started fishing more for reds and snook with my son, Stephen, in the mid to late 80s, I started to use them again. And the concept is just as good today as it was years ago.

Because of leverage (the fact that the rod is shorter and the weight of the line is closer to you), a short rod is easier to cast, less strenuous, faster to get into action, easier to make tighter loops, and more accurate. Then, once you are hooked up, the shorter rod is a great lever in fighting a fish and putting pressure efficiently. It's great in the summer when you want to release that fish quickly or if you're in lots of grass when you want to keep the fish off the grass during your fight. And when the red is tired and close to you, the short rod is more maneuverable, allowing you to guide the red to your hand or your friend's hand. Also it's easier to pull in and out of the rod rack.

But perhaps most important is the short rod's inherent accuracy. I talked to friend and master rod designer for Loomis Rods, Steve Rajeff, who has dominated the fly casting long distance and accuracy divisions for several decades. Steve had something to tell me about short rods in competition and on the water: "The short rods are much more accurate. For one, they point easier. And, when you cast, they don't magnify the mistakes, as a long rod does. For accurate medium and short casts when fishing, give me an $8^1/_2$-foot rod."

A shorter rod is not only good for accuracy casting and close quarters, but it's also great for fighting a fish at the end of the battle, when it is close to the skiff. Here Stephen Fernández fights a nice snook deep in the Everglades.

I know the difference between 8½ and 9 feet may not seem much, but believe me, it's huge. And it won't take you long to appreciate it either; all you have to do is pick a short rod and cast it a few times, and you'll know.

And by the way, while it's nice if you find a short rod that's marketed for salt water, there are a few 8½-footers on the market for heavy-duty fresh water that will do just fine.

ULTRA SHORT RODS

These are rods are around 8 feet long, more or less. They're specialized sticks for short casts or fishing backwaters in tight conditions. I own several of them and use them frequently in the backcountry of the Everglades and in heavy overcast days when visibility is nil. All the attributes of the 8½-footer are magnified here. By the way, some of these rods are marketed for bass, pike, and muskie, but they work just fine for reds and snook.

My friend Jerry Siem, great caster, angler, and chief rod designer for Sage Rods, has a predilection for short rods in close quarters and especially in low visibility. His simple statement was: "When the clouds come in, and you are fishing in low visibility only making short casts, a 9-foot rod is almost a disadvantage."

Action

A fly rod has two main characteristics that determine how it will cast: the taper, and the stiffness. And the combination of both is called the "action" of the rod.

Other factors also affect the rod action but to a lesser extent, like the materials used, guide size and their placement on the blank, the wall thickness, and more. And then, there's the wiggle factor. We'll talk more about the wiggle on page 89.

TAPER

The shape of a rod when it's bent is called the taper. And as you'll see, fly rods bend in many different shapes. If mostly the upper third of the rod bends when under pressure, the rod is called a fast taper, or fast-action rod. If the rod bends into the middle when pressured, it's called a mid or middle taper or medium action rod. And if the rod bends deep into the bottom of the blank, often almost to the cork handle, it is said to be a slow taper or slow-action rod.

A fast taper or tip-action rod can help you make some tight loops that easily cut into a strong wind and is also capable of holding lots of line in the air for a long cast. It's a popular taper for bones and permit for that reason. But it's not my favorite for the quick mid and short casts I often encounter redfishing. A medium taper rod is probably a better all-around rod for reds and backwaters, and I think in actual fishing situations, an easier rod to cast accurately. And the action is not as demanding of timing on the cast as the fast action. It's also a better taper for sinking-tip and sinking line that often need a little more open loop and a bit slower casting tempo. This is an action I like for reds. Also, there is a so-called medium fast taper, a taper between fast and medium, which I also find suitable for reds. The slow taper or slow action rods are almost nonexistent in salt water. In the extreme conditions of low visibility and for short cast requirements, then a slow action rod, probably well under 9 feet, will let you feel the load with little line in the air and help you form a loop and make accurate casts more consistently than other tapers. But we're talking about special situations here. I have a couple of slow-action rods in graphite and in glass. When and if you need that type of rod, you'll know it.

STIFFNESS

But any of the tapers mentioned above—fast, medium, and slow—can each have a degree of stiffness that resists bending the rod, independent of the shape of the rod when it's bent. This is the stiffness. A rod can be stiff, medium, or soft.

For me, stiffer rods cast a bit farther into the wind, because in good hands, they can hold more line in the air. But like fast rods, they are not my favorite for mid and short casts. And stiff rods are more demanding on your timing when casting. That is, they have a narrower margin of error while false-casting. That means you're paying more attention to the cast than the fish and the presentation—not good. Also, they are more tiring to cast, so you'll feel the difference at the end of the day.

I much prefer something closer to a medium stiffness, where the margin of error while false-casting is wider, so I can concentrate more on the fish and accuracy. I hook lots more fish with this choice. While the loop for medium stiffness tends to be a bit bigger, I still find the compromise more effective than stiffer rods.

Also, when the wind is blowing from my casting arm, my right side, and I have to backcast or cross cast from my left side, where I'm weaker, I find a medium stiffness rod much better to form a loop and hit my target. A stiff rod requires more effort on my part. This should be important to an angler sight-casting in the flats, since opportunities where you need to cast from the opposite side of your casting arm are an everyday occurrence.

A soft rod may be good for short casts, but is a very specialized, and has narrow use in salt water.

THE WIGGLE FACTOR

So now let's talk about the "wiggle factor." Everyone wiggles rods. Somehow, it's fun. And it looks like you may know what you are doing. Most people don't.

When I wiggle a rod, I am trying to determine the action by observing the combination of stiffness and taper. That is, I am watching how hard it is to bend and what the shape of the bend is. I usually make a fast downward stroke, ending on a stop. And at the moment of the stop, for a fraction of a second, I see how much the rod has bent and the shape of the bend. I repeat this a few times to engrave in my mind stiffness and shape. And then I come out with an idea of the action of the rod. But just an idea, mind you. I still have to cast the rod, preferably with a full leader and a fly. Then, if I like it, I'm ready to take it fishing.

OVER-LINING

It has become gospel in some circles of saltwater fly fishing to over-line any rod. That is, to fish your rod with one size line heavier. If you have an 8-weight rod, then you use 9-weight line. As a general rule, this is wrong. However, this approach works in some situations. For example, if you have a rod that's too stiff for the line labeled, and you are going to fish an area that requires lots of short casts, then go ahead and over-line.

The problem with these techniques is that there are enormous variations among the weights used by manufacturers of rods and fly lines. For example, 8-weight rods always vary to some degree in stiffness and taper, between manufacturers. And fly line manufacturers also vary in the weight and even the taper of their lines.

So without knowing the particular rod you have and the line manufacturer and model of fly line (like their redfish taper) you want to use, I can't tell you whether you should over-line that rod or not. All that being said, if you are dealing with a well-known and reputable rod manufacturer, I would start by using their recommendations. I have over fifty fly rods, from a 3-weight to a 14-weight, and very few of them do I need to over-line.

The Rod Grip

The grip should be of a shape and material that is comfortable to cast for long periods of time, yet gives you a good feel of what is happening as the rod loads and unloads during the casting process. A good grip can help you cast further and more accurately.

In terms of shape, the highly popular Full Wells shape is hard to beat for fresh and salt water. The increase of diameter at both ends has a good purpose. On the reel side, the reel seat can be partially buried in the cork, bringing the reel closer to the hand for better balance and less fatigue. And on the upper side, the rising diameter helps accommodate the thumb so it can comfortably push during the forward cast while giving you a good feel for accuracy.

Another option is the Half Wells grip, which only has the rising diameter on top, so the thumb still connects, but not on the bottom. It works fine, and looks smaller and less imposing on a small trout rod, I guess, but I prefer the Full Wells.

The Ritz grip, which is rarely seen these days, is also one of my favorites. It is a constantly rising diameter from the bottom where it meets the reel seat to the top. The changing diameter allows you to hold the rod up and down the grip to find the thickness that best fits your hand or just to change positions a bit to give your hand muscles some rest, like shifting around on your chair during a long speech. I like this grip.

A lot has been said about matching hand size to grip diameter. A big hand needs a big grip and a little hand needs a little grip. My hand is probably a little bigger than average, and I find that the average grip on the high end rods I use fits me just fine. However, Flip Pallot, who has larger hands than I do, prefers a thinner diameter grip than I like. And he does real well with it. So try the store grips—they should work just fine. And if after lots of use and experience you feel you need to go thinner or fatter, then go to a custom builder who can fix you up easily.

In terms of material, give me cork. It can be bitter cold fishing for redfish on a wet winter day in Louisiana or blistering hot on a calm August afternoon in the Everglades, but there's no noticeable change of temperature on a cork handle. It's always neutral. Also, cork never absorbs water, and it's easy to clean with a little dish-washing soap, no matter how dirty it gets. And if you take good care of it, it should last you for years—decades even. I just love that natural feel of cork. For me, there is nothing like it. Besides, when casting, I think cork gives you a better feel for the weight of the fly line than any other artificial materials. And I don't take good quality cork for granted either. It takes around thirty years for a tree to produce the quality cork needed for a fine fly rod grip, and some of these cork trees are several hundred years old. They're the real thing, man.

However, a great variety of foam grips will also work on a fly rod. And with the right firmness, they seem to cast fine. Still, for me, the ones I've tried still do not give me the feel of the cast like cork does.

Eddy Carman, owner of Biscayne Rods in Miami, has been building rods all his life, and so have his father and his grandfather. My dad use to take me there to buy rods or repair an old rod in the mid-50s. We go way back. So I asked Eddy what material he personally prefers. And he did not take long to answer: "For my regular fly rods, I still would take cork, although a firm EVA material is pretty close. However, for a big blue-water fly rod for marlin and tuna, where 20-pound tippet is often the norm, I feel EVA material is tougher and takes more abuse."

Multipiece Rods

Ferrules were always a problem, from the first bamboo rods all the way through glass, boron, and graphite. They were always the great limitations in making a smooth, multipiece action rod. And they were always, by far, the weakest link. Indeed, in the mid-80s, some rod manufacturers made fly rods in three pieces so there were no ferrules in the middle of the rod, to give the caster a better feel during the cast. I loved them. And in those days, it made a lot of sense. But not today.

At present, a good designer, with the latest advancements on ferrules, can make a rod smooth and in any action with a multipiece rod. And there's no need to buy a two-piece rod to minimize ferrules either. Those days went out before the twenty-first century. Designers like the fact that with four-piece rods they can experiment and use different materials and tapers for each section, making for some fantastic rods. Today, almost all rods are four-piece, which is a great compromise between the minimum amount of sections and portability when traveling. Besides, the new ferrules have proven to be tough. Witness the many four-piece rods used every day for tarpon, sharks, and billfish over a hundred pounds.

Some anglers like to buy five-, six- and seven-piece rods, because they break down into a smaller package. And while some of these rods have pretty good action, I still dislike putting that many pieces together. I don't think you even gain that much smaller a package than a four-piece to make a difference in traveling.

Finally, there are the one-piece rods. I remember when I went from my heavy two-piece, metal ferrule, bamboo rods to one-piece glass rods. They were ultra light, smooth, and very powerful. They were a dream. And for several years I didn't go to multipiece rods unless I needed to.

But today, with the latest technology in ferrule design and materials, a good rod designer can build a four-piece rod that is super smooth from tip to butt and very strong. I've tried a few one-piece rods in the 8-weight category, and I found them very smooth and with good feel all through the blank from short cast to long cast. But compared with a great four-piece, the difference was negligible while casting on land, and while fishing, I had some four-piece rods I liked better.

And if you travel by plane, the four-piece can be carried-on or checked easily.

The main use I see for the one-piece is big tarpon fishing, in an area like the Florida Keys, where the angler either lives close by and store his rods in this skiff, or lives up North, but leaves his rods with this favorite tarpon guide. So the rods don't travel.

But I do believe that for fighting big tarpon, or any other big fish, one-piece rods are stronger and tougher. So there's a place for them, but I feel that place is a specialized niche within the big-fish world—not the redfish world. All my light and medium weight fly rods are now four-piece.

Buying a Rod

So now that you have lots of knowledge about fly rods for redfish, let's talk about buying one, or several. First, let's assume this is your first fly rod for the salt, and you are mainly thinking of fishing for reds and the other fish in his world. If this is the case, not including extremely large redfish like those in Louisiana, then the chances are good that you should look into getting a 9-foot, four-piece, 7- or 8-weight rod. If you are a big guy or strong, you may lean toward the 8, but if you are small or maybe like me, you are well into your seventies and prefer less effort, you may lean toward the 7, and many ladies like a 7 too. You can't go wrong with either.

So now what? Now, if possible, I strongly recommend that you actually cast several rods before buying. Which is why I prefer you get the rod, or the complete outfit if that's what you are getting, at a specialty fly shop, where everyone there, even those with college degrees, are fly-fishing bums, as I am, and they really know their stuff. So come prepared to cast.

If you are just starting, and don't know how to cast yet, be prepared to also take a few casting lessons, with lots of practice in between lessons, as part of your investment. Most good fly shops have a caster or two that give lessons. Buy your rod and take a lesson. Right then, if you can. Go home and don't fish; practice what you learned at the lesson. A week later or so, go back for another lesson, then more practice. In a few weeks you'll be ready to fish. And I'm sure the gang at the fly shop would just love to advise you where to go to go fishing. Much more on this in the casting chapter.

Now for those of you who can cast, I want you to bring several things to the fly shop so you can reproduce, as closely as possible, the conditions of the flats. First, of course, bring your favorite fishing hat and glasses. It is safer and more realistic to cast with them at all times. If you are only buying a rod, bring the fly reel and the fly line you are going to use with the new rod. And rig the line with a 9- or 10-foot leader. If you are going to buy a reel and line also, then try the rod with a line from the store with a leader the length of the rod or so and a fly.

For a 7- or 8-weight rod, try a fly about 3 inches long with the hook cut at the bend, so it does not hang on the grass. This will be your practice fly. This way you'll know how the rod behaves, not only making loops, but also turning the fly over. A good fly rod is about casting the fly, not just the fly line.

Finally, I want you to understand this: *the difference between casting a rod in the grass without a fly—worse yet casting far—and casting that rod making short and medium casts with a 10-foot leader and a fly, is huge.*

Now take the rods outside and start by making many short casts, say 20 to 35 feet or so. Then go for medium cast up to 60 feet or so. Some rods will load easier for you, with more feeling. You may notice that you can turn the big fly easier with a particular rod. This is good.

Now, as you know, many of the shots you get while sight-casting are with the wind blowing from the side of your casting arm, forcing you to cast from the opposite side of your body. If you are right-handed, I mean from your left side. If you are left-handed, then from your right side. It's much harder, we all know this, yet few anglers practice that cast. Well, testing the rods, you definitely should see how the rod loads for you when you cast from the opposite side. So try now to make a 20- to 35-foot cast that way, and if you can, try a 35- to 60-foot cast. I find that for me, the softer rods usually give me better feel when I have to backcast to a fish or a shoreline.

After you've tried 20 to 60 feet from both sides with the rods you are testing, you'll probably have a pretty good idea of the rod that will fish best for you. Now, just for kicks, and because you've been wanting to do this all through the session, go ahead, strip lots of line out, and make a long cast. Now I want you to walk to the end of the cast, and see if the leader is fairly stretched out and the fly up front. If it's tangled, even if you cast 100 feet, it does not count. When it comes to making a long cast, it's about how far you can cast and still turn the leader and fly over. Then it counts. But not as much as the medium and short cast. And now you know what is the best redfish rod for you. Don't ask for a discount; just buy it.

If you have several rods already, and you are an intermediate caster, you may want to get a more specialized rod for reds to fit a particular niche in the areas you often fish. If you want a light rod to cast in super shallow areas, then maybe a 6-weight. But if your main redfish rod is now a 9-weight, then the light rod you want is probably a 7-weight. If it's a heavier rod you are looking for, to fish bigger reds and cast bigger flies, then probably a 9-weight, or even a 10-weight.

And if you're buying a 10-weight for reds, make it medium action and medium stiffness, not a powerful, stiff tarpon rod. This is a 10-weight you'd fish permit with, cast to big barracudas with, a comfortable-to-cast 10-weight.

Finally, if you need to cast in close quarters, with little room, back in the bushes, or you often face close-casting situations because of poor visibility due to muddy water or heavy overcast, then definitely try a rod under 9 feet, 8½ feet, or even an 8-footer. These rods can be deadly for short, accurate casts. And you can more easily form a loop while making these short casts. Less tiring too. And lots of fun to use. I have several of them, as short as 7 feet 11 inches. Love them.

Chapter 8

Fly Reels for Reds

A fly line may last a few short years or maybe just a few months if you fish a hundred days a year. And you certainly keep fly rods for years. But a fly reel is different: you may keep it for a few years, or if it's a good fit with your type and way of fishing, and touches your soul, you may keep it for a lifetime. You may even pass it on to your son or daughter. A reel my dad bought for me in the early 50s, a Seamaster S shaped handle, red knob tarpon reel, is still with me, and it's still capable of helping me land a big tarpon or sailfish, as it's done in the past many times. And I still use my circa 1960 Hardy Zenith, which have taken innumerable bonefish, snook, redfish, and many other species, since it was given to me more than fifty years ago. Other Tibor, Abel, and Nautilus reels in my collection I've had for years, and they get constant use, together with my latest acquisitions.

So when I take a new reel home, it needs to meet a series of requirements, starting with capacity, proportion, weight, and drag performance, followed by simplicity of design, anodized finish, rim control, clicker noise, looks and feel, and more. Let's start with capacity.

Capacity

On a fly reel, capacity means the amount of space there is on the reel's spool to accommodate the weight fly line you need, plus backing. Your fly line will be approximately 100 feet long. Long enough for the longest cast you'll ever make, or ever need to make. But not long enough to sustain a large fish's run. This is why you need backing line under your fly line.

In case of a redfish, even the largest of redfish, it's unlikely that you'll get a run much over 50 yards. Even fishing for the large reds in Louisiana. Nonetheless, I still feel you should plan to get a reel with capacity for the fly line, whether a 6-weight or a 9-weight, and about 175 to 225 yards of backing.

The reason for having what's apparently more backing than you need is partly because I want you to get a reel with a diameter large enough to be able to retrieve line pretty fast. Besides, the large diameter will keep your fly line stored in larger coils, so it will be less affected by "fly line memory." So when you get ready to fish and strip a few dozen feet of fly line of your reel, it will be much easier to stretch the fly line straight and ready to fish. It's a win-win all the way.

Besides, I'd like to think that in the future, you'll also take your redfish outfit bonefishing, where the runs will likely be much longer. Or you might take it to the Everglades, where an encounter with a big tarpon or a large shark is possible while fishing for reds—another opportunity to experience real long runs. If you feel that you are just going to fish for reds, in areas where you won't encounter big tarpon or sharks, then 150 yards is more than enough.

Now a few words about the type of backing you should get. When I recommended you get a reel with capacity of about 200 yards of backing, I was talking about 200 yards of 20-pound-test Dacron backing. You see, when a hooked fish is large enough to "run you into the backing," you will now have to handle the backing with your fingers to distribute line back and forth on the spool, while fighting the big fish. But not to worry, most 20-pound Dacron is "fat enough" that it should not cut your fingers while handling it during the fight. *No problema.*

However, there's another option on the market: braid or spun gel. This material is much more expensive, but it has the quality of being thin in diameter for its strength. So you could take a reel with the capacity for 200 yards of 20-pound Dacron, and put instead almost 400 yards of braid, in maybe 30 pounds.

In blue-water fly fishing, there are valid reasons to have lots of thin backing. One, there are situations with marlin and big tuna where more than 500 yards is

A few of the many fly reels I use for reds and other backwater species. All reels have capacity for at least 200 yards of 20-pound-test Dacron backing and a weight-forward fly line. Top, left to right: Nautilus FW 7—a very light reel, and a Nautilus NV 8/9. Bottom, left to right: Abel Super 7/8 N, Tibor Everglades, and my old 1960 Hardy Zenith clicker drag.

advisable. And two, the super thin diameter, when experiencing runs of several hundred yards can help reduce the water pressure of the giant belly that occurs during those fights. Having caught both marlin and big yellowfin tuna on a fly rods, I truly understand this, and agree.

However, fishing for redfish, snook, bonefish, permit, and the like, where 200 yards of backing is more than enough, I don't see the reason for getting a line that can easily cut your fingers when fighting a fish, just to get more backing that you don't need. It's trying to solve a problem that doesn't exist.

Given a choice, I prefer my Dacron backing in a bright color, such as orange or yellow, so I can easily see it in the water while fighting a big fish.

Proportion

To begin with, in terms of design, you want a large arbor fly reel. These are reels in which the arbor, unlike most old reels, is very large, so it keeps the fly line and backing on the outer third of the spool. Which, as mentioned above, gives you a faster retrieve and keeps your fly line stored on bigger coils. I think that most, if not all the reels that a good fly shop will recommend, are of this design.

Now you know that you are getting a large arbor fly reel with capacity for your fly line and about 200 yards of 20-pound. Is that it? Well, yes and no. There's still the reel's proportion to consider. You see, a reel could be big but narrow, or smaller but wider and still have the same capacity, just like a tall narrow glass may hold the same amount of eighteen-year-old scotch as a wide but short glass. And to tell the truth, both proportions will work. But given a choice, I'd rather have the tall and narrow—for reels, that is.

For me, if a reel is too wide, it tends to be harder to distribute the line evenly, especially during the fight with a nice fish. And the taller, narrower large arbor reel will also retrieve faster. So I tend to prefer reels with a narrower proportion. And a great many are large arbor too.

This nice red took a slider right on top for my son, Stephen—I got to hold the fish. He used a large arbor reel that is great when you need a fast retrieve close to the mangrove. STEVE HUFF

However, a big and narrow reel that isn't a large arbor reel will work just fine, as long as it's not too heavy.

Weight

An outfit that's well balanced is a joy to cast and to fish. You aren't aware of the reel or rod and only concentrate on casting and accuracy. And at the end of a day's fishing, you hardly feel tired. But a reel that's too heavy for a given rod will throw it out of balance, and your casting, accuracy, and fun will suffer, partly because you are constantly conscious of the imbalance. Plus, your wrist will probably be sore at the end of the day.

You want a reel that balances with your rod. That means you should be able to, more or less, balance the outfit in your middle finger when holding the rod's grip as you normally cast and fish. But this is not carved in stone: if the outfit balances in your index or ring finger, and it feels good to you, that's good enough. Go for it.

Also, remember that if you attach a new fly reel to a rod in the shop, just to see how it balances, keep in mind that it does not have backing or fly line, and they are also going to add weight to the reel. An 8-weight line will generally add over an ounce, and 200 yards or more of backing will add at least another ounce. Just be aware of this.

Old reels are often a problem, because today's fly rods are much lighter than they use to be, so it's not unusual for an old reel, maybe one you love, not to balance well with your latest fly rod. The difference in weight of old graphite rods compared to the latest ones is huge. The difference from bamboo or glass is even larger.

And yet, I'll often take one of my old reels, like a Fin-Nor size 3 Wedding Cake, or a Seamaster Tarpon S handle, and fish it, in spite of the fact that it's too heavy for the given rod. Just because some of those old reels have a soul. Just because it's fun. Remember fun?

Kristen Mustad, of Nautilus Reels, has been building and designing reels for many years. In a nutshell, this is what he had to say about reels:

> What's most important in a redfish fly reel is a large arbor for fast line recovery and lightweight

for balance. The fast line pick-up is to avoid tangles off the deck, and to keep a tight line during a fight. And it's lightweight, to balance today's light rods, making casting all day a pleasure. And a big handle on reels for an 8-weight or larger. I really like a big handle.

Drag

Just like conventional fishing reels, most fly reels also have drag to help you fight a good-size fish. Today you have two predominant drag systems on a fly reel: the cork drag, and the sealed drag. Frankly, either of them, from a good reel manufacturer, will give you a good, reliable, smooth drag, with little or no starting pressure. Let's examine them.

The cork drag on a fly reel goes back to the early 50s with the original Fin-Nor and Seamaster fly reel, and it's been doing a great job ever since. This system is reliable and has the advantage of allowing you to disassemble the drag in case sand or other debris gets inside. Just take the spool out, take the cork drag section out, clean, rise, dry the cork, put a little neatsfoot oil on the cork, and put it back together again. Done. I've done it many time since the 50s and the reels are still working today just as well as they did when I got them.

Just remember, at the end of a day's fishing, leave the cork drags on while you rinse your rods and reels with fresh water. That is, make sure that the cork is compressed so as not to allow any water to get in between metal and cork. Then, dry the reel, and always back off the drag. Cork is a natural material and compresses when the drag is tight. If you put it away tight, it will eventually deform, giving you an uneven drag. So back off all your cork drags before putting them away. I always do.

Now somewhere around the mid-90s or so, a new design of fly reel drag started to appear. It was completely sealed, unlike the cork drags. It looked strange to me. So as usual, I fought the change. Guilty until proven innocent is my motto when it comes to new systems, materials, designs, and such in fly fishing. After all, cork drags worked great. But little by little I started to use more and more sealed drag reels. Today, as I look at the few dozen reels I most often use, there are actually more sealed drags than cork drag reels on my shelves.

I took this 18-pound redfish in Louisiana, using an ultra light 6-weight rod and a light reel to balance the outfit. On a 10-pound tippet, the red ran way into the backing and was an exciting fight. CORBETT DAVIS

A sealed drag has many advantages. First, as a whole, they are usually lighter in weight, and simpler than cork. And they have proven to be waterproof, as the different manufacturers claim, at least for practical purposes. I've used them in rain and submerged them under water, either by accident or while fighting a fish. No problem.

They can be left with the drag tight, because the multiple drag surfaces they use, usually some type of carbon fiber, do not compress. And if you need to clean it because you dropped it in muddy water or got sand or debris inside, just take the spool off, rinse, put the spool back. Done.

However, do not try to open the seal drag yourself. If you have a problem there, you have to take it to the shop you got it from or send it to the factory. But I must admit, I have yet to have a problem with any of my sealed drags. And I take care of my reels, but I don't baby them.

Either way you go, cork or sealed, you won't have any problems. You may love the fact that you can take the cork drag apart and clean it yourself—full control of the situation. Or you may prefer the simplicity and light weight of the sealed drag. Either way, you can't go wrong. Just be suspicious of new reels that have more parts, making them more complicated and heavier, but that claim to have a smoother drag than the rest. Pass on them.

While shopping for a new fly reel at the fly shop, have the person helping you take the spool out so you can look inside of every reel you are considering. Be familiar with it. Learn to take the spool off and on when it's full of line. Sooner or later you'll have to do that in the field.

Other Miscellaneous Reel Features

All good fly reels today have a good anodized finish that effectively fights the salt, so here it's just a matter of your taste for a particular color. I'm told by some manufacturers that their black finish is the longest lasting. But since the few reels I have from the 50s and 60s, when the quality was supposedly not as good as today's anodizing, are anodized in gold and still in great shape, I stand by my belief. Any color you like is good.

You also want a reel with "rim control." This is the overlapping of a spool over the frame, whether full frame or not, so you can use your fingers during a fight to add more drag, or to let go quickly when a fish makes a sudden launch. Let's say you're fighting a big redfish with your drag set at about 2 pounds. During the fight, you lightly feather the rim control of the reel to add drag. Maybe at some point you add close to 6 pounds of drag, when suddenly, the fish makes a quick dash away from you. You wouldn't have time to back up the drag if it were set at 6 pounds. But instead, all you need to do is move your fingers from the rim control a fraction of an inch, an instant move, and you are back to the 2-pound drag. The fish makes his run, and you are still on the fight. You did not break him off. Most reels today have a rim control. Don't leave the dock without one.

By design, some reels are silent when you retrieve line in, or when the line goes out. But others have a clicker that makes a mild noise, either in, out, or both. I definitely like to hear a sound when the line goes out. I like to hear the reel scream when a fish runs. And I don't mind a bit of click going in, either. Some guides like to hear line coming in or out, because they are poling the skiff, so they are behind you and often don't know what's going on during a fight. But a click isn't necessary. It's just my taste.

So far we have been talking about direct drive reels, which are the great majority, as they should be. These are reels with the handle screwed on the spool. Simple. You crank and the spool turns forward. A fish makes a run, and the spool turns backwards, often lighting fast, which is great. This is by far the most efficient design to land a big fish on a fly rod, as proven by thousands of anglers landing billfish, giant sharks, big tarpon, tunas, and everything in the planet. They are also, by design, the lightest.

However, there's another design: anti-reverse or slip-clutch reels. These are reels in which the handle doesn't move when the line goes out. This means that when you try to reel line in during a fight, with the rod bent, the reel will slip and you won't gain any line, unless you bring the rod down fast enough to create slack. This is not good, or efficient. There are moments during the fight, especially at the end when the fish is close, where I need to crank a few inches, now. This is a moment for the direct drive reel. Period. So again, here, take my word for it, get a direct drive. And yes my old Seamaster S handle is an anti-reverse. I love it for all the memories, but I wouldn't get a modern anti-reverse design reel today. Enough said.

And finally, there is looks. What can I say? Well, my old friend, the late Mel Krieger, who spent a lifetime fly fishing had a saying: "There are two types of fly fishermen in the world: poets and engineers." I like to think I'm a poet.

So I believe strongly, especially when getting a piece of gear that you may keep for a very long time, that, providing a reel meets all the criteria needed, you should also select a reel that looks good to you. One that feels good when you reel it. Bob McChristian, designer of the Seamaster fly reel, use to tell me that you needed to get a fly reel you'd enjoy playing with in the living room; just cranking on it. I think there's a lot of truth in that statement.

The Great Spare Spool Myth

I've been fishing sinking fly lines since the days of lead core line and have always loved the change of pace of fishing deep. It's exciting to hook a big fish down deep, and watch it take line off the reel while wondering what species it could be, or how big it is. Or just the fun of taking a great variety of species of fish with your fly rod you would never hook with just a floating line. To date, I've taken well over a hundred different species of fresh- and saltwater fish, and sinking lines have been a great help.

Now let's say you have a new reel with a floating line, but you also want or need a sinking line. Or you already have a reel and want to start fishing your fly much deeper, getting close to the bottom in channels and the mouths of rivers and creeks. So, probably to save money, you feel or have been told that it's a good idea to just get a spare spool for your sinking line. Then if you are fishing and see a deep area that looks fishy, all you have to do is simply change spools, and you are ready to fish. I don't think so.

If you carry a spare spool with a sinking line, or any other specialty line in your tackle bag in the hope that when the opportunity presents itself you'll be ready to use it, you are going to be disappointed. To use that sinking line, you first have to cut the fly off the floating line, reel the line on the reel, take the spool off the reel, secure the loose leader end with a rubber band or something, and put the spool away in your tackle bag. Now take the spare spool with the sinking line, attach it on the reel, pass the line through all the guides (hopefully you rigged a full leader for the sinking line already), then look for the weighted fly you wanted to use, tie it on the tippet, sharpen the hook, and get ready to fish. By then many opportunities have passed, and you've wasted a lot of time. Then do the reverse a few minutes later when you want to go back to the flats and need your floating line. I bet you'll do this once, maybe, and then you'll never use the line again. The fact is, you are never ready with the spool in the tackle bag.

Instead, I have a reel for my sinking line, which is rigged with one of my fly rods, say a 9-weight. It has a leader, it has a fly with the point sharpened, and it's waiting for me on the rod rack of the skiff or boat all day long. When I see an opportunity, I put my floating rod down, pull the rod with the sinking line, and I'm casting in a Miami minute—that's fast. During a day's fishing for reds, it's not unusual for me to change back and forth between floater and sinking line outfits as opportunities present themselves. And why not? It only takes me seconds to change outfits. I may be fishing a mangrove shoreline in a foot or two of water with a floating line, come up to a channel, river, or creek, and in an instant I'll pull the outfit with the sinking line and soon be fishing a weighted Crystal Shrimp or Clouser five or ten feet down on the bottom. That's what you need to do.

Finally, on several occasions while hosting trips, I've had an angler who came with a fly rod, a fly reel, and two or three spools with different line—just in case, you know. But then the angler accidentally drops the reel on the ground and bends it. So the reel is out of commission until it gets repaired by the manufacturer. And the angler? Well, he's got many spare spools to play with. Had he brought a reel for each spool, he'd be fishing.

And if you already have bought a spare spool, no problem—I won't tell anybody. You just go to your local fly shop. As it happens, all major reel manufacturers sell the reel without the spool, so your local fly shop can order it for you, any color you want. And soon you'll have a complete reel, as it should be.

The Fly Reel Case

Every fly reel needs a protective case, the type that will fit over the reel and rod while it's rigged and ready. The case could be made of a cushioned cloth or neoprene—either works fine. Most good reels today come with one. But if you get a reel that does not have one, or you bought a used reel without one, get one. Make sure it fits easily over the reel and also over the reel while it's attached to the rod.

The case serves as a protector. When an outfit rides on the rod rack of most skiffs during rough weather, the constant pounding will often make the reel bang against the side of the skiff, or if in the lower rod rack, against the floor of the skiff. Either way it's not good for the reel. Also, in some weather conditions, a reel on a rack can get a constant spray of salt water, especially during a long ride. I've seen reels dry up with a crust of salt on them.

Other times, often while fishing in remote areas, the skiff is more basic, meaning no rod racks. Then the rods often ride with the reels laying on the floor of the skiff and the rod tips propped up against a cooler or tackle bag. This is fine if it's calm, but in rough weather, the usual flat bottom pangas or skiffs will pound your reels unmercifully against the floor. So you should get in the habit of always bringing your rods to the dock, fully rigged to the fly if possible, and with the reel in the reel case and wrapped around the rod. It's a good habit to get into.

The Clicker Reels

Okay, remember when I told you I was the poet type in fly fishing? Well, now we're going to make some exceptions

Landing small to medium fish in the flats with a clicker drag is something special. Here is my son, Stephen, with a nice snook taken on a light short rod and one of my Zenith clicker reels.

to what I said above. How about fishing a reel that has no drag, no rim-control, or even anodizing. Oh my!

I'd better explain. By 1960 I was well established in Miami. Doing a little work, dating, often studying and doing a lot of fishing. Life was good. And in those days, I was a proud member of what I like to call the Four Musketeers, an exclusive society of fly-fishing bums, which included Flip Pallot, Norman Duncan, John "Little John" Emery, and myself. That summer, Little John went to England with his parents on vacation. We kept on fishing. When he returned, he brought gifts for the three of us. I don't remember what he brought Norman, but he brought me and Flip each a brand new Hardy Zenith fly reel. It had the famous and dependable Hardy clicker drag system, which the company has been making now for over 100 years. And while the company designed the Zenith for seatrout, light salmon, and steelhead fishing, when Flip and I realized it held over 250 yards of backing, we immediately had other saltwater plans for our new reel.

Over the next fifty years, Flip and I have taken medium-size tarpon, big snook, redfish, bonefish, permit, big jack, a few bonitos and small tunas, salmon in Alaska, and many other species. This is all in spite of the fact that the clicker drag's spring and pawl, even when properly greased, barely keeps the reel from over spinning. And yes, the painted finish needs a little extra care, and it doesn't have a rim-control, so you must fight the fish by feathering the fly line with one or two fingers inside the spool as the fish runs. You also have to feather the backing if the fish has run that far. It's primitive, basic, and occasionally burns my fingers a little, but I love it madly.

And the sound of a plain clicker drag when a fish is making a long run is some of my favorite music. Right up there with jazz, classical piano, or an improvised Cuban tres guitar.

A clicker drag is simply a spring that applies pressure against a triangular shaped pawl that in turn puts pressure against a gear on the reel's spool to create drag. Very simple. Submerging the reel in water does not hurt it or alter the drag. And by way of maintenance, all I do to add a little more drag and lower the sound of the clicker to a deeper, more pleasant sound is add a little bearing or axle grease to the pawl and spring and also to the shaft. Done.

By the way, the old Pflueger Medalist is not a clicker drag. The Medalist has a large shoe drag. So if you fish one of these, you haven't experienced a clicker drag.

Fishing a clicker reel is great fun. Going back to basics. Nothing to adjust. Nothing to think about. If it gets wet or submerged, no problem. But be aware that when fighting a fish, you must constantly keep your hand on the spool when you are not cranking. Remember, you don't have a drag. This is something that a beginner may not like. But a seasoned angler may appreciate this, even come to love it, as I have.

The hard part is buying one. You see, most anglers are so used to a drag that having just a clicker seems unacceptable. It's like being used to automatic transmission, then going back to shifting gears with a manual transmission. Anglers today even demand drag on trout reels when they are going to use 5X tippet. Oh well.

Anyway, manufacturers don't make clicker reels for the salt anymore, and I don't blame them. Sales would be minimal. Still, when I want to use clicker drags, I get out some of my old Hardy reels like the Zenith or St. Aiden for my 8- and 9-weight rods. And for my 6-weight, I'll use a Hardy Princess or a new Abel Creek 2, which is still being made and holds a 5- or 6-weight line and 200 yards of backing. I've taken redfish over 20 pounds with this fine little reel and many baby tarpon and snook. Great fun.

So while a clicker drag is great fun, it is not my main reel in the salt. It's like owning an old Porsche with manual transmission or a Harley. It may not be my everyday transportation, but you always want to have one or two around. Drag reels are required purchases. But clicker reels are purchases of passion, because they carry in them the spirit, tradition, and sportsmanship of this old sport. And that for me is also a required purchase.

Chapter 9

Other Gear for Reds

Besides your rod and reel, you'll take many other items on a fishing trip. Some are just as important as your rod and reel, and others add to the experience or are just fun to take along. However, a flats poling skiff is small by necessity, so there's a limit to how much stuff you can bring and fit in the hatch. Also, if you travel to get to your redfish destination, your carry-on size is limited. And if fishing out of a kayak or canoe, room is often more limited. Fortunately, in the last few years, I've become a bit of a minimalist, always trying to bring less.

The good news is that all the important (and even not so important) fly-fishing stuff you need to bring does not take that much room. The trick is to know what is and isn't important to bring. So here is a list in alphabetical order of the gear, clothing, and other miscellaneous items I may be taking with me on a fishing trip,

Bags

On the skiff, canoe, or kayak, you'll carry your stuff in a tackle bag. If you need to wade far from the skiff, or your car, then you'll need a wading bag too. Meanwhile, you should be carrying on you: a hat or cap, a bandana or face mask to protect your face, high quality polarized sunglasses, a pair of pliers or forceps, and a file.

TACKLE BAG

A saltwater fly-fishing tackle bag should be big enough to carry all the stuff you need, but small enough to fit easily in the hatch compartment of the typical flats skiff. And if you fly to your destination, as I often do, it must be small enough to fit on the overhead compartment of most airplanes. So for starters, that makes it smaller than 45 linear inches when you add length, width, and height. And really, that's more than big enough—often I prefer smaller. So when I'm traveling to Louisiana to fish for those big reds, I use my tackle bag as a carry-on bag. Always have.

Here is a list of the items I often carry in my tackle box, so that you see that it doesn't take that much. And as you read it, keep in mind that most of the items I mention are very small: two or three fly boxes, six to ten spools of leader material, sun gloves mostly to rig or re-rig leaders, a small Moleskine notepad and pencil, sunscreen, fly line dressing and applicator or rag, a small flashlight, a tape measure, and maybe bug repellent. And sometimes, I include items to take out of the tackle bag when I get in the skiff, like my hat, polarized glasses, bandana, and pliers. And always, rain gear.

Your bag should be as waterproof as possible, because sooner or later, perhaps several times a year, you are going to experience heavy thunderstorms with lots of rain falling on you and your bag. Also, because you may have your bag out in the open while rigging or changing flies, the bag may get some or lots of saltwater spray. It happens to me several times a year, every year. And I love it; it's part of the adventure. It's also the reason that I always choose a waterproof bag. Besides, you may be carrying your car keys, wallet, and other items that can't afford to get wet. If the bag you like isn't waterproof, at least make sure that the bottom two inches or so are hard plastic, so it can sit in water for long periods of time. Sooner or later you'll be glad it does at least this. And then carry your keys, wallet, passport, and the like in a waterproof, Ziploc-type bag inside your tackle bag. That works too. Finally, make sure your bag has a good strap with an angled shoulder pad, so you can carry it through the airport or from your car or cabin to the skiff without using hands. Now, as you walk, one hand has the rod and the other can open doors, moves branches aside, and keep you balanced and safe.

Another solution for a tackle bag is to get a knapsack or small backpack. A sling backpack is also very compact. Just make sure it's waterproof and fits easily on a skiff hatch and overhead compartment of a plane. And with a backpack strapped behind, you can easily move from your room or car to the dock or across an airport, with both hands free to carry rods or open a door.

WADING BAG

If you are going wade more than a hundred yards away from the skiff, canoe, or car, you'll need to take with you spare leader material, extra flies, clippers or pliers, file, and a few other items. The best way I've found to carry all this so it's readily available when you need it and won't interfere with your casting and fishing is by using a small belt pack. Just carry it around your waist on your side or behind you, so that it's out of the way when casting and fishing. You can easily slide it in front of you when you need it. And remember, get one big enough to carry the minimal stuff you are going to need while wading. If you are aware of your belt pack while you are fishing, you have one that's too big or you've put too much stuff in it.

Some anglers also like to carry a water container, and plenty of fly-fishing belt packs come with a place for a water bottle. And by the way, a vest, even one made out of mesh, is too hot and cumbersome, and you won't need the extra pockets. The fishing vest has gone away with disco music.

Binoculars

Binoculars are one of those items you never think of bringing to the flats, until you use them. Let's say you're fishing with your buddy and it's his turn to fish. The guide is poling and you're in the middle of the skiff. Now since the guide is up in the poling platform and your buddy is on the front deck or on a casting platform while you are down in the cockpit in the middle of the boat, they are both much higher than you, so they are going to see most, if not all, of the fish before you do. However, if they're looking for surface action, like tailing fish, surface feeding, or reds pushing wakes, a pair of binoculars may help you see the action before they see it. Now you're helping and having fun.

Also, plenty of wildlife live all around you in the redfish world, and watching them up close, feeding or flying, is also part of the adventure of going fishing. Besides, this is the only time when I have better vision than my son, Stephen.

Finally, if you ever get lost in the backcountry, as I have, a pair of binoculars will let you spot markers and buoys a long ways off, and that's a big help when you are lost. So while binoculars are not a must-have item, you may want to give them a try anyway. I'd get a small, compact size so they don't take much room in the tackle bag.

Cameras

I've been photographing for well over forty years in the outdoors, in jazz joints in the old days, and while photographing birds and other wildlife. But any advice I could give you about what camera to get for your fishing trip would be obsolete well before this book got published. So without getting involved in the complex and highly emotional exercise of recommending a particular camera or a camera system, all that I want to say here is that you should consider, if you haven't done so already, bringing a camera to record your fishing experience with your friends or family—not just to pose holding a big fish. The memories, especially after some time, are priceless.

For a few hundred dollars, you can have a small high-end camera, often no bigger than your phone, that will take a scenic shot with an ultra wide setting, an angler posing with a fish, a macro shot of a flower or close-up of a fish's head with a fly in its mouth, and more. And some of these cameras can also shoot underwater. This way, you may have a better record of your trips and your experiences. On the other hand, if you are already involved in photography, and are carrying a couple of full frame bodies, a few prime and zoom lenses, and a tripod, you don't need the above advice.

Now for the real important advice. Taking a photo of your first or big fish should be a fast and coordinated operation. Take the fish out of the water horizontally, one hand either under the head or with thumb in mouth, and the other around the anal fin. The fish's exposure to air should be much less than thirty seconds. Take a quick couple of shots, and then gently return the fish to the water. There is more on releasing fish in chapter 17, "Landing, Photos, and Releasing." Please, don't take this advice lightly because it is vital for the fish's healthy release.

Clippers

Even though I always carry a pair of pliers with cutters or forceps with scissors built-in on all my fishing trips, I still carry a pair of clippers. You see, a good clipper can cut the tags of a knot extremely close and neat. This will leave a knot with a super smooth feel that can run through the guides if needed with a minimum of problems, and it's almost invisible in the water. When possible, I do all my knot trimmings on my leaders with a clipper. You'll always find one in my tackle bag and one in my wading bag, just in case.

Clothing

You want clothing that will keep you protected from the outdoors, yet comfortable, through harsh sun in the tropics, freezing cold weather in winters, rain storms, saltwater sprays, and other fun stuff. You also need to stay dry outdoors. And when you do get wet, you want cloth that dries very fast. Clothing that stays wet for a long time can freeze you to death even in the tropics and worse in cold weather. It's cool to get wet, but not cool to stay wet.

Also, to protect yourself from the sun's UV (ultraviolet) rays, it's a good idea to get clothing that is UPF (ultra protection factor) rated. Another way to get protection is to wear heavier clothing or clothing with a tighter weave material. For example, your legs will be well protected from the sun if you wear a pair of heavy jean pants. And some of my friends will often fish in jeans, especially during cold weather. But if they get wet, they stay wet.

In terms of design, a lifetime of fishing has taught me to wear clothing that is simple, with few pockets and no frills. So when you are in the middle of casting to a big redfish, you want nothing protruding or hanging that will catch your fly line, or draw your attention away, stealing your concentration. Believe me, buy good quality, but stay minimal.

SHIRTS

Make sure your shirt does not fit too tight; if anything, I prefer a bit loose. That way, in hot humid summer days, air can flow through, keeping you cooler. And in cold weather, when you need to wear an undergarment under your shirt for warmth, a slightly loose shirt gives you that room. For me, a tight-fitting shirt can be uncomfortable, somewhat restricting your movements, especially while fly casting. I want my long sleeve shirts to extend well past my wrist for good sun protection. And my short sleeve shirts to extend to my elbows, for the same reason.

Now, in keeping with that minimal philosophy I've mentioned, I fished with plain long sleeve cotton T-shirts for a few years, and they seem to worked fine. But eventually I found that if the fabric was too thin, I would often get some sunburn through the shirt after a day's fishing. And of course, if I got soaked, I'd stay wet for a long time. So today when I want to fish a simple no-pockets no-collar shirt, I wear a technical T-shirt, which has no cotton in the fabric and often UV protection. These types of shirts, preferably long sleeve, will protect you from the sun more than any cotton shirt ever will, and when drenched, will dry in minutes. They are great.

Sometimes, however, I want the niceties of a regular shirt, like a nice tall collar for extra protection from the sun. The extra pocket or two on the chest comes in handy to hold my reading glasses or a couple of flies, but make sure that the pockets fit nice and flush against your body. You don't want "accordion type" shirts that can stick out too far because sooner or later, they'll catch on something while you're casting to that big red. And I like my long sleeve shirts to have nice long plackets, so I can easily roll up the sleeve to my elbows, when I feel like fishing that way. A shirt is a more loosely fitting garment, so it just feels different than a T-shirt design. It's a good change of pace, and I own and use both types.

In terms of colors, I always keep in mind that I'm a hunter. So I prefer pastel colors like light blue or khaki. In winter I'll often use a bit darker colors too. Sleeve length is also a matter of taste, but long sleeves give you more protection from the sun of course. I generally use about 90 percent long sleeves while fishing. I find that on a really hot day with the sun in full force, I am cooler having the long sleeve shirt. But it's also nice to fish in short sleeves for a change. Just make sure you use plenty of sunscreen.

Some long sleeve shirts also have a build-in hood. I find that it's a good tool for sun protection, and the shadow that it creates helps me see fish better. And when I combine this hooded shirt with a face mask or bandana on my face, I can easily get away without using sunscreen on my face. Add long sleeves and sun gloves, and I will often fish for a few days without using sunscreen, and without even getting a tan.

Good friend and top angler Sandy Moret has used these hooded shirts longer and more often than anyone I know. And he is positive that with the large shadows that the hood creates around his face he sees more fish and is infinitely better protected from the sun. That's why I'm getting more of those shirts this year.

PANTS

My regular fishing pants are lightweight and sold specifically for fishing. They are light and comfortable, they have sun protection, and they dry fast when I get them wet, which is often. As always, I look for a pair that does not have too many pockets and gadgets. After all, you don't need to carry much on you when fishing on a skiff or canoe, and if wading or fishing on a board, a belt pack is much better to carry your stuff. For that reason, I also try to stay away from bulky cargo pockets, especially those with large loops.

But when it gets cold, I may use Dockers-type pants or even a pair of jeans. If I need to protect myself from rain or spray from the boat while running, then I'll also use the bottom pants of the raingear over the pants. And I prefer my fishing pants to go low, pressing against my shoes, not just for sun protection but for bug protection too. A deer fly will look for just those little unprotected areas, and when they find one, you'll know it.

As is the case with shirts, I also alternated between pants length but mostly use long pants, for the extra protection they offer. However, on a nice day, or if I am going

I like to wear clothing that is comfortable to cast all day, but not too baggy, or it will flop in the wind like a small craft advisory flag. BRAD MILLER

to wade, shorts are my preference because they are so comfortable; just make sure to use plenty of sunscreen. Also, on days that I know I'll just be wading a couple of hours during a specific tide, I may wear long pants but bring a light pair of shorts to wear while wading. Or if your pants have the zipper to convert to shorts, you can go that way too. Now, listen to this: *you'll never wade to a tailing fish more quietly than when wearing shorts in a place where you can also wade barefoot.* The difference is huge. Don't tell anybody I told you so.

GLASSES

A good pair of polarized sunglasses is imperative. They protect your eyes while outdoors, and of course, allow you to see fish in spite of the glare in the water. But also, and most anglers don't think about this, when driving a skiff in super skinny water, a good pair of polarized glasses helps you navigate safer and more efficiently, because it allows you to better see the bottom and helps you judge depth.

To protect my eyes from a lifetime of outdoor activities, I look for polarized glasses that offer full ultraviolet protection, that is, UVA, UVB, and UVC. Also, besides sun ray protection, wearing sunglasses when you are running in a boat can protect your eyes from any debris or bugs that come your way. Always wear your glasses while running in a skiff. Remember, there's no windshield in a flats skiff.

If you want to see more fish in the flats, the color glasses you wear will make a difference. Your eyes focus on blue light imperfectly, so you want a color of glasses that will block blue light. That's what brown base colors can do. So warm colors such as copper or amber are excellent for high definition and contrast, making it easier for you to distinguish fish from other shapes in the bottom. Another good color is yellow, especially when light levels are low, such as early and late in the day or when heavily overcast.

Yet another choice is an added mirror finish. Some anglers love them, but the mirror finish allows even less light to come through, and for my taste, at my age, it's a little too dark.

Now should you use real glass or plastic? It used to be that glass was always much better, but I find these days that a high-quality plastic is, at least for me, hard to tell from real glass. And the new plastics are very scratch-resistant. Still, nothing resists scratches like glass. So you either get the great total scratch resistance but heavier weight on your face of glass, or lighter weight but less protection against scratches of plastic. I've gone to plastic. But you won't go wrong with either. Frame is mostly a matter of preference, although a wraparound frame may give you less glare. Also, I find that some of the new frames with vented holes seem to help in air circulation.

Still a great pair of fishing glasses is of little use if you're lazy and let your glasses get dirty. The difference in a pair of dirty glasses and a squeaky clean pair can be huge when trying to see a redfish in difficult light. The problem is that I've heard so many different opinions on how to clean glasses that I wasn't sure who to trust. So I talked to my friend Ed Moody, who is an outdoorsman, hunter, and fisherman, and for twenty-five years has made his living as a vice president of product development for

Here is a big redfish, suspended just below the surface, on a day with lots of glare. But with a pair of polarized glasses, you could see it easily. PAT FORD

Costa sunglasses. I figure if anyone knows the best and most simple way to clean a pair of glasses, it's Ed. And since the following information is a blend of a few conversations with Ed, I'll paraphrase:

> The best material to clean glasses is a microfiber lens-cleaning cloth, because the soft but tight-woven fabric easily lifts sand, salt, and other debris from the lenses, where a loosely woven fabric might not perform as well. . . . However, in lieu of a microfiber cloth, I would prefer a clean T-shirt to a paper towel. In general, paper towels are to be avoided. They are highly abrasive and can do more harm than good. And in a pinch, you can use your shirt tail if the shirt has been tucked in, and therefore clean of salt, sand, and other particles. . . .
>
> Start by blowing first on both sides of the glass. Then, if you are going to use a sun lens cleaning solution or other cleaning solution, use it first. Just remember that you don't have to use liquid all the time. I recommend that you use a cleaning solution the sunglass company provides. But if not, select a dishwashing liquid that is PH neutral. Windex, for example, is too high on PH. But a dishwashing solution with a neutral PH is fine. The best I've found is Dawn. A good solution will get rid of oils and grease such as sunscreen. Put one drop of the liquid on your index finger and one drop on the thumb and gently rub on both sides of the glass then rinse. . . .
>
> When I go hunting or fishing, I may not carry the liquid with me that day, but I always carry my microfiber cloth with me. And if, after many months of use, the cloth starts to get dirty, just drop it in the washing machine. And don't hesitate to clean your glasses several times a day, as needed.

Frankly, in the last few years, I've become more aware of the huge difference it makes to keep your glasses clean. Now I always bring with me the microfiber cloth and the solution, and constantly check my glasses. Fishing the flats and running from one area to another, your glasses will get saltwater spray, and often without noticing it, you'll grab your glasses on the glass itself and get grease from your fingers on them, which may be sunscreen or bug repellent or what not. Anyway, I have found a marked improvement in my vision in the flats by keeping my glasses clean. What an easy way to improve your vision, no?

Personally, I like to bring two pairs of glasses with me, whether for a day's fishing or a week at a fishing camp. My primary pair today is either amber or copper color, and

Here on top, is the yellow color I like for hunting fish in low light levels, such as overcast days or early or late in the day. And on the bottom is the brown or copper shade I prefer in bright sunlight, 10 a.m. to 4 p.m., for great penetration of surface glare. They work like magic.

my second pair is the sunrise or yellow color which I use when the light levels are low, and which doubles as a backup should something happen to my main pair. Remember, if you drop your glasses overboard or break them somehow, you are basically done sight-casting, and have no eye protection. So a backup pair is not a bad idea.

GLOVES

Out on the water, your face may get rays of sun reflecting off the water, and the back of your neck may also get some direct rays, but the backs of your hands are constantly exposed to the sun, no matter what you are doing. It could be casting, tying a new leader, or eating a sandwich—the sun is on them.

So I either use a lot of sunscreen to avoid getting too much sun damage, or use my sun gloves and get no damage. They are great protection. But I also use my gloves to rig tackle. Tying good knots means pulling them tight until they "set." And that often requires enough hard pulling to cut my hands or at least give me some pain, which I don't enjoy. And since sun gloves are cut open to leave the tip of your fingers exposed, they allow full dexterity to tie knots and full protection for the backs of my hands. My gloves live in my tackle bag. Period.

HAT

Wearing a hat or a cap is imperative for sun protection and rain protection. It also blocks glare from reflecting on your glasses, which will greatly improve your ability to see through the water. Better to see that big redfish in front of you.

Personally, I prefer a hat with a full brim. I like the 360 degrees of protection it gives me, and frankly, I'm comfortable with the style. A brim around 2¼ to just under 3 inches will give good sun protection while not offering too much resistance against strong wind conditions. And make sure that the bottom of brim is of a dark color to cut down even more glare from reflecting on your glasses. My favorite color on the water is khaki.

A cap with a dark underbrim is a practical solution, protecting one's face and cutting glare from your glasses. Also, on windy days or running on a skiff, it's aerodynamic, catching little wind. For a while, many years ago, I even tried a pith helmet, but it was hard to travel with or store in the skiff and just did not work. Pity.

FACE PROTECTION

Fly fishing from an open boat of any kind means the angler is exposed to the elements for many hours, often from dusk to dawn. So every part of the body must be protected in one way or another. The face is, of course, no exception.

Now you can apply sunscreen, but this only gives you sun protection. Instead, if you use one of the many popular tube-shaped face masks, or an old fashion bandana, you'll get protection from the sun, and you'll also get protection from wind burn on windy days or while the boat is running, and it will help keep you warm on a cold day. Furthermore, especially if wearing mid to dark colors, you'll find that it can help visibility by cutting glare off your face. And that means you see more fish.

Tube-shaped headwear, such as the popular Buff gear, can be worn in many ways, but if worn over the

Here I am, fully protected from the sun wearing a hat with dark underside brim, face mask, and long sleeve shirt.

STEPHEN FERNÁNDEZ

head, so it covers you from the top of your head down including your neck, you have great protection. Since the material used by most companies to make the garment is very thin, it's comfortable and easy to breathe in, and it usually has UV protection too.

The old-fashioned square-shaped bandana has been around for hundreds of years, and it still works very well. It is used simply by folding the square cloth in half, forming a triangle, then bringing it to your face, just above the nose and tying the two longest ends on the back of your head, bandit style. I've used one most of my life. They are simple and they work great. While most bandanas don't come with UV protection from the sun, the fact that you need to double the fabric seems to give you all the protection you need. And when you need to take a quick sip of water, no need to take it off, just lift the bottom of your bandana and drink.

Both types of garment work, and I use them both. And on occasions, when I feel I need all the protection I can get, I'll even apply a bit of sunscreen on my nose or even lightly on my face before using the tube or bandana.

BELT

Most fishing pants and shorts are designed to be used with a belt, which is fine because it gives you a good place to carry your pliers. Today, I use a variety of belts, both in nylon, and yes, I've also gone back to using leather. Both types work fine even when wet. Just make sure they aren't too narrow. Most of my belts are 1¼-inch wide, and they work fine, but my only 1½-inch wide nylon belt is by far more comfortable while fishing and carrying pliers.

VEST AND JACKETS

For most of the fishing for reds that I do, I like the versatility that a combo of a vest and light raingear gives me during cool weather. I'll have my regular raingear and a light vest that takes little room in the tackle bag, perhaps one that rolls or folds to a tight and small size. Then if it starts to get cold, but no rain, I'll just put the vest on, and have the freedom to move my hands and cast in comfort. If we have to run, where wind factor will make conditions colder, then I'll also put the raingear on top as a wind breaker. But if it starts to rain and it's not too cold, I'll just put on the raingear and be fine. Lots of flexibility here.

A jacket that is totally waterproof is good both in the rain and in cold weather. But if it's cool but no rain, I prefer a vest. The jacket may be too warm and not as fun for casting and fishing. And if it's warmer and starts to rain, I prefer a light raingear without the vest.

However, if you know you are going to be fishing in very cold weather, like Louisiana or the Carolinas in winter, then I'll take a heavy waterproof jacket.

FOOTWEAR

Fishing Shoes

Today, most of my fishing is done in Crocs, or similar shoes. If I have to travel by plane, they are easy to remove at check points. On the skiff, at least for me, they are comfortable to stand in all day on a front deck or poling platform. And because they are easy to take off, they encourage me to remove them for a while, and either fish barefoot or with plain socks, which I always enjoy. However, I advise you to watch shoes for signs of wear, and discard them when the soles start to lose their tread, because they can be very slippery in wet surfaces. I know.

The natural feel of fishing barefoot is great fun and feels right. Besides, it has its advantages, because you can easily feel the fly line if you step on it while casting, and this can save you a big fish. However, you must make sure to apply lots of sunscreen on your feet. A sunburn on top of your feet is painful, to the point that you may not be able to wear shoes for a while. And it goes without saying that if you are going to fish with any kind of open sandal, you also need to use sunscreen.

A good compromise between using wading shoes and wading barefoot is to fish in socks. You'll still feel the fly line if you step on it, but depending on the socks you use, you may not need to apply any sunscreen, or at least, very little.

Wading Shoes

Wading for a tailing red is a wonderful experience. It's just you and the fish. If you're in an area where you can wade for them, I highly recommend it. However, you will be walking in a great variety of bottoms, often with different types of structures, rocks, and other hazards, which can damage the bottom of your feet or twist your ankle. So you'll need wading shoes, as least in most places. I like a wading shoe with a fairly hard sole for extra protection. When you go to your fly shop to buy a pair, try them with socks on, and walk around, making sure they're comfortable.

You'll find the heavy-duty pairs with laces can take a lot of beating. But the zip-up type are much lighter to wade on all day, and also less bulky. Your choice here. You can wade barefoot in a few places, but not many. That feels great, and it's quieter and less tiring that any shoe. I still remember how wonderful it was to wade barefoot for redfish with my son, Stephen, around the town of Arroyo, in southern Texas. Any chance I can wade barefoot, I'll take it.

Wading Socks

The disturbance you create on the water while wading stirs up sand and other debris that can easily get between your wading shoes and your skin. And even the smallest piece of sand or debris can rub your skin raw in a few steps. But not to worry: a good pair of socks in combination with your wading shoes will prevent almost all debris from bothering you, and makes wading super comfortable. My wading shoes and socks always travel together.

File

Today, more and more flies are tied on laser or chemically sharpened hooks, which have a needle sharp point so they are ready to fish. However, because of the huge selection of different hook sizes, shapes, and shank length, many saltwater fly tiers still use regular hooks, often made of stainless steel, which means they need sharpening. For those hooks, you need to have a file, not just to sharpen the hook when you first use your fly, but to keep it sharp throughout its use, since the hook's point may hit the boat while being cast, bump into rocks and structure on the bottom while being retrieved, face the mouth of a big tarpon, and more. And it's best if you keep a small file on yourself rather than in the tackle bag, so you can frequently check the point of the hook while you are fishing, and if needed, give the point a few strokes while remaining on the front of the boat. Otherwise you'll have to get off the front deck, go get your tackle bag, dig for the file, and so forth.

Your choices to perform this sharpening procedure are: a regular hard metal file, a diamond file, or a stone. The hard file can remove the most material off the hook per stroke. And if you are sharpening a big hook, say a 1/0 or larger, where you are going to make big changes on the hook—like lowering the barb size and reducing the point's length—then a hard file is a good choice. However, to be efficient, a hard file needs to be made of a real hard metal, and that means it will rust easily, especially fishing the salt. You could keep it oiled, and that helps, but then it does not cut as well. The bottom line is that you'll just buy a new file every year or two. Most saltwater anglers use hard files.

The diamond file takes less material off the hook per stroke than the hard file, but does not have the rust problem the hard file has. And I find that, for me, short of big 3/0 hooks or larger, I can easily sharpen any hook, and even file down a barb with a diamond file. I've been using a large heavy-duty diamond file, which I've stored in my tackle bag for years, and I love it. And I also have a smaller diamond file which I keep on my pocket while fishing.

The stone takes significantly less material off the hook per stroke than the other two choices above. They may be of some use to fine-tune a hook's point, but other than that I find it has little use in the saltwater world.

Flashlight

After years of going on fishing trips, local one-day trips and out of town trips, all kinds of "incidents" have happened to me for not having a light. So I came to the conclusion a few years ago that I simply had to carry a flashlight. On several occasions, while in my cottage in a remote fishing camp, I've experienced a strong thunderstorm in the evening or night, and the lights have gone out. When I say lights out, I mean an hour later, my eyes still saw pitch dark. And on several occasions while fishing deep into the Everglades and once in the marshes of Louisiana, good fishing has kept me a little too long into the evening, and I've had to pole out of a flat or run through mangrove tunnels, in the dark, slowly trying to make my way into deep water, and then look for the right marker, to get on plane and go home. Then there are a couple of times when I've had engine problems real late in afternoon, when I wanted to crank up and go home. In all these occasions, without exception, I would have given a lot of redfish flies for a good flashlight.

But no more. For the last few years I've carried a good flashlight with AA batteries, and already have had a couple of occasions to use it, with happy endings. So do consider keeping a small flashlight in your tackle bag.

Fly Boxes

Because redfish feed in so many different conditions, from clear water to murky, *café con leche*-colored water, and in the whole water column from surface to bottom, any angler fishing for them often must carry a great variety of fly patterns. Some patterns like my Seaducer, I prefer to store so that the delicate hackles are not plastered. Then hard head poppers and large deerhair Muddlers require lots of space in the fly box. And flies with long mono or wire weedguard are best kept so they don't bend or deform when stored a long time. So to properly carry a great variety of flies, you'll probably need different sizes and types of boxes. But before we talk about fly boxes, let's talk about your flies first.

If you're like many anglers I teach in fly-fishing schools or in hosted trips, you keep your flies in large compartment boxes, each compartment cramped full of flies. When it comes time to find a fly you need, say a light-colored shrimp pattern lightly weighted, it takes you a long time to find it, or maybe you find that you don't have one anymore, or maybe after finding it eventually, all crumpled, the hook is a bit rusted, and the bead eyes are twisted. Not a fly you want to fish.

You see, when you put too many flies in a small area, with time, the bad flies ruin the good flies. Rubber legs get destroyed. Feathers and deer hair get bent out of shape irreparably. So you are carrying maybe a hundred flies, with a few good ones buried in among them, like the needle in a haystack.

So I recommend that first, you take all your redfish flies and spread them out on a table. Now inspect every fly, deleting the bad ones—some of which may have lived in the box for years, rent free, without working for you. And by the way, if you find a fly that seems in good shape, but you can see rust somewhere in the shank of the hook, even the slightest amount, discard it.

Now separate the flies by patterns or conditions. Personally, I have a fly box for my surface flies, like poppers, deer hair flies, foam head flies, and such. Then a box with unweighted and lightly weighted flies with bead chains, such as shrimp patterns, baitfish patterns, marabou patterns, and such. I also have a box with weighted flies, mostly lead eye or big bead chain eyes, where heavy shrimp patterns, crab flies, and other bottom-dwelling flies reside. If I travel to Louisiana in winter for those extra big reds, I have a couple of fly boxes that contains my big redfish and backcountry flies. This way, when I want to fish on or near the surface, I reach for the proper box and find only those type of flies, and all are in good shape and fishable, or they wouldn't be there.

The most popular box for saltwater flies is the compartment box. They are sold in fly shops, regular hardware stores, and specialized container stores in a multitude of sizes and colors. My preference here are the popular 8 or 9 inches long by 4$^1/_2$ to 5 inches wide, with six compartments, in clear. And not the crystal-clear material that is so brittle, but the slightly opaque clear, which gives when you bend the lid, and doesn't break. This is a size that fits in every tackle bag, and will easily carry half a dozen midsize flies in each compartment. Of course, it's easy to cram a dozen flies in each compartment, but then you won't be able to see all the flies you have. That will require you to pinch all or most of the flies in the compartment and pull them out, in the outdoors, in the wind. So it's likely that some with blow off your hand, and so on. Besides, if they're all crammed in, with time, you'll damage your flies. For that matter, you could put hundreds of flies in a single shoe box, but I don't recommend it. You get the point.

There's yet another popular way to use a compartment box to carry flies, especially medium to big flies. Get a larger box than mentioned above, say about 11 x 7 inches, with six big compartments. Now take your flies and put each one in an individual fly bag, which you can get from your favorite fly shop. Then stack the bags on edge, side by side, in the compartments. The flies will stay nice and neat and no tangles between them. The down side of this method is that you can't see any of the flies at a glance. You have to take them out, inspect the fly, and if you decide to fish it, then take it out of the bag and put the empty bag back in the compartment. But for midsize and especially large flies, it's a good solution.

Then there's the foam box. Traditionally, you stuck the hook, barb and all, in the foam and it held them fine, but when it came time to pull them out, the barb would pull a small piece of foam. After a bit of use, lots of the foam was gone. Today, the better foam boxes have many slots along the whole foam to hold your hook. You just insert the bend of the hook in the slot and straighten the fly as you want. Now I can see all of my flies at a glance. And I can easily pull one out to inspect it without disturbing the rest. And, if not overstuffed, every fly stays in perfect shape, without damaging materials year after year. So you want a slotted foam fly box.

Also, when you need to select a fly on a windy day, a slotted foam box is less likely to allow flies to blow away. And in most boxes you can carry big and small flies, if you desire. To give you an idea of proper capacity, in a good quality foam box, approximately the same size as I mentioned, say 8 x 4$^1/_2$ inches, I can easily fit 24 midsize redfish flies, say tied in size 2s and size 1s.

You can also get a big slotted foam fly box, usually with a handle, that carries dozens of flies. The idea is to carry all of your flies in just one box. It sounds good, but these boxes are usually too big to fit in most tackle bags that I would use. And I don't like the idea of opening a big box with all of my flies I brought for the trip and exposing them to the wind. On the other hand, if you have big bulky redfish and snook flies, large poppers, and other surface flies, this box is high enough that it will not crush or damage them.

Sliding flies with weedguards into the foam slots, you have to be careful not to smash or bend the weedguard, because if left for a long time bent in the wrong way, it will set, and it will take you a while to straighten it. And unlike the compartment box that only takes a couple of minutes to dump all the flies in, the foam box takes more time, more planning. Yet the foam box is worth the trouble.

Another way to carry flies is to put your flies in the same individual bags mentioned above, and then put the bags in a large Ziploc bag. I usually use this method when I'm carrying big bulky flies and want them to take the minimum amount of room in the tackle bag. A couple dozen big and bulky flies, Louisiana-style let's say, when carried this way will take very little room in the bag.

Now every fly you have is in top shape and ready to fish, and you can find them in very little time.

Insect Repellent

Insects are a big part of the redfish's world. Early and late in the evening, close to a shoreline, in the close quarters of the backcountry, sooner or later, you'll need insect repellent. Just make sure you have enough. There's nothing quite like running out of repellent while you are desperately spraying yourself under a fierce black cloud. This is why, when fishing out off my canoe or other craft that does not have an engine to leave in a hurry, I always carry repellent in a spray and in a bottle.

Also remember that many insect repellent today use DEET, which works well as intended, but is also an effective solvent and can damage your fly line. And if you get it on your flies, the fish won't like them either.

Leader Materials and Leader Container

You need some type of container or wallet to carry your leader and your leader material. Just remember that your leaders, whether hand tied or knotless, are going to require little room. Twenty leaders in their individual bags flatten out to almost nothing. Don't take them out of their containers because important information such as length, diameter of the butt section and strength of the tippet section are written there. Just store them as they are in a leader wallet that fits them or in a plain Ziploc bag.

Now if you tie your own, as I mostly do, that's a different story. Now you'll be carrying at least half a dozen to a dozen spools, ranging from about 40-pound-test to about 12-pound, if you are fishing for reds or fishing the backcountry. Now these spools require more room to carry. You can put them in a plastic box or in a Ziploc bag, but I have a better solution. For years, I've been carrying about a dozen different spools of leader material, from about 50-pound to 10-pound, on Flip Pallot's Leader Wallet. And I still have room for readymade leaders and a few small tools. When I open it, all the different spools are exposed, and I can easily pick the spool or spools I need. It's the best solution to carrying leader spools I've found.

Notepad and Pencil

I think an angler will gain a lot by bringing something to take notes with, whether on a day trip or a long trip. It could be things you keep forgetting and want to remember to bring next time, the email or phone of someone you meet, a good tip or advice from a guide you want to remember, or simply the happenings of the day. I have kept notes on all fishing trips away from home, some of my local fishing trips, and all of my canoe fishing trips for more than twenty-five years. And I have notes from some of my trips in the 60s and 70s. My only regret today is not having taken more notes in the early days.

You'll be surprised how much you forget about what really happened, even after a few weeks, and what great memories these notes will bring to you when you read them, especially with close family and friends. Also, when going back to a fishing camp or fishing spot you haven't fished in a while, just a couple of pages of notes taken the last time will tell you volumes about what to bring and what not to bring this time around. So I advise you to consider doing it. It only takes a few minutes. And besides, years from now, your kids and grandkids will love reading about it. I guarantee it.

My favorite way to take notes in the field is with pencil and paper. I know you could bring a laptop to a fishing camp or a tablet while fishing, but for me, that's too much like bringing the office to the field. I'm trying to forget the office, hence my organic ways.

My notepad of choice, for many years, has been the Moleskine, in the light and thin model Cahier. With a sewn spine to allow it to lie flat while writing, ivory colored acid-free paper, rounded corners, an expandable pocket inside the rear cover and many other features, depending on the model, it has worked great for me. It was inspired by a handmade notebook in Paris in the nineteenth century and is said to have been used by many writers and artists such as Oscar Wilde, Vincent van Gogh, Picasso, Hemingway, and others. Today, the great outdoors writer, fly fisherman, and world traveler Charles Gaines carries one everywhere he goes.

To write while fishing outdoors, where it's often wet with rain or spray, my writing tool of choice is a pencil or a mechanical pencil, because it uses graphite, which is a very stable material. You see, graphite doesn't fade with the exposure of light, or bleed when it gets wet. So my words are not going to fade away with the years. And if it smears a little, I've also got an eraser.

So Chico's Outdoors Word Processor consists of a Moleskine, a couple of pencils with a small sharpener or mechanical pencils, a rubber band and three business cards for luck, all inside a heavy-duty Ziploc bag. It never crashes, and it doesn't need no stinking batteries. It even floats.

Pliers and Forceps

Fly fishing requires that you have a tool or tools to cut leader material, plaster hook barbs, remove hooks from a fish's mouth, rig leader and fly lines, and many other uses. In fresh water, with generally smaller hooks and lighter leader, anglers must use forceps, and in salt water,

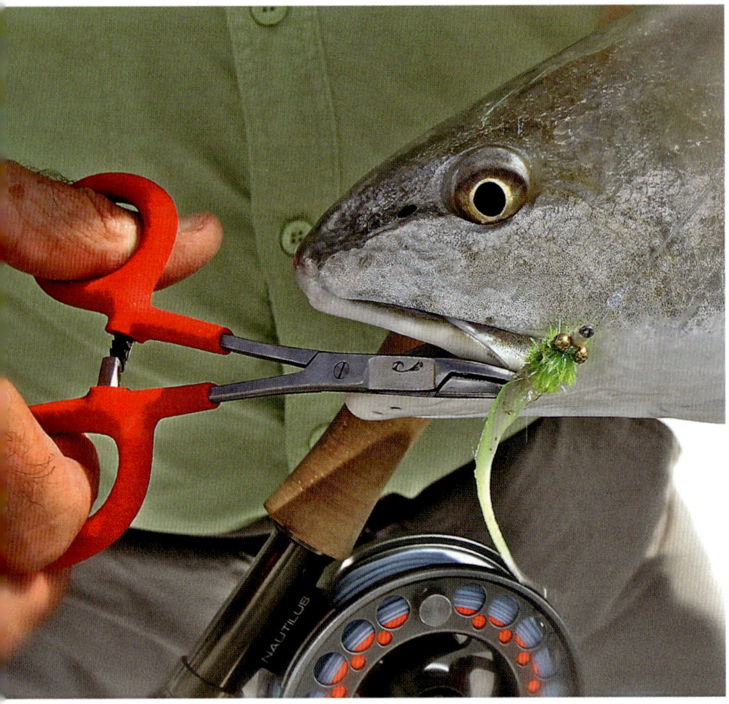

You need a tool to cut mono and extract hooks. Most anglers in the salt use fishing pliers, and that's fine, but I prefer a good pair of stainless steel forceps. Here I'm removing a white shrimp pattern from a red's jaws.

with larger hooks, much heavier leaders, shock tippets and wire, most anglers use pliers. A good heavy-duty pair of pliers that is saltwater resistant, either by anodized aluminum, stainless steel, or other methods, can do all of the things you'll need. I own a few of them, and use them from time to time in my fishing.

However, in the past few years I've made a change, using mostly a large locking forceps with scissors about six to seven inches long, in stainless steel. Bent nose is my preference, but there are straight noses too. I like this size forceps mainly because the long nose is perfect when I need to take out a hook that's buried deep in a fish's mouth. It makes the procedure easier and faster, so I can release the fish sooner. Often, design of the short and chubby pliers makes it difficult to reach down and maneuver deep in a fish's mouth.

Also, a good scissor forceps will easily cut heavy mono, even 80 pounds. So it will certainly rig any redfish or backcountry leader you need. And it has the power to plaster down barbs to convert hooks to barbless. Being stainless, they require little maintenance, and they are very light. About the only drawback I find right now is that I have not been able to find a good sheath to carry my forceps on my belt.

Then there's another type of pliers, one that Flip Pallot and I started using more than a half century ago: parallel pliers. While this type is still being made by several manufacturers, it's no longer in vogue. Their advantage is that the jaws move parallel in relation to each other, so they squeeze an item evenly, unlike regular pliers in which the jaws are at an angle. And this does give the parallels a mechanical advantage when gripping. However, they are not stainless, and the salt likes them, so they need maintenance for rust, like fresh water and oil. Still, they are great and fun to use. I lost mine years ago and didn't replace it. But Flip, not willing to tolerate this, gave me a pair with a custom-made sheath, so I keep it on my belt. I now use mine when I'm not using my forceps. Flip is always wearing his.

In reality, I use my scissor forceps for 80 percent of my fishing and the pliers for big fish like sharks, bluewater fishing, or when I just feel like bringing pliers that day. Again, it's about fun.

Rain Gear

You're going to be outdoors in a skiff or some other type of watercraft that does not have a roof, or any other

Sue Moret, a good friend and avid fly fisher, holding a nice snook caught on a fly during a rainy afternoon in the backcountry. Notice she's got her rain gear, both jacket and pants. SANDY MORET

A thunderstorm is approaching, and this is the moment when you're glad you bought good rain gear. I never leave the dock without it. PAT FORD

protection from cold weather, severe rainstorms, saltwater spray, and lots more. I wouldn't have it any other way. Still, I always carry rain gear. I mostly use just the top jacket, which generally comes down to my thighs for warm weather. But in colder weather, I'll also bring the pants portion of the outfit for complete protection. I can't tell you how many times I left the dock on a beautiful day and come back that afternoon bundled up in soaking wet rain gear. Let me put it another way: I never ask anyone whether they think it's going to rain; I just bring my rain gear. I encourage you to do the same.

Purchasing your rain gear is not the time to go cheap. Good rain gear lasts for many years and protects you from rain and the elements by not leaking and keeping you warm. And it's a super windbreaker too. The first time you face real tough weather, you'll be happy you got good gear.

I suggest you make sure your new rain gear does not fit too tight. Remember, you may be wearing several layers under it in cold weather, and you want to be able to move freely. Also, I prefer a top that comes down well past my waist. Take the time to try the pants, too, to make sure the whole outfit fits well and feels comfortable.

Sunscreen

Sun damage is cumulative over a lifetime. So you must think of applying sunscreen as part of your ritual every time you are going fishing in the daytime. Nighttime anglers are spared.

I generally use 30 SPF sunscreen that is labeled "broad spectrum," which means that the product is effective in blocking UVB (ultraviolet shortwave) rays and UVA (ultraviolet longwave) rays.

My ritual is as follows: I apply a liberal amount of sunscreen on areas that will be exposed, usually indoors, and I return the sunscreen bottle to my tackle bag. Then, I step out with tackle in hand, ready to go. Later in the day, while fishing, and remembering that the peak hours of sun are between 10 a.m. and 4 p.m., I'll probably apply again. I know I should do it several times and go through this procedure whether it's very bright and sunny or cool and cloudy. You'll burn either way.

Finally, remember that, like insect repellent, most sunscreen is harmful to your fly line. So wash your hands after applying, every time.

Stripping Baskets, Mats, and Wet Towels

My experience fishing the salt is that there are more windy days than calm days—a lot more. And while a bright, windy day with good visibility can be advantageous, allowing you to approach a redfish much closer, you still have the problem of managing your fly line while casting.

A pile of loose fly line on a deck will move by itself and catch anything and everything around it, even on a calm day—let alone on a windy day. So while I don't like bringing any extra items I don't really need, the truth is that on very windy days, well, you just may need some sort of line tamer.

Trying to sight-cast on a windy day requires that you concentrate on your casting and most of all on presentation. The problem is that while you are trying to move the fly in front of the fish, your fly line will also be moving, often catching on your shoes, sliding overboard into the water, falling off the front deck and into the cockpit where there is lots to tangle with, and more. So while making a presentation, you need to keep your fly line from moving.

There are two well-proven devices to control your fly line on windy days: the stripping basket and the stripping mat.

THE BASKETS

The stripping basket is a fairly large standing basket, round in shape, like a garbage can, that you place in front or to your side to strip line inside so it stays protected from the wind. When you need to shoot line, it will freely come out of the basket. Works great.

However, the basket needs to be wide enough to comfortably toss fly line in without having to look at it or pay much attention to it, because you should be looking at the fish you're trying to cast to, not the basket. And because the basket is quite large and cumbersome in a small skiff, I like the ones that collapse. So when not in use, you can collapse them and even store them in one of the skiff's hatches, totally out of the way. I also like the idea of mesh material because it does not catch as much wind.

Even when it's not super windy, a stripping basket can be useful. If you like to sight-cast high on a casting platform, even a mild wind will blow the fly line in the water before it reaches the deck. In this case, having a stripping basket by your side is a good idea. And if you often fish on a skiff by yourself, where you have to do it all, a stripping basket is a great help.

While I never wear the small shooting or wading baskets on my waist while wading for reds or bones, I do wear one if I'm fishing the beaches. You simply cannot strip line on the water on a beach and attempt to shoot it. If you're fishing mostly on the water, the constant wave action will simply drive you crazy. And if you are mostly on the sand, then the fly line will pick up sand that will get on your guides and eventually to your reel. Don't try to fish the beach without wearing, low on your waist, a small stripping basket. You'll thank me for this.

THE MAT

The mat is basically a device, usually made of rubber with spikes, design to lay flat in front or to the side of a caster, so when you throw fly line on it, the spikes grab the line and keep it from moving, in spite of wind, so the line does not tangle. Yet when you make a cast, the line will come off the mat freely. It really works.

The great attraction of a stripping mat is that they are lighter, smaller, and more compact than big standing baskets. And, when not in use, you can roll them like a newspaper, taking so little room that they'll fit almost anywhere in the skiff, or a duffle bag if traveling. It's a more portable solution than the basket. And laying flat on a deck, it won't catch virtually any wind, unlike the basket. Besides, for me, it's much easier to throw fly line that catches on the spikes while looking at my target fish, than to throw fly line inside the basket. And as long as a few loops of line are caught by the spikes or prongs, the fly line will not move, yet will shoot as easily as if laying loose on the deck on a calm day.

I tend to prefer mats that are oval, or at least with rounded corners, because I feel the fly line is less likely to be caught under one of the corners, and, in strong winds, it will not catch the wind as easily as 90 degrees corners. Also I like the spikes to be soft, so if I accidentally step on them, I won't twist my ankle or damage my foot.

Sandy Moret, an old friend that has won many bonefish, permit, and tarpon tournaments, has his own way to use the mat, especially for long casts. Sandy will first strip line off the reel and into the cockpit, then strip the last 20 or 30 feet or so on the mat. This way, the fly line on the mat cannot move, so it's not moving the rest of the line on the cockpit. I've witnessed Sandy make 60- and 70-foot casts to permit on really windy days and watched the fly line run through the guides with no problem. Cool.

NO BASKET, NO MAT? THROW IN THE TOWEL

If you don't have either of the two devices mentioned above, and are caught sight-casting on a very windy day, you may try wetting a towel on the deck instead. It's not remotely as good as spikes, but if it's not blowing up a storm, the towel will help. And a wet towel will fit the configuration of an uneven surface and still work

All of that being said, personally, I love the simplicity of a clean deck without any gadgets, and that's how I try to fish. But on very windy days, I've been known to resort to a stripping mat, maybe even the basket.

Tape Measure

This is not one of the necessary items to carry, but I like to have a plastic tape measure, bought at a sewing store, to measure the length of fish. I find this is a quick way to get a more accurate estimate of weight than guessing, without having to actually weight the fish. Besides, when rolled up, it will take very little room in the tackle bag.

I measure the whole length back to the tip of the tail, not the fork. An 18-inch redfish is about 2 pounds, a 24-inch red is about 5 pounds, a 30-inch red is about 10 or 11 pounds, and so on. This way I have a good idea of how big my fish is, so my notes are more accurate. And yes, I know that there are weight variations between redfish taken in different parts of its range, but this is just an estimate. And on the occasion when I want to take a red, mangrove snapper, or a seatrout for dinner, I need the fish's length to know if it's legal.

Chapter 10

Rigging Backing to Fly Line for Reds

The stories of poor rigging of backing and fly lines are legendary, and fun to tell over a drink. But it's not so funny when it happens to you. I've seen more than once a fly shop or an angler rig a fly line backwards, so that the angler ended up trying to cast the thin, light running line, an impossible feat. And there are many stories of anglers hooking a large fish, clearing the line, the fish making a long run well into the backing, and then, poof, the connection between the backing and fly line fails, and the angler is left holding rod, reel, and backing. The fish kept the fly line, leader, and fly. Depressing when it happens, but completely avoidable, if you learn to rig right, or have a good fly shop to help you. And even if you have the fly shop or someone else do it for you, I feel that you should know what a proper rigging of your backing and fly line looks like, so you can recognize if the people doing it are doing a good job. Know what you are paying for.

Properly done, a well-rigged fly line should run through the guides easily. And neither the knots connecting to the backing or the leader should have any problems sliding through the guides. If you find that any of the knots clicks hard going across the guides, you've got a problem. And sooner or later, during a fight, you'll break a good fish off. And even if you don't break it off, knowing your rigging is not up to par, you will not fight with the same confidence, and you'll also lose fish for it. Instead, you should be able to pull on a good fish with confidence, often to the limits of your tippet, knowing your connection will hold.

With this in mind, let's start with an empty fly reel and a spool of backing.

Left to right: an empty reel ready to install backing, a reel with 200-plus yards of backing, and a reel with backing and a full fly line. Notice the reel has been rigged full, not just to have the most amount of backing possible, but also so it yields the fastest retrieve.

Putting Backing on a Reel

The first thing I do before starting the long process of winding a couple hundred yards of backing or so is to inspect the reel, whether new or old. You want to make sure it's in good working order. Check to see if it needs grease on the gears, if the knob turns freely when you crank, and if it's a cork drag reel, to see if it needs lubricant.

If everything seems in order, you are ready to attach the backing to the arbor of the reel. And as we talked about in the reel chapter, you'll be using 20-pound Dacron or similar backing.

Now you want to put enough backing on so that when you add the fly line and leader, the leader just about scrapes on the outer post of the reel when you crank. That is, filled to the rim, so to speak. This way, you have the most backing capacity the reel can yield, and the fastest retrieve possible, while the fly line, stored in the biggest diameter possible, will have the least amount of memory. A win-win situation.

The problem for a beginner or someone that does not do this with some degree of frequency is knowing how much backing to wind and still have room for the fly line. Well, the reel manufacturers give an approximate guess, but since different manufacturers of 20-pound backing and fly lines have slightly different diameters, this is just a guess. I'll tell you that after many years of doing this, I simply put a bit more backing on than I think I need, and try the fly line. If it doesn't fit, I take a little more backing off. I do this until the fly line and leader just barely fit. Works for me. If you're a beginner, just let the fly shop guys do this. You just make sure the backing is nice and tight, and it's filled to the rim before you pay.

Now take the backing and tie it to the arbor of the reel using a uni knot or Duncan, a clinch knot, or any other cinch knot. If you want a knot that is a 100 percent, just tie a Bimini twist, which makes a double line, and then use this double line to tie to the arbor with any of the knots mentioned above. I usually use a Bimini followed by a Duncan cinched tight.

Whether you have a machine to wind the backing, or like me, you have to crank it yourself by hand, you need to pack it in real tight. To make sure you're doing it right, halfway through, take your thumb and index finger and press on the backing you've wound. If it feels soft and spongy, it's no good. Take it out and do it over. Sorry. And if you decide to leave it as is—and you shouldn't—then when you're fighting a big fish, the backing, pulled tight during the fight, will get buried in itself and break off, leaving you to carve the rest of the backing with a knife and start over with new backing and fly line. This, too, I've learned by experience.

The good news is that backing lasts for a long time, especially on small and midsize fish, so you don't have to worry about doing this exercise again, on this reel, for many years.

Backing to Fly Line

Today, most fly lines come with loops on both sides. So if you have a fly line with built-in loops, all you have to do is make a strong loop with your backing, making sure it's big enough to pass through any reel, and then just use a loop to loop connection for the backing and fly line.

You can make the loop with your backing using a variety of knots. If you are using Dacron, which is what I recommend, the best knot is a Bimini twist, tied with twenty turns or a bit more. If you are using one of the many types of braid or gel spun, which I mostly recommend for bluewater fishing, then I may use a surgeon's loop.

The loop to loop connection is an easy and quick procedure; just make sure that the two loops tighten, or intertwine, forming a figure eight. The thinner line, in this case the backing, should not overlap over the fly line loop. Once you have it right and snug, pull it tight so that the two lines "set" and keep in memory their new configuration. This will keep the figure eight loop constant, even when there is slack on the line.

You'll find this an excellent connection that runs pretty well through the guides, with only a minimum of occasional bumps, and it's just short of 100 percent strength, which is more than strong enough. And with a loop, you can easily change to a different fly line when you choose to, say, for a sinking line or a new line.

However, some fly lines still do not come with a loop. In this case, you can attach your backing to the fly line either with a permanent knot or by making a loop on the fly line and then using the loop to loop method. With a permanent knot, changing fly lines would require that you cut the knot off and retie the new line.

If you want to be quick, you can use a nail knot or an Albright, with at least seven turns, and it may yield 60 percent the strength of the backing or fly line, whichever is weaker. But I really do not recommend this. You are gambling a big fish and a fly line. Instead, use the loop to loop way, since it's almost 100 percent and you can change lines in a few seconds. To put a loop on a fly line that does not have a loop is not really that hard. You take the back end of the fly line, and form about a 2-inch loop. Now secure the loop with a pair of six-turn nail knots, about half to three quarters of an inch apart. And pull them firmly so the knots bury themselves a bit in the double fly line. Then trim the tags close. Done. In the time I wrote this paragraph, I could have long finished making this loop.

Now, with this loop you've made yourself, you have a connection that will go through the guides easier and is super strong. It's the connection I use for sailfish, marlin, and big tuna on the fly, when I get the mood to do such things.

My friend David Olson, who is great at rigging, goes one step further, and adds a bit of wrapped fly-tying thread at the end of the second knot, to make an even smoother connection. It works—his are the smoothest, and you can do that, too, if you want to take the time.

Fly Line to the Butt Section of the Leader

There are several ways to connect your leader to the front of your fly line. Just keep in mind that you want not only a strong connection, but also the smallest, slickest knot possible, so it can slide through the guides with ease.

The easiest way to make this connection is simply to buy knotless leaders or handmade leaders from a fly shop that makes them, which come with a loop at the butt section. Then simply loop to loop them together, and you are done. This will be a strong connection, but it will also be a bulky one. And on occasion I'll use this method because I'm in a hurry or being lazy. However, it does work.

A better connection, and one many fly shops use, is to add at the end of the fly line about a foot of 30- or 40-pound mono with a nail knot and put a Duncan or perfection loop at the other end. Now you can loop to loop any leader that has a loop. And this method does go through the guides much easier than using the loop of the fly line. If done right, it's worth it.

But there's a better way. Unlike the backing to fly line connection, where tying a knot was weaker than a loop connection, the fly line to mono connection allows for a variety of very strong knots, and with less bulk. Let's look at a few of them.

The most popular connection, and one of my favorites for anything but very large saltwater fish, is the nail knot. You'll find that on most fly lines with a braided core, a well-tied nail knot, say with seven to nine turns, should get you over 20 pounds of strength, probably lots more. And the connection is super small, long, and slick.

And by the way, the only reason I don't talk about the needle knot, my favorite, is that today's saltwater lines do not have hollow cores, so there is no way to insert the butt section inside. Too bad.

Another good connection, but a little bigger and bulkier than the nail knot is the Albright special. And well tied, pulled tight, and with a finishing knot using the tag, you can pull on any fish. One of the best fishing guides I know, Captain Rob Fordyce, uses the Albright special for all his fly fishing, from bones to billfish. Rob finishes the Albright with three turns pulled very hard to reduce size and set the knot, and he tells me he has had no problems with the knot going through the guides.

Another knot you can use that will not slide is a knot I wrote about in my bonefish book, what I call the Steele connection. Many years back, several of us learned about

At any time you may hook into a big redfish, snook, or other fish in your area, and when the fish runs into your backing, taking your fly line for a ride, your rigging had better be right, and a full reel will help you with a faster retrieve. Here I am with a big snook, taken in a foot of water with an 8-weight rod, when I least expected it. STEVE HUFF

this knot from angler Frank Steele. Well tied, this knot will not slide, and for practical purposes, it's 100 percent strength. It is a bit smaller than the Albright and easier through the guides. But I think it's also a bit harder to learn.

To tie the Steele connection, you peel an inch or more of the coating at the end of the fly line, leaving the bare core. Take the core, make a figure eight knot, insert the butt section through it, and tighten it. Then tie a regular nail knot right against the figure eight knot, and pull it tight. It makes a pretty slick, kind of longish knot that will run mostly free from guide to guide. And it cannot slide because the figure eight knot acts as a stopper. Pretty clever.

The Strength of Knots

Finally, to give you an idea of the strength of the knots we have been talking about, I spent a couple of afternoons testing a great variety of knots and leaders with angler Dave Olson, who has a Black Max scale that is certified by the IGFA (International Game Fish Association). And scales have no opinions. Mind you, this is only with 40-pound butt sections and 8-weight fly lines. With 50-pound butts or heavier and 12-weight lines it would be a higher number.

Looping the butt section of a leader to a manufacturer's fly line loop, several tests averaged above 20 pounds.

Using the Albright special, several tests averaged above 30 pounds. Most of my nail knots came between 27 and 31 pounds.

Using the Steele connection, tests averaged above 30 pounds and just edged the Albright special. However, I wonder if Rob, who is an expert at the Albright, was tying the knot, if the Albright would have beaten the Steele connection. I'll have to arrange that meeting some day.

KNOTS FOR CLEAR LINES

Today, we have some fantastic lines, both sinking and floaters, that are as clear as a leader. They are great for blind casting or for sight-casting in situations when the fish are tough. When I fish the backwaters for reds and snook, I always keep one rod rigged with a clear line, whether floating or sinking line.

However, what makes these lines so clear is not only that the coating is clear, but that the core is made of a clear single monofilament line. And some clear lines, at least in the past, have not had great adhesion from core to coating. So a simple nail knot often slides off easily with minimum pressure. Now again, most of these lines come with loops, so you can simply loop a leader to the front of the line as mentioned above with the colored lines. But that method is still bulky and does not go through the guides as well as I like. So for a smaller, less bulky connection, you can use either the Albright special or the Steele connection, and you won't go wrong.

However, as of the April 2014, testing results with David Olson on new clear Cortland and Monic lines has led me to change my mind on butt connections to clear lines. And it may be because these new lines now have better adhesion from core to coating. But testing knots with clear lines, again with David's IGFA certified scale, the results were surprising. David tied the Albright and the Steele connection with 40-pound-test butt, getting the expected results of about 25 to 29 pounds. The surprise is that when I tied a few eleven-turn nail knots, I got breaks of 26 to 29 pounds. I guess we have more good choices now.

COATING KNOTS

Just to make the knots smoother, lightly coating the knots with head cement, Hard as Nails, or a UV knot glue, which dries very fast, is a good idea. Also, when dressing your line, it will help if you run the dressing past the knots. The silicone on the dressing will make the knots slick, and that also will help. But let's make one thing clear: the coating does not make the knot any stronger. It's just to make it slicker.

Finally, I want you to know that in the many years I've fly-fished, I have broken fish off, had guides ripped off the blank of a rod, and have even seen broken rods, when a big fish was on and a knot got stuck on one of the guides. So yes, I'll do anything to make sure the knots run free though the guides. It's a big deal.

CHICO'S CHOICE

Fishing a 6- to 9-weight in the backwaters for reds, snook, and the like, I use a seven- to nine-turn nail knot. It's plenty strong, even with 16-pound tippet, and it's small. When I go for big tarpon, sailfish, marlin, shark and tuna, then I either use an Albright special, or, if I feel I may need to change complete leaders, I'll make my own loops with nail knots as explained above, and loop to loop.

However, with the new results mentioned above, I may go back to using an eleven-turn nail knot for clear lines, because I'm comfortable tying it, and it's pretty long and smooth through the guides. I may even try it on bigger fish. We'll see.

Last Words

I recommend that you mark your fly lines right out of the box as you are rigging them. Otherwise you won't remember whether a particular line is an 8-weight or a 7. The best way to mark them is with an indelible black pen. Make about half an inch mark for a 5 and an eighth-inch mark for a 1, much like the V and I of the Roman numerals. So an 8-weight line would have a long half inch or so mark around the line and three small marks, eight. Do this a couple of feet from the end of the back and front of the fly line. You'll thank me for this in the future.

Also, remember that no matter how well you tie your knots when rigging a fly line, they don't last forever. Depending on how often you fish, a few months or maybe years later, with the fly line bending and forming loops, being pulled by fish, exposed to sun and rain, eventually, the knots will wear and weaken. The fly line's coating will crack, creating a hinge, which besides showing weakness, will hurt your cast and your ability to turn over a fly. So inspect your line periodically, and when needed, replace the knots.

Finally, you may wonder why, if you can have some or all of this rigging done by a good fly shop, I've gone to the effort to give you such a long explanation. Two reasons. One, many of us (and maybe you, too, with time) prefer to rig our own. And two, even if you'd rather pay for the rigging, you should learn enough to know if it's been done right.

So now that we have backing and rigged fly line on the reel, let's go tie a leader.

Chapter 11

Leaders for Reds

A leader is simply the final extension of the fly line. With one end tied to the front of the fly line and the other end to the fly, a leader needs to perform several important functions, not only during the cast, but later while fishing.

When casting, a well-designed leader will slow down the end of every false cast so that the fly turns around in a smooth motion, without the feel of a kick or bump and the end of every false cast. This is a very important function, because it helps the caster's timing, loop control, and accuracy. And during the final cast, the presentation, a leader with the proper taper can turn a fly over on a windy day with authority or on a calm day, drop a fly like a rose petal, softly on the water's surface.

Once you've completed the cast and your fly is close to the fish, a good leader should show as little as possible of itself to the fish, its last few feet thin and supple, al most invisible, creating the illusion that the fly is actually a crustacean or fish, moving naturally in its environment. It's a tall order, but a well-designed leader can do all of the above. And this chapter will show you how to make or select such a leader.

The Essence of a Leader

For a leader to transfer energy from the fly line to the fly, it needs to be tapered. That is, it needs to be thicker and heavier on the fly line side and progressively thinner until it reaches the fly. Some anglers, either because they don't know any better or because they are being lazy, make a leader from a single piece of leader material, like 8 feet of 20- or 30-pound-test for example. But such a leader will turn over poorly even on calm days and probably not at all on windy days. Besides, with such a leader, loop control (and therefore accuracy) will also suffer with these simple nontaper leaders. You want a tapered leader.

In essence, a well-designed leader has three sections or parts. Each section contributes its own particular function to the overall performance of a leader. These parts are the butt section, the mid section, and the tippet section. And by properly changing the length and thickness of these sections, you will have the flexibility to construct a leader to match almost any fishing condition.

The butt section is the backbone of the leader. This is the strongest and thickest portion of the leader, and its function is to deliver the largest percentage of the energy that comes from the fly line down the leader to the fly. This is the section of the leader that is most responsible for turning a large fly over in the wind, and it also has the most influence in accuracy. One end of the butt section is tied to the fly line and the other end tied to the mid section. The butt sections should be the longest section of your leader. Selecting the right butt section for a particular fly line is the single most important factor in the performance of a leader. Once you have the right butt section, in diameter and length, it's all downhill from there. Further below, I'll get into more detail on the selection of thickness and length for your fly line.

The mid section, the smooth one, is located in the middle of the leader, and it's joined by the butt section on one end and the tippet section on the other end. It is usually made of several pieces, and its function is to make a smooth transition between the powerful butt section and the delicate tippet. This often-neglected section is an important part of the leader. A leader tied with just a butt and tippet section will be jerky in the air. You tend to lose loop control and therefore accuracy. You want a smooth, controlled turnover, even during your false-casting. A nice progressively tapered mid section can be a joy to cast.

The more sections you use to go from the fat butt's diameter to the thin tippet, the smoother the transition. However, while a mid section composed of four or five

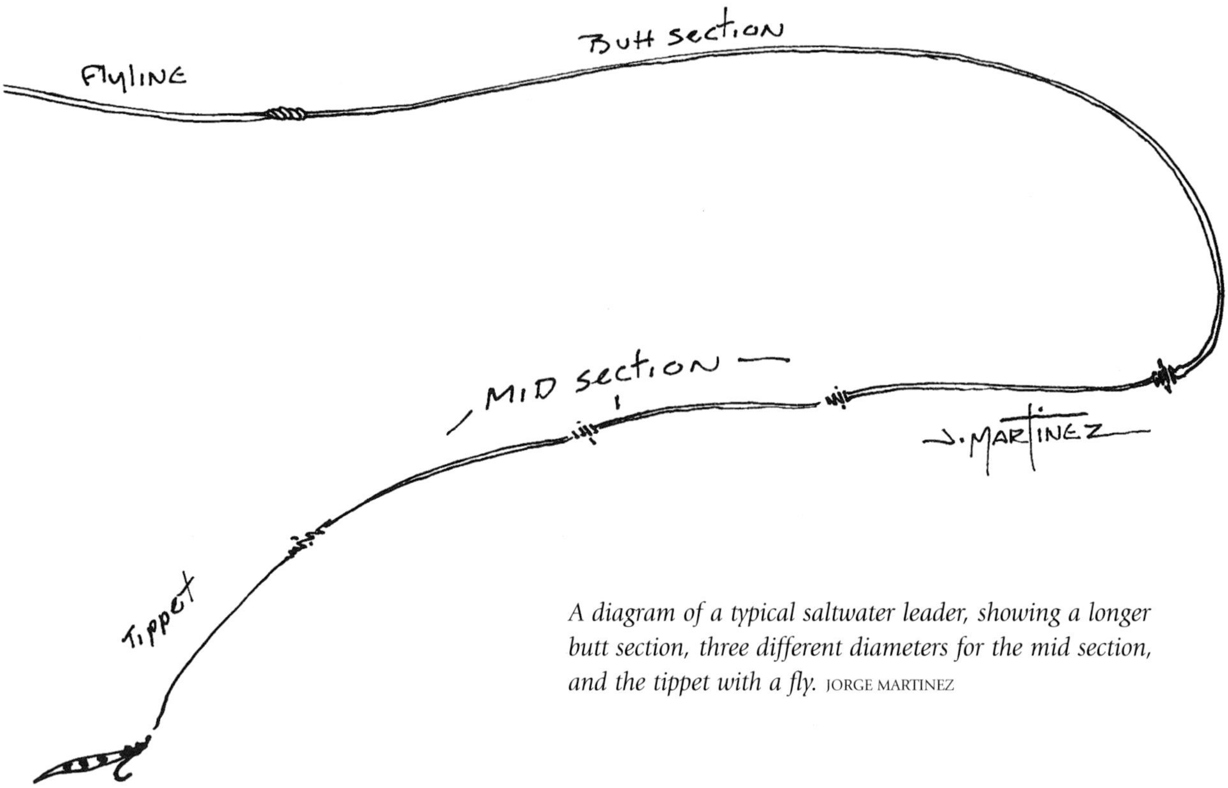

A diagram of a typical saltwater leader, showing a longer butt section, three different diameters for the mid section, and the tippet with a fly. JORGE MARTINEZ

sections would turn over very smoothly, I find that so many sections is not practical, especially in salt or brackish water. Most of the mid sections of my leaders for redfish or other backwater fishing are composed of two pieces. And on occasions where I am using a lighter tippet, I may use three pieces. More on this later.

The mid section is also called the taper section, which describes its anatomy well. But I find that many still call this section by the old name of hinge section, and this is wrong. There certainly should not be any hinge in your leader or it will collapse at that point, before it ever finishes turning the fly over. So I prefer "mid section."

The tippet section is the illusionist, because it's most important function is to create the illusion that the fly is unattached and swimming freely. This is the last section of the leader, with one end connected to the end of the mid section, and the other to the fly. A good tippet needs to be thin and supple to be as invisible as possible. Yet it needs to be strong enough to fight a big redfish and to some extent, also overcome some of the abrasion that will result from the tippet rubbing on the red's teeth, against mangrove roots, stumps, or other structures in the environment during the fight.

So, being the thinnest, the tippet section is the weakest link in the whole outfit. If you break the fish off, unless there is a major error in the rigging, it should be on the tippet section, whether the tippet itself, or one of the knots connecting on either side of the tippet.

The shock tippet, often called bite tippet, is the tough one. Basically, this is a small section of heavier leader material, usually less than a foot long, added at the end of your tippet to overcome the abrasion that may result from a fish's teeth rubbing against the leader material closest to the fly.

Bonefish and permit, of course, do not need a shock tippet, since they have a rubbery mouth with no teeth up front, and usually you don't need a shock tippet for redfish, other than perhaps fishing for big reds in special situations. Still, you may want to add shock tippet when fishing for reds in places where you also encounter other fish species that do abrade mono easily, such as snook, tarpon, and ladyfish. There's more about when and where to use shock tippet further down in this chapter.

Also, because the shock tippet is heavy and it's at the end of the leader, the extra weight does not help your casting at all; as a matter of fact, it makes it more difficult. Still, when it's needed, it's needed, and that's what the heavy butt section is there for, to turn over the fly no matter what.

Leader Length for Reds

When I first fly-fished for reds in the late 50s, mostly in South Florida, they were easy. The philosophy those days was that all one had to do is make sure the red saw the fly. "Just slap it on his face" was a common motto, and it worked. And to make extra sure the reds saw our offering, we used large and bulky flies, often in bright colors. It was not unusual to go out in the flats and take dozens of reds, not only out of a big school, but also casting to singles and small pods. My best day, around 1961 or so, was seventy-nine reds. I'll never forget it. But those days are long gone.

Today, while you can still have days where you take quite a few reds, fishing pressure has made redfish and other gamefish smarter and spookier in most parts of their habitat, making the use of longer leaders necessary. A leader should be long enough to let the fly land on the water a good distance away from the splash of the fly line, so as not to alarm Mr. Red. How far away you need that splash to be will depend on the fishing conditions you're facing.

Day in and day out, I've found the best all-around leader length to be about rod length or a little longer. And since most rods are 9 feet, that makes my average leader about 9 or 10 feet long. So with a 7- or 8-weight outfit and about a 10-foot leader, I can sight-cast to tailing or cruising redfish, mudding reds in deeper water, blind cast a shoreline, and many other situations. It's a great combo.

However, it's not uncommon for the above outfit to spook reds, and other backcountry fish when conditions get more difficult, such as: flat calm days, clear shallow water, and reds feeding so shallow that their backs are out of the water, to name a few. These are all conditions that dictate a more subtle presentation, and while using a smaller fly will help, it's usually not enough. Besides, often the fish are spooking just from seeing the fly line in the air, so that's one more reason for a longer leader.

Faced with one of these conditions, I usually lengthen my leader to about 12 or 13 feet. And while these longer leaders are harder to cast, if it's calm, then it shouldn't be too hard to turn over—if your butt section is long enough and you are a decent caster.

If in spite of the smaller, lighter fly and the longer leader, the redfish are still spooking when I make a presentation, then I give up increasing leader length. I've found that if a 13-foot leader isn't long enough, a 14 footer won't help, and I'm not casting a 16-footer. So my next move is to go to a lighter fly line. I'll put away my 8-weight and probably go right to my 6-weight with a 12-foot leader. I find going two sizes lighter on the fly line will make a bigger difference than adding a couple of feet of leader to a heavier line. So quite often the lighter outfit helps me trigger a strike. Happy day.

If that doesn't help, you could still go to a lighter saltwater 5-weight outfit. But personally, I don't like fishing any lighter than a 6-weight in the salt. So I do the next best thing. I put the 6-weight down, and reach in the cooler for one of my big homemade sandwiches, and when finished, I run to another flat.

Another way to gain the clear look of a long leader is to fish a clear-tip fly line. As you know from chapter 6, this is a weight-forward fly line where the first few feet are clear and the rest of the fly line is colored. So let's say you line has 10 feet of clear tip and you have attached a 10-foot leader; then you have 20 feet of clear line that the redfish is less likely to see. This works. However, those 22 feet of clear line is also hard for you to see while false-casting to a tailing redfish, and therefore, it's harder to be accurate. It's a good solution, but not perfect.

Just for fun, I thought I'd mention to you a couple of difficult conditions that don't happen often, but when they do, they can force you to push the envelope or give it up. Some anglers, however, don't give up easily, and when faced with almost impossible conditions, they still manage to hook fish. Tournament caster and fly fisher David Olson is well acquainted with the spooky reds in Mosquito Lagoon in mid-Florida. These fish get a lot of pressure, and if you try to fish them on a bright, calm day and low water conditions, well, they may sit with their backs out, feeding all over, but they are nearly impossible to present a fly to, let alone get a hit from. On one such day, David started fishing these reds with his 7-weight rod and a 12-foot leader. He soon found that every cast, even long casts, would spook them.

Determined to take one, David pulled out his 5-weight rod, rigged with a clear tip and a 12-foot leader, so he had 22 feet of clear line. Using a lightly dressed size 4 fly and making casts well over 70 feet, his presentations were so quiet he hardly could see the impact on the water. Even when part of the fine light leader landed over a red's back, it did not spook. So when David moved the fly, which was among several reds, of course, he had one on. He took several that day when no one came close to landing one. It was the right tool for that day. Too cool.

Another difficult situation you may face that truly requires long casts and long leaders, especially if the water is shallow, is casting to reds with a white, sandy bottom. A good friend and great fly fisher, whose clients have won many tournaments, Captain Rob Fordyce is well aware of this situation. One day, while discussing the reasons for the reds' acute awareness when in sand, he came up with a good parallel to explaining the reason for a fish's behavior in sandy bottom flats. He said:

> Imagine looking for your friend in a busy parking lot at 5 p.m. in the afternoon. A multitude of people going in and out, everyone moving, it'd be hard to find your friend. But imagine if you had set the time of the meeting at 5 a.m. in the

morning, as we do on a fishing trip. With no one in the lot, the minute your friend pulls in, you see him. Well then, imagine now looking for reds on a flat with lots of seagrass. A good current moving the grass back and forth. The grasses hold lots of life, so a variety of shrimp, crabs, and small fish are constantly moving or darting about. All of this distracts the redfish, or any fish, so it is much easier to present the fly without spooking him. But in a plain sandy bottom, with practically no grasses and few crustaceans or fishes darting about, a cruising redfish has little to distract him, and he'll see you.

So on a bare sandy bottom it is likely, especially if it's shallow and calm, that you will need a long leader and a long cast to make a successful presentation.

Just be aware that longer leaders have their disadvantages. Even with a good long butt section, it is harder to maintain good loop control for good accuracy or to turn a heavy or bulky fly over into a strong wind. And long leaders work best at medium and long casts. They do not work well in situations where short casts are the norm.

But it's not always about the long leader. Many fishing situations require short casts, and therefore, medium to short leaders. Wind, rain, and other factors can make the waters you are fishing off-color or even muddy. And while you may still be able to spot reds if the flat you are fishing is shallow enough, you'll only spot them when they're close to the boat, often well inside 20 feet. I've hooked reds a foot or two from the skiff or canoe, where I even had to move or lean back a little to present the fly. The fish simply was not aware of the craft or at least not scared of it. The red was surprised to find a shrimp to eat right in front of its nose, and more surprised to find itself hooked up.

Overcast days can happen in a minute and often last for hours or all day. Again, you can see fish, but only when they are close to the boat. And on very windy days, where the fish's window, the surface, is broken up by the waves, the fish don't see you and you don't see the fish. Most of the casts you'll get in these conditions are going to be short and quick. And finally, if you fish far back into the narrowest areas of backwaters, where the creeks and openings are small and you are in close quarters, most of the casts needed will be short.

When a redfish is tailing in shallow and clear water, as this one is, it usually takes a long leader, probably about 12 feet long, to land close to the fish without spooking it. PAT FORD

If you face one or several of these conditions, it may be time to shorten your leader. I may start by using a 9-foot leader, but if pressed, I'll reduce my leader to 8 feet, even a bit shorter. This way, the rod will load better when I only have 15 feet of line in the air, because I have less leader and more fly line, which has the weight. Anyway, in all the cases above, usually shortening the leader makes a huge difference in making a quick, short, and accurate cast. Some anglers faced with super muddy water or poor visibility will go to as short as a 6-foot leader. And it does work. But somehow I don't feel I need to go much shorter than 8 feet. It's your choice. Another place for a short leader is when fishing a fast-sinking line in off-color or muddy waters. Then I'll go to an 8-footer. But if the water is clear, I'll stay with a 10-footer or so. And with a clear sinking line, I generally still use a 9-footer or so.

Finally, I've also found that fishing over heavy grass, such as spartina grass, you're better off using a leader shorter than 9 feet. But we're talking about fishing reds in areas where there's often more grass than water to cast on. I've had occasions where my 20-foot cast landed right in front of the redfish, but no strike. The problem was that neither the fly line nor the leader, let alone the fly, was touching water. Everything was suspended a foot or so in the air. This happen often. I even had a red come a few inches out of the water to take the fly, and I hooked the fish! Don't you love it?

Selecting a Leader

You can get a leader two ways: buy a premade one, or learn to tie your own. As you can probably guess, there are advantages and disadvantage to both choices.

Premade leaders can be knotless or pretied. A knotless leader is manufactured by an extrusion process, starting with a larger diameter and progressively decreasing in size through the whole length of the leader. This way you have a leader with all its parts integrated (butt, mid, and tippet section), and no knots. And most knotless leaders come with a loop at the butt section so you can loop them to the loop of your fly line. A good knotless leader will turn over fine.

The other choice in premade leaders is to buy a knotted leader that is made in a fly shop. I find that if the individual person making the leaders knows what to do, then you are fine. Unlike a knotless leader, a hand-tied knotted leader is made from leader material of various sizes, tied together in a decreasing order of diameters. So you may start with 40-pound-test tied to piece of 30-pound-test, then to a piece of 20 pounds, then 15 pounds, then maybe tie the fly to it.

Learning to tie your own is not too hard, but it takes a little time to understand the concepts and then learn to tie a couple of knots. I feel the main advantage of making your own leader is flexibility. Since you control every aspect of the leader, from length and taper to tippet strength, you can make a leader to match any changing conditions in your fishing. And that, ultimately, is what makes the "tie your own" leader so great. It does things a knotless leader can't accommodate. The probabilities are endless, and the process very satisfying (and I must admit, habit forming). I love designing and tying leaders.

Personally I tie most of my leaders. But occasionally, when the need arises, I have no problem using a knotless leader. You have to keep an open mind, or you stop learning. Now, let's look at the knotless leader in more detail to see if they fit the bill for you.

Knotless Leaders

Just a few years back, knotless leaders, as far as I was concerned, were good for some freshwater applications, but none had the longer and fatter butt section needed to turn over saltwater flies. Besides, they were very soft, which in the cold water temperature of a trout stream it was fine, but in the warm waters of the tropics they acted like long, wet linguini.

But today most major manufacturers have knotless leaders designed for the salt, with adequate butt sections, both in diameter and length, that are stiff enough to endure warm weather. So an angler can now buy a good leader for redfish that will cast well with a 7- or 8-weight line.

And while a knotless leader still cannot have the flexibility of a leader you tie yourself, it has many advantages. For starters, it is great for a beginner, who can buy a good redfish leader, say a 9-footer with 12-pound-test tippet, take it out of the bag, straighten it, loop it to the fly line's loop, tie a fly to the tippet, and be ready to fish with a leader that works. Can't beat that.

And knotless leaders aren't just for beginners. If you are fishing for reds in areas with lots of loose grass, a knotless leader has a great advantage because it does not have any knots. A knotted leader, no matter who tied it or how tight and closely trimmed the knots are, is going to pick up grass. Often a knotted leader can pick up a lot of grass, making you waste fishing time while you remove it. Personally, in these cases, I'll gladly switch to one of my knotless leaders, which I also carry in my leader kit.

So who should get a knotless leader? First, a beginner. I feel when you start to fly-fish, you have quite a learning curve. Between learning to cast and finding fish, you have your hands full. So I say, get a knotless leader, go fishing, keep practicing your cast, and have fun. Later, as your cast gets better and you appreciate the need for flexibility in different conditions, then learn to make your own leader. And even if you are an expert, don't be hard-headed when there's lots of floating grass; change to knotless. Or if you are in a rush, or feel a little lazy that day, it's okay, go knotless.

Knotless leaders for redfish come in a variety of lengths and tippet strengths. If you are a beginner, get mostly the 9-footers. Leave the 12-footer for more delicate presentations in shallow water or for tailing fish, provided you can cast well enough to turn it over. In tippet size, you may want to get 12- or 16-pound-test for most fishing. If using small flies, maybe use 10-pound-test, and for the big reds like they have in Louisiana, 16- or 20-pound-test will get them.

Read the label and make sure the diameter of the butt is at least 0.024 of an inch; 0.026 may be better, and if using a 9-weight, even 0.028. I'd mainly get monofilament (really nylon), but if you are fishing in areas where you want the fly to sink, besides using a weighted fly, then try a fluorocarbon leader. More on leader materials further down.

I tie my knotless leaders by one of three methods, depending on how my fly line is rigged, or how lazy I feel that day. The fast, easy way is to use the loop that is on your fly line and loop it to the loop that comes with the knotless leader. Done. It's quick, but it has one disadvantage: it's bulky. And it does not go through the guides well.

Another way, which many fly shops use, is to cut the loop in front of the fly line and tie a foot of butt section with a nail knot or some other knot, then at the end of this short butt, add a loop. Then you simply loop to loop both loops. The advantage here is that the nail knot and the loop to loop connection of both mono sections are less bulky and go through the guides much better. And yes, with the added foot, a 9-foot leader would now be a 10-footer. As Miles Davis would say, "So What?"

And finally, you could take the 1-foot butt tied to the fly line, and instead of looping it, you don't use the loops but tie a neat blood knot. This yields the smallest knots, and they go through the guides much better. However, if at this point you already know how to tie a blood knot, chances are, you also make your own leader. Anyway, I often use this method.

However, with time, your knotless leader will change, and not for the better. You see, knotless leaders are manufactured so that when the taper gets to the tippet, there's usually 2 to 2½ feet of level line. This is where you'll attach your fly. But as you keep changing flies, the tippet section keeps getting smaller and smaller, until you are tying your fly close to or at the point where the taper starts to get fat, the mid section. For practical purposes, you can no longer use this leader. You'll have to dispose of it, as many anglers do, by unlooping it and looping a new leader.

But there is another way, and one that I often use. You buy tippet material of the same strength, let's say 12 pounds, and you now add a couple of feet or more to your leader with a blood knot. Presto, you now have a good leader again. That requires that you learn to tie a blood knot—not a bad thing.

Soon you may start to experiment, and instead of adding a mono tippet to your mono leader, you now use a blood knot to tie on a fluorocarbon tippet, which will sink faster and catch less wind during a turnover. You are way out there now.

One day you'll realize that, if you can make one blood knot, you can make three or four and tie a complete leader. Then, you'll be a purist, tying your own leaders. With more time, you'll start to go back and use knotless leaders where they apply and knotted most of the time. That's when you've arrived.

Formulas

The first thing you should think about when you start to make a leader is how long each section is going to be. A leader formula answers that by showing what percentage of the leader's length is butt section, mid section, and tippet section. For example, one of the most popular formulas, 50/30/20, simply means a leader in which the butt section is 50 percent of the total length, the mid section (the total of all pieces used) is 30 percent, and the tippet is 20 percent. So to make a 10-foot leader with this formula, you simply use 5 feet of butt, 3 feet of mid sections, and 2 feet of tippet. Following a leader formula is the best way to consistently repeat the same taper every time you make a leader, no matter if you change the length of the leader or use a different size fly line. Just apply the formula, and you can't miss.

For me, the most important part of the leader, the part that will determine most of what the leader will do and will not do, is the butt section. Within reason, the longer the butt section, the more energy the leader will have to turn the fly over, but the harder it will land on the water. The shorter the butt section, the harder it will be to turn a fly over, even against a mild wind, but the more delicate it will turn over a fly on a calm day. This is why a good angler may change a leader's formula or length, to adapt to changing conditions.

I find that a formula that uses 50 to 55 percent butt section makes a great all-around compromise between power to turn over and delicacy of presentation in the salt. If the wind picks up or I decide to change to a bigger, bulkier fly, I may go to a 60 percent butt section when making a leader to turn over a bulky or heavy fly line or a big popper, for example. Either way, I usually don't work with a butt section much smaller than 50 percent of the length of the leader.

Here are some of the formulas most often used in the flats, some very good, some not so good (so you can avoid them):

50/30/20. This is the most popular formula and, I feel, the best all around. I use it frequently, but still, when I want to use a longer tippet, I may use something like a 50/25/25. Now my tippet, instead of being 2 feet, is 2½ feet. Also works great.

60/20/20. This is Charles Ritz's famous formula from the 1930s, perhaps the oldest formula. This is the formula I go to for big flies or windy days. The longer butt section has power. I know many great anglers who fish this formula, whether windy or calm.

40/30/30. A formula designed for delicacy. For me it does not have the power to turn over except on calm days. If you have one rod, say an 8-weight, and you want delicacy, it may be okay. I would still use a 50 percent butt section on a longer leader, say a 12-footer with a 6-foot butt, if I needed delicacy.

4 feet of 40 pounds / 3 feet of 30 pounds / 2 feet of 20 pounds and 2 feet of tippet. This formula has been around for a while. And it's probably popular for its cute pattern of length matching the pound test. But I don't do cute, and I suggest you don't either. This leader is 11 feet long, so a 4-foot butt would be only 36 percent of the leader. That's too short to turn over well, even with a longish 3 feet of 30-pound following, acting as a compound butt. I think you know how I feel about it by now.

Rule of Halves. This is a loose formula. You simply select a butt section you want, say 5 feet. Then the next section 2½ feet, the next 1¼ feet, then the tippet. The greatest proponent I know of this formula is Sandy Moret. Being very laid back, Sandy just measures a butt section the length of his hands spread, then ties the next section by measuring casually from one of his hands to his chest, or roughly half. Then one section that is half again, then the tippet. Then he goes fishing—smart guy. And when I do this formula and measure the butt section, it's usually a "casual" 50 percent, like Sandy uses. It works.

Butt and Tippet. This is a quick tie formula that consist of about two-thirds butt section and one-third tippet section, or a 67/33 formula. It's usually used with short leaders of less than 8 feet. Because it does not have a mid section to help smooth the turnover, it doesn't cast as well or have the smooth, controlled turnover that you need for a good and accurate presentation. I know it's a little bit faster to construct, but if you don't have the time to tie a couple more blood knots, I strongly suggest you use a good knotless leader.

I've never gone wrong with 50/30/20 and 60/20/20, from bluegill to redfish to permit. So I encourage you to use these formulas, and go from there.

Materials to Make a Leader

Now that you know about leaders and the formulas to build them, you need to select leader material. Either monofilament (nylon) or fluorocarbon. Both come in a great variety of diameters, strengths, degrees of stiffness, and colors. So you can build just about any leader you can think of with either material. I find monofilament (I'll call it mono from now on) to be the best all around material for leaders. Fluorocarbon has its place, which I'll talk about later.

Mono is strong for its diameter, and it's soft and slick, making it easier to tie knots with great strength. Knots set tight and small with mono. Also, mono stretches easily, so when your heavy butt section is all in a coil from being in your fly reel too long, a good stretch brings it back perfectly straight and ready to turn over. A butt with a coil memory will not turn over well, if at all.

And because mono has a specific gravity very close to water, it is great to use when fishing a surface fly like a popper or a deer hair fly that needs to stay dancing lively on the surface.

When using mono for leader material, I much prefer medium stiffness. If the mono is super stiff, it's hard to tie good knots, and the butt section is almost impossible to keep straight for a good turnover because the stiffer mono is hard to stretch. If you can't stretch it, you can't straighten it. On the other hand, if you use a super soft, limp mono, it will not turn over a leader well, and you'll be more prompt to get wind knots on your tippet when you cast, which will reduce its strength.

I find Ande and Maxima lines to have that medium stiffness I love, and I've used Ande for fifty years and Maxima for at least twenty years to make leaders. RIO also has, along with its stiff and soft offerings, a medium stiff line. And there are other manufacturers that also offer medium stiff mono, although they never mention "medium stiffness" by name. Sorry.

Fluorocarbon is more dense than mono, with a specific gravity of about 1.75 or so, to mono's 1.1 (water is 1.0), and this has several advantages and disadvantages depending on conditions. Being so dense, fluorocarbon will sink faster than mono, and this can be an advantage if you need your fly to sink fast or if you want it to stay deep while you retrieve a fly. Then a full leader made of fluorocarbon will work well for you. Fluorocarbon is also a bit more abrasion-resistant than mono, which can be an advantage when using a fluorocarbon shock tippet for redfish in an area that also has snook and tarpon.

Also, while not the magic that many anglers make it to be, fluorocarbon is less visible because it has less glare underwater than mono, which could help trigger more strikes when reds are in very clear waters. On the other hand, when the material gets frayed by a redfish, snook, or baby tarpon, the frayed part can actually be more visible, especially when the sunlight hits it at the right angle.

Another place to use a full fluorocarbon leader is when using a sinking line, whether a slow-sinking clear line or a fast-sinking line. The dense material together with the sinking line will help keep the fly deeper than it would be had you been using a mono leader. Fishing a beach with a slow-sinking clear line, you could use a fluorocarbon leader to keep the fly riding just a little bit deeper. And being dense means being heavier, so casting against a strong wind, a fluorocarbon leader cuts through the air as easy as a sinking fly line does.

However, I find that often in shallow flats, a full fluorocarbon leader keeps dragging my fly on the bottom, where it picks up grass or simply gets hung on the bottom. Here I use mono.

And fluorocarbon is not good for surface flies. You see, a great surface fly needs to be buoyant, to the point that it's practically alive on the surface—that's the magic of a great deer hair streamer, a slider, or even a long pencil popper. But fluorocarbon will drag a surface fly down as you try to retrieve, killing its action. Use mono on the surface.

Finally, being stiff, fluorocarbon is harder to tie good knots with, and you may find that your knots don't have the strength that a similar knot tied with mono. Just make sure when you tie your knots that you lubricate them well before you pull.

Personally, I mostly use mono in most of my fly-fishing with floating lines, and it works great. But sometimes I want the quality and feel of mono but with a bit more sink rate to a fly in the flats, without adding more weight. Then, I'll use a full mono leader, except that at the end I'll tie a fluorocarbon tippet. This keeps the more buoyant mono just under the surface, while letting the more dense fluorocarbon tippet and fly go down a bit faster. It works great for casting to tailing reds and being able to get the fly down at their level, while still using a lightly weighted fly that won't spook them when it lands on the water. This is another advantage of tying your own leader.

And when I want to get my fly down, I do like using a full fluorocarbon leader with my slow-sinking clear lines and my fast-sinking line. And the fact that their higher density helps me turn over a fly into the wind is another added bonus. So there's a place for fluorocarbon in the salt, and since the material keeps getting better every year, I suspect I'll use it more often in the future. For the time being, I'm still mostly into mono, but we'll see.

Durability

All light, but especially UV light, is harmful to monofilament, degrading it and making it weaker. So it's wise to keep your leader material away from light, preferrably in a dark cool place, as you should do with fly line. Fluorocarbon holds up better than mono under UV light, but I still take care of it as I do with mono. You'll find that often some spools of line will be with you for years, so proper care can make a big difference on how strong they stay.

Recently, I learned a good tip on taking care of leader material from friend and top fly fisher Raz Reid. He told me that when he gets new leader material, the first thing he does before storing it away is to take an indelible ink felt pen and write on the label the day he got it. This way he'll always know how long he's had a particular spool of line.

Well, after Raz shared this idea with me, I went home and looked at the dozens of spools of line I had in my closet. To my surprise, I realized some spools had been there for almost twenty years! And indeed when tested, some were not as strong as they once were. Well, I now own a third of the spools of material I use to have. But they are fresh and strong. Thanks, Raz.

Color

A lot has been written about matching the colors of leader materials to the color of the water or the bottom. But since fishing for redfish often means a variety of water colors, from clear to muddy and bottoms from bleached white sand to dark grass, often in a single day's fishing, I don't see the logic.

Throughout a lifetime of fly fishing, I've always used clear leader materials. They seem to blend well with a great variety of environments and have produced a lot of fish for me, often in difficult conditions. Still, I'll always be curious and ready to learn, so from time to time, I'll try different colors. I've done well with light green, and lately I've played a bit with pink, since that seems to be the hot color these days with some top anglers. And so far, the colors, if very light, work fine, but I see no difference or improvement. So I'll stay clear. Frankly it's going to take a lot to make me change my opinion on this one. Still, I am open for debates over an adult drink—if color mono advocates pay the tab.

Leader Knots

While many different kinds of knots can be used to tie a leader, the truth is that you only need to learn a knot to tie the different sections and a couple of knots to tie your fly. That's it. The knot I recommend you learn, to tie the different size sections of your leader, is the blood knot. Well tied, it approaches 100 percent strength, and often achieves it. When set properly, it is small and the tags can be trimmed tight to form very little profile. And it doesn't use much material to tie, which is important.

Other knots, like the surgeon's knot, work fine, but for that knot, the tags stick out at an odd angle, so it tends to pick up grass easily. Even worse, it takes a lot of material to tie. The problem with this is not economy—you can afford to buy a few more yards of material. The problem comes when you have a full leader made, and you decide that you need to shorten a section. With a surgeon, you can't. The small sections of the leader, other than the butt section, are not long enough. So you simply have to construct a new leader. Using two uni knots back to back has that same problem. But with a blood knot, you can cut the part of the leader you want to change or shorten, and with just a few inches of material, tie them together.

Whether you use mono, fluorocarbon, or you are mixing them in a leader, a blood knot can do it all. For the upper part of the leader, where you may be tying 40-, 30-, or 25-pound-test line, and strength is not as important, I'll tie my blood knot with five turns of the thinner line and three turns of the fatter line. So, for example, five turns of 30 and three turns of 40. But when tying the tippet section, which is the weakest connection and where you want maximum strength, I'll use six turns to five turns, which test very strong, sometimes right at 100 percent. Another option, and one I have also used, it to tie an improved blood knot. This is simply a blood knot in which you first double the thinner line and then tie a blood knot, as if the thinner doubled line was a single line. It's a good knot, too. I'd also use six turns on the thin doubled line and five turns on the thicker line.

To tie your fly to the tippet or shock tippet, you have two choices: to loop or to cinch. In almost every case, I'd rather tie my fly with a loop, because it allows the fly to move freely and with more action, almost regardless of the pattern. Sometimes, I think it also hooks more fish.

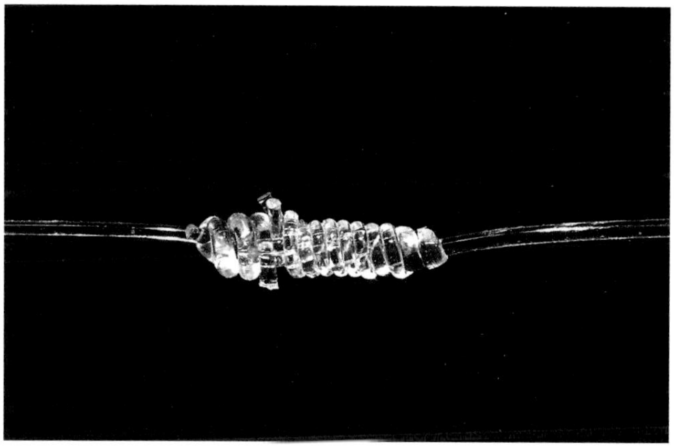

A close-up of a blood knot that I tied, pulled tight, and "set" to give you an idea of what it should look like.

On top: the fly tied with a clinch knot will allow less action and keep the fly sinking slower, often suspended if the fly is not too heavily weighted. Below: a weighted fly tied with a loop knot will allow the fly to move more freely and with more action, and it will also sink much faster. It's a matter of what you need the fly to do. JORGE MARTINEZ

Also, a loop lets the fly sink faster, which is often what you need.

To tie a loop on the fly with a tippet of 20 pounds or less, I use either a six- or seven-turn Duncan loop (created by my friend of half a century, Norman Duncan) or a variation of the no-slip knot with four-turn. If I am tying a loop on a shock tippet that may be 30 to 50 pounds, mainly to overcome the fray of snook and tarpon while red fishing, then I'll use three or four turns on the Duncan loop. And maybe three turns for the no-slip variation.

However, sometimes, especially in shallow water, you don't want the fly to sink fast, but rather stay suspended, or even close to the surface. In these cases, I'll cinch the fly. A cinched fly is more restricted and has less action, but produces a good minnow-like darting action. But be careful: the knot on a cinched fly, if it's not tied tight to the ring eye of the hook, will often move slightly to the left or right of the eye, creating an unnatural movement on a fly when retrieved, because it cannot be pulled straight. And a fly that is cocked to the right or left of the eye of the hook will not fly as straight in the air either, making casting and accuracy more difficult. A loop does not have that problem.

To cinch a fly to a plain tippet of 20 pounds or lighter, I either use a seven-turn clinch, or a six-turn improved clinch. Both, if tied properly, test well over 90 percent. More turns may improve the strength a little, but they are much harder to set. And if cinching with a heavy shock tippet, then a plain clinch knot with three or four turns will work fine.

Top angler Sandy Moret tying a big redfish fly with a loop, for more action.

Now, regardless of the knot you choose, it's imperative that you "set" the knot every time. Let me try to explain this. When you make a knot, you first form it, rearrange it with your fingers if it needs it, wet it, and then you pull it tight. When you pull it tight, it is important that you pull in one continuous motion until the knot cannot be pulled any tighter; that's when it is "set." If done properly, the knot almost looks like one piece, like a diamond. This way, it cannot slip, and no matter how hard you pull, it will stay the same until something breaks. This is good. However, if the knot is not quite tight, if you feel you have to pull it tight one more time, chances are, you won't be able to do it. This is a weak knot. It's not "set." Believe me, you need to cut it off and tie it again. So "set" each knot.

And to help you set every knot, you need to wet it, lubricate it. This way it will more easily slide and tighten as it should. What most anglers do is to wet it with saliva, which works much better than trying to pull it dry. But if you want to really see your knot slide and tighten to a set, easily and quickly, use water. Works great. Just put a little bit of water on a saucer or glass and dip the knot before pulling. And when I'm fishing, I try to wet the knot on the water before pulling it tight. I even use the melted water in the cooler.

Also, I have found that twelve-year-old Scotch or eighteen-year-old single malt works the best, if you happen to be sipping some while you are tying leaders one evening. I'm not kidding. You don't need to be drinking a little Scotch while building leaders in the evening, but it's encouraged.

Making a Redfish Leader

I'm going to choose a good all-around leader for redfish—a 10-foot leader for an 8-weight line with a 16-pound-test tippet—and use the popular formula of 50/30/20. You can't go wrong with that. Just remember that while the explanation below takes some time, when you learn to make your leader, it only takes a few minutes.

First, let's gather the tools. Get 40-, 30-, 20-, and 16-pound-test leader material. To cut materials and trim the knots, pliers or forceps with scissors will work fine, but clippers are my first choice here because they usually can trim knots much closer. To lubricate the knots before pulling them tight, get a saucer with half or a quarter of an inch of water on it, to dip the knot.

Also get a yard stick or a measuring tape to measure the sections. And if pulling hard on the sections hurts your hands, use your sun gloves or a light pair of garden gloves. I generally don't use gloves, except when I'm tying big game leaders. Just make sure you can comfortably pull hard enough to set the knots. For those of you more advanced, a micrometer may help you, especially when using material where the manufacturer doesn't show the diameter. But it's not necessary. And if you're a beginner, don't even think about it.

Whatever material you choose, use the same make throughout the leader, so that stiffness and other properties remain constant, from the butt section to the tippet. The only exception of this rule is if you decide to use mono for the leader and carbon for the tippet or a shock tippet. About 95 percent of the leaders I make are composed of the same material, usually mono, from butt to tippet or shock tippet. For medium stiff mono materials, I like Maxima and Ande, but I've tried some saltwater RIO and some Umpqua that also work well. And frankly, there are many line companies making good medium stiff leader materials. These are just the ones I mostly fish. But if and when I find better, I'll change.

We'll start with the butt section, but first, I want you to know how I arrive at the right butt section, not just for the 8-weight line but for 5- to 10-weight lines. The ideal butt section should mimic the fly line it's attached to, in density and to some extent, in stiffness in order to have a smooth transition of the cast's energy, from the fly line to the butt section, and later all the way down to the fly. But leader materials are stiffer than fly lines, so what has worked out throughout the years, to match stiffness, more or less, is to use a butt diameter that is 60 to 65 percent of the diameter of the tip end of the fly line.

Since the tip end on an 8-weight line measures around 0.040 of an inch, then 60 or 66 percent of that is around 0.024 or 0.026 of an inch. And that, in most average medium stiff leaders is 40-pound-test. That is why most good saltwater anglers, either by knowledge or experimentation, now use 40-pound-test butt section on an 8-weight.

Still, the pound test is just a guide. You're really building the butt and mid section of leaders by diameter (which really means weight), and the tippet by pound test, that is, strength. Now, let me give you an idea of the "approximate" butt section diameters that I like to use in lines from 5-weight to 10-weight. I can't see using any lighter or any heavier outfits when fishing for reds.

Just remember to guide yourself by the diameter (which is often on the spool label these days, and that's nice). The pound test is another guideline.

On the next page, I give you some of the companies whose materials I often use to make leaders—as a guideline to you. With the years, all of this will change—there will be other line manufacturers or distributers, perhaps better, perhaps not—but the basic principles stay the same. And that reminds me of a story I want to share with you:

5-weight	0.0205–0.022"	Use 25-pound-test butt.
6-weight	0.023"	Use 30-pound-test butt.
7-weight	0.023–0.025"	Use 30- or 40-pound-test butt.
8-weight	0.024–0.027"	Use 40-pound-test.
9-weight	0.025–0.029"	Use about 40- or 50-pound-test butt.
10-weight	0.025–0.029"	Use 50-pound-test butt.

About thirty years ago, in the early 80s, I did thorough research on fly line to butt section diameter. It took me months of experimentation. But I had more time those days, probably because the Internet and cell phones weren't around. Anyway, finally I came up with roughly the facts that I'm giving you here. So now I knew that for the 8-weight line I used for bonefish, snook, and redfish, a good butt section was something close to 0.025 of an inch or about 40-pound-test. I was proud of it. A few weeks later while fishing for bonefish in the Keys, I ran into my friend Lee Wulff as the docks. I immediately told him that I had done an exhaustive research on butt sections for bones and backcountry fishing, using 7-, 8-, and 9-weight lines. Then I waited for him to ask me what I found. But instead, Lee scratched his head slowly, while looking far into the horizon, seemingly lost in thoughts for a few seconds (Lee was an engineer), and then told me that since the 1940s, he had always thought that 0.025 inch was an ideal butt sections for 7-, 8-, and 9-weight lines. He asked what I'd found.

I don't even remembered what I answered, and I guess it doesn't matter. But the point of the story is that basics stay the same, no matter what new leader material you get, even if it's pink.

The chart on the next page shows the materials I often use for butt sections.

Needless to say, the principles are the same for knotless leaders, where 0.025 to 0.028 inches works well for reds. This info is generally on the package.

Now, if you bear with me a little longer, I'll tell you another story about butt section diameters. In the early 90s, my son, Stephen, was still in high school, life was much simpler, and we both had lots of time to fish together. But when we only had half a day, we would often

Pound Test	Brand	Diameter
25-pound-test	Ande	0.0205"
25-pound-test	Maxima	0.0205"
30-pound-test	Ande	0.0235"
30-pound-test	Maxima	0.023"
40-pound-test	Ande	0.0245"
40-pound-test	Maxima	0.0245"
40-pound-test (fluorocarbon)	Ande (fluorocarbon)	0.0246"
40-pound-test (fluorocarbon)	Maxima (fluorocarbon)	0.0243"
50-pound-test	Ande (Back Country—a softer mono)	0.028"
N/A (Recommended for 7- to 9-weight)	Umpqua Butt Material (a softer mono)	0.027"

go fishing for snook and baby tarpon in the famous Tamiami Trail canal, on the west side of Florida, an hour and a half from Miami, where we lived. I had fished the Trail since early 1959, with Flip Pallot, John Emery, and Norman Duncan. I knew it well in those days.

The Trail canal goes east and west, so a strong northern wind will push all the water out of the north sloughs and into the main canal, and with it, all the minnows that are living in the sloughs. So it's like nature's natural chumming. It can be great fly fishing, with snook, tarpon, and occasionally redfish and bass all feeding against the shoreline as the minnows come out. It's a good day for the fish, but a bad day for the minnows. The only problem is that to fly-fish in this situation, you need to cast against the northern wind and reach the other side of the canal.

Well, at this time I was late with an article assignment and didn't have the time to rig the day before. Stephen quickly offered to rig, make sandwiches, and even drive the next morning. Anything to go fishing. Fine, I agreed and went back to my writing.

The next morning before daylight we drove to the area, well past the road that goes to Everglade City. When we got there, just at dawn, snook and baby tarpon were popping near the opposite shoreline as a strong north wind blew into us. Knowing that both of us could cast the 60 or more feet into that wind, I anticipated no problems.

We quickly took out a pair of 7-weight rods with small Muddlers that imitated the size of the mud minnows and started to cast. But to my surprise, every time I shot a loop into the other side of the canal, the fly line would unfold fine, but the leader would not, leaving the fly 10 feet behind the fly line. No matter how hard we tried, the leaders couldn't penetrate the wind. Frustrated, I examined the butt section and found that it looked and felt like 20-pound-test, or thinner. So I turn around and explained to Stephen, probably in a loud and frustrated voice, that 7-weight rods needed 30-pound-test and that he should know better by now. But he swore up and down that he had used 30-pound. Well, the fish were popping on the other side, so I was not going to have a dissertation about leader diameters. We ran back to the car, changed the whole leader with thicker butt sections and were back fishing just in time to take a few snook and jump a tarpon or two before daylight put an end to the action.

Back at the house a few hours later, I found out what happened. Stephen knew that a 7-weight took a 30-pound butt section to turn over, but that's all he knew. So when he got back from school that Friday, in the rush to get ready for the trip the next day, he picked up a spool of 30-pound-test ultra thin mono that I had laying around. The diameter of that mono was like normal thin and light 20-pound-test. So of course the leaders did not turn over; they would not have turned over on a calm day! We needed the weight that comes from a thicker diameter, not the strength of 30 pounds. Stephen learned another lesson, and I threw the spool away.

Anyway, following the 50/30/20 formula, cut 5 feet of 40-pound-test for butt—actually a few inches longer to allow for tying the knot to the mid section. Also, the measurements do not have to be exact to the inch, a close approximation is fine. Now the mid section, which is simply a smooth transition from the fat 40-pound-test to the thin 16-pound-test tippet. Here 20 and 30 pounds will work well. And since the formula said the mid section should be 3 feet, you can either cut each section $1^1/_2$ feet, or cut 2 feet of 30 pounds and one of 20 pounds. Either will work. Now blood knot the 30-pound section to the butt section and then blood knot the 20-pound to the 30-pound.

Now let's tie the 16-pound tippet to the end of the mid section, which, by the 50/30/20 formula, is going to be 2 feet long or so. At this point you are about to tie what is usually the weakest connection, often more so than the tippet connection to the fly. So to make that blood knot as strong as possible, tie five to six turns. That is, use six turns of the thinner material, the 16-pound tippet, then use five turns of the fatter material, the

20-pound lower mid section. Make sure to lubricate it, then pull it steady and firm so the knot sets.

Now you have:

Butt = 5 feet of 40-pound

Mid = 3 feet (about 2 feet of 30-pound and 1 foot of 20-pound)

Tippet = 2 feet of 16-pound

Your leader should be about 10 feet long, and all you need to do is tie a fly to the tippet.

I know it took a lot to explain, but in reality it only takes a few minutes to tie.

Choosing a Tippet

Unlike the rest of the leader, the tippet's job is to take the fly to the right depth, allow the fly to move as freely as possible to entice a fish, and be strong enough to hold the fish during the fight. To keep a fly swimming deep, you can use a longer tippet or a lighter tippet or use a fluorocarbon tippet with its higher density. If you're fishing a big bulky or heavy fly, such as a popper or a deer hair streamer, a shorter tippet, say 18 inches or less, will turn over in the wind much better.

When using small redfish flies, say a size 4 hook or smaller, use a 12-pound tippet or lighter, even 10 pounds. The thinner lines are softer and don't obstruct the natural swimming action a small fly needs. But if you attach that 2-inch streamer to a 20-pound tippet, the heavy line will kill the little fly's action, and you'll probably get few strikes and lots of refusals. And in clear water, especially if it's calm, it's a good idea to stay away from the heavy tippets.

Also, when fishing for big reds, 16- or 20-pound tippet is a good choice, and if you are a beginner, use 20 pounds. Not just to be able to land them (you can land a big redfish on 8-pound tippet if you know what you are doing) but to be able to land them without going through a long fight, which often kills the fish. Personally, my everyday tippet for reds is 12 pounds. On big fish I'll go to 16 pounds. And sometimes, if we are fighting many big fish, I'll even go to 20-pound tippets.

When fishing a light rod, like my 6-weight, for medium and small reds or sheepshead in Louisiana, I may even go as light as 10 pounds. With good knots I can pull pretty hard with 10 pounds. Fishing Louisiana in the winter months, where reds and black drum often are over 20 and even over 30 pounds, a 9-weight rod with 16-pound tippet is my standard rod. If a bit lazy, I may just go to 20-pound tippet.

In situations where reds are in extremely shallow water, often with their backs out of the water, it's exciting to fish for them. But it's also frustrating because they seem to spook from the slightest noise, or even from the fly line in the air. In these conditions, what I often do is tie a much longer tippet on my leader, say over 3 feet. Now I can often cast right among several reds, the tippet even over their backs sometimes, without disturbing them, and get a strike. And yes, I know, casting a longer leader with a very long tippet is much harder, but it beats spooking them. I've taken some tough reds that way.

Below are a few examples of tippet materials I use for redfish. Consider the diameters approximate figures, just to give you some guidance.

Pound Test	Brand	Diameter
10-pound-test	Ande (clear mono)	0.012"
10-pound-test	Ande (fluorocarbon)	0.0113"
10-pound-test	Scientific Anglers (fluorocarbon)	0.0118"
10-pound-test	Scientific Anglers (clear mono)	0.012"
12-pound-test	Ande (clear mono)	0.0145"
12-pound-test	Ande (fluorocarbon)	0.012"
12-pound-test	Maxima (clear mono)	0.0155"
12-pound-test	Maxima (fluorocarbon)	0.0125"
12-pound-test	RIO (IGFA)	0.0135"
12-pound-test	Scientific Anglers (clear mono)	0.013"
15-pound-test	Ande (clear mono)	0.0165"
15-pound-test	Ande (fluorocarbon)	0.014"
15-pound-test	Maxima (clear mono)	0.016"
15-pound-test	Maxima (fluorocarbon)	0.0138"
15-pound-test	Scientific Anglers (fluorocarbon)	0.0137"
20-pound-test	Ande (clear mono)	0.018"
20-pound-test	Ande (fluorocarbon)	0.017"
20-pound-test	Maxima (fluorocarbon)	0.0165"
20-pound-test	Maxima (clear mono)	0.018"

Shock Tippet

While I have fished for redfish in most if not all of their range, from Virginia to South Florida and from there all the way to the Mexican border, living in Miami, I do a lot of red fishing in South Florida, mainly in the Everglades. And that means I am constantly encountering a mix of reds, snook, and tarpon. Yes, I know, you don't feel sorry for me. Anyway, I am intimately familiar with shock tippets and all its variations.

First, do you need a shock tippet for redfish? Basically, no. Yes, they can fray a little but not enough to require a shock tippet. Even in Louisiana I've taken big reds to over 30 pounds with straight 16 mono, and seen other friends take them just as big with 12-pound fluorocarbon. Also, Captain Lance Ledet, owner of Dulac Charters in Louisiana, tells me that after many years of taking big reds on 16- and 20-pound tippet, he does not remember having a fish fray a tippet bad enough to break off. And I remember one morning, while fishing with Lance, I took an 18-pounder and a 21-pounder on a 7-weight rod with straight 12-pound tippet, no problem. However, it's not unusual, after a long fight or after landing a few reds, that on close inspection, I find my tippet too frayed for my comfort. Then I simply cut off the few frayed inches and retie the fly or change to a new tippet, and I'm ready to go again. And if you are still a little uncomfortable, either because you are fishing a light tippet or because you are fishing big reds, you can use fluorocarbon, which has more abrasion resistance.

The problem is not the redfish then, but other raspy-mouthed fish. Tarpon can fray your tippet and cut you off, but pound for pound, snook are much worse, fraying a 16-pound tippet sometimes in seconds if hooked deep. Even an undersize snook can fray you off. When you feel a shock tippet is necessary, you first need to decide how heavy a material to use. Too thin, and you still get frayed; too heavy and you don't get strikes. After a lifetime of this dilemma, I have settled on the following shock tippet sizes. My first choice is 40-pound mono, which is abrasion-resistant enough that I've landed countless snook between 10 and 18 pounds or so, a few over 20 pounds, in years past, plus a few big tarpon too. And I've been frayed off very few times, so I'm quite comfortable with 40 pounds.

However, when fishing areas that do not have many large snook, say mostly under 12 pounds, or if I'm fishing a 6-weight outfit with light tippet, then I may go to 30-pound mono—lately I'm using 30 more and more when red fishing. If I need to use a small redfish fly, say one tied on a size 4 hook, where a fat heavy shock tippet would kill the action of the fly, I have been known to go to 25-pound shock tippet. But I tell you, I've also been known to lose a few big snook that took the small fly, frayed me off, and kept my small fly. It's a jungle out there.

By now, you may have noticed that I've only mentioned mono. The reason is that I often use surface flies like sliders, Muddlers, and Hot Lips, which are designed to ride right on the surface, and if I use a heavy fluorocarbon shock tippet, it will sink the fly and kill the action. But fluorocarbon is a great material to use for shock tippet, and if you know that you will only be using underwater streamers, such as weighted Clousers or unweighted Seaducers, there's no reason you couldn't use fluorocarbon and take advantage of its extra abrasion resistance.

Also, regardless of the material you use, make sure that the shock tippet is as straight as possible. A heavy shock tippet with some memory will have a negative effect on the way your fly swims. To make sure that a fly is swimming naturally, always straighten your shock tippet as much as possible.

Finally, when adding a shock tippet, don't use one that is too long, or it will be tough to cast. Cut about 18 inches of material to allow extra room on one side for tying an improved blood knot to the class tippet, and one on the other side for the loop or for any knot you want to use that cinches tight to the eye of the hook you want to use to the fly on the other side. You'll end up with a shock tippet no longer than a foot.

Loop to Loop Connections for the Tippet and Shock Tippet

This is simply a method of quickly connecting or disconnecting the tippet and shock tippet from the end of the mid section of your leader. It was popular with big tarpon anglers years back, but not anymore. We all carried tippet stretcher boxes with a couple of dozen tarpon flies pretied. But tarpon anglers don't do that anymore.

Anyway, you simply make a loop at the end of your mid section. Then tie several tippet, shock tippet, and fly combos, tying a loop at the end of the tippet. Then, if your shock tippet is badly frayed after several fish or you want to change flies, you can simply unloop the frayed combo and replace it with a fresh one—faster than tying the whole thing.

Some anglers carry several pretied tippet, shock tippet, and fly combos in their tackle bag, to quickly change when needed. One such angler is my friend Vince Maggio. Vince loves to use this loop to loop connection method to change his tippet and frayed tippets. Since the area he fishes has lots of snook and tarpon mixed with the redfish, he needs to fish with a shock tippet.

But Vince uses the smallest loops possible to make his interlocking connections. Just big enough to pass a fly through, he always says. This way he feels there is a better transfer of energy with no hinge during the turnover. And once the connection is made, then he advises that you pull it tight for a few seconds so that both loops set, like in a mold, taking a shape that will not easily loosen up.

Vince, who is very organized, preties many shock tippet and fly combos before a fishing trip and puts each one on its individual clear plastic bag. Fish, shrimp, and crab patterns are all well represented in his tackle bag. So if he needs to change in the middle of the action, he can do it very fast. And since Vince often fishes by himself, this works well for him. Actually, I have seen him change flies while a redfish was tailing in front of us and be back fishing in no time.

Personally, I have tried this method several times, in different ways, throughout the years, but it has not worked for me. First, the leader is not as clean. The loop to loop connections are bulkier than the plain knots, of course, and therefore more visible in clear water and more likely to pick up grass. So, in the final analysis, the method does work, and it's a valid alternative for those that have to use a shock tippet when red fishing, but it's just not for me. I guess I'd rather change by just cutting and retying, keeping a very clean leader with minimal knots in it, the old-fashioned way.

Final Thoughts

When it's all said and done, getting the best leader reminds me of getting the best apple pie. If bought from a good store is can be very good, but my wife, Marilyn's, made-from-scratch Pennsylvania apple pie is to die for, and there's simply no comparison once you know the difference. And just the same, once you know the difference, a good old-fashioned made-from-scratch leader, especially if it's tied for a specific condition, can't be beat . . . once you know the difference.

PART III

Catching Redfish on a Fly Rod

Chapter 12

Casting for Reds

Before we start all the technical stuff about fly casting, I want to share with you how I feel about fly casting after a lifetime in the sport:

With fly rod in hand and a hookless fly at the end of my leader, I begin to practice false-casting while watching the fly line slowly unroll in front of me. I watch it again, and again, until soon, other senses take over. It's not just the visual of the line in front of me anymore, for now I am conscious of the kick of the rod unloading the line behind me, the backcast. Then the process of false-casting becomes whole, becomes one; I can visualize it, as it should be. There is a rhythm now that just feels good. I'm in rhythm with my inner self, in rhythm with my soul—like standing in another dimension. Problems are forgotten, because there's no room for problems between a backcast and a forward cast. And I am no longer aware of the casting tool. Rod is no rod. Line is no line. There is just the constant movement of the fly line, back and forth, back and forth, back and forth. And once more, I've fallen into a spell, I've fallen in love.

Well, that's how it feels to me. And just as relaxing as my Tai-Chi practice.

One day, if you fish long enough, you'll go fishing, and realize that while you aren't catching many fish that day, you're having a great time just casting. Then, my friend, as far as I'm concerned, you are now a fly fisherman.

Becoming a Better Caster

But not only is the ritual of fly casting very enjoyable, it is also something that is absolutely necessary if you want to be a good angler, and especially if you want to sight-cast, which to me is the ultimate skill in saltwater fly fishing. And you can't buy your way out, either. Remember, you can travel to the best fishing destinations and hire the best guides, but when you get within 50 feet of the fish you're after, no one can help you: you're on your own. Casting then, to me, is the most important fly-fishing skill, especially if you're a beginner. The better and more accurate you cast, the more fish you'll take. Period.

This is very true when fishing with a guide. You see, a good guide is really fishing through his angler's hands. That is, he learns your skills and limitations and then chooses fishing spots and conditions that best match your casting skill level. For example, there may be a shoreline he didn't take you to that day, even though he feels it may have fish, because maybe that day conditions were such that you'd have to backcast to work that shoreline, and he knows that is your casting weakness. But had you been a better caster, able to backcast with fair accuracy, you would have fished there. And probably caught more fish that day.

Remember, guides don't gravitate to their profession because they want to become rich—they simply love guiding, fishing, and the outdoors. And the effort a good guide makes to learn the areas he fishes well enough not only to find fish, but to make the best and easiest presentation for each individual angler's skills, is monumental. And still, a guide does not mind the effort. What he does mind, and what frustrates him to no end, are anglers who simply do not want to take the time to learn how to cast well. I've always felt that even though you pay guides, you still should bring good casting skills. You owe your guide, and yourself, that much.

Also, among a group of fly fishers, casting is what separates you from other anglers. And by that, I don't mean just how good you are at it, but the way you do it, how you do it. You'll develop a style of your own. Other anglers can buy a fishing shirt like you have, or the same expensive rod model you fish, but your casting skills and style are yours—no one can copy that. And I find that so great.

Let me tell you a quick story. A few years back, I traveled to a fishing show to give a couple of clinics and

Here, I'm making a long cast to a school of reds pushing large wakes. PAT FORD

casting demonstrations. After I checked in, the show owner mentioned that two of my old friends were also there giving casting presentations: Flip Pallot and Joan Wulff. And if you want to say hello right now—the owner said—they are both outside working already.

I stepped out of the building to see over a hundred anglers, fly rods in hand, all over the place, some casting and some watching. I took a couple of seconds to look around, and then just smiled. Even at a good distance, Flip's powerful overhead casting style and Joan's precise, delicate casting were easy and obvious to see, even among a hundred or more anglers, many of them casting, others just holding one or two rods.

To say that each one of my friends had their own individual casting style would be a great understatement. No one could match their style, and no one will be able to match yours, either. So take casting lessons, practice, learn to cast well, and you'll be rewarded, in many ways, for the rest of your life. I guarantee it.

Skills Needed

The typical scenario when fishing redfish is a window of opportunity that usually appears well under 50 feet, often under 20 feet, requiring you to get the fly in motion, and then make an accurate cast. This is not always easy, and it certainly is not intuitive.

Getting the fly in motion, and making a short, fast, and accurate cast is difficult because you're casting more leader than fly line, and it's the fly line that has the weight to load the rod. So it's hard to feel any load on the rod and therefore, to form a loop or to get accuracy. And as you get more line in the air, casting gets progressively easier but accuracy is still difficult because in most cases, the redfish you see is moving as it looks for food, and your target is roughly ahead of the fish and not easy to pinpoint. Now add to this that of all the fish that anglers sight-fish in the flats (such as bonefish, tarpon, and snook), redfish probably require the most pinpoint accuracy. Often you need to have the fly pass right by a fish's lips. But don't despair. A redfish will often give you a second and even a third chance to make that cast—you won't often get that many chances from a nervous bonefish!

Now, while a short, fast cast is the quintessential redfish cast and the one we most often talk about and discuss, there are many other scenarios while fishing for redfish that require longer casts. A tailing redfish, being so visual, presents a very exciting target. But here, especially in clear water, seldom will you get a short cast. Most casts to tailing reds seem to be much further. And unlike the short, fast casting we discussed above, tailing fish generally require that you slow down a little, and then "read" the fish to determine where to cast the fly so that the red sees it. So with tailing fish, you usually have more time to make the cast, but have to cast longer, and often with a longer leader, even a lighter rod sometimes.

Schools of reds, generally found in deeper water, are usually moving, often fast, and pushing wakes, and since they are looking ahead, you seldom get a chance at them close to the skiff. So here is a situation where you may have to make a long cast fairly fast. The good news is that often you get a few shots at each school.

Also, when working a shoreline, especially at the lower stages of the tide, getting too close will spook fish. You'll have to keep the skiff 50 feet away or further from the edge of the water. On the other hand, this type of fishing does give you time, so concentrate on making a good accurate cast as close as you can from the edge. This is one of my favorite ways to fish reds and snook.

How to Cast

Now that you know what you need to do, I'll get a little technical. And while I don't believe you can learn to cast just from a book, any more than you can learn to swim from a book, I do think that if you have a good idea on what to do and why, it's going to help you.

So let's start with the short and fast type of casting scenario. Let's say that you're covering ground in a flat, either by being poled or by wading. The bottom is dark and visibility is only fair. So by the time you see a redfish, it's 30 feet away and approaching. The distance between you and the redfish is shrinking. There isn't much time before the red sees you and spooks. First, you need to get the fly in motion. Then, with a minimum of false casts, you must get enough line out of the tip to be able to make a short, fast cast. And then when you have the amount of line you need in the air, make an accurate cast in front of the red, so when you start to retrieve, it sees the fly moving away from him, trying to escape and takes it. Nothing to it.

THE FAST DRAW

The average beginner and even some intermediate casters who come to the redfish flats from another type of fly fishing other than sight-fishing, after spotting a red, will start waving the rod back and forth in a frantic series of false casts, usually with the rod held too high and while rocking the boat.

Now let's look at this scenario from the redfish's point of view. The fish is covering ground in a flat, looking for good *tapas* to eat. It probably noticed a big, dark object floating about 30 feet away, but since it does not seem to be moving fast, if at all, the fish continues to look for food, perhaps keeping an eye on the dark object, just in case. Then, all of a sudden, something in the dark object is moving back and forth furiously, and the dark object is now starting to rock back and forth, sending a series of loud wakes which the fish can easily feel. The redfish is scared—this doesn't sound good, so it either stops feeding and moves away from the dark object, or bolts away, pushing a big wake.

There's a better way of getting the line in motion without doing fast or abrupt movements and rocking the boat. This method is well known to good anglers. And I've always called it fast draw, because you have to draw your gun out with minimal movements but maximal speed. What makes this cast so challenging is that trying to false-cast a leader and a few feet of front taper fly line, both weighing very little, makes it difficult for you to feel the rod load. Yet with practice, and time on the water, you'll get to where you are fairly consistent in executing the cast.

To get ready for a fast draw, I usually like to stand with my feet at about a 45-degree angle. And being right-handed, that would mean with my left foot forward and my right foot behind. A left-hander would do the reverse, of course. Then, I strip as much fly line off the reel as I think I'll need considering the conditions. Your guide will help you here. Now the more line you have out of the tip of your rod, while holding the fly, the faster you'll be able to get a long cast out, because you have more weight out and will be ready to load the rod in one false cast. But more line is harder to manage, and it can drag on the water as the skiff moves, picking up more grass and potentially getting tangled on structure, like a mangrove shoot. So it's all a compromise, as usual.

I have found that for me, keeping the leader and approximately a rod's length of fly line out of the tip is an ideal amount for almost all conditions. So let's say I have a 10-foot leader and 10-feet of fly line—20 feet out of the rod tip. Then, holding the rod with my casting hand, and holding the fly by the bend of the hook, with my stripping hand, I'm ready. Now, when I see a fish close to me, I can make a quick backcast, and when I come forward, I can stretch the fly line and leader, sending the fly as far as 20 feet or so, if I need to, in almost no time at all.

To give you an idea of how fast this cast should be, I'll give you my own experience when I get to fish with an old friend and renowned captain for over forty years, Steve Huff. Having lived this situation requiring short, fast casts, not just for redfish, but also for snook, permit, tarpon, and many others species, Steve uses a method that tells the angler right where to put the fly. He does this with the clock system, where 1 o'clock is slightly to your right and 11 is slightly to your left. (More on this in chapter 14 on page 159).

Anyway, I'll be on the bow, rod in hand, looking for reds and snook with Steve poling in the Ten Thousand Island area of the Everglades. Then he'll spot a redfish at 11 o'clock, let's say. So I'll hear, "Turn it over at 11." That's it. When I hear that, I know I need to look for a fish very close at 11 o'clock. Since I know there's little time before the fish spooks, I'll start my fast draw, getting the cast in motion while desperately trying to locate the fish, so I can present the fly. I don't ask Steve any questions, since there's nothing else to say. He's already told me all I need to know.

In terms of the loop, generally, there is no loop because you are mostly casting leader. Notice Huff said to "turn it over," not meaning to throw a tight loop, but turn it over, roll it over, kind of a loopy cast. And since the cast is so simple, you don't have to do it fast and frantic where the fish may notice it, just go slow and smooth and you'll get there in a couple of seconds.

Also, keep in mind that the closer the redfish, or any other fish, is to you, the easier the fish can see the movement of your rod. So when very close, if possible, keep the rod at a lower angle, so it's less visible to the fish. But as the distance needed increases, the visibility of the rod is less important, so you're then better off to cast a bit more vertical if you want more distance.

THE SHORT AND MEDIUM FAST CASTS

Well, the fast draw is great for the quick, ultra short cast, where the red is close and ready to spook. But many casts are going to be in the short to medium distance range, say between 20 and 50 feet or so. These casts require that you still move quickly to get a fly out there, but perhaps more importantly, they require accuracy. So what to do?

Well, if you see a red in that short to medium range, you do the fast draw, making the quick but smooth backcast and forward cast where you have about 20 feet out, but instead of making a presentation, you simply continue false-casting and releasing line until you have just short of the amount you need, and when you come forward this time release a few feet and drop the fly in front of the fish. And it should take you only a few seconds.

THE LENGTH OF THE STOKE

Now, let me compare the length of the stroke during false-casting to another sport. When you see a third basemen throw to first base, you'll notice he has to make a long stroke with his arm to reach that far. But when the shortstop catches a grounder and makes a quick flick with his forearm to throw the ball a few feet to second base, to get his man, his stroke is very short—because the distance is much shorter.

Well, casting is just the same. You don't want to make long strokes when you only need to cast to a red 20 feet. With your 9-foot rod, that's just a relatively short stroke. So, remember, when you're false-casting, use short strokes for short casts. And as you carry more line in the air to make longer casts, increase the length of your stroke. Keep this in mind when you practice.

"FAST" DOESN'T NECESSARILY MEAN FAST

What I meant when I said that you had to make a "fast" cast before the opportunity disappeared is that you have to get the fly in front of a red quickly. But I did not mean that you have to move fast when you see the red or false-cast furiously. Making a quick or sudden movement when you see a red shifts the skiff abruptly. Even if it's not a big move, it still sends waves that spook fish. And moving your rod too fast won't help you feel the load of the line on your rod.

So don't move too fast, don't make abrupt movements, and start your casting at a medium speed, as fluid as you can, trying to feel the line's weight as it loads the rod to a bend. Stay loose. Don't put so much into it, and you'll get more out of it. And keep it compact; don't stretch your arms up in the air. You have a long rod, so you don't need it any longer. Just accelerate to a stop. And as soon as you have enough line out to feel it, try to produce a loop, the tighter the better (within reason). You'll find that making a good, fluid loop with a minimum of false casting and unnecessary moves is the way to get the fly on the water, fast. And yes, I know this is hard to do when you see a fish and are very excited. I get nervous and screw up too.

THE LONGER CAST

When you find redfish in conditions where you simply do not dare get any closer, you must be able to make long casts with ease. The advantage when casting from a distance is that generally the further the fish are from you, the more time you have to get a fly to it.

The only way to make long casts consistently is to carry a lot of line while false-casting. You see, the line will only advance while it's unrolling, and once it unrolls to the end, gravity claims it and it comes down. So if you false-cast 30 feet of line with a good loop and try shooting it far, it will shoot forward for as long as it's unrolling, but when the 30 feet has unrolled, it will then come down. Maybe you shot 10 in the process and with the 30 feet you held in the air, you got a 40-foot cast. Now let's say you can hold 50 feet in the air, which has more weight to drag loose running line from the deck, and takes much longer to unroll than the 30 feet did. Now you cast the 50 feet, and as it is unrolling, you can shoot the 30 feet that was lying on the deck, making a nice 80-foot cast. That's more like it. The angler who can carry more line in the air while false-casting, with a good controlled loop, is going to cast the furthest and exert the least effort.

This, of course, is with a regular weight-forward line. Shooting heads and super thin running lines will cast long distances while needing less line to false-cast in the air, but they lack the accuracy needed in the flats, and the ability to make a second cast without stripping in most of the line first. And the super thin running lines needed are nearly impossible to manage in actual sight-casting conditions. Forget heads for sight-casting.

Accuracy

Many anglers spend more time looking for that magic redfish fly pattern that will catch more fish than they do practicing their accuracy. Believe me, there is no magic fly. If you want to see magic, make a good accurate presentation to a redfish on your first attempt, and I'll show you magic.

A great part of accuracy is concentration. Most anglers don't concentrate when they're fishing. Ever seen a great dart shooter at a pub? He concentrates. And a golfer when putting, he concentrates too. Just the same, when you're casting to a fish, the motions of the casting should be second nature, done automatically, while you concentrate on two things: reading the fish to figure out where to present the fly so the fish will see it trying to escape, and, once

Classic conditions for short casts in open water often occur when casting to mudding rays. Here Flip poled me close to let me achieve good accuracy. BRAD MILLER

you have decided on the target—and it's often a moving target—then hitting the target accurately. It can be hard, but not as hard as it sounds in writing.

Where to cast is about reading the fish. Selecting the right spot to place the fly, the target—especially when a fish is moving—takes practice and lots of time in the water. You must compute how fast the fish is moving and how much time you have to allow for the fly to sink to the fish's level, among other factors. In other words, you have to read the fish. And that's a long subject that we'll tackle in coming chapters. Just know that selecting the right target is vital. Obviously, accuracy won't help you if you pick the wrong place to cast the fly and make a perfect cast.

Humans are programmed to try and hit what we're looking at, so even when you have selected the right spot in front of the redfish, if you are looking at the redfish, chances are you'll hit it right between the eyes and spook it. So you look at the red, you select the spot to cast, maybe even looking at the red from time to time, but, at the last moment, you should take your eyes off the fish, look at the spot you selected, and concentrate on that spot, the target, when making the cast. This is important.

Now, when you've got your line out, you're false-casting what you feel is the right amount of line, and you've selected a target, it's time to try and see the fly in the air to check if it's going in the right direction to hit the target. If conditions are such that you can't see the fly in the air, maybe the fly is too small or visibility is poor, then look at your fly line, and see if the loop is unrolling in the right direction. If not, then adjust the direction of your loops to the right or left as need be with your next false cast, so that it is going toward your target.

By the way, this is the reason clear lines, which can be deadly when used by a good angler but are difficult to see in the air, are so hard to cast accurately. That is why I usually like fishing clear lines with big flies that I can easily see in the air. That way I can be fairly accurate with them.

ACCURACY ON SHORT AND MEDIUM LENGTH CASTS

For that average redfish cast, I prefer to cast off the tip of the rod, making tight control strokes. I find long strokes less accurate. Also, smaller movements are more consistent, and you won't rock the boat, or canoe, when you're casting to that big redfish. It's about minimal movements, so don't move anything you don't have to and just keep it simple.

ACCURACY ON LONG CASTS

The trick for accuracy on long casts is to hold more line in the air and shoot less line. For example, if you need to reach a tailing redfish 60 feet away, you are more accurate if you can hold 50 feet of fly line in the air with a controlled loop, and then carefully shoot 10 more feet to drop the fly close to the fish. But if you false-cast 40 feet and then try to shoot 20 feet and land in front of the tailing fish, you'll be less accurate. The more line you can hold in the air, with good control, while false-casting and the less you shoot, the more accurate you'll be.

Imagine you see a redfish tailing 45 feet away, so you make a pretty good cast, but as the fly was on its way, the red moved to the left a couple of feet and continued feeding. So the fly landed just to the right of the red and two or three feet away. The red is still tailing. You have a second chance. Now if you strip in 20 feet, pick up the line and attempt to shoot line and land in front of the tailing red, your chances are slim. Shooting line is a good way to get maximum distance, but it's seldom accurate. On the other hand, if you had just stripped in 5 feet, picked up the rest of the line with just one false cast and shot 5 feet to drop the fly, your chances of a good presentation are much better. On long cast accuracy, carry more, shoot less—no doubt about this.

LEG POSITION

Being right-handed, I've always like casting with left foot forward and my right foot back. This way, much like when throwing a ball, I can easily move my hand back, or make adjustments as the target moves. This stance is also ideal for longer-distance casting. However, tournament casters have long known that if you are right-handed, for example, you cast more accurately with the right foot forward, and your left foot back. Reverse if you are left-handed of course.

Joan Wulff, who has won multiple tournaments and who wrote the book on accuracy, literally, has mentioned to me many times that you are more accurate to cast from the right foot if you are right-handed. And she recommends that you keep your rod hand in front of you for maximum accuracy.

Also, another friend of many years, with whom I share fly fishing, fly casting, and the love of jazz, is Steve Rajeff. Steve, head rod designer for Loomis Rods, has dominated the world of competition accuracy and distance casting for four decades, besides being a top angler. Also, Steve has perfect score record on every accuracy event in the ACA (American Casting Association). The following is advice Steve has told me many times, so I'm paraphrasing:

> Accuracy is a matter of two factors: direction and distance. For direction, have the right leg forward if you are right-handed and the weight also on the right leg. Remember, dart and basketball players put their right foot forward when they throw. This way you align foot, hand, and eye. And keep the casting hand in front of your shoulder. Then, I imagine or visualize a straight line in the water. Also, the backcast has to be straight and aligned with the front cast. To help judge distance, allow the leader to completely turn over, unfold, to get a glimpse of the fly hovering. Also, a false cast to one side and then the other of an intended target helps gain parallax. This can help judge distance. Then aim straight on the final cast.
>
> But for distance . . . it's a matter of experience. Time practicing. Fly casting for distance has similarities to throwing a ball. When throwing, there's weight transfer from back foot to the front, body rotation, chest, shoulder, elbow, forearm, and finally wrist, in that sequence. In long distance fly casting, these are the same, with the added challenge of keeping the hand travelling in a straight path. The trajectory of a fly cast is lower than for a long throw of a ball, but is a factor for optimum results.

THE CASTING ANGLE OF THE ROD

Fishing conditions sometimes dictate that we cast with the rod canted from a few degrees to completely horizontal. If I am casting to a shoreline with branches above the water, leaving a shadow, you bet I'm going to try and get my fly way back under that branch. A big snook or redfish may be hiding there ready to ambush prey or just enjoying the cooler water temperature the shade provides. That situation often requires that you make a side cast with the rod almost if not completely horizontal to the water. Also, when a redfish gets too close to the skiff before I see it, if the fish is still not spooked, instead of raising my rod and casting with a vertical rod position, I will more often cast with the rod horizontal so the fish does

Angler Corbett Davis making a tight and low riding loop to cut through a strong wind. If I recall, we fished all day with that strong wind. We took reds, but we had to work for them.

not see it. But casting with the rod canted that much also reduces your accuracy because you lose alignment with your eye. Yet it's a compromise I'm willing to take to remain inconspicuous.

However, even when making mid to long casts, I still find that I don't like casting completely vertical, with the line and fly flying directly over my head, so I mostly cast with my rod canted a few degrees or maybe as much as 60 degree or so. This is just my own habit, I guess.

ONE LAST TIP ON ACCURACY

Jerry Siem, head rod designer for Sage Rods, is a top caster and angler and a personal friend from whom I've learned a lot about rod designs and casting. A few years ago, we were teaching at the Florida Keys School, and during one of the breaks, he gave me this tip on accuracy, which I now use frequently, especially in low or difficult light conditions. What Jerry does to gain more accuracy in some conditions is tilt the rod to the side when casting to the point where he can place the loops against a background that makes them more visible, like a dark portion of water or the dark foliage of mangrove trees. And when he can see the loops better, he can also better judge distance in relation to his target. This trick has worked well for me in the backcountry, where I not only need accuracy for sight-casting, but also to fish shorelines. Thanks, Jerry.

Different Types of Casting

Imagine you're joking with your friends while fishing the flats, then one of you sees a redfish coming into range. Still joking, you make a couple of false casts and send the line the fish's way, and miss, lining the fish. This happens all the time from lack of focus. If you want to get good at fishing, you'll find that there's a time to joke around or have lunch, which I love to do, and a time to concentrate, be aware, and focus. I think anglers miss more fish because they're not really paying attention than any other factor in the equation.

When you see a fish, concentrate and forget everything else. Try to read the fish's movement, how fast it's coming at you, where it is in the water column, the position of your guide behind you. And when you do select an area or spot to cast in front of the red, pick a small spot, a spot within a spot. Then just focus on the fly in the air and the spot, and try to put the fly in that spot. Don't take this lightly—someone could write a whole book on this subject as it applies to sight-casting. Besides, those moments of concentration, just you and the fish, are precious, often unforgettable.

CASTING IN THE WIND

Flip Pallot has a saying that I really like, because while simple, it is so true: "The wind is your friend." I'll often hear him say it to a class, when he and I are teaching a fly-fishing school, and it always brings laughter. But since we've heard this before, we just wait. Then, when the laughter subsides, Flip will repeat the statement, and this time let them know that he is serious, not joking. And that this is a statement that every fly fisherman, especially those who love sight-casting, should fully understand. Now the whole class is listening.

Ask a good flats angler what he dislikes the most, and it's never wind—it's visibility, or lack thereof. Usually, as long as you can see, wind is not a problem, and often it's an advantage. You see, on windy days, fish cannot see you or the skiff as well, and there's more noise, more wave action, and just a lot more to distract the fish, so almost always, you can approach much closer on windy days. Situations that on a calm day would have required a 60-foot cast or further, on a windy day may only require a simple 30-foot cast. Which, with a shorter leader and a short head fly line like a redfish taper, is an easy cast.

In the many trips I've hosted over the years, I've seen decent casters in calm weather make drastic changes in their good casting style when faced with a stiff wind, and start making casting strokes that wouldn't have worked even on a flat, calm day. So first of all, even on fairly strong winds, if you make a good tight loop, it has a great chance to cut through that wind. Still, there are other things you can do.

The lower you cast, the less wind affects you, so the easier it is for the loop to unroll and make a presentation. If you raise your hand way up on a strong wind, as I have seen anglers do when attempting to make a powerful cast, the wind will get you. So stay low. And of course, a tighter loop will better cut the winds, catching less of them. So, in the wind, stay calm, don't overpower, and just try to make a smooth tight loop off the tip of the rod, fairly low or close to the water. Remember, if you are home and it's very windy, it's time for you to practice your casting. And I don't mean downwind—wind blowing from your casting arm.

Few anglers want to cast from the opposite side of their casting arm. They usually feel it's too hard and not as much fun, so they never practice that cast. And of course, they never get better. Most anglers are terrible at it. It's like being a tennis player but only concentrating on your forehand, never learning the backhand. Yet, on a day sight-casting or working a shoreline, many of the opportunities will require that you cast from the opposite side of your casting arm. It's an everyday occurrence. And in the field is not the time to practice.

When the wind is blowing against you casting arm, but it's just a mild breeze, you can cast with the rod low and horizontal to the water to get the line, leader, and fly further away from you and still make the cast from your preferred side. However, when the wind is strong, it blows the fly line, leader, and fly against you as you false-cast, and this, besides ruining your presentation, can get you "hooked." In these conditions, you need to cast with the fly line, leader, and fly on the opposite side of your casting arm. If you're right-handed, then the cast has to occur on your left side. And this can be accomplished

Author using a backcast to cast from the opposite side of the casting arm. Use a backcast when the wind is blowing from your casting arm side or when there are obstructions on that side. PAT FORD

by several casting methods: backcasting, overhead casting, or cross-casting.

BACKCASTING

I think this is by far the most common cast anglers use when the wind is blowing against the casting arm. Its advantage is that since you already know how to make a backcast, if you turn your body toward your left (if you are right-handed) and twist your wrist, you can make your backcast go forward. It's a bit awkward, but it works. And, using a longer stroke and a good hard stop, you can make a real long cast this way. However, it can be tiring to cast for prolonged periods, and you are not facing the target very well, so it's harder to be accurate.

OVERHEAD CASTING

This cast is accomplished by casting with your arm in the regular position, but with the rod's upper third or so canted over your left shoulder. Now the fly line, leader, and fly are being false-cast downwind. It works well. The disadvantage for me is that you must make this cast with your arm higher than I like, and the fly line travels very high above water, where a fish, especially in shallow water, is likely to see it. For me, it does not make for the best presentation—the ideal presentation being a low cast.

CROSS-CASTING

Not many saltwater anglers use the cross-cast, but I think it's a good tool in the right conditions. If you're right-handed, just move your right hand across your body so that it's now aligned with your left shoulder and left eye. Now the fly line, leader, and fly are being false-cast on your left side, or downwind.

The advantages of cross-casting are that you're facing the target naturally for more accuracy, unlike backcasting, and that you can still make a low cast presentation, unlike the overhead cast.

The disadvantage is that having to bring your hand across your body leaves you less arm movement than the other two alternatives. So cross-casting is good for short and medium distances. But remember, a lot of red fishing is short casts.

Personally, I use the backcast most of the time, but if the cast is short, say 30 feet or less, I often use the cross-cast. Now, what I think you should do is try and learn all of these casts for a short time. Soon you'll find one, or a couple, that suit you. Then, incorporate that cast into your practice repertoire, and as always, make sure that you make a good stop at the end of every cast. You do have a casting repertoire, right?

Casting Heavy Flies

The tightest loops you'll ever see are at fly-fishing shows. Why? Because most demonstrations are done without the weight and bulk of a fly. So it's easy to build up speed, since you're not dragging anything. Everyone looks good! Unfortunately, you need a fly to catch fish. Which, by the way, is why you should practice casting with a real fly—hook cut at the bend so you don't snag on grass.

The heavier and bulkier the fly is, the harder it is to build up speed, so the harder it is to cast. And even when you're able to cast the big fly, you'll notice that when you do get a tight loop going, it "kicks" at the end of every cast. The problem is that the big fly cannot make such a tight turnaround smoothly at the end of each cast. The heavier the fly, the bigger the loop you should use to false-cast; the smaller the fly, the tighter the loop you can use. I don't mean giant loops, I just recommend that you open the loop a bit, as needed. Also, don't feel that you must cast needle-nose loops day in day out. Fishing a midsize loop is comfortable and efficient, except in the windiest conditions or when you need pinpoint accuracy with small flies. It's all relative.

And even if the fly is not too big, but you need to add a shock tippet, say for snook or tarpon, that too adds to the weight you have to cast and turn over. So here too is a situation where a bit wider loop will serve you well.

Calling a fly heavy is relative to the size of the fly line you use. A size 2 redfish fly, lightly weighted, is not too heavy to cast with tight loops using an 8-weight fly line, but with a 6-weight, I'd probably cast a wider loop. And with a 10-weight line, you wouldn't even know the fly was there. So for the purpose of casting, a fly's weight is only heavy or light in relation to the size of the fly line used.

RIGHT-HANDED WITH A LEFT MASTER EYE

The dominant or master eye is usually, but not always, on the same size as the master hand. I'm not that lucky. I am right-handed with a left master eye. The reason I mention this is that for the purpose of accuracy, this situation may cause a problem in aligning. And while I've fished and sight-cast all my life, and won a few accuracy contests with fly, spin, and revolving spools, still I feel I should talk about this.

Seeking some help, again I turned to Steve Rajeff, who has won more accuracy titles in the last forty years than anyone I know. I'll paraphrase what Steve told me: "For right-handed casters with left master eyes, or vice versa, your choice is to use parallax. That is, learn through practice where that straight line is, so you can stay aligned. Which is how you get accuracy."

So it may be a little harder for casters like me to get accuracy, but not much really. And when casting from the opposite side of our bodies, like cross-casting or backcasting, we are then casting from our master eye side, and the rest of the anglers are not!

WHEN YOU MISS

So you spotted a couple of reds in a foot of water, about 40 feet away. You made some false casts, sent a nice loop their way, and landed about 5 feet too far to the left. The fish have not spooked; they don't even seem aware of you, so you have a second chance. How do you handle this situation?

If you're excited, and I can understand that, you may rush to make a second cast, but in that rush, you rip the line off the water, making a loud noise and hurting your timing when the line breaks off the surface of the water. We've all done this at one time or another. By the way, the redfish left. Or you may decide to strip line in, false-cast, and shoot line their way. Well, this is better, but it's still not a good idea because, as mentioned earlier, shooting lots of line is not the best way to get accuracy. And doing an extra false cast while a couple of reds are sitting only 40 feet away is probably not helpful.

A better, simpler, and faster way to get to those fish, quietly, is to slowly pick up the whole line, and try dropping it 5 feet to the right. You have the range, all you needed was to move the fly a bit to the right. In other

Casting at dusk, when there's not enough light to see the fly line, an angler needs to cast by the feel of the fly line loading the rod. It's harder and it takes practice, but it's worth it. Here angler Dan De Aguiar makes it look easy.

words, if you shoot line, you can be too long or too short. But if you pick up 40 feet of line to land 40 feet to the right, you aren't going to miss the range.

So how to pick up that line quietly? Slowly lift the tip of the rod, higher and higher, and watch the fly line lift off the water until only a few feet of fly line, leader, and fly remain in the water.

Now without stopping, in a fluid motion, start your backcast, helping yourself with a smooth double haul. And at the end of the your backcast make sure you make a definite stop.

Now, because most of the line was out of the water, pulling just a few feet of front taper fly line and leader off the water is not going to make any noise, even on a calm day. So the reds will not know you are planning a comeback.

Now false-cast once to get control and aim, but make sure you aren't casting over the heads of the reds. Then drop it in place. The whole procedure should take you a couple of seconds, even though you should have done this in what looks like slow motion. Be prepared for a hookup.

PRACTICE, PRACTICE, PRACTICE

If possible, select a spot that has enough room not just to make a long cast one way, but to be able to cast upwind, across wind, and downwind. For practice a 7- or 8-weight is great, but a 6- or 9-weight is also good. Use a floating line and a leader about the length of the rod. If you're a beginner, you can cast with a leader and no fly until you reach the point that you're making loops with little difficulty. Then, tie a fly on. Ideally, the fly should be about the size you use for reds, say a size 2 hook or so. Get a brightly colored unweighted fly with some bulk so it's not too easy. And then cut the hook at the bend so it does not snag on the grass.

Using a fly is the only way to be realistic. This way, when you are able to make good control loops in practice, with a fly on, you'll see little difference when you go fishing. So the practice will help. I've seen anglers cast well without a fly, then go fishing and find that with a little wind and a fly on, they can't get the fly out of the boat. Also, by using a fly during practice, you see if the leader you tied or bought is transferring enough energy to turn the fly over. You want to find this out while practicing, not on the day you get to go fishing. Also, bring the cap or hat you fish with and a good pair of polarized glasses, so you can see the fly line in the air and inspect your loops, but also as a safety device in case the fly hits you.

It will also help if eventually you bring a tape measure to the practice area, so that you get familiar with what 30 feet or 60 feet is really like. From time to time, I'll get a student call me for lessons and tell me over the phone that he (it's seldom a lady) can cast 80 feet fine, but just can't seem to reach 100 feet. Almost invariably we'll get together, and his 80 feet is a 60- to 65-foot cast that is landing in a pile. So bring the tape measure, which, like scales, have no opinions. And for a practice target get a 2-foot stick or a wooden redfish, or something that you can identify as having a tail on one side and a mouth on the other. I don't want you to get a round target, because I don't want you to get used to hitting what you see, but instead presenting a fly a few feet in front.

The beginner can practice without a fly until he develops a consistent loop, which shouldn't take long. But once the angler has a good loop, you need to vary your exercises during your practice. Don't just practice at 40 feet. And whatever you do, don't practice trying to make the longest cast. Here are a few things to practice:

Start by making a good control loop at 20, 30, 40, and then 50 feet. Then practice the fast draw. Start with the fly in your hand, the leader and a rod length of fly line out of the tip of the rod, then make a backcast and try stretching the 20 feet of line with some accuracy. Then try doing another false cast and hitting something with your fly at 30 feet. Then at 40 feet.

As you get better, start thinking about casting from the opposite side of your casting hand. Try the backcast and the overhead cast, and see which works better for you.

Eventually, when you have pretty good control of your loops, you may want to start increasing distance. Sometimes it's good to be able to cast the whole line or so. To do this, start false-casting as much line in the air as you can, with a good control loop. Say when you start, you can false-cast 45 feet. Mark your line at the place where your hand is holding the line with a black marker. Then, as you keep practicing, you'll hold 50 feet of line, then 55 feet of line. The markers keep creeping further and further, and as time goes by, it will get harder to add a foot or two. But, in the meantime, if you can hold 60 feet in the air with a good loop, you can shoot lots of line and reach way over 80 feet.

Another way to practice, if you have the room, is what I called in my bonefish book "Casting around the Clock." You stand with your fly rod ready to cast in a field with lots of room all around you. Face any direction you like, and we'll call it 12 o'clock. Now try casting 30, 40, and 50 feet, if you can do them. Fine. Now face 2 o'clock, and do the same, then 4 o'clock, then 6 o'clock, then 8 o'clock and so on. What will happen is that you'll be forced to cast with the wind, sideways to the wind, into the wind, and with the wind on your casting arm. When you can do that consistently, you'll have no problems catching reds, or any other fish in the flats.

Also, do try to find a good instructor, and take lessons. Someone has to oversee you to correct bad habits. You only need a few lessons spread out over lots of practice. And as far as the amount of practice you should do, I have a motto: "Practice very little, but practice very often." So don't try to improve quickly by practicing many hours in one day. Sessions of 20 to 30 minutes, in which you concentrate while practicing, are the best way.

And through all this, don't get frustrated; try to have fun and enjoy it. And by all means, don't be too hard on yourself. Give yourself room to make mistakes because that's how we all learn.

Finally, the day you go fishing, maybe at the dock that morning before you get in the skiff, or when you just stopped to start poling the flat, if you can, it's always a good idea to "warm up," by making a few casts. You don't need many casts, just a couple of minutes can make a difference.

And most of all, have fun.

Chapter 13

Getting Ready to Go Fishing

Packing one's gear to get ready for a fishing trip is the art of bringing everything that's essential and leaving all the "what ifs" that you don't need at home. You'll find that the more you learn, the less you'll pack to bring with you.

How long this packing will take depends on how organized you are and how often you go fishing. Just don't leave everything until the evening before the trip. It takes time to get tackle together, select flies, maybe rig a couple of leaders, pack a lunch and water, and much more.

The first thing I do is select what fly rods I am going to bring. If you have one 8-weight, then of course that's it. But if you have several, then you need to make a decision on what rods, lines, leaders, and flies to bring and how they should be rigged. And to do that, you need to know the area you're going to fish, the tides, and the weather.

If I'm fishing with a guide, I'll call him the night before and find out how the fishing has been, and what conditions he feels we'll face the next day. I've always found a good guide more than willing to give his customers all the information and advice they need. After all, he wants you to have a successful day on the water. If I am fishing with a friend or my son without a guide, then I'll check weather and decide which flats and at what stage of the tide I'll be fishing them.

So let's say I'm fishing with a group, and we plan to fish early tomorrow morning on a low incoming tide. We hope there will be tailing reds in much less than a foot of water, as the water level slowly rises. Then by late morning, when the water level at the first flat gets too high to see tailing or cruising fish, we'll move to another flat that's well known for mudding redfish or reds following mudding stingrays. Water level will be high but we should still be able to see a mud or even the actual redfish as they swim around the ray.

If I only had my 8-weight, I'd rig it with a 10- or 12-foot leader and a lightly weighted fly, such as a small crab or shrimp pattern, or an unweighted fly to fish the tailing fish early in the morning. By midmorning, as the tide rises, there will be less tailing activity, and the targets will be mostly cruising reds. Then I may switch to a larger fly, with a bit more weight since the water is now deeper. By early afternoon, when I'll be trying my luck at the mudding fish or rays, I may still fish it with that mid-weighted fly. With two rods, I'd rig the lighter one, say a 6- or 7-weight with a 12-foot leader and the light fly. And I'll rig the heavier rod, say an 8- or 9-weight, with a weighted fly, like a shrimp pattern or a Clouser. So I'll have two rods ready.

Now that the rod, or rods, are rigged with a fly, let's get them ready to put away. I'll strip enough line off the reel so the fly line clears the tip-top, then bring the leader around the reel and back up the guides, probably the second or third guide from the bottom, and hook the fly on the guide—if it's one of the stripper or bridge guides, bring the hook around the bridge, not the actual ring. This way the butt section of the leader, just a few inches out of the tip of the rod, will remained straight, avoiding the kink that occurs when the heavy butt section makes that sharp turn around the tip-top. My fly line may have a mild kink, but it's easier to get rid of this by straightening the fly line than to have the kink on the butt section, where it'll never go away. This exercise is important because if my butt section stays in the reel, I'll have to stretch it out once in the skiff, and that's one more thing to do. But if it sleeps all night nice and straight, it's going to turn over much better at the end of a cast. It's the little things.

If I can't make up my mind what fly to use, or my guide told me that he'll figure it out once he stops the boat, then I'll rig the rods with the full leader, just as I've told you, but when I reach the right guide, not having a hook, I'll secure it by just making an overhand knot with the end of the tippet. This way, when the guide suggests the fly he wants me to use, all I have to do is pull the tippet lightly off the guide, and tie the fly. Everything is ready to fish.

Finally, I never show up with my rods in the aluminum tube. If you did that, your friends, and mostly your guide, would hate it, and so would I if you were fishing with me. Always be ready to slide your rods, rigged, in the rod racks.

Now I probably won't forget my rod and reel, but there's so much other gear to bring that it's not hard to forget an item or two. And leaving one item, say a fly box or polarized glasses, can ruin a trip. So for many years now, I've kept several fishing travel lists in my Mac. When packing, I'll print out the appropriate list and work from it. I have one list for a day's fishing locally, that is South Florida; one for a week's fishing trip, whether the Bahamas or Louisiana for those big reds; one for trout fishing; one for fishing the Northeast; and so on. And while I can hear a few of you laughing, you should know that since doing these lists, I seldom, if ever, forget an item. And as I get new ideas, I update my lists.

On a typical day, with list in hand, I'll be carrying at least two fly boxes, with at least a couple dozen flies in each. One box may have surface or close-to-surface flies, such as poppers, foam head Hot Lips, unweighted Seaducers, and fish patterns. The other box would have weighted flies such as crabs, shrimp, and larger fish patterns, and some heavily weighted flies such as larger shrimp patterns, Clousers, and such. Occasionally I may also have a fly box with larger flies for tarpon, sharks, jacks, and other big fish. This way it will take me little time to find the fly box I need. And once the box is opened, I can see all the flies at a glance.

I also take a leader wallet or some other container to carry leader material, probably spools of 40-, 30-, 20-,16-, and 12-pound-test, or a few knotless leaders in 9 and 12 feet, with the desired tippet strength—or both.

I apply a liberal amount of sunscreen, usually indoors. I find, especially in hot weather, that is more efficient to apply sunscreen before you step outdoors and start to perspire. Of course, I often forget and apply it while we are running in the skiff.

Fly line dressing and applicator to dress my lines during the day are important. So is bug repellent, if needed. And I take sun gloves, which I use sometimes instead of using sunscreen on the top of my hands, and other times I use to tie leaders. A tape measure will be useful for fish and sometimes while constructing a leader to help me measure leader sections. Also, I carry a small Moleskine notepad and pencil to take notes and make observations. This practice has being quite useful, not only to write down information for articles and books, but as a journal of the trip. It's simply amazing how much we forget, often in a few hours, let alone in days or weeks.

And I always bring cameras—either a case with two full frame interchangeable lens cameras, or a large sensor point and shoot. Whatever you choose, bring something to record the fish you catch or something fun on the trip. Just keep in mind that a wide angle, even an ultra wide angle zoom, is useful in the close quarters of a skiff or canoe. If you're in an area where you are going to wade for reds, then bring your wading shoes, and a small belt pack that will fit a small box of flies, clippers, a couple of spools of tippet, forceps to remove hooks, and not much more.

Bring plenty of water on every trip. And of course, I never forget lunch—never have, never will. And I always bring rain gear.

On me, I usually have my hat, polarized sunglasses, a bandana or face mask to protect my face, maybe a hook file, and a pair of pliers or scissor forceps on my waist. Then, I'm ready.

Finally, I bring a tackle bag. For this, I advise you to lay on a table all the items I mentioned above, and see how little room they really take. My present tackle bag, an old Mangrove bag, fits in the hatch of any skiff, holds all the items mentioned above and a nice size DSLR camera, easily—soon, I'll only be using one of the small, mirror-less cameras. Don't buy a giant bag. It shouldn't be any bigger than 45 linear inches—preferably smaller.

Now, in the morning, when I leave home to drive or walk to the dock, I only have a tackle bag over my shoulder, which needs no hands, rods in one hand, and a free hand to open doors and move about as I head for the dock.

Arriving at the Dock

Imagine now it's early in the morning when you arrive at the dock. And since this is usually the best time to fish, the sooner you get going the better. You can talk on the way. So you put the lunch in the cooler, slip the rigged rods on the rod holder, drop the tackle bag on the skiff's floor or inside one of the hatches, and you are gone. This is vital. I've seen anglers get to the dock, which required several trips to the car to bring all the tackle, and then start constructing a leader. That's a waste of prime time. But I know you won't be doing that from now on.

After a thirty-minute or so drive, the skiff is finally stopped, and your guide or friend is getting ready to climb on the poling platform. I know you've been waiting for this moment.

Arriving at the dock at dawn, this angler has his rod rigged and ready. All the tackle is stacked up in front of the center console ready to be put away. These anglers will be on their way in minutes, and that's the way it should be. MARKUS HAUGG

Selecting a Fly

We've already discussed fly selection, so by now either you or your guide has selected a fly, and it's tied to your tippet. But the fly is not ready to be fished, and you probably don't have much of an idea what the fly will do in the water. So here is the rule that I go by: first, wet the fly, then test the fly.

Most flies, especially marabou flies and flies that are heavily dressed, need to be thoroughly soaked to really "breathe" or realistically swim in the water. So plop the fly in the water, let it sink a bit, and give it a couple of sharp jerks, so you get all the air out of it. Then, bring it back and squeeze it between your thumb and index finger to get water and air out. For a bulky fly with lots of material, you may need to repeat the procedure twice to get every hair in the wings wet. But now the fly will work as it was supposed to work from the first cast you make. It will swim and undulate in the water looking lively.

Now that the fly is wet and ready to fish, you may want to test it, especially if it's a weighted fly. Take the fly and plop it in front of you and watch it sink. Get a mental picture of how fast it sinks, or how long it takes to sink to the bottom. This way, when you see that big red in 2 feet of water with the tested fly, you have a pretty good feel of how long to wait before the fly is at the redfish's level or below. Then, you can start your retrieve. It can make a big difference. Be one with the fly you are fishing.

Straightening Your Leader

Well, if you rigged the night before as I suggested, your leader should be pretty straight. If you didn't, then take the time to straighten is by stretching it, starting from the butt section all the way down to your tippet.

Warm Up

Now this is just a suggestion, but usually at this point, and before I get into line management, I like to cast. Think about this. No one in any other sport would start a match or even a practice session without warming up. You have been working all week, maybe in the office, and probably have not had a chance to pick up your rod much, and you got up this morning extra early to go fishing. Now do you think you're going to stand in front of the skiff for a while until you see a fish to cast, and then make a perfect presentation? Probably not.

What I like to do at this point is make a few warm-up casts, from about 20 feet to 50 feet or so. Then, maybe I'll make a long cast shooting whatever line I've stripped off the reel. This should take two minutes, that's all. And if I'm fishing with a guide, I'll let him know ahead of time that I want to make a couple of warm-up casts before getting on with the hunt. This practice has worked well for me throughout the years, even though I cast at home all the time. I encourage you to do the same.

Line Management

The secret to good line management is to strip all the fly line you need for the occasion, and no more. Most anglers, especially after they learn to cast far, will strip lots more line than they need, and so their line is often tangled.

The main factors that will dictate how much line to strip off the reel are visibility and water quality. And in the redfish's world, both factors are likely to change constantly throughout the day, as you change locations, as it gets cloudy or sunny, as the tide goes up or down, and so on. So you should constantly monitor the amount of line needed.

On a bright, clear day, with good visibility or fairly low water, you'll see fish much further, so it's not unusual to have enough line out to make a 60-foot cast or longer. But on an overcast day, or a windy day with fairly murky, off-color water, most of the casts are going to be extra short, so you will not see a fish until it's fairly close. In that case, why strip all your line? Why not strip only what's needed and avoid more tangles and having to clear too much line when a large fish is hooked?

Actually, on a day with low visibility, when I expect I won't see the fish until they're much less than 20 feet from me, I may not strip any line and just fish with a rod's length of fly line and leader. This way, I can make a fast, short cast, with no chance of tangles. And by the way, these conditions are common in the Everglades and up in the Louisiana marshes too.

An exception to the above is when you're fishing in low-visibility conditions, where you can only see fish say to 30 feet, but the guide, more experienced and standing much higher off the water, tells you he can see to 50 feet, and advises you to strip that amount of line. Now when he sees a fish you cannot see, he'll guide you as to angle on the clock and distance, so you can make a fairly accurate cast. This is fine. I've landed many fish I did not see, guided by the angler or guide poling.

STRAIGHTEN THE FLY LINE

Now that you have the right amount of line out for the present conditions, you need to straighten the fly line. A fly line casts best when perfectly straight—with no memory coils from living in the reel. Also, you'll find that a straight fly line tangles less when lying flat on a deck, free of coils, partly because it's less likely to be caught by the wind. So take the time to straighten all the fly line you cast. And if you reel in and run for an hour to another hot spot, some lines, in some conditions, will gain some memory again. I would advise you to take the few seconds again and straighten the fly line and leader.

PILE IT UP RIGHT

In order for the fly line to come off the deck smoothly and with no tangles, either when you shoot line or when a fish is taking line from your hand, the fly line needs to be piled so that the back of the line is on the bottom and the front of the line is on top of the pile.

The easiest way to do this is simply to cast the line out and strip it in. Now the front of the fly line is on top of the pile. This is important, because otherwise the line will tangle as it tries to come off the pile from the bottom.

As you fish throughout the day, the fly line pile will need to be constantly watched and managed, arranged and rearranged, moved to one side of the boat, and later to another. The wind and the movement of the boat are constantly moving that line a bit. So I always make it a habit to repile the line every so often, even if it looks right. I make a cast and stack again. Often, the line was tangled. Go figure.

And whatever you do to move the line around, do *not* push it away or to the side with your shoe. That will twist the line so that it's difficult to straighten just right again. Bend down and pick it up, or restack it in another place.

WHERE TO PILE THE LINE?

If the wind isn't too strong, I'll pile my fly line on the front deck with me. When it gets windier, then I'll strip it directly behind me, down in the cockpit, where the wind can't catch it. If too windy to control, occasionally, I let it run between my legs and into the cockpit.

If really windy, I'll use a stripping mat to help me hold the fly line as explained in chapter 9 on page 112. If it gets even windier, I go home.

The Old Fast Draw

Now with the fly line piled correctly, all you have to do is hold the rod with your casting hand, the fly with your stripping hand, and let out of the rod tip a rod length of fly line and leader—you know, the old fast draw we talked about on page 138.

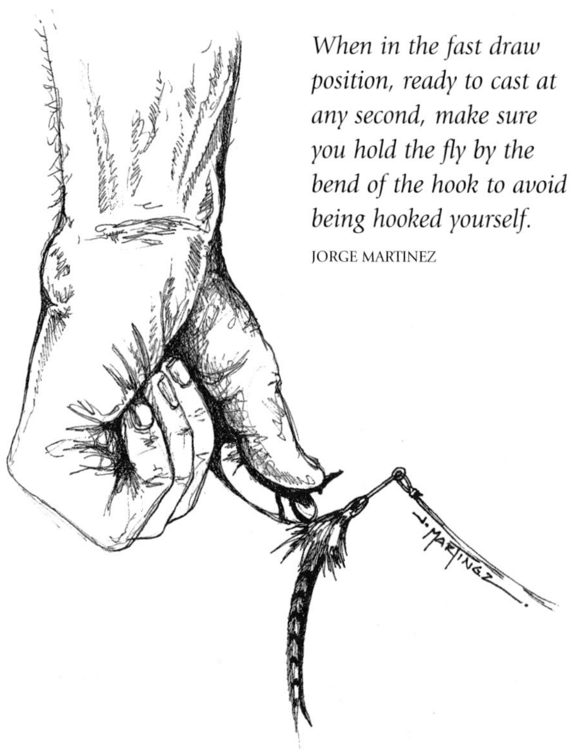

When in the fast draw position, ready to cast at any second, make sure you hold the fly by the bend of the hook to avoid being hooked yourself.
JORGE MARTINEZ

Just make sure that as the skiff moves forward covering ground, the big loop of fly line and leader is not so long that it drags on the water. If it is, sooner or later, it will catch floating grass and other debris, and you won't be ready to cast then. Worse yet, it could catch on one of the many mangrove shoots or other vegetation in your area and then the line will pull on the fly in your hand, maybe snagging the point in your finger and pulling. This is not good, believe me. It's one reason why you should always hold the fly by the bend of the hook, or by the wing of the fly depending on the pattern. It's also why you should never hold the tippet a few inches above the fly, as I see in many magazine photos. Please be aware of this.

Rod Position

I usually like to hold my rod on the downwind side. That way, the fly line and leader blows away from the boat; besides, it takes less effort to hold the rod downwind. Some guides like to have you hold the rod straight forward, at what would be the 12 o'clock position, so the rod is not distracting as he looks for fish. This may be fine, but you have to watch out that the line and leader loop does not get under the skiff or tangle on the front eye of the skiff. Your choice.

Well, now we're getting ready to start looking for redfish.

Chapter 14

The Hunt for Reds

Hunting for redfish, or any other fish in the flats, requires that you know how to look for them and what to look for. Looking for reds, in most situations, is an exercise in moving your head as you constantly scanning the area. Your eyes will be darting all around. And depending on light and visibility conditions, you may be looking for fish on the surface or through the surface.

Early in the morning, with the sun low in the horizon, your polarized glasses can't help you much to penetrate the water. So the hunt is usually done by looking at the surface of the water, searching for wakes or tailing fish, which you can easily see even with some glare on the water. But as the sun gets higher, your polarized lenses can start to help you see in the water, often all the way to the bottom. Now, you transition into looking past the surface and through the water, preferably with the sun behind you. So in these conditions, try to look "through the water," not "at the water."

Top fly fisher Sandy Moret has a good way to explain this to beginners at our school in the Florida Keys: "Looking through the water, past the surface, is like looking at a store window. You can look at the reflection of yourself in the glass, or you can look past it, and through the glass at the items in the store." I've hear him say that to countless students throughout the years, and seen how easily they soon grasped the concept.

For beginners, who have difficulty seeing fish, Captain Dave Denkert often has them pick a window of little or no glare, and only look for redfish there, while he looks for them everywhere. This way he finds that the anglers, being able to see the bottom and perhaps see rays and other miscellaneous small fish, are more encouraged and keep their concentration the whole day. It really works.

Often, while trying to see through the water with polarized glasses, you'll find that glare is still getting in the way. This is probably because the direction you are looking and the sun's position are not ideal. But if you tilt your head right or left to get the best polar effect for the time of day and direction you are facing, you'll often eliminate all or part of the glare that was bothering you. I find this really helps me. Anyway, in essence, when looking through the water, you are focusing on the bottom until you see a fish.

Now, let's discuss "what to look for."

When looking for tailing fish, sometimes you may find them tailing so hard that you can see the whole tail, often even the wrist of the tail, waving frantically as a red searches for food on the bottom. In those conditions, everyone in the skiff can see the fish, even at a long distance. But other times, redfish may be moving slowly or standing still in deeper water, often showing only half an inch or less of tail sticking out of the water. Then they can be difficult to see, and you need to concentrate hard.

Still, seeing that little portion of tail may not be enough, especially if the fish isn't moving or is moving slow. Because now you need to look closely at the triangle of tail that sticks out of the water, and try to determine what direction the fish is facing. That's right, you need to know whether to cast right or left of the little triangle, because a red won't eat from the wrong side. Again, time on the water gaining experience is the only answer here.

Sighting a cruising redfish or a pod of them can often be easy. Maybe you can see the whole fish, or just the bronze-colored backs, and you put a fly 2 feet in front and hook up. That's great. But other times, in deeper flats, in low visibility situations, or when the reds are not moving much, they can be tough to see. Then, it's mostly about subtleties. In those situations, you'll be looking for just a movement of the body, maybe the actual shadow of the fish on a light bottom, or just a glimpse of a blue tail. Or it can be a shape or color that does not match the environment, or the formation of the bottom. You notice the odd difference, you look hard, and all of a sudden,

Sometimes, as in this case, seeing redfish tailing and finning is easy—and what a beautiful and exciting sight it is—but other times it takes a keen eye and good concentration to spot them. SCOTT SOMMERLATTE

you've found the fish. And when you do, it's such a special moment.

Another exciting way to find redfish is by spotting them while they're cruising right under the surface, pushing a wake. A wake can be traveling slow, but more often it's at a medium or fast speed. Maybe it's a single fish or several fish, even a school of a hundred fish. You'll find that a knowledgeable angler or guide can often spot a school of reds pushing wakes several hundred feet away. And in these situations, the poler or guide will start to make the long approach, trying to intercept the school, while you strip more line from the reel to make the longer cast that surely will be needed, but know that if you get a fly in front of the school, you are going to hook up. I just love that moment.

However, it's not enough that you can find a wake; you need to identify it too. You see, many other fish in the flats also push a wake when moving under the surface. So the trick is to learn by experience the difference between the wake of a red, a mullet, a catfish, a sheepshead, and so on. Basically, the red's wake will have more bulk to it. But I've fished places where really big mullet pushed wakes similar to a redfish. Again, bottom line here is that you need time on the water, especially with a good guide or angler in the skiff, to help you learn the difference.

If you fish flats with lots of tall grasses sticking out of the water, such as spartina grass, chances are, you won't be able to see the redfish itself, even when it is within casting range. Yet, the hunt is exciting. And when you finally detect a fish, it's even more exciting, in spite of the fact that more often than not, you still cannot see the red. In such conditions, you look out and most of what you see is grass. Yet there's also lots of water all around you. And when a redfish enters such a flat, often all you notice is the grass parting as the red pushes its way, with little or no effort, toward shallower and shallower water. You must look hard over a sea of grass, until you notice that something is pushing the grass aside, advancing further up the flat with the incoming tide. When you find a red, do not take your eyes off of it. The fish may be easy to notice parting the grass, but at any moment it may stop, perhaps to feed, and then you won't see the grass moving. If you haven't kept track of exactly where the red was when it stopped moving, you'll never find it in that sea of grass.

Just looking away for a couple of seconds may be enough to lose a fish. Stay focused as the skiff is poled

Often, spotting one or several reds waking is easy, but look closely and learn to tell the difference, because catfish, big mullet, and other fish also push wakes in the flats. PAT FORD

within casting range. Then, if you can see your red or if it has started to move again, you can make a cast. If you can't see the red when you get to the area where it was last seen, you can do a bit of blind casting in the few pockets of open water as you pole around, very slowly, to try and find the fish. Other times you'll notice redfish tailing in pockets where there's less grass and more water. In these cases you can usually get fairly close, so you should be able to identify which way the fish is facing and make an effective presentation, casting close to the fish.

As they come in the flats, redfish are opportunistic and do not only look down to find food—they also look up. You'll love this. With the rising tide, fiddler crabs try to stay out of sight from the redfish that will surely come looking for them as the level of water allows the fish to move in. Most fiddlers will go into their borrows, but others will climb as high as they can up stalks of the grass, totally out of the water, to stay out of sight of Mr. Redfish. However, some old reds have been to these flats many times and know the drill. Well, all a red has to do is simply push the grass down with its nose, and let the blade of grass slowly come down to the water, allowing for an easy meal when the crab, still holding on to the blade of grass, enters the water. I love that procedure, and I'm sure the redfish does too. The fiddler crab, probably not so much.

Where to Look for Reds

If you have a good guide, problem solved. A good redfish guide can't be beat. He knows his area well and understands the movements of redfish and other gamefish on different tides and times of year. Besides, chances are, he fished for them yesterday. Have a nice trip.

Personally, I have a lot friends who are fishing guides, and so I often fish with them. I love it. Yet I also like taking my Hell's Bay skiff to one of the many redfish flats and sharing a day of fishing, poling, and hunting for fish with my son, Stephen, or a good friend who isn't a guide. So if you can, given a choice, I strongly suggest you treat yourself to both experiences. And if one day you're fishing with a friend on a spot that one of your guides taught you, and you see the guide there with a client, have the courtesy to move to another spot. It's the class thing to do.

Now when learning a new area, it's helpful to have a friend tell you about a spot, or use a spot you learned from a guide, but to me, one of the most exciting things about learning an area is exploring. Nothing beats it.

When I'm exploring a new area with a good tide movement, I know it will have redfish and other gamefish at one stage of the tide or another. But there's nothing more frustrating than to being caught high and dry on an outgoing tide. You sit there, eventually surrounded by mud and oyster bars, your skiff with a few scratches on the bottom, and you with nothing to do for a few hours. Did you bring a book? If the bottom is hard enough, I may try to step out and push, which I've done in the past. If the bottom is soft, then I can't step out, so I've tied leaders, eaten lunch (sometimes twice), told jokes, and taken naps. I've been there. You want to avoid this.

So when I'm exploring a new tidal flats, I try to arrive early in the morning with a dead low tide or at the very beginning of the incoming. This way I have several advantages. First, I can't get stuck with a rising tide, so I'm relaxed. Second, with a very low tide, I get to see the whole bottom configuration: the highs and lows, ridges, small channels, and more. Remember, a flat is not flat. If against the mainland or large key, it probably tapers somewhat, getting deeper as you move further from shore. And while I may have to wait a bit for the water to be high enough to float, which in my case is just about five inches or so, when I can finally get in, I'll have a few hours of fishing with no danger of getting stuck. Later that afternoon, on a falling tide, I may fish a portion of the flats that's closer to channels and other deep-water areas, just to avoid getting stuck. I've done this for many years, and it works for me.

Sometimes a tidal flat will force you to fish into the sun in order for you to move the skiff into the incoming fish. However, in areas with little or no tide movement, other than wind, I like to position myself with the sun at my back so I can have good visibility, which is vital.

Another thing I do, and I know many guides do the same, is look for wading birds, say, white herons, flamingos, often pelicans, all feeding in shallow water. And if those birds are feeding, that means there's food in the area and that reds and other gamefish will soon be feeding too.

Sandy Moret poles renowned photographer Brad Miller. It's windy, and the water has turned a bit muddy. In this case they'll be looking for fish within 30 feet, often much closer. Brad will have to make a short, fast cast to hook up.

Captain Rob Fordyce, who has won more tournaments in the Keys and Everglades area than I can remember, gave me this advice about looking for reds:

> The first thing I do in a new area is look for the fish's reservoir—that is, the deeper area, usually adjacent or close to the flats where the fish would be when not in the flats, like at low tide. Then, I know what direction they'll be coming in the flats, and I'll know what direction to pole when the tide is right. Next, I make sure that, especially at low tide, I don't run over the reservoir, where the fish will be holding.

Good tip—I've never heard that one.

I also want to give you an idea of the thinking process of other top guides in their local areas.

Captain Nick Sassic, an expert on redfish for many years, fishes the mid East Coast of Florida, and he told me:

> In the summertime, especially on calm days, I'm going to go shallow for reds, but in winter, I usually fish deeper because most crustaceans in our area are deeper then. Otherwise, I look for schools of mullet working the flat, or look for bait, then fish around them.

Captain Dave Denkert has won many tournaments in the Keys, and when it comes to hunting reds with a fly rod, I know no one better. Dave and I have fished for reds and snook for over thirty years. This was his advice:

> For me, looking for reds and snook in the Florida Bay and Everglades area, it doesn't get any better than when I can find muds or mullet muds. But there is a right and a wrong way to fish around these muds. When you find the muds, fish the deeper side of the mud—that's where the reds and snook will be. On the shallower side, which is often ahead of the mud as mullet move into shallower water on an incoming, you'll see mostly catfish. If you see catfish, you are usually too shallow. So fish behind the mullets, not ahead of them.

Great angler, tournament caster, and an old friend, David Olson, has fly-fished reds all over Florida for many years. Mostly referring to the mid East Florida, he said:

> In our area, summertime is about very hot water temperatures. In these conditions I often find them in the white sand potholes where the water is cooler, often as much as 5 degrees cooler than the dark bottom flats. Also, in winter, when the water is often very clear, I am often able to see reds only by their bright blue tail. I've taken many reds where I only saw the blues.

A friend of almost half a century, Captain Steve Huff is one of the best who ever poled a flats skiff. His specialty in the Glades is snook, and big tarpon, but he sure can find reds. He told me:

> If I know I'll be fishing in muddy waters, I'll try to fish early in the day on a low incoming tide to see them better. But if I can find a bay with clear water, and mullet muds, I know I've found reds. I just need to fish the edges of the muds.

And some guys can find them in unusual places. Captain Chuck Naiser has been fishing for Texas reds for over twenty-five years. And I've had trips with him where my friend Mike Wilson and I easily took several dozen reds on fly. He said, "Redfish are given to the influence of tides, and they can go places other gamefish won't go. In flood tide I have even seen them in cattle trails!"

Actually, talk about reds and cattle trails, I went fishing with Captain Steve Huff for reds and snook on an unusual high tide. Everything was covered with lots of water, and the flats were so deep, you couldn't have seen a school of reds if they bumped the skiff. But Huff had an idea where to go. After an hour or so, we went through a creek, ran to the end, and found that an area that was usually a bone-dry cow pasture was now covered with a foot of water. You know what? The reds were all around it.

Personally, when looking for reds or other gamefish in the backwaters, I like to see life in the flats. When I stop to fish a flat, and I see mullets mudding, a stingray passing by, a fish that just spooked from the boat, baitfish, wading birds feeding, sharks, or any combination of the above, I'm staying to pole this flat.

Covering Ground

Now that we've talked about how to look in the water, what to look for, and where to look, let's talk about covering ground with the minimal amount of disturbance. First of all, you're hunting, so try not to make any noise by bumping into something in the craft you are fishing or talking out loud. Many top anglers believe that reds hear you talk. Personally, I've caught myself yelling back something at a guide or fishing friend, only to find I've spooked a red. Captain Eric Herstedt, who has fished reds

Even when I'm running to a particular spot I want to fish, I'm always hunting, often running my skiff at half speed, say 20 miles per hour, while I look around. I may spot a large amount of wading birds in a flat or fish crashing bait on the surface. Don't just blast to the spot at full speed; instead, when you're going through areas that look good, slow down a little and hunt. It's paid off for me over the years. STEPHEN FERNÁNDEZ

and bonefish in South Florida for years, often says that he has "no doubt that redfish can hear you talk better than any other fish—certainly much better than bonefish." This from a guide who often fishes bonefish in Islamorada, the toughest bones in the world. So keep noise to a minimum.

In terms of direction, when there's a tide, most of us pole with the tide to run into reds and other gamefish that are often hunted into the current. This way you get lots of shots, mostly head-on shots. Captain Fordyce, however, gave different advice: "I often like poling cross current when fishing a flat, and this way I get more angle shots, which are easier than a head-on shot because you don't have to be as precise with the cast."

Here again, Captain Steve Huff has more to share. He's a guy who doesn't want you to share your favorite spots with him because he prefers to learn it all himself. How does he do it? Well, Steve has told this secret to just about anyone who'll listen: "Most people are too quick to crank up. The secret is to pole, and pole, and pole. This way you are hunting and fishing for a longer time of the day. Pole long enough, and the fish will find you, I've always said." To illustrate Steve's point, I'll tell you a short story:

A couple of years ago, I got another call from Steve inviting me to fish the area of Everglades City for reds and snook. I try never to miss a chance like that. After the usual big breakfast, we launched his 16-foot Whipray on a ramp in Chokoloskee, on the northern part of the Everglades, and proceeded to run to the Lostman's River area. As we zig-zagged through the many bays and flats on the way, I was asking questions about different spots. And Steve had lots to say about each one of them. Finally, after an hour's run, covering many miles of mangrove shorelines, I asked him how come he knew so much about every spot I asked. He looked at me and smiled: "Chico, over the last few decades, I have poled every foot of shoreline you have just seen. That's how I know." Now, look at the area I just mention on a map or Google Earth to see how many miles of coastline we ran by, on our right and left, and you'll understand the significance of that statement. That's about twenty-five miles of coastline on each side, so maybe fifty miles of mostly mangrove coastlines!

So, personally, if I've learned anything about looking for reds in the past half-century, it's to pole a lot, but pole slowly, as if you knew you were close to a red and didn't want to spook it. Too often, many of us give up on a place and crank up the engine for a "better spot." Think twice before you do that. I always say, "No one ever caught a redfish while running."

Wading for Reds

Just like poling a skiff or canoe after redfish, I find most anglers wade too fast, too loud, and often without concentrating. Remember, you are hunting. And if you finally see a red, stop, concentrate, then cast. Don't ever cast to a fish while you're moving. You'll make too much noise.

Another good friend, Captain Scott Sommerlatte, has guided, fished, and photographed redfish for many years. He has waded many miles in Texas and parts of Florida after reds. I like his simple advice about wading: "If you can hear yourself while wading, you are moving too fast. Slow down."

The Clock System

So you've done all your homework, and you are now being poled in a skiff through prime redfish water. You are totally immersed in the hunt. Then you hear your guide whisper, "Okay, I have one: 11 o'clock, 50 feet." This is sight-casting talk from the clock system, a very effective method to indicate the position of a fish, relative to the front of the skiff, using the numbers of a clock's face. Directly in front of the craft is 12 o'clock. Other positions to the left would be 11 o'clock, 10 o'clock, and so on, and positions to the right would be 1 o'clock, 2 o'clock, and so on.

Be aware that many anglers unconsciously think of 12 o'clock as the direction they're currently facing. This is wrong because 12 o'clock is always directly in front of the skiff. If the angler is facing a bit left of the front of the skiff, then the direction straight ahead of him is 11 o'clock, not 12.

And while most shots are between 9 o'clock and 3 o'clock, don't be surprised if you get called to cast at 4 o'clock or 8 o'clock. Mr. Red can show up anywhere—that's part of the challenge.

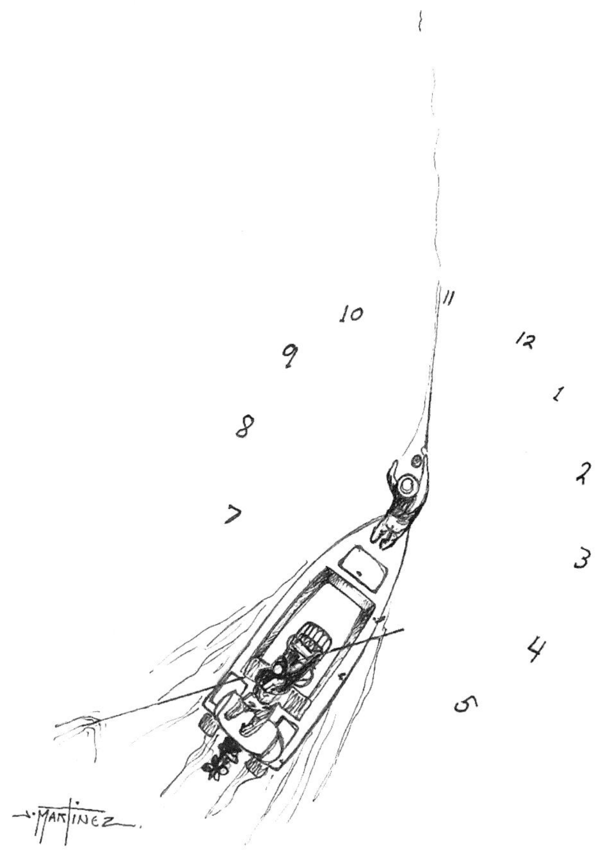

In the clock system, 12 o'clock is straight ahead of the skiff. The angler in this drawing is casting slightly to the left in the 11 o'clock position. If he does not see the fish, all he needs from the guide or poler is the distance, and chances are, he'll soon spot the fish. JORGE MARTINEZ

DISTANCE

"Okay, I got him: 11 o'clock at 40 feet, moving left to right. . . . Can you see him?" says the guide. Well, you heard the instructions, and there's no time to lose. You look at the 11 o'clock direction. No fish. Fine, maybe the fish is moving left to right so you look around 12 o'clock or so. No fish.

"Can you see him? He is now 30 feet at 12 o'clock!" The guide now yells with a little impatience, as you look around frantically. But you don't see it. Then, the red sees the boat and spooks. Now you see it. Turns out you were looking much further away.

The problem was that your 40 feet and the guide's 40 feet were different. It happens all the time. The clock system only helps you on right or left direction. Distance is another matter. What to do?

First, I would make sure that your 40 feet is really 40 feet. This is why I recommend that you practice your casting accuracy with measured distances. Most beginners

With line piled up and fly held by the hook bend, Diana Rudolph is ready and hunting. She is facing around 12 o'clock and looking at 10 o'clock. It's flat calm with good visibility, for her and for the redfish. So she may need to make a long cast.

and even intermediate anglers, when they make a 40-foot cast feel they made a 50-foot cast or further. Let's just say they are very optimistic. But what happens then is that when the angler poling tells them they see a fish at 40 feet, they usually look further than they should.

So develop a good feeling for distances. Not just within range but even out of range. Often a guide will tell me he sees a red tailing 100 feet away and starts approaching the fish. He does not expect me to start casting; he just wants me to lock my eye on the fish and get ready to make a cast when we're in range. Since I have a good feel for what 100 feet is, I'll probably see the tail. And it's the same when a guide tells me in a rush that we have a red 15 feet from the skiff at 10 o'clock. I have a good feel for 15 feet, so I probably will not be looking for the red 20 or 25 feet away. And I'd better not, because at that distance I have only a few seconds to find the red and pass a fly right by its lips.

Now that you're practicing accuracy with props at measured distances and developing a good feel for it, you need to find out what your guide calls 20, 40, or 60 feet. Just make a cast and let him tell you how far it is. In other words, get in sync with him. You'll find that in tournaments, there are always a few angler and guide teams that are constantly on the top three places. Partly it's their superior knowledge and abilities, but it's also that from fishing together so many times, when the guide says a fish is at 11 o'clock 50 feet away, the angler is going to put the fly right there most of the time. Teamwork gets fish. Teamwork wins tournaments.

So now that you know how to find a red and lock it in your vision, your guide or friend is going to start an approach, while you get ready and your heart beats a little faster. So let's talk about the approach and cast next.

Chapter 15

Approach, Cast, and Presentation

Every approach is different. In one area reds may be tailing hard, while in another, they're laid up still on the bottom and not feeding or cruising fast while pushing a wake. And even when you do find a tailing fish feeding with gusto, by the time you're in casting range, the fish may have changed its tune. Maybe you or your boat made too much noise. If you watch closely, you'll know when a fish has changed its body language. Now catching that fish is going to be more difficult than it seemed when you started the approach. So you are constantly reading the situation all the way to the hookup.

The Approach

During the approach, two different anglers, the caster and the poler, are reading the situation with different objectives in mind. As a caster, I read the fish as we get closer, trying to decide where to place the fly. If a red is happily feeding, then I'll place the fly nearby. If the red looks nervous, maybe I'll cast a few feet in front and wait for the redfish to move to the fly. I do all this while making sure that the loose fly line on the deck doesn't get tangled.

As a poler, if the fish is far, I'd be poling pretty hard to close the gap quickly because I know a fish won't stay there long. Whether a school or a single fish, reds are just covering the flat, feeding as they go. So I don't have all day. Once I'm near casting range, I will start to slow down, not wanting to make noises or push a bow wake that a red will either hear or feel.

All the while, I've been thinking of the best angle I can give my caster, trying to avoid giving him a backhand cast, while moving to a side that will give us the least amount of glare for best visibility. I lock my eyes on the fish so as not to lose it. As I get closer, I also try to determine the fish's body language to see if it is still happily feeding or if it feels our presence and is getting nervous.

When I'm close, and my angler has not cast yet, I move the boat slowly and try to keep the push pole as low as I can to keep the lowest profile possible. At the last moment, I push the boat a little to the side to make sure the caster's backcast does not hook me—very important.

If I notice that there are more reds around when we make the approach and can see that the red we're working on looks spooked, I let it go. There's no sense in really spooking that fish and every other red within our immediate area. But if the fish stops to feed again, and I can't find another redfish, then I'll chase it again.

Also, I find that you can get much closer to a redfish when it's coming straight to you. But when moving away, it can feel you easily. And if you try to catch up to a red by poling faster, it'll just swim a little faster. You'll probably never catch it.

But as careful as I think I am on approaches, some of the top guides I've fished with are way ahead on me. That's partly why, in spite of constant fishing pressure in some areas, the good guides still catch plenty of reds. So here's some of the advice they have given me over the years:

Captain Dave Denkert, who is one of the best redfish guides I have ever fished with in South Florida, is always careful to show the redfish the least visible silhouette when positioning the skiff for a cast: "I find that when the boat is facing the fish, it shows him the smallest silhouette, as opposed to showing him the boat sideways where he sees the big boat and engine. I find that has made a big difference."

Captain Eric Herstedt, winner of many tournaments, has always shown me lots of redfish when we go hunt for them in the Everglades: "I always pole quiet when close to them, but I am especially quiet when poling on grass. They seem to spook easy to that noise. I tell you, Chico, they are worse than bonefish!"

Flip poled a long way to get me within 60 feet, and rather than get any closer on this bright sunny day, we decided to take the shot. Notice a 6-foot spinning rod hanging from Flip's back pocket: if I hook up, and there are more reds around, Flip will draw that short rod faster than Doc Holliday. BRAD MILLER

Captain Jared Raskob has become a master of the quiet approach, allowing the angler to cast to a feeding or traveling redfish that is relaxed and more likely to take a fly. This really makes a big difference on the hook-up percentages: "In some areas they can be so sensitive to noise that I have started to use a 24-foot pole so as not to crunch the pole on the bottom too often. And I found it has made a difference in many cases. Also, I try to ease on them with wind and current. They are the only fish that is visibly affected by your voice."

Captain Rob Fordyce, one of the best guides I've ever fished with, is a master of turning a hard approach into an easier one:

> I take into account the sun angle. Early in the morning, the long push pole will cast a shadow over 50 feet long. And the same with the caster's rod when held up. I always look to see how the shadow is casting on the water at a particular time. So I try to make an approach so that the fish is not straight down from the sun. Also, go slow. The harder you push the skiff, the more a bow wake you push ahead of you. And reds, and many other fish in the flats, feel the bow wake and leave. So when approaching a fish 100 feet away, I may push hard for the first part of the approach, but at the end, I push very slow

Captain C. A. Richardson, an expert on West Coast Florida redfish, is big on poling more and running less, a philosophy I fully agree with:

> Some anglers do too much running and not enough poling. Personally, when I'm approaching a flat and see at a distance mullet or other bait activity, rays, and other fish around, I will make the commitment to pole the flat. I don't think of running if I don't see reds right away; I pole the flat. This works for me day in and day out. I say, don't wait 'til you catch the first red. Enjoy the poling, enjoy the hunt. I do.

Anyway, you can see that in the final moments, slow is the way to go. But how slow? Well, a couple of springs ago, Flip and I took his super light Glades Skiff and went looking for redfish in the area of Yankeetown, on the West Coast of Florida. We launched the skiff and soon found some backwater shallow areas with shorelines covered with large black mangrove trees. The tall trees were just right to protect us from the wind, so we were fishing in flat, calm waters.

Soon we found reds. They were moving slowly, lazily, with only the very tip of their fins showing from time to time, so they were hard to see. The dark bottom didn't help visibility either, so we spooked lots of reds and only took a couple of small ones. We had to find that half inch or so of fin out of the water, and then guess which way the fish was facing.

Then, for just a second, a very large fin stuck out at least 6 inches above the surface, maybe 80 feet away and

They saw the redfish show its tail, push a subtle wake for a few feet, then disappear. So they proceeded slowly, so as not to make noise and not to push too much of a bow wake—smart. Markham Cronin holds a fly rod at the bow, and Chris Peterson was doing the poling that evening. PAT FORD

straight at 12 o'clock, before it was gone. It was the fin of a big red, no doubt. We both saw it. Since it was obvious that we needed to get closer, I urged Flip to get going, *muy pronto*—Flip speaks Spanish fluently, so we are fine here. But Flip didn't get us going right away. Actually, he didn't get us going at all. He just stood there, looking at the spot where we'd seen the large fin. I looked at the spot too. Nothing. Flat calm. We waited and looked for the fin to show again. Nothing. I hinted that we should get closer. But Flip said that he didn't want to spook the red, and, that he was quite sure the fish was still near in the same spot. I kept trying to get Flip to push us forward. Finally, he moved a few feet, stopped, waited, then repeated the process. It was an eternity.

At last, we were 30 feet or less from the spot we saw the big tail, and all we could see was dark water. Couldn't even see bottom. And then, we saw it. Keeping still, sideways to the narrow skiff, the fish was facing left and only 20 feet away. So it had actually moved closer to us, but not much. I only made a backcast and placed the fly, a small unweighted Seaducer, close enough to pass the fly a foot away from the fish's lips. It made a powerful thrust with its tail overtaking the fly, and inhaled the fly. The red was well over 30 inches and very dark. What a beautiful fish. But I know that if we had pushed forward when we first saw the big tail, even slowly, we would have spooked the fish.

Casting

As I've said before, when you finally see the red, one of the worst things you can do is to make a fast, abrupt movement, which I guarantee you the redfish will notice, most likely causing it to bolt. And even if you're lucky and the red did not see the move—perhaps it was looking down for prey or in another direction at the moment—it will feel the waves created by the skiff as you rocked it with your sudden move. And now the red is less likely to take the fly, even if it has not left yet.

Act immediately, if you have to, but slowly. In other words, immediately start to get your cast in motion, slowly. This way, you'll be able to execute your cast with good timing, while deciding where you need to cast to properly show the fly to a fish, and then concentrate on accuracy.

If possible, don't move your feet; they make noise and also can rock the boat. And don't rock the boat as you false-cast, which sends waves to the red you're casting to and all others in the vicinity too.

Here are more thoughts from top guides and anglers I know well:

Captain Richard Black, a young guide who has already won several tournaments in the Keys, and from whom I've learned much about redfish in the Florida Bay and shark fishing on fly, had this to say: "In low visibility, anticipating mostly a short, fast cast, keep little line out of the reel, and be ready to make a quick, short cast, without false-casting—just a backcast and a presentation. Get good at this, and you'll take lots of reds over the years."

Captain Jon Cave, an expert on the redfish in the Indian River area of mid-Florida had some advice on casting to reds: "Never hover cast over a fish. It will spook him. I prefer to start a side cast and then for the last false cast, straighten the rod and present the fly. This way he never sees the fly line in the air."

Angler Vince Maggio, a specialist on super shallow water redfish, who fishes out of the small Devil Ray skiff: "In very shallow gin clear water conditions, an overhead cast spooks too many fish. I like approaching the fish as close as possible, and then making a side cast parallel to the water for the lowest profile possible."

Presentation

Presentation is the art of showing a gamefish a prey imitation trying to escape. It's not just casting right in front of a fish. There's a big difference. Where to cast in a given situation, how long to let the fly sink (if at all), and how fast to move it depends on a great variety of conditions, such as whether you are imitating a fast-moving baitfish, a hopping shrimp, or a slow-moving crab pattern.

You want to present the fly as soon as possible, since windows of opportunity in the flats are fleeting. You simply never know how long a fish will be feeding within range before it leaves. All I can tell you is that it won't be very long. Ideally, and I know this is hard, if you're able to present the fly on your first cast, this is a great advantage. After that, while you may still have a good chance to get the fish, you should know that with every subsequent cast you make, your chances of a strike decrease. This is especially true in clear or shallow water. So really concentrate on that first cast.

Also, on your presentation, don't make a high cast. Instead, cast a low loop. I find that a fly traveling low has two advantages. One, the fish cannot see the fly line and fly in the air as easily, so they're less likely to spook. Two, a low-traveling loop will make a more quiet presentation than one cast high.

Personally, I tend to be a bit aggressive on my presentations to reds. It really is about passing the fly close—right by a fish's lips. And while casting so close you take a chance on blowing a fish, I still bet you'll take more reds with this attitude. For years, my saying has been: "Hook them, or spook them," meaning, be aggressive, take a chance, and place the fly close. I've taken many reds with that philosophy. The muddier the water, of course, the closer I put the fly.

On the other hand, some days Mr. Redfish will not tolerate a close cast. Don't know why. So what I do is start the day by casting my usual close and aggressive. Usually, it works. If it doesn't, I back up a little. If I'm still too close, I'll give the reds as much lead as they need that day.

Now if you don't get a reaction after you made what seems to you like a good presentation, it could be that the red did not see the fly. If it's tailing, its head right on the bottom, or maybe it's just laying on the bottom resting, then you may not have gotten the fly down to the fish's level. The redfish probably doesn't know you are there, which is why it didn't take the fly but hasn't spooked either. In this case, don't be persistent. If the fly is too light, and letting it sink a little longer has not worked, change to a heavier fly, maybe lead eyes instead of a bead chain, so you can get down and really show it to the fish. To me, the correct fly weight is the most important factor on a fly. If a fish doesn't see the fly, then size, pattern, and color are immaterial.

Generally, after sighting a cruising redfish and deciding how deep the fly needs to travel, I'll try for a cast a foot or two ahead and beyond the fish, depending on its speed and location in the water column. This way I can bring the fly and "coordinate the meeting." Once the fly lands and I've let it sink the proper amount, if it needed sinking, I'll slide it forward a bit until I feel it has entered the redfish's area of awareness. Then, I start to give the fly the action it needs. The fly will now pass by the red's eye that's further away from me, and then by the eye that is closer to me. My chances of getting a strike are very good.

Area of Awareness

As a redfish moves along the flat looking for food, its area of awareness can increase, especially if it's chasing baitfish, like pinfish or finger mullet. On the other hand, the area may reduce drastically if a red is digging for a single crab on the bottom. Just like the area of awareness that you "look at" when you walk around a shopping center may be dozens of yards in front of you, but on the other hand, the area you "look at" when reading a mystery novel is only a few inches.

Often a redfish concentrates so hard while hunting for food, that it seldom looks any further. This is why you can often get very close to a redfish that is busy feeding, but it's hard to approach red that is just lying there, looking up, with a large area of awareness. And this is partly

Here's a bird's-eye view of the approximate area of awareness of reds. It's narrower when they're focusing close on prey, but much wider when they're looking a few feet away while hunting for food. JORGE MARTINEZ

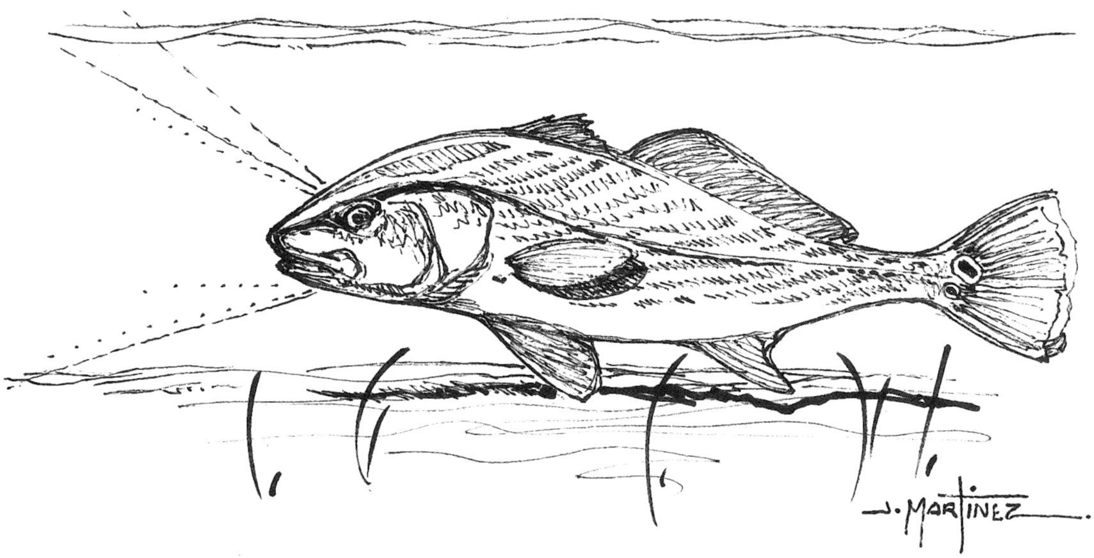

This side view of a red's area of awareness shows that a redfish can be hunting anywhere within the water column, from top to bottom. JORGE MARTINEZ

what you do when you read a fish: you should judge its body language, seeing how close you can get before the fish notices and leaves.

Also, since redfish find food from the surface to the bottom, their area of awareness is really a three-dimensional area, with length, width, and depth. You need to keep all three dimensions in mind when you're presenting the fly. The depth dimension will tell you how long to let the fly sink, if at all.

By the way, another name for this area of awareness is "the plate," a name coined by Tim Borski. So when you hear, mostly in South Florida, that a tailing redfish has a small plate while tailing, you'll know the red has a small area of awareness. If you know this term, you can blend in like a native when you're in the Keys. Tipping your guide well also helps.

Tailing Reds

When approaching a tailing redfish, you need to decide where to place the fly. You know by now that the fish is paying attention to a small portion of the bottom (that is, its area of awareness is small). So however you do it, you need to pass the fly very close to the fish.

Now I wish I had a magic presentation for tailing reds, but I don't. There are just too many variables. After many years experience, and many days fishing with some of the best in the world, I can only tell you that there's more than one method to get the fly close enough for a tailing red to see the fly and inhale it.

One way to show a fish your fly, especially on a red that's actively tailing, is to drop the fly close, say, 8 to 16 inches, using a fly that makes a soft but definite sound when it hits the water. I'm talking bead chain eyes, not lead eyes. This is the old classic way, and it sure works.

But in shallow and clear water, where I detect "nervous body language" while a red is tailing, then I may cast close with a weightless fly, like my shrimp pattern. This fly will not sink much, maybe a few inches from the surface, but since we are talking gin clear water, chances are, the red will see my fly as it moves around. And in these conditions, I'm usually fishing a 6- or 7-weight outfit with a 12-foot leader or so. If you need quiet and subtle, this is a good way.

One method that makes me nervous, but works, is to cast over and pass the tailing fish by about three to five feet, where the mid section of the leader is right by the fish's tail. Then, retrieve the fly slowly until you reach the redfish and pass it by. This way, even if the red is spooky, there's no noise as the fly passes. Now I know this works, and many guides and anglers use this method with success all the time, but I've seen the leader touch a redfish tail, and that fish really didn't like it.

Another method that works well is to wait until the tail goes down, and the red pushes to another location, then cast as the fish moves or pushes a wake. This works too, but it's not for me. Frankly, I'm excited when I see the tail, so I'm not waiting for it to go down; I'm going for it right now. Also, keep in mind that some places may be easier to get a hookup or better for a particular method of presenting the fly. Surely it's different casting to a red in a Louisiana marsh than in Mosquito Lagoon in mid-Florida in clear shallow water.

Captain Bou Bosso, of Islamorada, Florida, suggests yet another way to present to tailing redfish. I've had some great days fishing redfish with Bou and always look forward to our next trip. And since I know that Bou loves to fish tailing reds and has a different approach, I asked him about his methods:

> With the increasing pressure on redfish these days, I've come to embrace what I call a delicate, romantic presentation. I mean, Chico, I get out the tablecloth and candlelights for them. I tie on a fairly large fly but with no weight, usually in brown or olive, and a big heavy hackle, so it lands with no noise at all. They don't even know it's there. Now casting past them, I slowly bring the fly back. Then when I feel it's in their area of awareness, I make a long pull and pass it by their face. They have to take it.

Cruising Reds

Casting to a cruising red in any type of water requires you to put the fly close to the fish. Captain Richard Black, who at his young age has already won several tournaments in the Keys and Everglades and fishes all the flats species in the area, was emphatic about what the angler needed to know about reds: "Fly casting to a cruising redfish is *the* most accurate casting there is. No other species demands such pinpoint accuracy." And I've never heard a redfish guide question that statement. Let's face it: quite often Mr. Red wants to be spoon fed.

However, a cruising red in clear water looking far ahead has a much larger area of awareness than a tailing fish. So in this case, I may intercept the red by casting about three feet ahead with a fly that does not sink fast, wait until the fish get closer, and then retrieve it so that the red sees it with one eye first and then the other.

But in muddy waters, when visibility is minimal, it's best to use a big bulky fly that has a big profile and moves lots of water—probably in dark color like all black, black and purple, or brown with some orange. Then I try passing the fly as close to the red's lips as possible. And don't worry, you won't spook it. If the fish sees the fly, it'll take it. On the other hand, in clear water, I like bright-colored flies or fish patterns with light colors on the side, a bit of flash, a dark back, and big eyes, too.

However, I find that when fishing spoon-type flies, I don't need to cast as close to attract a red's attention. I find that a well-designed spoon fly pattern pushes a lot of water and produces lots of flashes, so it's better to make a more conservative presentation with them. Captain Jon Cave, creator of the Wobbler, and an expert on fishing spoon flies for reds, had this to tell me: "When using a spoon, don't 'spoon' feed them; that is, don't cast too close, but instead lead them a bit. They'll see it, I assure you. My usual drill is to pull it slow, and when they see it, I start manipulating the fly." I've used spoon flies with success in areas where I needed to cover lots of water blind casting. Also, I've caught tailing reds and sheepshead using gold spoon flies.

When you find reds on the move, you have a better chance at catching them than when they are laid up. Captain Lance Ledet, of Dulac Charters in Louisiana, has spent years fly-fishing for the big reds in that area, and he says: "Reds that are moving slowly or mid-speed are hunting, this is the guy you want. Often early in the morning the reds will just be laying still, and you'll find them difficult to entice into taking a fly. But once they start moving, they'll take flies." Sure enough, most of the big reds I've taken with Lance, during several trips to his camp, were cruising fish, if not tailing. Laid up was always tougher.

Finally, another piece of advice on cruising reds, and something that I always forget to do, from Captain John Turcot in mid-Florida: "Whenever possible, put the fly so a redfish does not have to turn toward the boat, where he now has a chance of seen it and spooking." This is a good one, and seldom mentioned. I'll try to remember it next time, John.

Laid Up Reds

Sometimes you fish the flats, and the fish aren't moving. Usually it's because they haven't started to feed. They may need the tide to start moving, or they may have other reasons. Anyway, you'll find a red just laid up, usually close to the bottom, sometimes in a pothole, just hanging out. It's always exciting when you see a red, but a laid up red may be a bit more challenging. After all, it isn't hunting. So, what to do?

Well, the one advantage you have with a laid up red is that since it's not moving, as long as you don't spook it, you can take your time in making a good presentation. So don't rush. Most laid up reds will not move far to take a fly. This is the time for a cast accurate enough to pass right by the fish's lips. And so I would start by making an approach that places me where I can make a good cast. If the fish is facing away from me, I'd take the time to maneuver the skiff so I can get a head-on or a side shot. If a head-on shot, I'd probably cast to the fish's right or left, so that as the red moves for the fly, it is less likely to see the boat. That works too.

This is a big red drum, easy to see, just laying there. But it's facing away, and casting past it would bring the fly toward the fish—not good. If the fish is close to the boat, as this one is, I'll still cast and try to move the fly as sideways as I can to avoid having the fly "attack" the red. But if the fish is 30 feet or further, I may try to move the boat around to get in a better casting angle. It's often worth the time. PAT FORD

Captain Mark Krowka, of South Florida, another tournament winner, uses a technique I've used in Louisiana for reds with good success, but which always makes me nervous. He told me: "Even in clear water, when facing a laid up red, especially in a bit deeper water like 18 inches, I'll cast past his tail, and run the fly past him. When he sees it, he hits it. Period."

Pushing Wakes and Schools

Redfish will often push a wake as they move just under the surface. And since they have massive heads for their size, the wake is generally easy to spot, even at a distance. So even in low light levels, like early or late in the evening, it's easy to spot the bulky wave of a red and sight-cast to those wakes. And in good visibility, you can often see the fish or a semblance of it in the wake.

You're fishing a flat when you see a wake coming. It's bulky and very visible, so you figure no catfish or mullet could produce this size wake. You guess it's a redfish—and you're probably right. So you get within casting range and you present the fly a couple of feet in front of the wake. Looks perfect. You pick up the little slack from the cast and retrieve the fly with some action, but no strike. You try to get closer but can't, so you make a desperate long cast and land very close. You again impart action to the fly, but the wake continues on its way undisturbed. And you probably decide the fish wasn't in a feeding mood or didn't like the fly. But the fact is, that red may not have seen the fly.

Now how can that be, you may say, if the cast was perfect? Well, it may have been perfect for the wake, but not for the redfish. A redfish swimming under the surface leaves a wake that starts to form behind its head, so the head and part of the body is ahead of the wake. The fly landed ahead of the wake but behind the redfish's head. No strike.

Just remember, you have to cast well ahead of the wake. If the fish is moving slow, about three feet ahead may be fine. If it's moving fast, which is often the case with waking fish, especially in deeper flats, lead it at least five feet or more. And remember not to cast too close to the V of the wake, or your fly will be behind the fish by the time you start to retrieve.

Also, if you're a beginner, chances are that even with a good presentation well in front of the wake, your line will land with plenty of slack. This means you'll have to take time to strip all the slack, and by the time you actually start to move the fly, the red will be long gone. So you may want to factor a little more lead time. While I'm at it, when you practice your cast, try to land with minimum of slack. Watch a good caster fish or cast for accuracy and see how straight his line lands. One strip and the fly is moving. This is very important.

If you're a good caster, often it's much better if you can reach a waking fish with a long cast, say, over 70 feet. Here is what Jerry Siem, head rod designer for the rod company Sage, likes to do on a fast-incoming fish: "When I see a red headed my way pushing a fast wake, I make a long cast well before he is in casting range to the area I feel will intercept him. The fish may still be 100-feet-plus away. Then I wait and see if he is going to meet the fly. If I feel he is going to go on the right or left of the fly, I may have to pick up and cast again." Now, you may think that the possibility of Jerry's fly meeting the incoming redfish within a couple of feet seems improbable. However, keep in mind that a cruising red, especially one traveling fast, has a large area of awareness because it's looking straight ahead and far. So yes, there's a good chance that Jerry gets his fish.

Casting to schools is a different thing, and usually, an easier thing. When you present a fly in a school, try to place it so the greatest amount of reds can see it. This way, if a few fish part from the school after the fly, the spirit of competition will make them receptive, as they often lose all sense of caution, to taking a fly before their buddies get it. It's fun to see them fight for it.

But if the school is just traveling, they aren't feeding, meaning they're less likely to take a fly. What I try to do if I get a refusal is make a cast in front of the school again, but this time I let the fly pass the first fish or two, and then start to retrieve to see if the fish in the middle of the school are interested. Often it works. However, if after a few attempts, you're still having problems getting fish to look at the fly, or worse, they're spooking from the fly, then I suggest you leave the fish, and go find some that are feeding.

In most situations, you want to strip at least at the speed a fish is moving. To a slow-moving or tailing fish, you could cast a fly that only works moving slowly or not at all, such as a crab pattern. To a red moving slow or medium speed while it hunts, you could use a shrimp pattern and hop it midspeed. But if you need to move a fly quickly, then I want a fly pattern that is meant to be retrieved fast, and to me, that is a baitfish pattern for sure. It can be retrieved at medium speed, but if you have to retrieve it fast, it still looks natural. Normally, I'd be using a fly about $2^1/_2$ to 3 inches long, but for bigger fish, I may use bigger flies. For example, the fly patterns I cast in Pensacola to schools of reds that measured well over 45 inches long were about 5 inches long. And they inhaled those flies.

LARGE SCHOOLS OF BAITFISH

On occasions, you may find schools of baitfish being rounded up by gamefish, such as jacks, snook, or redfish. I've seen reds beating up a school of glass minnows right against the beach. It's exciting to see them crashing all over the surface. But where to cast?

Using a fly that imitates the baitfish as closely as possible, cast the fly a foot or two into the school of bait, and then retrieve it out into the open. You see, the school stays tight, often in a dark ball, for protection. If a baitfish, or a fly, swims into the open, a predator will try to take advantage of the "mistake" this bait made.

Fishing the Thick Grasses

When fishing thick grass areas, such as spartina grass, it's essential that you present the fly very close, or the red won't see it. Even a foot away in some cases may still leave lots of grass between the red and your fly. So quite often you have to be "in its face." It's about trying to get close enough to make a pinpoint accurate cast. Also redfish often move in a fairly straight line in these conditions, so when one starts to move, you may be able to anticipate where it is going, cast a couple of feet in front, wait until it's inches away from the fly, and then move it.

By the way, a crab pattern is good for this fishing. Another good pattern is a lightly weighted shrimp pattern, with a weedguard, of course. And when you impart action on the fly, don't move it much or too far, or you'll be out of his area of awareness, his plate.

Potholes

Many flats have depressions, often somewhat circular in shape, that mark a bit deeper water than the surrounding bottom of the flat. They are potholes. And they are a great place to find redfish, as well as snook, tarpon, seatrout, and other species. Their usual light bottom makes quite a contrast to most flat's darker colored bottoms, so they are easy to spot. Often you can even spot a fish just laying there waiting for food to come to it.

I love fishing potholes. They can hold such a great variety of gamefish that you never know what will come out of one of them to take your fly. I've even hooked big tarpon while fishing them. But since this often happens when using a 6- or 7-weight outfit, the tarpon has won every one of those encounters so far.

Usually I fish potholes in tidal flats. In those conditions, the best results by far come in the mid to low outgoing stages of tides. Fishing at these times, by the way, is the most common way to get left high and dry if you're not careful. The fishing can get hot at the very low outgoing, and often an angler wants to fish "just one more pothole," and then finds he can't move the boat anymore. I've done that.

Anyway, reds and other gamefish will station themselves just under the lip of the pothole, facing the current, just hiding there until a crustacean or small baitfish going with the current tries to pass by, then it gets the last surprise of its life. In these conditions, I often approach the pothole from the side, cast quarter upcurrent between 1 o'clock and 2 o'clock, and let the fly swim downcurrent into the pothole. If I'm downcurrent from the pothole, I'll cast the fly past the pothole and into the flat, making sure that only the leader landed on the deeper pothole, so as not to scare any fish. Again, let the fly swim into the deeper water. I don't like this approach as much, but often I can't get another angle.

If the pothole is not too deep, I like using a lightly weighted shrimp pattern. But if it's deep, then a heavily weighted fly, such as a Clouser, will get down once it enters the pothole. On the other hand, in conditions where the water is very clear and I feel any red in that pothole can see a good distance, I may use a surface fly, popper, slider, or foam head. The strike I may get could be the highlight of the day.

The Surface Fly

Since most redfish are looking down when hunting for food, the position of their mouth just perfect for that activity, then why use a surface fly for reds? For fun, that's way. And yes, there are conditions where a surface fly is best for reds, but that's not the reason I use it. Again, it's for fun.

During a working trip to Texas, I got invited to fish for reds out of a kayak. I accepted right away. The next day we headed for the coast in two Suburbans with extra-wide racks to accommodate two kayaks each, carrying more tackle than a local fly shop.

The plan was to launch our kayaks, cross about a quarter mile of open water, and get to the flats. Then, we would fish by wading, towing our kayaks behind us with ropes tied around our waists. It was a little awkward at first, but it worked.

The flat had big clumps of grass, often many yards long, and there were plenty of reds tailing around the edges of these clumps. Their area of awareness was small, as they concentrated on the bottom, so approaching

Often when working a shoreline, if the area is shallow, say, 2 feet of water or less, I love to use a surface fly like a slider or a Hot Lips. The strikes it can yield are worth the effort, even if I don't hook up. GEORGE CONTORAKES

them within casting range was not a problem. I just knew I was going to hook up right away.

But after an hour of casting weighted shrimp and crab patterns, no one had a strike or even a follow. In the meantime, the reds were feeding happily, seldom spooking from our attempts. Basically, we were ignored. This led me to realize that the reds didn't know we were there and hadn't seen our flies, and if we kept doing the same thing, they weren't ever going to see those flies.

But, I had seen these conditions before, so my next fly was a dinner bell: a small popper with a short tail. On the first cast, I dragged the popper to within a foot of a tailing red and gave it a couple of light pops. I saw the red stop tailing and keep still for a moment.

I popped the fly again a couple of times, and the red turned around and headed for it. The red's body language showed excitement. Then one more pop, and the fish rushed over, its mouth open wide, and crashed the fly. But somehow, the red missed it. I popped the fly again, and the fish turned around and missed it again. The popper was less than 20 feet away. One more pop, and this time the red hit it hard, missed it and glided toward me, saw me, and with a big puff of mud, headed back to a clump of grass. It was funny.

From then on, I'd wade to a tailing fish, call it with the popper, and often get it to strike. I took three nice reds that afternoon before the action stopped. Surface flies are great, and poppers are something special in the fly fisher's arsenal. I never leave home without them.

But there are plenty of conditions where you can take reds on the surface. When you see a red that's off the bottom, either in the middle of the water column or close to the surface, it may come up for a fly. Tailing redfish will often come up to the surface to take a fly that is lightly popping or making soft noises. Just wait for them to move to another area and cast in front. Or see if making a little surface noise attracts them. A Hot Lips or any other gurgler-type fly will work. Just make sure you don't make a loud pop with a popper, or you'll clear the flat.

When you find a tailing redfish in very shallow water, you can often convince it to take a small surface fly. Just remember, you need a soft-landing fly that doesn't make too much noise. I've seen them crash it with vigor, or just sip it quietly. But redfish that are actively feeding on the surface on juvenile mullet or other small baitfish will take a surface fly readily, even a popper. Just try to match the size of your fly to the baitfish. And finally, reds pushing a wake, whether singles or in schools, will often take a fly on top.

A Spooked Redfish

You can spook a bonefish, a snook, a tarpon, or a permit. It's easy to do, and it's final. You may see that fish again, but not today. However, a redfish is different: it has many degrees of spook. A red may spook, run 20 feet, and start feeding again, begging to be fished. Or, it may spook and go 100 feet and stop and start feeding, as if it had forgotten the incident that spooked it a few seconds ago. Then the red may spook, leaving the flat, but at a slow or medium speed. And finally, yes, it may spook and leave at high speed, bonefish style.

This is certainly strange behavior for a flats fish, but the fact is that many spooked reds can still be caught. I've seen this happen with bonefish, but rarely. Whereas I've had many days of landing several spooked reds. It's a matter of reading just how spooked the red is this time.

Anytime I spook a red and it only runs a few yards and start to feed, or stops, I know I have another chance at it. If it spooks but does not run directly out of the flat, but runs parallel to the flat, and not directly to deep water, I may have another chance at it. In running, if the red changes speed and starts to slide, slower, that is also a good sign you may get to try the same fish again.

A good technique for these "semispooked" reds is to cast way ahead of them, wait until they're close to the fly, and strip. But if you see that the fish reacts by simply going around or under the fly, don't waste your time—go look for another red.

Bonefish and Redfish in the Same Conditions

For years, I've been mulling around the idea that if you take a typical redfish and bonefish, say both about five pounds, feeding in a foot of clear water, tailing or cruising, I would think you would use the same casting technique, same 7- or 8-weight rod with a 10- or 12-foot leader, same shrimp or crab fly, and same retrieve. No difference.

So when I started to talk or interview all my friends for the redfish book, I took the opportunity to ask them whether they agreed. And I made it very clear that I didn't mind if they disagreed. I was just curious, since both fish generally live is such different worlds.

Out of the dozens of top redfish and bonefish fly fishers I know, 95 percent agreed completely, and 5 percent agreed, but added a small change. They would select a little bit bigger fly for the red, and a little bit heavier fly for the bonefish—that's all. I thought you'd get a kick out of that. Now let's go talk about retrieving the fly and hooking Mr. Redfish.

Chapter 16

Retrieve, Strike, and Fight

Well, we're moving to a different dimension. We're no longer going to talk about the mechanics of fly casting or the formula for a well-designed leader; we're leaving science behind. Now, we are going to talk about art—basically the art of seduction. It's the art of making a gamefish, in this case a redfish, believe that a bunch of natural or artificial materials tied to a hook and danced in front of its face is actually live, delicious food, trying to escape. And while a red may even be aware of the tippet tied to the fly, if the dance is done correctly, chances are the red will ignore suspicions and take the offering.

Years ago, when I was a boy in Cuba, my parents took me to see the *marionetas*. At the time, I didn't know what they were, or even knew what to expect. But as soon as they appeared on the little stage, I was fascinated. And I was fooled into thinking that they were moving by themselves, since all my attention was focused on their movements as they danced, played, and even fought all over the stage. They did all this while talking to each other, and occasionally even to us kids in the audience. Little did I know that on top of the curtain was a puppeteer pulling the strings—the "puppet master," as they often called him. In retrospect, I should've been able to see the strings that manipulated the puppets, but maybe I wanted to believe so badly I ignored them. Like a puppet master, a skillful angler can fool most redfish into taking a fly, despite the line attached to it. This is primarily what this chapter is all about. After the seduction, striking and fighting the redfish is a lot easier.

But before we talk about enticing fish with a good retrieve, let's get the fly so it enters the area of awareness. If you make a presentation and it lands almost right but not good enough, it can be corrected if you are careful. Say it's two feet ahead, which is great, but too far past the fish. Now you know you have to quickly move the fly forward to intercept the area of awareness in front of the fish. Well, the best way to bring the fly forward quickly, and without causing alarm, is to slide it forward making a long steady pull. Then, when you think it's in the right place, or if the fish notices it, start your retrieve. Just don't try to bring the fly into the right place by working the fly. This could spook the red.

If the fly lands in the wrong place, and the fish is not aware of your mistake, slowly pick the whole line off the water, if possible, and drop it back in the place you want. I mentioned how to do this on pages 145–46.

Getting Ready to Retrieve

To be effective at imparting action to a fly with your stripping hand, you need to have the minimum of slack between you and the fly. So the first thing you should do when the fly lands is strip in the excess slack. This isn't about moving the fly; it's just getting rid of the slack. Next, you want to lower the tip of the rod all the way down to the water, so there's no fly line slack between the water's surface and the tip of the rod.

This way, every move you impart with your hand will transfer precisely and immediately to the fly. This is vital if you're going to fool a fish into eating your fly consistently. Also, you'll have a straight line to the fly, allowing you to feel a strike right away, and increasing your percentage of hookups. Often a fish will strike hard and hook itself before I have a chance to set the hook. And by the way, as you get better at this game, you'll have less slack, if any, at the end of your presentations.

A rod held high above the water when stripping a fly causes the fly line that's above the water to slap the water and make lots of noise. Often a red following the fly may spook from it. But with the tip of the rod on the water, you are dead silent. Dropping the tip right down to the water is truly a win-win situation. But if you find that you are too high to reach the water with the tip of your rod,

Keep the tip of your rod down, even to the point that it touches the water, so that you'll have the minimum amount of fly line between the tip and the water. This reduces slack, which not only makes any manipulation of the fly more responsive but is also a quieter retrieve. In this photo, since the Glades Skiff is low, it's easy for me to keep the tip close to the water. BRAD MILLER

maybe because you're fishing from a casting platform, then at least try to minimize the distance, say to a few inches, and that should be enough.

To fool a redfish, or any other fish, into taking your fly, you have to concentrate. You should start to retrieve your fly while watching the fish's reaction to the fly's movement. At that moment, you should be completely engrossed by the fly you're using.

Sandy Moret has an expression to denote how much you should concentrate: "If you are imitating a shrimp, for example, be the shrimp." That is, become that which you are trying to imitate, perhaps like an actor becoming the character he's portraying. In being the shrimp, you may swim the fly slowly like a shrimp usually travels, or you may hop it with sharp jerks as a shrimp does when it's trying to get away. So "be the shrimp" or whatever food you are using at the moment.

The Retrieve

There are many good ways to retrieve a fly for redfish, depending on fishing conditions and the food you're imitating. We'll cover them later in the chapter. But for now, I want to give you one good, universal redfish retrieve that anglers and guides (including myself) use often and with great success.

Let's call it the "classic redfish retrieve." It consists of a short, choppy, and erratic retrieve that looks alive, like it's trying to get away, but really, it's moving very slow. Actually, it wants to be caught. I think more reds are caught on this retrieve than any other. The retrieve looks alive, but it moves forward slowly so that it stays in redfish's area of awareness as long as possible. The longer it stays in the fish's face, teasing the red and looking like it's getting away, the better the chances of the red eating it.

You want a short, choppy, even pulsating retrieve, and if you think about it, it makes sense. You're mostly imitating juvenile crustaceans, like shrimp and crabs, that even at their best are slow and erratic swimmers. You don't see a 2-inch shrimp trying to escape with quick foot-long strides. No way. So the action described above is a pretty good imitation of the typical food a redfish finds in the flats. Make sure your fly enters the area of awareness moving away from the red with whatever retrieve you've decided to use. This is what the redfish should see. In terms of speed, I generally work the fly as fast as the fish is moving. And if possible, I'll try to select a fly to accommodate that philosophy. So when fishing cruising reds, often pushing a fast wake, I'll use a fast retrieve, preferably using a baitfish pattern that is meant to be moved fast. On the other hand, fishing a flat with tailing reds or reds lying still, I may select a fly that is meant to work slow, like a little shrimp pattern or a crab pattern. And in areas with real big redfish, I use big flies and work them much faster than I'd work a small 2-inch shrimp pattern.

Also I've found that, especially using large bait imitations, it's popular to use a long, steady pull retrieve instead of short and choppy. Perhaps this is a better imitation of a larger baitfish swimming. Indeed, I remember the many times I've had the pleasure of fishing with Captain Lance Ledet and his father, the late Captain Leland Ledet, in Dulac Louisiana, when we mainly fished flies 4 inches long or larger with a long, steady retrieve. We did very well. We also used flies that breathed easy in the water, such as marabou and rabbit strips; just pulling them through the water was enough to add lots of action to them. Anyway, I've caught lots of big reds that way. Another angler who often uses the long strip retrieve is Captain Nick Sassic, of mid-Florida. He tells me that when reds are spooky, a long, slow retrieve works much better for him and his clients.

Some fly patterns are designed to be fished or retrieved in a certain way. Crab flies are a good example. They're designed to be fished slow or dead on the bottom. Often, you should just cast close enough to get the red's attention, then let the fly drop to the bottom. Let the fish dig for it. And if my cast is a bit too far from the red, and the fish didn't see it drop, then I will slide it so it enters the red's area of awareness. When I see the red notice it, I let it drop. Or I will let it settle in the grass, then move it gently, just so the red sees it's alive.

Well-known marine artist and angler Jorge Martinez likes to fish areas of the Everglades with clear water and spooky redfish, and his choice of fly in these conditions is often a crab pattern. Here's how he does it: "I like to cast a crab fly in front of a red, and let it sink to the fish's level. Then, I use a long, slow, and steady retrieve, watching the red's reaction. And because there is no slack on the steady retrieve, if he takes it, I feel him immediately."

All of my shrimp patterns are weighted with bead chains, brass eyes, or light lead eyes and fished with a loop knot. This way, they'll hop up with every small pull of my retrieve, dropping when I stop, creating hopping action, like a shrimp makes when trying to get away. The shrimp pattern is perhaps my most often-used fly for reds in the flats.

When using baitfish patterns, especially in the flats, I like them to dart forward—not hop up and down like a shrimp. So most of my baitfish patterns aren't weighted up front, and tied with a clinch or improved clinch knot, so at the end of every strip, during that stop, the fly will not dive down. This way, I'll strip a little pinfish imitation in a foot of water, and it will dart forward with every strip like pinfish swim. Redfish love a pinfish meal.

As I've mentioned, a spoon fly is also effective on redfish. First, it pushes lots of water as it's retrieved so reds can find the spoon even in muddy waters. Then, when the reds get close enough to see it, the multiple flashes it produces have proven irresistible to redfish. I must admit that I don't use a spoon often, but when I do, I've taken reds.

Fly fisher David Olson, who has fished for redfish all over Florida and other states, has had plenty of experience with spoon flies: "Those days that I can't seem to get a reaction from a redfish with any of my favorite flies, I'll turn to a spoon fly, and always get them to react—usually in a positive way. I've taken reds with a spoon when nothing else would work, using a smooth and even retrieve, no jerks."

Captain Jon Cave, who designed the Wobbler spoon fly, gave me this advice: "With a spoon you have to lead them more than with a regular fly. I pull it slow until they see it, then I start to manipulate the fly."

With surface flies for reds, I try to make just enough noise to attract them, but not enough to spook them. So with a popper, I pop it lightly, often kind of dragging it. With a slider, I just worry about putting lots of action on the surface but not moving too fast, but I don't worry about making too much noise. And with a foam head like a Hot Lips, I retrieve it in 6-inch pulls or so, and it makes just the right amount of noise. Often I'll get a red to take a Hot Lips while it's just lying on the surface. And I use surface flies for reds any time I can because I'm addicted to those wonderful strikes. Always carry some in your fly box.

In low-visibility conditions, like muddy waters, I like to use a bigger and bulkier fly that pushes water so a red can sense it even when the fish can't see it, and in a dark color, so that once the red is attracted close enough, it can easily see the fly's silhouette.

The best retrieve here is a slow, steady retrieve, so the fish has a chance to track the fly down and find it. And then, once the red does see the fly, keeping the retrieve slow will allow the fly to stay in its vision. You don't want to retrieve so fast that the red loses the fly again in all that muddy water. So slow and steady is the way to go in low visibility.

In areas of thick turtle grass, reds may dig under the grass to take crustaceans, but if you cast a weighted fly down into the grass, it'll get lost and the red will never see it. What I often do in this case is use a small baitfish pattern and try to fish it just above the grass. So in 2 feet of water with long turtle grass extending, say, 9 inches from the bottom, I try to get my fly to swim a few inches above the tip of the grass. Slap the fly on the water in front of you, watch it sink, and see how long it takes for it to sink a foot or so. Reds love to pick a fat little fish for breakfast.

Now I've given you lots of advice on what fly and retrieve to use. But what happens when the fly you selected doesn't seem to work? You've tried it a couple times, and you're not sure what to try now, since the fly that was "supposed to work" didn't. Maybe Mr. Red has not read my book yet. Well, Jorge Martinez has advice for these occasions that I really like and have found useful: "I find that when the fly I am using does not work, it is best to go to extremes. That is, if I was fishing a small fly, I go with a big fly. If using a bright color, I may go to a black fly. Extreme changes have worked much better for me than subtle changes."

I have found Jorge's advice of making extreme changes, which he gave me years ago, to work well for me. However, before you change flies, make sure that the red actually saw your fly. It's not enough that your presentation was close to the red, so to find out, you have to watch the red's reaction when the fly passes by. Look for a subtle move that shows the red saw it. This could be a small move toward the fly and then a rejection. I say this because often an angler keeps changing flies, and in reality the reds have not even seen the fly yet. As always, time on the water helps here. And if you fish with a good guide, he can teach you how and what to look for in a red's reaction to the fly.

I'll finish the retrieve section with a quote from an old friend, who, according to some of the best guides in the business, is as good at talking a fish into taking his fly as any they've ever fished with, Sandy Moret. So it's appropriate that he finishes this section:

> The beginner has a tendency to cast to a redfish, or any other fish, and strip the fly in a somewhat mechanical motion. That's not it; it's much more than that. I find there is an intuition to be developed, that some anglers start out better than others, but it can be learned with time on the water.
>
> For starters, try to see the fish as well as you can, so you can read his reactions. For me, it's about closing the distance between the fish and the fly. You are trying to accelerate the closing of that distance. Perhaps as I move the fly, I see him react, so I strip faster as if trying to escape. That's why I prefer a 30- or 40-foot cast to a red, so I can read him well. Can't do that at 80 feet. Just remember, every fish, every presentation, is different.

The Strike

That moment of a visual strike is special. Some strikes are so memorable, as I've written elsewhere in this book, that you talk about them with friends for years. And to make it even more interesting, every strike is different and exciting, no matter how many strikes you've seen. Surely an experienced guide has seen a million strikes, and still, I know he loves to see new ones.

But because the visual strike is so exciting, it's tough for the angler to set the hook in an efficient and effective way. I can't tell you how many times I've seen a redfish rise to a fly, open its mouth, and as it starts to inhale the fly, the angler, striking with the rod high, pulls the fly right out of the red's mouth.

Some anglers and guides tell you to strike when you feel a fish. That works, and avoids the mistake of striking too soon as in the example above. However, here's my philosophy on setting the hook: sometimes the strike is visual, other times, perhaps because of low visibility or because you're blind casting the area, you just feel it. Well, if you feel it, then strike. But if it's visual, I find that it's best to read the fish as it's coming to take the fly, because some strikes require different ways to strike back.

If the red rushes to the fly from the right or left and takes it, I'm probably going to feel the fish an instant

Pat Ford beautifully captured this violent strike of a big bull red to a surface fly. You don't forget these kinds of strikes. I live for them. PAT FORD

after the fly disappears if I've been stripping to keep the line tight with no slack. Certainly I am going to strike. The proper strike here is what is called a "strip-strike." Just strike with the same movement of the stripping technique you've been using to move your fly.

What I do here is try to make a long, slow strip to set the hook. How long depends on how much slack there is, if any, at that time. If the fish is moving toward me, then the strip will be longer to pick up the slack. If it strikes sideways fast or going away from me, then the strips may be just inches, or even none if the red tightens the line before I have a chance to strike. That's fine with me.

Either way, don't be too gentle: strike hard. You want the hook to penetrate, especially when using larger hooks on larger flies, and you have the stretch of the fly line and leader to contend with. But whatever you do, be slow and powerful—not fast or jerky. It's a pull.

The slow pull has another advantage. If the fly comes out of the red's mouth or the fish misses the fly, it will only travel a foot or two away from the red. Chances are, the fish will rush and grab it again. But had you raised your rod and pulled back, when the red missed the fly, you would have made a backcast and you'd probably never get the fly in front of that red again.

And since you're pulling straight to the fly, without the rod, this method has huge leverage, and therefore power. With a strong enough tippet, this is the most common method for big tarpon, sailfish, marlin, and other big fish. So you should have no problem setting the hook on a redfish. And this is why, as soon as you feel you've hooked a fish, you should raise your rod. Now the cushion of the raised rod reduces leverage so you don't break the tippet.

Other times, a red will rush to get a fly from behind, coming straight toward you. It'll take the fly and keep on coming toward the skiff, creating lots of slack. If you've been reading the fish, you should know that a simple strip-strike pull won't pick up all the slack it has created. Now you have a couple of seconds to eliminate the slack and set the hook before the red spits the fly. What to do?

One way is to strip-strike, and at the same time, also strike with your rod. This way, you can pick up a lot more slack. Often this works. However, I've seen reds, and other fish, take a fly coming toward me and not stop until they were very close to the boat. The amount of slack in this case is huge. And no strip-strike or rod strike is going to pick up all that slack. In this case the only thing you can do is keep stripping line in, fast, hoping that you'll come tight before the red spits the fly. I've hooked many fish in this situation by fast, frantic, stripping. But I've also lost lots of reds this way. Still, it's the best I know how to do.

Other times, especially with reds, the strike occurs very close to the angler. Either because the cast was to a fish close or because the fish followed the fly all the way to within a few feet from angler before it decided to take the fly. Now with the fish so close, it's best not only to strip-strike with your line hand, but also to strike with the rod to the opposite side of where the fish is going. So if the fish strikes going to the left, you need to strike with your rod toward the right.

This way there's less chance of pulling the fly out of the red's mouth, and you also tighten on the fish that much sooner. This is the most effective way I know of setting the hook on a strike close to you.

If the strike occurs far from the boat, then moving the rod left or right has no effect because you won't have much of an angle on the fish.

IF YOU DON'T GET THE FISH

I feel you should get in the habit of asking the guide or other angler, if knowledgeable, why you don't get the fish you miss. You'd be surprised how much knowledge a top angler or guide has accumulated throughout the years. And if you ask, I'll bet he'll be glad to tell you. Often it's just that your fly wasn't getting down to the red's level, or you are leading the fish too far, being too cautious. Anyway, this is a great opportunity for you to learn in a relatively short time. It's a great way to improve. I still ask those in the skiff, and I'm still learning.

Clearing the Fly Line

Now the line is tight, your rod is bent, and you've hooked a redfish! Great. You're excited and watching the red in front of you. But now is the time to take your eyes off the hooked redfish for a moment and look down at your feet. When you do, you'll find that the fly line you were stripping during the retrieve is all around you. Some of it on the deck, other parts are in the cockpit, maybe around a tackle bag—it's a mess. Your job now is to make sure that line is free to run out through the guides as the fish pulls on its first run. If the line tangles anywhere and you can't get it free, you'll break the fish off. And it's a shame to lose a fish like that because you've already done all the hard stuff. So let's talk about clearing the line.

While looking down at the fly line, separate your hands, which will help in monitoring and clearing the line. Now make sure the rod hand keeps the fighting butt of the rod against your wrist to prevent the line you're trying to clear from wrapping around the butt, which happens often. And keep the rod at about a 45-degree angle or lower. Any higher and the rod starts to throb, making it hard to release line smoothly.

The hook is set and the rod is bent, but this angler still has fly line to clear, and a strong wind blowing the loose fly line all over. It's challenging, but it's also great fun.

As the fish pulls the loose line, you should let it go with mild pressure from your stripping hand. This slight pressure gives you control of the line. If you release it with no pressure, practically loose, it will rattlesnake all over the place and is sure to get caught on something. But holding it too tight, the line will often burn your hands a little, and worse, it will come off your hands in sharp erratic motions, making the fly line jump all over, again increasing the chance of a tangle. And if you hold it real tight, well, you'll break the fish off. Just apply light pressure as it goes out. Meanwhile, as the line is running out, the line hand may also be moving around, helping untangle the line from different places. It sounds harder than it is, really.

When there's just a few feet of loose fly line to clear, it's a good idea to slowly move your hand toward the first guide, maybe within a foot, so that you won't let go of the line. Letting loose the last few feet of the running line because you think you've got the fish will often send the loose line crashing and tightly wrapping around a guide. And with no give, the fish is sure to break off. I've broken fish off at this last stage of clearing the line, just because I let go of the last few feet of line before I should, and it's a heartbreaker. Now that all the line is gone, you're "on the reel" and fighting your fish.

If you've never cleared a line before, I think it's a good idea for you to practice doing a few times. You can learn it quickly. Go outdoors to an open field or grass area, and just have a friend act as a fish and pull line out, slowly first, as you clear the line. Then have him do it faster, let him run, and clear the line. It will soon become second nature to you. And it's better than doing it the first time with a real fish on.

But what if you set the hook on a redfish, and the red won't run like it's supposed to? It's not unusual for a hooked fish, a redfish, a snook, even a big tarpon to move around, confused, and not run away from you. Often they'll even run toward the skiff. I've had a hooked redfish run toward me and then hide under the boat for a while. Eventually, with my friend stomping on the bottom of the boat and me trying to pull the fish out, it ran out into the open and made a decent run. Crazy redfish.

In these cases your job is to keep a tight line so that the fish doesn't dislodge the hook by keeping the rod bent, and then applying pressure to bring the fish to you. If it's a small red, you may land it by stripping. You can land many fish "by hand," especially smaller ones. Or you may play the red for a few seconds before it realizes it's in trouble and finally makes a run for it. Then you clear the rest of the line as described above until you're on the reel. You're back on the fight—no problem.

The Run

If the redfish is of decent size, once it feels the hook, it'll make a run for it. Your reel's drag should not be set too tight, maybe a couple of pounds of drag—enough so that you don't get an overrun on the spool, or maybe a bit more. If you need to add more pressure, perhaps because the red is running toward a mangrove root or other structure, you should only add more pressure by palming the rim control on your reel.

And if you have an old reel without rim control, then feather the fly line or backing inside your reel with a couple of your fingers. This way, if you need to decrease drag right away, just pull back your palm or fingers. It's instant. You can never be as fast decreasing your drag knob.

As the fish runs, just rest your rod around your belt or stomach at about a 45-degree angle, never higher, and let it run. Enjoy this moment: you've earned it. The one exception to this rule is if you are fighting a red on an area with lots of mangrove shoots or other small plants

David Olson palming the rim control of the fly reel as a big red makes a run for it. By palming, he can put all the pressure he feels he needs, yet he can reduce the amount of pressure instantly. Definitely practice and get a feel for palming.

or structure. Then you need to raise the rod high to let the fly line clear the structure and avoid getting tangled.

The Fight

It's okay to enjoy the fight. It's fun to see the red, usually in shallow water, make lunges and splashes as it fights against the pressure you are applying. However, it's best that you fight a red hard and land it in a reasonable amount of time. You see, the longer you fight a red, the harder it is for the fish to recover when released. This is particularly true during summer, when temperatures are high and oxygen levels are low. Many reds that look like they recover fine, slowly swimming away from the boat, actually die. Some get caught on vegetation and are too exhausted to fight it, so they can't move, can't breathe well, and soon turn over on their bellies and die. And in the Everglades, where several species of sharks abound in the flats, I've seen many reds being released exhausted, only to be eaten by a shark after swimming a few yards.

But all this can be avoided. Just fight reds reasonably hard, keep constant pressure to avoid any slack so they are less likely to dislodge the hook, and still, enjoy the fight. Then, go get another one. If the redfish you have on is a big one, and it runs well into your backing, then you should try to get the fish back on the fly line. The closer you are to the red, the more effective the pressure you are applying with your rod will affect it. That's why your guide will pole after the fish, allowing you to gain line.

When you're close, say in the belly of your fly line, try to apply pressure by pulling directly against the direction the red is facing. Place the tip of the bent rod at a low angle and right down its spine. If the fish moves to the right, you swing your rod to the left and apply pressure. If it the turns around and moves to the left, you change directions too and now apply pressure from the right side. This will tire the fish faster.

And if the redfish manages to tangle the fly line or leader on loose grass, you should try to get rid of it. Grass is heavy and resistant to any move you make. If possible, try to lift the grass off the water with your rod and shake it loose. If too heavy for that, then just with your hands or with a friend's help, try to shake it loose.

Often during a fight, a red will try to get under your skiff. One way to avoid this is to fight the fish on the lee side of the boat, which is opposite to the direction it is drifting. In this way, the boat is not trying to "run over the red," but rather drifting away from the hooked redfish.

But sooner or later, one of your hooked reds is going to get under the boat. When this happens, be careful on

When a red tries to get under the boat, make sure you don't high-stick it. That is, don't keep the rod high, or you may break it. Instead, keep the rod low while maintaining pressure, as angler Nick Curcione is doing here.

Palm the reel while keeping constant pressure on the redfish. Notice how there's a good bend on the middle low portion of the 7-weight fly rod, putting lots of pressure on the redfish. BRAD MILLER

the type of bend you put on your rod, or you'll break it. So avoid what is commonly called "high-sticking" a rod, which is simply pulling back on your rod to create too sharp an angle.

And when a redfish does get under the skiff, besides not high-sticking the fish, you must also be careful that as you are keeping your rod angle low, your bent rod does not touch the hull or gunwale of the skiff. If it does, the chances of breaking the rod right where it touches the boat are very good. Many rods are broken that way.

Finally, when a hooked redfish (or any other fish you're fighting off the reel) runs toward you fast, you must pick up the slack created so as to avoid the fish spitting the hook. This involves fast reeling—often crazy fast reeling. But invariably, a beginner will face this problem, and, noticing that no matter how fast he reels, he isn't catching up with the incoming red, he'll try to reduce the slack not just by reeling fast, but also by raising the rod and bringing it back over his head. Don't do this. If you do, what will happen most likely is that with the tip of the rod high behind you, the fast reeling will make the rod wobble, and that wobble will eventually get the line wrapped around the first couple feet of the rod. Now you can't reel in, and worse yet, if the red decides now to make a run, you can't yield any line either, so you'll break it off. But don't worry, there's a much better solution to this problem.

When a hooked fish rushes your way at speed and your reeling isn't catching up, what you should do, besides still reeling like crazy, is just to stick the tip of the rod in the water so all the fly line is in the water. That's it. Now, helped by the tension of the full line on the water, anywhere the fish moves, it is dragging the whole fly line, and that's a lot of tension, so there's no slack. That's what I do, and it works. It's also used by most top anglers and guides I know.

Now that you have that big red by your side, let's talk about landing him.

Chapter 17

Landing, Photos, and Releasing

Of the fish you'll find in the flats, the redfish is among the toughest when it comes to surviving being caught and released. But still, they need proper handling. How you handle a redfish while landing, photographing, and releasing it can have a big effect on its chances for survival.

Terminal Tackle

Just a couple of changes in your terminal tackle can greatly increase the redfish's chances for survival when you release it. Many fly hooks come with large barbs, and removing these hooks from a fish's mouth takes much longer as the angler wrestles and pulls in different directions. And when he finally succeeds, it's always by tearing flesh, which is the only way the barb can be dislodged, often producing extensive damage. But if you pinch down the large barb with a pair of pliers or forceps, you'll greatly reduce the time it takes to remove the hook, and there will be much less damage, if any, to the flesh. Mr. Red will be back swimming and feeding in no time. In terms of hooking a red, the lower the barb, the less resistance and easier it is for the hook to penetrate. So hook rate increases too. Also, if you hook someone, or yourself, you'll be real glad it was a barbless or low barb hook.

When a fish is hooked too deep to remove without extensive damage, just cut the tippet as close to the hook as possible and release the fish. Once in the water, and with a barbless or very low barbed hook, most fish are able to get rid of the hook in a relatively short time.

Now in terms of holding the fish with a very low barb, I have been a bit skeptical in the past. Aaron Adams fishes barbless all the time, and he tells me he doesn't see a significant difference in fish lost because of hooks coming off. Well, I have to admit that often trying to dislodge a hook with a pinched barb from a redfish, the hook still held pretty well. So now either I pinch the barb, or use the super low micro barbs. And I often reduce those big barbs with forceps or a touch of my file.

Also, I strongly feel that forceps, being long and slim, are a better tool than a fat pair of pliers for removing a hook, especially if the fish is hooked deep. I always carry forceps. Finally, don't use any "lip-holding devices" to land a red. They punch a hole on the lower jaw which is harmful to the fish, probably more so on bigger fish.

Landing a Redfish from a Skiff and While Wading

Once you have a red beat, you need to maneuver it within reach—either for you or for the angler helping

If someone in the boat is going to help me land the fish—in this case Corbett Davis is going to use a net—then, with the rod low and bent on the lower third section, I ease the fish toward the net, while Captain Leland Ledet holds the boat steady. MARKUS HAUGG

If I'm going to land the fish myself, once the fish is tired and close to the boat, I'll reel in line to the point that the fly line and part of the leader are inside the rod. And then, while keeping the rod low, I ease the fish toward me. BRAD MILLER

you. But a typical 9-foot rod, great as it is for casting, is an awkward tool at best to bring a fish close to a skiff for landing. Here a shorter rod is much easier. If an angler or guide is going to help me, I usually move to one end of the skiff, preferably the bow end, and then try to work the fish toward the middle or last third of the skiff, where the other angler is waiting for it.

Another way is for the angler who is going to land the fish to kneel down against the gunwale of the skiff, usually around the middle of the boat depending on the layout, while I stand a few feet behind him and work the fish toward him.

Just make sure that you don't bring the rod back too far—as in high-sticking—in an effort to bring the fish closer, or you are sure to break your rod. Pull back, but keep the rod angle as low as possible—horizontal if you can. In all types of saltwater fly fishing, more rods are broken during the end of the fight or landing than at any other time.

When a fish is within reach, if I'm landing it, I usually try to grab it either by putting my hand under its belly or by grabbing its tail—and since the fish is in the water, my hand will be wet too, so I don't have to worry about taking off the fish's protective slime.

If the fish resists, thrashes about, or tries to swim away, I can control it somewhat by holding the tippet close to the hook. This way, it may take a couple of attempts, but I'll manage to get the fish in a position to lift for a photo or to take the hook off.

Captain Richard Black has a good method for initially handling a red: "I usually start by grabbing their tail first, because I find this hold takes less slime off him." I like that idea.

When wading, it's hard to get a tired but still fighting redfish close enough to grab the leader. What I usually do when the fish is tired enough is to extend my rod hand as far back behind me as I can. I hold the rod vertical or tilted toward me a bit. With my other hand, I reach out

Quite often, the angler or the guide will just lead the fish gently and slowly by the tippet, and then grab it by hand. It's my preferred way. MARKUS HAUGG

and get the leader. Then, I give myself some extra slack and put the rod under my casting arm.

Now I have both hands free. One will hold the tippet close to the red, and the other I'll use to grab the red under the belly or by the fork of the tail. And since the red is in the water, my hands are wet, as they should be when handling a fish. When wading, I like to fish a rod shorter than 9-feet. Short rods let me make a more accurate presentation, and landing a fish by myself is infinitely easier.

The Landing Net

Personally, if I'm going to release a fish, I usually prefer to do it by hand. Besides, since I have the somewhat minimalistic philosophy of carrying only what I absolutely need, I seldom keep a net in my skiff or canoe. But if you want to use a net, the right one is fine, if used properly.

I seldom use a net for reds, unless I intend to keep them.

The right nets are knotless with rubber coating, which removes the least amount of the fish's protective slime.

When you're ready to land a red with a net, bring the fish to the net, not the net to the fish. A red, even hooked, can move pretty fast, and you'll find that the net has a lot of resistance when you try to move it through the water, so there's no way you're going to catch up with a fish to scoop it. So hold the net steady while you bring the fish to the net. Then as the red is almost all under the net, bring the net up so that the rim is a bit out of water.

Once you have your red in the net, keep it in the water. Let the fish recover from a hard fight. And since the red is still in the water, free to move a little inside the net, there's little friction, if any, between the net and the fish. But, whatever you do, don't lift the red out of the water with the net if you intend to release it.

Also, I think it's best if you get a net large enough so that when a big red is in the net, it's not bent in a U, but instead laying straight, able to move its fins while breathing comfortably.

Removing the Hook

Whether you're holding the red by hand or you have it in a net, it's much better to keep the fish in the water. And the less you handle the red, the better. So if you can use your forceps to remove the hook without touching the fish, while the fish is still in the water, this is ideal. But if the red is thrashing around and making things difficult, you often have to hold it. You can try holding it under the head or with a finger in the jaw, and the other hand around the anal fin, or holding the fork of the tail. Again, make sure your hands are wet. If you have to take the fish out of the water because you can't get the hook out,

Sandy Moret lands a red for me by hand—a method many anglers prefer. BRAD MILLER

definitely don't use gloves or a towel to hold it, as they will remove more slime than bare wet hands.

Another way to hold a red, especially if it's being difficult, is to hold it upside down. Turn the red belly up, and it will relax and stay still; this state is called "tonic immobility," and you can take advantage of this tranquil moment to remove the hook. Just don't take any longer than you need to remove the hook, and it shouldn't do the red any damage.

Photographing Your Catch

You just landed a significant fish. It could be your first red on a fly, a big redfish, or maybe your daughter's first redfish, so you want to take a few shots on your camera. I understand that: I've been photographing fish and covering fishing trips most of my life. However, you need to think of the redfish first. Make sure you keep the fish alive and healthy, and work around its needs.

Now your red is comfortably sitting mostly still in the water, breathing, and moving its fins. Great. This means you have plenty of time to get your camera, and decide how and where you want to pose, what the settings on the camera should be, and what instructions to give the photographer. When you're ready, wet your hands, gently pick up the red with a two-handed horizontal hold, and pose. And please don't hold the fish up into the camera with your hands extended, while biting the rod's cork with your teeth. Instead, just hold the fish naturally close to you. You'll both look great. The water should still be dripping from the fish, and its fins will be erect, making for the best photograph. Let the photographer take a few shots, then put the fish back in the water. Believe me, done this way, thirty seconds is more than enough time.

Another way to photograph yourself with a red, and one that I've started to do more often, is to lean over the gunwale, and hold the red only partly out of the water while the photographer is shooting you also from the gunwale. It looks great and fresh, and the fish only comes partly out of the water for two or three seconds at a time.

And finally, why not take a few shots while fighting the fish? That's memorable too.

How Big Is He?

So you've been fishing reds now for a couple of years and have taken your share. Now you're starting to dream about landing a big one. But when you do land the fish (and if you're persistent, you will), how do you know just how big it is?

Well, my question to you is: how accurate do you need to be? If you want maximum accuracy, you need to get a good scale and have the IGFA (International Gamefish Association) certify it for you. My scales are certified by them. However, unless I'm looking for a world record, I seldom need an exact weight. Give or take 10 percent is good enough for me. And that is one of many reasons why I always carry measuring tape in my tackle bag.

So in checking the chart Aaron supplied for page 20 of this book, a 30-inch redfish—measured to the fork of the tail—is about eleven pounds give or take depending on the location where it was caught. I can live with that. If you can too, get yourself a measuring tape. And if you can't, buy a good scale and call the IGFA. They'll be glad to certify your scale. And tell them Chico sent you.

Releasing Redfish

You got a red, maybe took a couple of photos, and now you are about to return this nice redfish (all reds are nice regardless of size) back into the wild. And it wants to go back, but only if it is in good shape. Remember, not only does it have to continue to make a living chasing a variety of foods, it has to do it while staying away from predators, like sharks. And if it's tired, a predator can recognize that in a second. That red is as good as dead. So take the time to revive a redfish.

Gently hold the fish under the head and the base of the tail, and give it time to regain its strength. Try not to decide when to push it off, but rather let it decide when to leave. An exhausted fish may need a few minutes to recover. This is especially true in the summer months when they are more stressed and exhausted because of the lack of oxygen.

I remember Captain Greg Dini, who chases lots of reds in Florida and Louisiana, telling me how hard it can be in the heat of the summer to release a redfish: "Yes, they may kick hard and get away from your hands, but soon their heads may be stuck in the grass and they can't even move. What I often do is find a sandy pothole, with cooler water, and release him from there."Also, you can help a red revive faster if you can get some water passing through its gills by moving it forward. Try placing it facing forward on the skiff and have someone pole for a few yards. It'll love that.

When you are ready to release a fish, take your time, making sure it is fully recovered and ready to go back to its world.

If the red finally starts to swim away, only to stop, maybe tangled in grass, get it on a clear spot and try the same procedure again. The fish probably needed more time. Keep judging its condition—you are its doctor now.

Captain Nick Sassic says, "I take my time when releasing a red. But even when he finally breaks away, no matter how strong he looks, I watch him and watch him until I lose sight of him. Then I know he has a good chance of making it."

After Releasing Your Red

You've just landed a redfish, and you can't wait to get another one. I understand. However, your tackle just went through a fight. Let's make sure it's ready for the next one.

First, wash your hands of any slime. You don't want slime on your tackle, but most of all, on your fly line. If your fly line needs dressing, this is the time to pass the applicator. The difference in casting performance and ease of use between a dry fly line and well-oiled line is huge. Go down the leader checking for any nicks or frays, especially on the tippet, which is your weakest section. Now check the point of the hook for sharpness by using the method I mentioned earlier and testing it against your thumbnail. If it sticks, fine. If not, touch it with your file. You want that point to stick on flesh at the slightest touch.

And finally, make sure the fly isn't tangled. Just one feather wrapped around the hook, and you won't get a strike, even after a perfect presentation. After inspecting it, I like to test it by slapping it on the water and swimming it in front of me. I'll even cast it back by the angler poling just to see how it looks to him. Confidence is important in any game. You'll find that all of the above takes only a couple of minutes, and it's absolutely necessary. Now you can go back fishing, knowing you are ready for any size redfish. Good luck.

Chapter 18

The Other Fish in the Redfish's World

The shallow water world of the redfish, whether in the marshes of Louisiana, the flats of the Carolinas, or the mangrove backwaters of the Everglades in South Florida, contain an incredible variety of food. And such rich quantities of crustaceans and fish also attract many other gamefish, like black drum, seatrout, tripletail, snook, tarpon, sharks, and more. But to fly-fish for them, it's best if you understand their own peculiarities as to how they feed, what foods they prefer, and where in the water column they feed. For example, you'd certainly present a fly to a black drum a lot different than to a seatrout, as you'll see further below. So let's examine each species in detail.

Black Drum

Like Rodney Dangerfield, black drums get no respect. Yet you can sight-cast to them in shallow water while they tail, cruise, or mud on the bottom; they are plentiful; they grow to over 100 pounds; and they fight hard. Besides, if you get good at catching them, you'll be practicing casting accuracy, fly manipulation, and fish-fighting skills as a bonus. I have always thought that when you learn to fish for a new species, you can't help but learn more about its environment and the different foods in their habitat, in turn helping you become a better angler. So if you haven't tried casting to a big tailing black drum, you are missing out.

Pogonias cromis, the black drum, is a member of the croaker family, and closely related to the red drum or redfish. It has a shorter, deeper body than the redfish, and that causes the black drum to often show their backs out of the water when a similar-size but slimmer redfish would not show at all. This can often make a black drum highly visible in the flats. Like the other members of the croaker family, black drums have the ability to use their air bladder to make a loud drumlike sound. Actually, they're louder than any of the other members of the family. They have to be the most vocal fish in the flats. Often when a school passes your boat, you can hear them.

When young (under eight pounds or so) the fish tends to show vertical bars. The mature individual varies in colors, probably depending on environment and color of the bottom it frequents, from a silvery gray to a very dark, almost black color. And a black drum doesn't have spots close to the tail, like the redfish does.

Unlike redfish, black drum have whiskerlike forms underneath the chin called barbels. These barbels perform a dual function in taste and feel, helping a black drum to find its prey. Its diet consists mostly of crustaceans and mollusks, so it feeds mostly on the bottom. A dark weighted fly worked on the bottom is a good choice.

Black drums grow slow—a 30 inch fish is about ten years old, and old fish are often over fifty years old. Fish

A young black drum showing vertical bars that will fade as it grows past 8 or 10 pounds. Notice the barbels under the chin, looking like whiskers.

A copper-colored black drum taken on a crab fly and 9-weight rod. Captain Lance Ledet, who made a difficult approach in the wind, holds the fish for me. CORBETT DAVIS

Corbett Davis holds a 45-pound black drum taken on an 8-weight rod. It was a long fight.

between 5 and 25 pounds are quite common in many flats. And they can grow to over 100 pounds. I've taken a few over 40 pounds on a fly and have seen them in the flats over 60 pounds. And I've fished for them from the Carolinas all the way to the end of Texas. Depending on the area, I've seen them in the flats in every month of the year.

Also, they are often confused with redfish while tailing, since they may tail in the same area. But keep in mind that the black drum has a more translucent tail, and if you look closely, you'll be able to tell the difference. It's not unusual for a beginning angler to cast surface flies to what he thinks are tailing redfish without a strike for hours—only to find out, eventually, that he has been casting to black drum, which rarely if ever will come up for a fly. We've all done that at one time or another!

Captain Bou Bosso, who often fishes the backwaters of the Everglades, had this to say about distinguishing reds from black drums when mudding in shallow water: "I can tell black drums from reds when they are mudding because unlike the single, more defined mudding of the redfish, the black drum muds all over; they can make a mess of the place." I asked Bou if they were sloppy eaters, and he laughed and said, "Yes, they are very sloppy."

I'm usually not looking for black drum, but they find me while I'm looking for redfish, snook, or baby tarpon. And if the conditions are right, meaning actively feeding or tailing, I may decide to go for them. I'll take a solitary fish or a few fish in a small pod, especially if well spread out so I can take my time and work each one. Then a well-placed weighed fly will have a good chance of a take. Frankly, I've always found the black drum moody and unpredictable when fished with a fly, but I think this also adds to its charm. Aaron Adams always tells me: "They feed just like redfish, Chico, only slower."

THE PRESENTATION

Fly placement is of the essence when you're trying to catch a black drum. You must strive to put the fly right under its "chin." Remember that they use their barbels to feel and smell—that's how they locate shrimp, clams, crabs, even some minnows. So they seldom will go far out of their way to chase a fly. Try to keep the fly close and in front of the fish for as long as possible while still moving the fly slowly. Even let the fly rest for a few seconds from time to time. Especially a crab pattern. So when casting, first make sure you determine which way the head is facing, or which way the fish is moving so you can place the fly a little ahead and let the black drum run into it. Trying to cast close to the fish itself is seldom going to be accurate enough to yield a strike.

Captain Scott Sommerlatte, who has fished black drum in Texas, Florida, and Louisiana, put it this way: "The trick to catch black drum is to tickle their whiskers. Do that and they'll probably take your fly." So you can't appeal to their sense of smell, and their sight is not that good if the area is all muddy, so you need to make sure they can feel your fly. Yes, it has to be that close. And remember: cast and cast until you either get a hit, or spook the fish. As long as you don't spook them, and they keep feeding, you probably have a chance.

In setting the hook, remember that the strike will probably be subtle. So as you retrieve, make sure you have a tight line, with a minimum of slack. This way, if there's the slightest bump during the retrieve, you'll feel it. Also remember to keep the rod tip close to the water for no slack and no slap on the water. We've already talked about this in previous chapters. And when you do feel a fish, set the hook by the strip-strike method, as always. But remember that black drums have a hard, rubbery mouth, especially big fish, so strike hard.

When the black drum feels the steel in its mouth, you never know exactly how it will react. Sometimes it'll shake its head hard several times, sometimes it'll move slowly away eventually gaining some speed, and other times it may just take off. You just need to look down to manage the clearing of your fly line and start fighting.

Think of big black drums as heavyweight boxers—slow but powerful, with plenty of endurance. And if they manage to drag you into deeper water, they never seem to give up. I fought a drum over 40 pounds with 12-pound-test tippet, and it was quite a while before I could get my hands on the fish and remove the hook. On the other hand, on summer days with temperature in the 90s, a fight may not last that long.

Use a fly line heavy enough to cast the fly. In this case it's much like for reds, a 6- or 7-weight works for light flies, 8-weight is the best all around, and a 9- or 10-weight works for big heavy flies, when casting to larger fish. A 9- to 12-foot leader with 12- or 16-pound tippet is fine. And a fluorocarbon tippet will help get the fly down, if you want. But regardless of how tough black drums can be, since the fight is usually in open water, you can land a big fish with an 8-weight, no problem. Then there are days when they can be hard to approach. Days of clear water, extra shallow and calm, will make the black drum (or any flats species) extra spooky. Then, I may go to 12-foot leaders and lighter rods. And the challenge of those conditions can be fun too.

Most flies I use for black drum are black or dark color combinations of brown and olive. I've also done well using a spoon fly, mostly on dark colors, but I do remember taking them on gold spoons too. Another fly that has worked for me and other anglers is a fly with a rattle. It seems the noise also attracts them. Weighted flies, like Clousers, dark shrimp patterns heavily dressed, and crab patterns, have all worked for me. I recommend using weedguards, since you're often dragging the bottom with the fly.

Seatrout

Seatrout can be one of the easiest fish of the lot if you blind cast for them in a few feet of water, or they can be one of the hardest to take on a fly if you sight-cast for

The seatrout can be the easiest fish to take in the world if you blind cast for them in a few feet of water, and one of the hardest if you sight-cast for the big one in shallow flats.

them in shallow water. You can find seatrout in grassy open areas of three to six feet of water or so, often with potholes and maybe some structure. Basins are good places too. Since you need to cover water, you can best fish these open areas by drifting. As you drift, it's best to cast to one side of and slightly ahead of the boat. You stand with your back to the wind that's pushing the boat and make a side cast.

Then you let the boat pass the fly as it swings around its side. This way, the fly will be swimming for a long time, with more chances of getting a hit. And by the time you finish your retrieve, the fly will be on the upwind side of the boat. Then you turn around and make another cast. Don't cast directly ahead of the drift, especially if you're drifting rather fast, because you won't be able to retrieve quickly enough as the boat quickly catches up with your fly. Besides, the time that you would actually be moving the fly in these cases is very short. If two of you are fly-fishing, you may have to move or lower your fly rod while the other caster makes his cast. With practice you'll get a rhythm going that will allow both anglers to cover lots of water from both sides of the boat.

Now you would think that in this depth you'd be better off with a slow-sink line, but that has not been my experience. Instead I prefer to have a floater, or even better a clear floater if I have one, with a 10-foot leader or so, and a weighted fly. This way you can keep the fly down, but keep the fly line on the surface and out of sight of trout, which are mostly on the bottom or close to the bottom. Only when the water gets so deep that the fly when retrieved cannot stay in the lower third of the water column, will I go to a clear slow-sink line—say, over 6 feet deep.

If the water is clear, I also like to use a popper. Some of the biggest trout I've taken in these conditions have been while using a big popper. And by the way, trout like a big mouthful, like a snook, or even a black bass, so don't be afraid to use a big shrimp or fish pattern for them.

Also if you find areas with schools of baitfish, like finger mullet for example, they will probably have seatrout, and other gamefish, feeding on them. But even though you are in a bit deeper water than a regular flat, you should still approach these schools of bait as carefully and as quietly as you do in the flats. Believe me, it will pay off in big fish.

Captain Nick Sassic often fishes for trout when they're working a school of bait in deeper water, and has his own method:

> In a big school of bait, don't just cast over the bait, but instead, fish under the bait, where the trout will be. I like to use a large Seaducer with pink wings and chartreuse hackle and big lead eyes, so it swims under the bait. And yes, Chico, it's ugly. But this fly will cast a big silhouette they can see, and it's something quite different than all the other bait. If I don't get results, then I'll change colors to all black. I've taken many big trout throughout the years this way.

But in the flats, it's an entirely different story. Many of the seatrout that you encounter in the flats are big trout. They're wise big trout, sitting still, waiting in ambush, and mostly looking straight ahead—not looking down tailing like a redfish might. So they can often spot an angler or skiff at a distance. It's all about long, accurate casts here.

Some of the longest and most difficult casts I've had to make have been to a laid up big seatrout in a clear shallow flat or sitting on a pothole. So be prepared to make long casts, with a 12-foot long leader, minimum. Try to make the first cast count, because these guys don't give too many chances before they leave. The tricky part

Diane Pallot with a large seatrout, taken the hard way, by sight-casting in shallow, clear water with a 14-foot leader. Caramba, *that is tough!* FLIP PALLOT

Flip Pallot releasing a big, dark seatrout taken in a shallow flat in mid-Florida. Notice how gently he is handling this big trout as he puts it back in the water. That's respect for the fish. DIANE PALLOT

is to be able to spot these big trout before they see you. Unlike redfish, these guys are harder to see, even in shallow water. So stay focused, and if fishing with a good guide, let him help you.

My favorite flies for big trout are either a 3- to 4-inch Seaducer, unweighted, in white and red, all chartreuse, all black or white, yellow, and grizzly or a baitfish pattern in white with a dark back in green or gray and big eyes. And for a surface fly, I use a lightweight slider mostly, in all white, all yellow, or all chartreuse. And by the way, the strike on these sliders can be spectacular for all in the boat to watch.

Captain Richard Black in the Everglades area says, "Use an unweighted fly, but one that is bushy, maybe with lots of hackles, so it pushes water. This way it will attract that big trout to look up. This can make a difference."

Sheepshead

With a range from around Cape Cod through Florida and the Gulf of Mexico to Brazil, the sheepshead inhabits most places you find redfish. And while they like structure, like rock piles and jetties, fortunately, they also like to come in the flats and feed. They can grow to over 20 pounds, and I've seen them in the flats over 10 pounds. Personally, I think they are pretty neat fish and hard to confuse with other fish, with six or seven wide, black vertical bars over a silvery body. And you should know that their large front teeth and rows of molars often make it hard to set the hook on them.

Most of the sheepshead I've taken on a fly have been in Louisiana. My best day was four. But I've caught very few elsewhere. They can be hard to approach, and it's hard to make them take a fly. Only in the past few years have a few guides and anglers started to develop methods to take them consistently.

I more or less fish for them as I do for permit. I use a small fly, mostly a crab pattern but occasionally a small shrimp pattern too, in colors that mimic the bottom I'm fishing, or darker. So I use browns, olives, black, and combinations of those colors, usually in size 4 hooks or so. I keep the fly right on the bottom and move it slow, crawl it, occasionally letting the fly just sit there on the bottom for a few seconds. I try to make the fly look alive while not moving it much. A 6- or 7-weight is ideal to cast the small flies and makes for a quiet presentation, which is often needed.

Captain Lance Ledet with one of several sheepshead we took that day, some tailing, while using small weighted crab and shrimp patterns.

And while I'm retrieving, I make sure to have a straight line, with no slack, so when a fish takes it, I can feel it immediately. Then I strike hard, because I find these fish difficult to hook. It's got to be those big teeth.

One of the toughest places I've fished for sheepshead is my home waters of the Everglades. They can be spooky and difficult. And I know many good anglers who have tried to catch a sheepshead in the Glades and have yet to succeed. Some anglers call the sheepshead "the permit of the Everglades," and I can understand why. But Captain Jared Raskob, one of the top guides in the Keys and Everglades area, has made a project out of figuring out how to catch them consistently. And by now, he has had many days of taking one or two fish, with the best day taking four sheepshead. We all lost money on that bet. So, of course, I had to ask Jared how he was doing it. He told me:

Actually, [sheepshead] are a lot like permit. I use a black crab pattern in size 4 hook, but only an inch long. And I put root beer–colored legs, and two small brown feathers sticking out the back. I cast the fly 2 or 3 feet in front of the fish and let the sheepshead come to the fly. But when he gets close, I pop it hard, a 6-inch pop, then I barely move it, and wait to feel the strike.

So, a hard 6-inch pop, eh? I've got to try this method next time I'm in sheepshead territory.

Snook

We were over an hour away from the dock, deep in the Everglades, while dark clouds covered the sky. It had been a good day's fishing, and going home would've been the obvious and mature thing to do. But we were fly-fishing, and when you're fly-fishing, you don't always make mature decisions. We stayed, of course. The reason is that we'd come to a cove with a promising shoreline. An outgoing tide had dropped the water level of the cove to the point that we could just about see the bottom in many areas. This meant that we'd be able to see and sight-cast to any decent-size fish swimming along the shoreline. We weren't leaving.

So with low visibility caused by the clouds and time of day, I felt conditions were just right for a surface fly. I don't remember why, but among many to choose from, I chose a yellow popper that had a rather slim body with a small, cupped front. I felt the small cup's sound would imitate the light noises a small shrimp or baitfish would make on the surface—just enough noise to attract a predator, but not so much that it would spook the fish. At least, that was my thinking.

As we poled 50 feet or so from the edge of the mangroves, we started to spook fish, probably redfish. The problem was low visibility caused by a heavy overcast sky, and strong wind rippling the surface. So I mostly blind cast ahead of the skiff or against the mangrove roots on the shoreline.

Finally, we came up to a fishy-looking slough, only a few feet wide, where the mangrove branches crisscrossed over the top, making a tunnel. I remember it was dark back in there. Light only fell on the entrance of the tunnel at the mouth of the slough; after that, it was all in shadows, too dark to see. The slough looked deep. The obvious cast was to get the popper way back and see what was there. After a couple of attempts, I finally got a tight loop back into the shadows. I couldn't see the popper or hear it pop as I retrieved, trying to produce minimum noise. But we had no problem hearing the loud characteristic pop from a big snook, as the fish took it.

As I set the hook, the fish's first reaction was to come right out of the slough. And as soon as it found itself in open water, it headed for a large fallen black mangrove tree trunk a few yards away, and soon had me wrapped around several of the small branches of the fallen tree.

We poled the skiff right to the fallen tree, and by quickly breaking a few of the dead branches, I was able to untangled the leader, now a bit frayed, and set the snook free to continue the fight. To our delight, it made the mistake of dashing for open water. The snook made a strong run, but we knew we had it. And sure enough, after a few more minutes of fight, and the skiff now 60 or more feet away from the many structures of the shoreline, it was over.

Full of confidence, we congratulated ourselves. My friend came down from the platform and dropped the push pole. Then, noticing that the hook had torn part of the lip and was barely holding on, we decided to get the net. But the net turned out to be too small. So we figured we should use a gaff to slip the point around the lower jaw. The gaff was in the front hatch way back toward the bow. Soon my friend's body was half into the hatch as he fished for it. And I had reached into my bag and had my camera on hand while keeping the rod bent so there was no slack. I wasn't about to lose the fish.

Meanwhile, during all this, a strong wind had been pushing the boat back to the old fallen black mangrove tree. And soon, we were only a few feet from it. The snook was the first to realize we had not staked the boat. And like Brer Rabbit who lived among the thorns, this fish had lived all its life among those mangroves. The rest was history. Actually, after a lifetime of fly-fishing for snook, I should have known better. This idiosyncratic, unpredictable fish has given me more frustration and more delightful moments than any other fish I have fly-fished for. It was the first fish I caught on a fly rod, back in Cuba in the 50s, and I confess, it is still my favorite.

Captain Steve Huff, releasing another big snook taken on fly. More big snook on a fly in the flats have been taken with Steve at the pole than with any other person I know.

Even if you've never seen one before, a snook is hard to mistake. Its prominent black lateral line, running from the top of the gill to the end of the tail, is unique. It also has a purpose. That lateral line serves to detect movement and vibrations in the surrounding water. It is used to find food and to avoid predators. A snook makes good use of both lateral lines!

Also, a long protruding lower jaw makes snook very obvious. And like other fish in brackish waters, they change colors as they move from lighter to darker bottoms to better blend in the environment. They also often exhibit beautiful bright yellow pelvic and caudal fins. You can't mistake these either.

The common snook, the one you're most likely to catch, is *Centropomus undecimalis*, and it can grow to well over 50 pounds. But anytime you catch a double-figure snook on a fly, you've got a nice one. There are many other snook species and subspecies, but most don't grow as large as the common snook. I have taken a few of these species with a fly, such as the fat snook (*Centropomus parallelus*), the tarpon snook (*Centropomus pectinatus*), and others. I've caught a few over 20 pounds, a couple under 6 inches, and the 30-pound-plus snook of my dreams on a fly rod is just that—a dream. So far, I've hooked two fish I thought were well over 30 pounds but have never landed them. One frayed my 30-pound shock tippet, which is why I mostly use 40- and even 50-pound shock tippets when I'm in areas that have big snook. The other fish made a powerful run deep into the mangroves during a high tide, and actually cut the belly of my 8-weight fly line when it ran across an oyster bed. This snook was hooked from shore in the Marco canal that joints the Tamiami Trail. I'll never forget either one of them. Anyway, I'm still looking for that 30-plus-pounder.

I'll leave the last comments on snook to an old friend who has spent a lifetime fishing and guiding for them. As far as I know, he has guided fly fishers to more snook over 20 pounds—while sight-casting or working a shoreline, not chumming—than any other guide I know. I'm talking about Captain Steve Huff, who says:

> For me, after a lifetime of fishing and poling after snook, they are still a mystery fish. They don't tail like a bonefish or redfish, or roll like a tarpon, so they don't usually give themselves

A snook hunting for food over turtle grass, one of its natural environments. PAT FORD

away, even when fishing areas where I just know they are around. I find them the most challenging of the flats gamefish to figure out. Yet, they are an honest fish. By that I mean that if you get the fly to them before they see you and do all the right things, you'll get a bite. Which is not usually the case with permit, or heavily fished tarpon . . . you know? When it's all been said and done, snook is still my favorite fish.

I'll mention more about where to find them, retrieve, flies, and tackle, after we talk about the mighty tarpon, because you fish for baby tarpon and snook with similar techniques.

Tarpon

Running into tarpon while fishing for reds, even the baby tarpon you'll most often encounter, is exciting and fun. But before we get into tarpon, I need to share with you my most memorable tarpon story.

It was mid-June 1969, tarpon season for sure. And in those days, tarpon were plentiful and dumb as rocks. And better yet, I went fishing pretty much whenever I wanted to. Those were the days. The phone rang late one evening. I was probably half asleep when I picked up the receiver, but I could sense the urgency in the voice of the caller. It was one of my fishing *compadres*, Flip Pallot, telling me that tarpon were thick in the Lower Keys, and if I wanted to go, he knew just were to find them.

"When?" is all I remember asking.

"Tomorrow," he said.

"Let's go," I said.

"I'll pick you up tomorrow at 5 a.m. Get some sleep. You can rig on the drive down," he said, and hung up.

I remember being surprised. I thought he was going to say next week. But in a few hours was fine. Actually, in those days we did a lot of last-minute rigging in the car on the way to some fishing destination. And packing took little time those days, probably because we didn't have that much tackle.

I took a small bag with a few large, bright tarpon flies on 4/0 hooks, leader material, pliers, file, hat and sun glasses, and placed it by the front door. Then I grabbed my tarpon rod—a fiberglass Fenwick, with a slow action to the butt, designed for a 10-weight floater or an

11-weight shooting head, with a Fin-Nor size 3 that had a 10-weight white floating line and 175 yards of 30-pound-test Dacron. I placed the rod also by the door. Done.

Then I went to the refrigerator to get a couple of Cuban sandwiches I knew my mom had made—Cuban bread, ham, pork, Swiss cheese, real butter, and mustard . . . and as Flip always said, "just the right amount of thinly sliced pickles." He still says that.

Done packing, back to bed. In retrospect, I find that life was so simple then. Today it takes me hours to pack, even when I try to be as minimalistic as possible.

Next morning, before 5 a.m., Flip was at my door, trailing an early 50s Challenger skiff, fully reconditioned and named the Last Flat. The skiff, minimally rigged, was squeaky clean, as always. On the transom hung a black Mercury 50 horsepower engine with a tiller steering. Attached to the port side gunwale was a kill gaff, with rope knots tied by the legendary Captain Jimmy Albright that were a true work of art. On the starboard side was the push pole, always with a guava fork; Flip's favorite to this day. No instrumentation, no poling platform, no nonsense.

Soon we were riding south. I remember Flip driving, a little above speed limit to "catch the tide," while I rigged tarpon leaders. When we reached Summerland Key, he pulled off the highway and launched at an old ramp on the Gulf side. No one was around. Soon we were on plane, and headed for a place tarpon anglers called Hommell's Corner off Loggerhead bank.

Flip had fished this bank in all tides, but the high outgoing we had that morning was what he wanted that day. I remember having some action as the tide receded, maybe we jumped some fish, but that was it. By noon, I called for lunch. Flip staked us out on the edge of the bank, the water now much lower, and we pulled out the Cuban sandwiches. Soon I was fully concentrated on lunch, but Flip, always the angler, also kept a watch on the surroundings.

I was halfway through my sandwich when Flip saw a fish coming around the edge of a mullet mud. It was moving. We threw the sandwiches and sodas aside. I reached for my fly rod and began to strip line off the reel as fast as I could, while Flip grabbed the push pole and poled hard to intercept the tarpon. It was soon evident that the closest point of interception was still going to be a fairly long cast. So, at the last moment, Flip turned the Challenger so I had a clear backcast, and then gave me what he thought was good reassuring advice. As I remember, it went something like this:

"No pressure Don Chico, but the fish is huge, and he is moving fast. This is your tarpon of a lifetime . . . Get him." You think I had a little pressure?

I remember false-casting the large 4/0 grizzly and orange streamer and trying to send the fly well in front of the tarpon, since it was moving pretty good. The cast unrolled nicely, but by the time it hit the water, the tarpon was right on it. The fish didn't hesitate—didn't even slow down. The strike was instantaneous, and the fish's head came out of the water as it inhaled the fly—funny how I can still see that fish break the surface of the turbid waters of Hommell's Corner.

I set the hook, and the fish was in the air immediately, leaping and greyhounding in the shallow water. But then it decided to run, and soon most of my line was gone from the reel. Meanwhile, Flip was poling fast and furious. As I remember, the fish stayed in relatively shallow water, did not jump much toward the end of the fight, but exhibited tremendous endurance. Finally, the steady pressure from the fiberglass rod took its toll, and Flip was able to slip his small release gaff into the lip of the giant female tarpon. And then he handed me the gaff while he went and got his Pentax camera loaded with black and white Tri-X film.

However, we had a problem. I couldn't lift her. She was too big and I was too tired. So Flip suggested I step out on the flat for the photo; this way, the fish partly on

Well, this is the tarpon I fought with Flip at the push pole in the Lower Keys. Notice the Challenger skiff from the early 1950s, a killer gaff on the gunwale as was customary in those days, my old Rolex watch I've had since 1955, a guava fork on the push pole, a Fin-Nor size 3 wedding cake reel, and a fiberglass Fenwick rod. Those were the days! FLIP PALLOT

the water, so I wouldn't have to lift the whole body. And so, we took a few photos at last. I was exhausted, but emotionally on a high. That high is still there every time I think of our adventure. For me, nothing beats an adventure you share with a good friend. It can be a big fish you caught, or a fish you lost after a long fight, or enduring a severe thunderstorm, or any other exciting experience in the outdoors. For me, the adventure beats the actual catch or number of fish caught. So many years have gone by since that day, a lot of fishing trips and a lot of salt spray, yet Flip and I often talk about that big tarpon. We speculate about how big she was. The photo taken with a standard 50-millimeter lens does not show it as big as today's photos with ultra wide lenses. But is that important? Also, we talk about the tackle we used in those days: how simple, basic it was, yet how well it worked. Yes, adventures like that are never forgotten.

And by the way, when we finally climbed back in the skiff, neither one of us could find any trace of the Cuban sandwiches. Whatever happened to them?

Well, back to finding tarpon while fishing for reds. You'll find that, especially on the redfish's warmer range, you'll often encounter tarpon. And to make this encounter more exciting, with a tarpon, it could be a 10-pounder, a 40-pounder, or even one over 100 pounds. I've hooked quite a few big tarpon over the years while looking for redfish and snook. And regardless of how light a fly rod I'm holding, I'm going to try to hook that tarpon. But the average tarpon in the shallow redfish and snook flats is probably 5 to 30 pounds or so, and just perfect for the outfit you are using for reds.

Author holding a baby tarpon that took a Hot Lips on the surface. STEPHEN FERNÁNDEZ

The tarpon you'll find in the redfish's range is *Megalops atlanticus*, or the Atlantic tarpon. It grows to over 8 feet and just under 300 pounds. Tarpon close to and over 200 pounds have been taken on a fly. My biggest was "estimated" around 170 pounds. But on the other hand, I find most fishermen's opinions on weight to be a bit on the high side, while scales have no opinions. Your choice.

To me a tarpon is "uniquely silver," not just silver. They glow for me and have a coloration of their own. With big eyes, some soft ray fins, and a bluish or greenish or dark back, they are gorgeous. And they are different in that they must breath air. If they can't get to the surface to gulp air, they die. And they do this by a rolling motion that gives them away to any angler hunting for them. I've seen tarpon rolling in deep water that I guessed at close to 200 pounds, and then I've also seen them rolling, and caught them, in tiny creeks, canals, and mosquito ditches where they measured well under 6 inches.

You'll find that a 2-pound tarpon rolls faster than a 20-pounder. And a 100-pounder rolls slower than the 20-pounder. But other than that, a tarpon rolling is a tarpon rolling. They are truly spectacular fish.

Tactics for Snook and Baby Tarpon

I find that the snook and baby tarpon that one encounters mostly in the southern parts of the redfish's territory share a lot in common in terms of where they feed, the salinity they prefer, how they like their food or flies presented, and more. So I've joined them together at this point to avoid being repetitive.

One of the best places to find snook and tarpon in the backwaters is during a receding tide in creeks, rivers, around mangroves or sawgrass, and even in flats with small channels or potholes.

What happens is that during the high stages of the tide, and when large quantities of water flood the area, baitfish and crustaceans can find places to hide from predators, by looking for cover among the flooded sawgrass, mangrove roots, or other structures. Here they are relatively safe, often in just a few inches of water. And while still attacked by a variety of wading birds, it's still worth it for them to stay hidden.

But once the tide starts to ebb, the water level will eventually drop to the point that the baitfish and crustaceans cannot remain, and they're forced to come out of cover into more open water, where snook, tarpon, redfish, and many other species of fish are waiting. Also, the wading birds that were trying to feed on them way back in the "bushes," during the high stages of the tide, are now at the mouths of creeks, small channels, sloughs, and so on, where water is pouring out and carrying food. So the bait is out, and so are the wading birds that follow them, and the predators. And so you should be there.

One easy way to find these conditions is to find birds feeding around an opening, like a slough or mouth of creeks and rivers, for example, where water is pouring out. This will indicate that baitfish are pouring out, especially if you see birds feeding, the chances are there will be gamefish feeding with them. And it's a very exciting moment for an angler, when he approaches a group of birds feeding on a shoreline, and as he gets closer, he sees the strikes all around the area, often spooking the birds up in the air as they pop the baitfish on the surface.

For this type of situation, you want to see a good moving tide (or a strong wind that is blowing in the right direction to empty the water). And you will find that the action continues to move slowly with the tide until, at its lowest stage, the fish are around the mouth of the creeks, rivers, or canals, and around some of the usual small flats in the area.

And you'll find them in tidal flats, where redfish may also be present, as long as the tide is moving, incoming or outgoing. But on a flood or ebb tide, with no water movement, you're usually better off to move to another place.

Anyway, when you encounter a snook or baby tarpon, first keep in mind that unlike redfish, who are more often looking down for food on or near the bottom, snook and tarpon prefer their food at eye level or above. It's awkward for a snook or tarpon, with their protruding lower jaws, to go down for the fly, but natural to rise to it. So, you want a fly that is not going to dive to the bottom, but rather stay at the fish's level or above. An unweighted or lightly weighted fly, or even a surface fly is usually best.

I don't retrieve for them much different than for redfish. If I'm using a shrimp pattern, then retrieving at mid-speed with hops may be best. If using a baitfish pattern, I will usually fish it a bit faster. And maybe, in some situations where they are feeding hard and furious on baitfish, I may retrieve a mullet or other larger baitfish pattern faster than I would have for a redfish.

But when working a fly to feeding fish on receding water, I cast the fly as close as I can to the action, which is usually right against the shoreline, and try to keep it acting alive while not moving it forward much. I want the fly to stay close to the action as long as possible.

One of my favorite fly patterns for snook and baby tarpon is a white, yellow, and grizzly Seaducer. As far as I know, this color combination goes back almost a hundred years. I also like bait patterns in light colors like white or yellow with a dark-colored back—or in all black or black and purple, especially in off-color waters. And if I think they may take flies on the surface, then a slider or a Hot Lips are my first choices. When I use a popper, I usually don't pop it too loud.

Once hooked, a snook may come out of the water on a clear jump or it may do one of its famous head shakes with head and pectoral fins out of the water. But if there's any cover nearby, the snook will head for it. Your job is to try and stop that fish. So keep the rod low while you put on as much pressure as you feel the tippet will stand. And if the snook reaches cover and tangles you, then ease pressure, and quietly approach the fish, trying not to excite it, then gently untangle the mess from whatever structure you're tangled on. But before you resume fighting, try and look at the leader and see if any parts are severely frayed. If so, resume fighting, but apply less pressure now, so as not to break the fish off. I've landed hundreds of snook after a tangled mess and with frayed leaders that were about to break.

But a hooked tarpon, whether 5 pounds or 50, is a different fight. If a hooked snook is an alley fight, hitting below the belt and throwing garbage cans, then the tarpon fight is usually a clean fight, Madison Square Garden–style. Once hooked, a tarpon most likely makes a short to medium run and then jumps—once, twice,

Often when fishing small creeks and canals, you can encounter tiny tarpon, from less than 6 inches to a couple of pounds or so. If I know I may encounter them, I'll bring along one of my trout rods, say a 4-weight or so, and fish them with an inch long size 8 streamer. Here, Stephen is releasing one of many tiny tarpon we took that day while fishing out of our canoe.

many times, you never know. And more likely than not, every jump will be different. No angler that fishes for them, even after many years and many tarpon landed, ever gets tired of seeing them show that display. There has never been, or will ever be, a boring tarpon jump.

Then, as if that's not enough, if you hook a real active fish, it may make a long run away from the skiff, or run toward the skiff, or run to the shoreline. I've had more than one hooked tarpon jump over a tree branch that stood several feet above the water, and land on the other side. Of course in these cases the leader will be tangled all over the branch, and you'll probably ruin your leader, break the fish off, and lose your fly, but who cares?

In terms of tackle, as long as the fly line is heavy enough for you to cast and turn over the fly, you are fine. Just keep in mind that the raspy mouth of both these fish will require a few inches of shock tippet to overcome the abrasion that will often occur during the fight. So as I mentioned earlier, use about 30 pounds for smaller fish, or 40-pound-test for bigger snook and tarpon. And keep in mind that, pound for pound, a snook will fray a leader much more than a tarpon.

Tripletail

I find the tripletail a very unusual but wonderful gamefish for the fly fisher. Here is a fish with a body shape reminiscent of a huge bluegill, taking streamers and even surface flies, fighting hard, and at the end of the fight, also a good one to invite to dinner. And considering the body shape, it's the last fish I would guess to jump when hooked. But they jump often when hooked, and I think that's kind of neat. They can grow to 40 pounds, but the average fish a fly fisher targets is well under 10 pounds. Their huge range more than covers all the redfish's range. So if you're fishing for reds, there's a good chance you don't have to go too far to find them.

Normally a solitary fish, tripletails can be found in bays, sounds, estuaries, and other bodies of open coastal water. And the large adults a fly fisher would be looking for are often found in open water near the surface, close to structure. Other times they will float on their side, perfectly still, just under the surface, mimicking floating debris to escape the eye of predators like sharks.

Juveniles are colored in mottled yellows, browns, or darker colors. But adults are much darker, in colors ranging from a dark brown to a reddish brown, often with a bit of silver gray to them.

I've taken a few big ones, to 12 pounds or so, by sight-casting to them in the flats. But this is not common anywhere I've fished for them, so don't count on it. And the few I've taken in the flats I didn't recognize immediately, but just saw a dark spot in the flat that "didn't look right," made a cast, and hooked up. Lucky me.

Generally, tripletail are fished by running on calm days, checking every marker or buoy, and stopping a hundred feet or so from the structure to determine if it holds fish. If it does, then judging the wind and drift, you should let the skiff pass within casting range. If you're serious about catching them that day, bring an electric engine to make a better approach.

My favorite flies are weighted Clousers, shrimp patterns, and weighed crab patterns, mostly in dark colors. I usually try to make a close presentation and either work the fly back, or often let it sink and watch them dive and take it. But as you can imagine, there are other ways to approach and cast to them. And many places fish different than others.

Captain Scott Sommerlatte, who fishes them mostly in the Texas coast in areas where they are often fished hard, has his own methods: "I like a very calm day to find them. I cast an unweighted fly upcurrent and dead-drift the fly back toward the fish. But the main key here is to use a light tippet, because they can be very leader shy. Definitely no shock tippet. If you've been snook or tarpon fishing, cut the shock tippet off and tie the fly directly to the thin tippet. It makes a huge difference."

Captain Bou Bosso fishes tripletail in the southern parts of the Everglades: "I like to fish them when there is

Tripletail love to hang out against structures. Brooke Black found this one laying right against a buoy. It jumped twice and fought hard in the open water before she landed the fish.

A big lemon shark is cruising in a foot of water, but since the water is fairly muddy in this flat, the shark will be easy to approach within 30 feet or so. It should be an easy cast. Now whether this shark takes the fly or not is another story.

some current. And since this area has lots of shrimp that drift with the tide, I like to mimic that. I cast an unweighted shrimp pattern and when he sees it coming it's very natural, so he eats it most of the time. I just let the current do the work."

Captain Nick Sassic of mid-Florida gave this advice: "Tripletail are always on the down side of the buoy. So you need to cast and past the fly close to him so that he eats close to the structure he is hanging out. Don't want him to have to chase the fly too far. And also don't drop the fly down or he may dive with the fly, not take it, and disappear."

Sharks

Some redfish areas also have a great variety of sharks. Some are small and attracted to the same food the reds are eating, but there are also bigger ones attracted to redfish, snook, trout, and other gamefish. Certainly in the Everglades I see lemons, bulls, spinners, black tips, and even tiger sharks in the flats. I've seen a shark in redfish flats to well over 500 pounds. I didn't cast to that shark, by the way. But I have taken many sharks on a fly over 100 pounds and a couple over 200. They can be exciting to hook and fight in the flats, and they're a great way to learn to fight big fish with your fly rod.

Some of the shark species like spinners will make great jumps, crash a popper on the surface and give you the fight of your life. And if the fish you see within casting range is too big for your taste, don't cast to it. Wait for a smaller one. Still, for all their advertised ferocity, many of the sharks you see in the flats often ignore flies, even large, juicy shark flies. Usually, when I decide to fish large sharks on a fly in the flats, I do it by chumming. This way, you get to cast to many sharks, they are more excited and maybe willing to take a fly, and you can often pick a species or size.

The procedure I use is one used by many fly fishers. I select a flat with 3 to 4 feet of water, often close to deep water. And I like the current, if any, moving toward deep water. You can choose to drift while chumming, which covers lots of water with a good wind, or to just anchor.

This big lemon shark took a big orange streamer. PAT FORD

Many great guides drift and do great but I don't seem to keep sharks long when drifting. So I anchor the skiff by staking it with the push pole. Then I take out the chum, which usually consists of a couple of barracudas or lady-fish—whatever I can catch that day. I open the fish up with a knife, maybe filleting each side 80 percent, and I hang one fish on the port and one on the starboard side of the transom. Each fish is right against the boat. You don't want them too far or the shark will just come in and eat it and go away.

This way they often come very close, say within a yard of the boat, and still not touch the chum. But other times a big shark will crash against the stern of the skiff, rocking it, as it eats part a fish or the whole thing. You want exciting? That's exciting. Anyway, as the sharks start to circle around the back of the skiff, you can cast a fly to them. And if they are excited enough, they'll take the fly.

For murky or off-color water, I like an all-orange fly in 5- to 7-inches depending on shark size. And in clear water, I'll use a baitfish pattern in white with a dark back, flash on the sides, and big doll eyes. Also, I like using a large popper in the same sizes and colors mentioned above. And if a shark takes it, you'll remember the strike.

I try to pass the fly by one of the shark's eyes. They don't see well if you put the fly directly in front. But other times, I may be fishing the flats for reds and snook and see one or several sharks with their fins out, and just rig one of the above mentioned flies on a 9- to 11-weight rod and cast to them. Often they won't take a fly, but when they do, it can be lots of fun.

Also, in terms of size. You'll see sharks from 5 pounds to several hundred pounds, depending on where you're fishing for reds. I usually don't care to cast to anything under 40 pounds or so, depending on my mood.

Once hooked, some sharks like the blacktip will make spectacular jumps. Others can run far enough to empty your reel if you don't follow them. But for all their reputation, they are not strong pound for pound like a big jack, for example. So you can land an 80-pound shark, especially a lemon, with your 9- or 10-weight rod and 16-pound tippet in a reasonable amount of time if you know how to fight fish. And, of course, make sure to use 8 to 12 inches of wire to overcome the bite of those teeth.

Captain Richard Black tells me he has been doing a lot of shark fishing with flies lately. And his clients have done well in the Key's shark tournaments. So I asked him to give a run down on how he is doing it:

> First of all, I like staking the boat instead of drifting. I find that the sharks will come to the chum, where we get to make a few casts, then they'll move away, say, 150 feet, and circle back, where we get to cast to them again. My preferred chum is ladyfish. But I do not cut a fillet 90 percent like most, but instead I cut only about 3 inches, and put it on the water. Then I shake it a lot, every few minutes, to disperse the scent. Then, after a while, I make that 3-inch cut 6 inches, put it back on the water and shake a lot. Works great.
>
> Also, if I get big lemon sharks, which are often lazy, I wake them up a bit by throwing a few 1-inch pieces of ladyfish their way. The pieces soon go to the bottom and as they dig for them, they muddy up the place, and once they do that, they get excited and often take the fly easily.

One final piece of advice on sharks: if you've never done this and are not too familiar with sharks, you're probably much better off to hire a guide that has done this type of fly fishing. You'll see more sharks, learn a lot about how to fish them and how to fight them effectively, and be much safer.

Even More Species of Fish

Regardless of where you're fishing for redfish, you'll find many other species to fly-fish for besides the ones mentioned above. Big jacks, cobia, flounders, goliath grouper, and many other small species can be fun on lighter fly rods. Be open to other species. The more you learn about them, the more you'll learn about the redfish's world, and the better an angler you'll become. I assure you.

On one of the hottest weeks of summer last year, I got a call from a friend of many years, Dr. Lloyd Wruble. Lloyd founded the Herman Lucerne Memorial tournament, in honor of his friend, the late Herman Lucerne, who was a pioneer and legend in his vast knowledge of backcountry fishing in Everglades National Park. This is a wonderful nonprofit tournament where all proceeds go to benefit Everglades National Park. I've often participated in this tournament and fully support it.

Big flounders like this one often will lay in ambush waiting for food to come by with the current. SCOTT SOMMERLATTE

A nice mangrove snapper in a grassy flat. PAT FORD

Anyway, in the many years that Lloyd fished with Herman, he learned those backwaters inside and out, and is now a legend himself. I love it when he takes me way back in those remote areas, but that's usually in the winter time. But as I mentioned, this was the hottest time of the year, so we ended up fishing up front in Florida Bay. We reached the flat we wanted to fish, right by a deep bay area well known for its big reds and big snook, but the tide, while already rising, was still too low, and the flat itself had only a couple of inches of water. It would be another hour before the water level would be high enough for us to pole in.

So, just to kill time, I started to pole the perimeters of the flat, in about two to four feet of water, while Lloyd cast a light 6-weight rod using a weighted shrimp pattern. He took a couple of small jacks and seatrout but not much else. Then we came to a deeper area with a light bottom and a big clump of turtle grass that rose about two feet from the bottom. Lloyd cast the shrimp fly at the clump, let the fly sink a bit, and had a fish on. The fish fought hard for a few minutes but we couldn't see what it was. When he finally brought it to the boat it was a pretty big mangrove snapper. A beautiful fish.

After some discussion, we decided not to keep the fish for dinner. But Lloyd cast again to the clump and hooked another one. By the time the snapper quit biting, we'd taken six of them. It was great fun. But by then the tide was just about right and we poled into the flat.

Dr. Lloyd Wruble with a nice goliath grouper he sight-cast to in the flats. It's another species the fly fisher can find when fishing reds in the southern part of their range. FLIP PALLOT

We actually took some reds and no snook that day. But what Lloyd and I remember distinctly is that big clump and all those beautiful, hard-fighting mangrove snappers on his 6-weight. It's all fun.

Chapter 19

Mr. Redfish Needs Your Help

With more and more anglers moving to the coast, developments, pollution, and fishing pressure, among other factors, have all deeply affected the redfish's world, which needs help more than ever. So as far as I'm concerned, any angler, beginner or experienced, should make sure to join and support one or several conservation organizations. After all, their minimum yearly dues are often much less than the price of a fly line.

I'm aware of our right to go fish for redfish, and enjoy their environment, but I am even more aware of our duty, our responsibility to make sure the next generations also enjoy the beautiful backwaters of the redfish's world. And while we're at it, let's try to leave it better than it is today.

With that in mind, I've always supported, with my money or my time, a variety of organizations. Presently I'm a Florida representative and lifetime member of the International Game Fish Association. I'm also a founding

Brooke Black about to release a good-sized red. PAT FORD

and lifetime member of Bonefish & Tarpon Trust. I am a charter member of the Board of Governors, emeritus status, and a lifetime member of the International Federation of Fly Fishers. Finally, I'm director at large of the Florida Council Board and advisor to the Snook Foundation

These organizations, and many others, are working hard, in one way or another, to help keep a healthy environment for us to enjoy, and they need your help, your money, your time, and your support. Please help in any way you can.

I thank you. And the redfish thanks you.

—Chico Fernández

Below are messages from some of the organizations I support.

Bonefish & Tarpon Trust

A fisherman who's spent as much time on the water as Chico knows that healthy habitats are essential to having quality fisheries. In his time on the water, Chico hasn't just learned about the behaviors of the fish he pursues, he's also learned about the important connections between these fish and their habitats. In fact, it was Chico who once said, "Gone are the days when we could have a good day of fishing, go home, and forget about it. Now we have to become involved in conservation to make sure we have fish in the future." It's this understanding of the importance of fish and habitat conservation that brought Bonefish & Tarpon Trust and Chico together—Chico is a founding member of BTT (founded as Bonefish & Tarpon Unlimited in 1998), and remains on the BTT board.

Since its inception, BTT has been working with fishermen, fishing guides, scientists, and resource managers to design and implement better regulations and conservation measures for bonefish, tarpon, and permit. Since we still have a lot to learn about bonefish, tarpon, and permit biology in order to design effective conservation plans, BTT funds and conducts scientific research, and then applies the findings to conservation and education. For example, new knowledge about juvenile tarpon and their habitats has led to a juvenile tarpon habitat restoration program. And research about the effects of catch-and-release fishing on bonefish has led to an important education campaign—Best Handling Practices for Catch-and-Release Fishing.

Why does this matter to redfish, the focus of this book? Because much of what we learn about bonefish, tarpon, and permit, and the conservation strategies that result, is also applicable to redfish. The Best Practices for Catch-and-Release, for example, are also applicable to redfish. And BTT's pursuit of habitat conservation and restoration helps redfish as well—tarpon and redfish in the Everglades, bonefish and redfish in the Florida Keys.

At BTT we have learned that, just like in human medicine, proactive care is most effective. And much of this proactive care needs to come from recreational fisherman—from getting involved in conservation and joining conservation groups like BTT. So please enjoy Chico's book—he is after all one of the best in the business—but also take Chico's advice and get involved in conservation.

Tom Davidson
Chairman
Bonefish & Tarpon Trust

About Bonefish & Tarpon Trust

Bonefish & Tarpon Trust is a nonprofit, science-based conservation organization dedicated to ensuring that bonefish, tarpon, and permit populations, and the fisheries they support, remain healthy and helping to restore the fisheries that have declined. BTT accomplishes this mission by funding conservation-focused research; working with local, national, and regional resource management agencies to improve regulations to protect these fisheries; and funding and conducting education of anglers and the public. BTT uses scientific findings to advocate for fisheries conservation and works to ensure coastal habitats used by bonefish, tarpon, and permit are protected. For more information, www.BTT.org. ■

International Game Fish Association (IGFA)

Like to fish? Then get involved.

We anglers all want the same things: more fish and the ability to pursue them. However, if you are passionate about fishing, it's important that you understand what's happening in your fisheries and find ways to participate.

One way to accomplish this is to be a member of a recreational fishing conservation organization, such as the International Gamefish Association (IGFA). Since 1939, the IGFA has played an active role in fisheries management worldwide. This means that in addition to being the world's keeper of fishing records, such as Chico's 12-pound tippet redfish record, the IGFA is also constantly working to ensure that our fisheries are healthy.

Stephen Fernández taking all the time needed to put the redfish back in its world.

Currently, the IGFA has several projects that are geared to help ensure that redfish, and other species, get the protection they need. The IGFA weighs in on state fisheries management actions that affect redfish to represent the recreational angling community. We are also working on alternative methods to help collect recreational catch data, which in turn helps fisheries managers do a better job in managing fish such as redfish. However, managing gamefish directly may not be enough. Ensuring that there are ample amounts of forage species to feed redfish is also very important. As such, the IGFA is currently working with other groups to highlight the need for better forage fish management around the country and particularly in Florida.

These days, the annual membership fee for the IGFA costs about half of what a new fly line costs. In becoming a member, you not only become part of one of the world's oldest and most venerable recreational fishing organizations, you are also helping support an organization that works hard to ensure we have abundant redfish populations, as well as the other species that we like to fish for.

Jason Schratwieser
IGFA Conservation Director

Coastal Conservation Association—*United in Conservation*

Anglers are optimistic by nature. We are great believers in what is possible every time we cast a fly or lure. We are driven to prepare and practice and plan every last detail. We may not catch a single fish, but great hope rides on every effort; a fervent belief that something good is about to happen accompanies every cast. This combination of diligence and optimism is what makes recreational anglers such effective stewards of our marine resources.

In 1977, hope for conservation was a little hard to find on the Texas coast, even among recreational fishermen. Years of intense commercial pressure had driven redfish and seatrout to the brink. A group of fourteen anglers met in a Houston tackle shop and decided that something had to be done to improve not just the management of those two species, but also attitudes toward marine resources in general.

The spirit of conservation and stewardship of the "Save the Redfish" campaign swept across the entire Gulf Coast. By 1985 Gulf-state chapters had formed from Texas to Florida. By decade's end, state chapters were founded through the mid-Atlantic region, and by the early 90s, development of the New England state chapters was completed to address state and national issues as a united Coastal Conservation Association. Through CCA's efforts, gill netting for redfish has been outlawed in most Gulf and Atlantic waters, and gamefish status has further protected them.

As American jurist Oliver Wendell Holmes once said, "Greatness is not in where we stand, but in what direction we are moving. We must sail sometimes with the wind, and sometimes against it, but sail we must, and not drift, nor lie at anchor." That statement effectively sums up the evolution of CCA into the national, grassroots organization that it is today. The battle against wasteful commercial fishing practices suddenly cast a harsh light on many others. Our message of the wise, sustainable use of marine resources appealed to tens of thousands of anglers in states all along the Gulf and Atlantic coasts.

That CCA is such an effective organization is due entirely to the relentless effort and commitment of our members. Becoming a member of CCA does not end with the mailing of a check. CCA members fuel the conservation agenda for their states by organizing banquets and other fundraisers. The funds they raise stay in their states, and are ultimately used to enhance and improve the condition of local marine resources and expand fishing opportunities.

We could paint a glowing picture of how far we have come in less than forty years, but more important is what lies over the horizon. Our oceans, bays, and estuaries face new threats every day, and we will have to protect our gains with vigilance. But we should not lose sight of the fact that we also live in a world of great opportunity. CCA will continue to fight for the health and conservation of our marine resources for future generations, and we will do so with diligence and optimism.

At CCA, united in conservation, we always believe that we can make good things happen. To learn more about us, you can call 1-800-201-FISH, visit www.joincca.org, or write to the Coastal Conservation Association at 6919 Portwest, Suite 100, Houston, TX 77024.

Ted Venker
Coastal Conservation
Association

Every angler I know wants to see a scene like this one: lots of redfish tailing in a healthy environment. But for this to continue, and to improve on the areas where this is no longer the case, we need to support the organizations that are doing something about this problem. This is the most important message in my book. I help all I can, so please do the same. SCOTT SOMMERLATTE

International Federation of Fly Fishers

Chico Fernández is well known for his writing and lectures on the subject of saltwater fly fishing and is a strong advocate for conservation. He also is a long-standing member of the International Federation of Fly Fishers (IFFF) and serves on the Board of Directors of the Florida Council of the IFFF. I therefore was delighted to receive an invitation from him to write this brief message for his new book about redfish and tell you a little about the conservation activities of the IFFF and why you should consider joining Chico and our organization to support conservation of redfish and other fisheries around the world.

The IFFF will soon celebrate its 50th anniversary and from its beginning has recognized that conservation of our wetland and fishery resources is fundamental to our present and future enjoyment of fly fishing. We have for many years advocated catch-and-release fishing, use of barbless hooks, and safe handling of fish by all fisherman. And we recently played a key role in supporting adoption of new rules that designated bonefish and tarpon as catch-and-release species in Florida because of their high economic and recreational value to our members from around the world. We also have supported regulations in Florida that allow reasonable "take" of redfish for the table, while managing redfish in healthy and robust populations for those who choose to fish for the species with artificial flies and release them safely for others to enjoy. The IFFF maintains a National Conservation Committee with members who serve on several steering committees with agencies to assist them in the development of biologically sound plans for managing fisheries and their habitats collaboratively across state and other political boundaries. Our primary focus is sound biology as a basis for management, allocation of harvest among all commercial and recreational users, and recognition that the many aspects of recreational fly fishing is of high economic importance to our members and the economy.

It is an honor to contribute these comments for this fellow "Chico" who has done so much for fly fishing. You are encouraged to join Chico and become a member of the IFFF by visiting www.fedflyfishers.org and support our conservation efforts for redfish and other species, and help preserve fly fishing for future generations.

Tom H. Logan
Certified Wildlife Biologist
VP of Conservation, FL Council IFFF
Senior Advisor for Conservation, IFFF

Acknowledgments

Like most anglers, I started fly fishing by trying to catch a fish with a fly rod. Then, it was trying to catch many fish. That followed by trying to catch a big fish, and soon the biggest fish—a world record even. Somewhere along the line, I noticed that my outlook kept changing. I started to pay more attention to the different environments fly fishing was taking me to, and the solitude of being "out there." But eventually I realized that nothing is more important than the many friends I've been lucky to meet over a lifetime of fly fishing. And I am very aware, that in one degree or another, I've learned from every one of them.

Now this book is a long one, and I've procrastinated on it for many years, yet many friends kept helping me with their time and encouragement, contributing in many different ways. I shall not forget that they did not give up on me. So I want to thank them now.

Friends who contributed to this book in one way or another are:

Tim Borski, well-known artist, fly tier, fly fisherman, and snake catcher. Tim has a preference for fishing reds in muddy waters, so I got great information on the big bulky flies he loves to use, and the super close-up approaches that are needed in low visibility.

Ray Box, for the use of his fishing camp in Arroyo, Texas, where we had such great fishing wading and taking photos for the book. Thanks.

Eddie Carman, Biscayne Rods, Miami, Florida—an angler, fly fisherman, and rod builder—for his help on custom rod designs and building me custom push poles for skiffs and canoes.

Cathi Comar, executive director of The American Museum of Fly Fishing, Manchester, Vermont, for her efforts in the fly-fishing history of redfish.

Marshall Cutchin, founder and publisher of MidCurrent, for much information on tackle, skiffs, and publishing advice.

Corbett Davis, a friend, master jeweler, and fly fisher, who took me for the first time to fish the big reds in Louisiana and Pensacola, Florida. And for contributing photos and always helping promote my work.

Mike Duckworth, Islamorada, Florida, for the great fishing trip in Brunswick, Georgia, to fish reds in the tangle of spartina grass.

Norman Duncan, a friend since 1959, a great fly fisher and light-tackle angler, inventor of the Duncan Loop and the Outside Fly, was one of the early influences, and one of the members of the Four Musketeers.

Vince Maggio, a jazz pianist, fly fisher, and fly tier, who has great passion and love for the redfish, for all the info, especially fishing them is super shallow water, and contributing several redfish fly patterns.

Jorge Martinez, a close friend, well-known marine artist, fly fisherman, and fly tier, for contributing numerous drawings and paintings for the book, and many redfish fly patterns. Jorge is mostly responsible for getting me to start using clear floating fly lines for sight-casting a few years back. We also share a love for Cuban cuisine. *Gracias*, Jorge.

Jimbo Meador, great angler and fly fisher, for expert info and know-how about fishing on kayaks and surfboards.

Sandy Moret, of Florida Keys Outfitters, an old friend of forty years, is one of the great fly fishers, especially sight-casting. He also runs the famous Florida Keys Fly Fishing School, where I have taught with him and others for over twenty-five years. I've learned a lot from teaching the school and from Sandy. His encouragement on this book was endless. Also encouraging and helpful was Sandy's wife, avid fly fisher and expert on outdoor clothing, Sue Moret. Finally, thanks to both your guys for contributing images.

Kristen Mustad, Nautilus Reels, Miami, Florida—a fly fisherman, reel designer, and friend—for the info on fly reel manufacturing and especially sealed drag designs.

David Olson, of Fly Shop of Miami, a great friend, fly fisherman, tournament caster, and fly tier, who has fished for reds in most of Florida and elsewhere for over twenty years. David's input on redfish, tackle, and flies has been and continues to be invaluable. He has been a great supporter of this book, helping me immensely and even participating in the editing. Besides, we also share a love for jazz, rock and roll, and Cuban cuisine.

Flip Pallot is one of my oldest friends. We met in early 1959 when I arrived in Miami. I literally could write a book of the stuff we did in those early days—and that's just the stuff that's printable. He is a member of the Four Musketeers, with Norman Duncan, John Emery, and myself. He is truly a great fly fishermen, author, captain, hunter, archer, and very knowledgeable on small crafts and canoes. Besides the love of fly fishing and the outdoors, we also share a great love for canoes and Cuban music. What we've learned from each other goes way beyond redfish and fly fishing. I'm delighted that he wrote the foreword and contributed some important photos.

And Flip's wife, Diane, also a fly fisher, has also been a great supporter and often helped in photo sessions. I love fishing with her, but beware; if there are manatees or dolphin around, she will often jump in the water to join them for a while, and they always love it. Flip and I always stay in the boat.

Jeffrey Pill, a fly fisherman and accomplished outdoors film producer. Jeff has done his best throughout the years to help me and my career, often when it wasn't easy. Thanks.

Steve Rajeff, head rod designer for G. Loomis, who is many times a world distance and accuracy casting champion, and who has spent a lifetime designing rods. A friend of many years, he gave me great input about rods for sight-casting and accuracy casting. We also share the love for jazz.

Tim Rajeff, of Rajeff Sports, is a great tournament caster and fly fisherman, and he's very knowledgeable on fly-fishing tackle. I got great input on rods and fly lines, especially as it pertained to sight-casting.

Raz Reid, tackle rep and great fly fisherman, has been a great help in my business, often helping me get tackle needed for this book, and he gave me the right contact to fish reds in the North Carolina area.

Bruce Richards, of Scientific Anglers, is an old friend and great fly fisherman and technical fly caster who really understands the dynamic of a cast and the anatomy of a fly line. His input on fly lines was great and extensive, as I knew it would be.

Jason Schratwieser, Conservation Director for IGFA, for his info on reds as a marine biologist, and poling time way back in the Everglades to produce photos.

Jerry Siem, head rod designer for Sage Rods, a great angler and caster who understands rod design as well as anyone today. He had great input on rod selection for sight-casting up close and long.

Mike Wilson, of Angler's Edge in Houston, Texas, is an avid fly fisherman, with a great preference for redfish. He has facilitated numerous red fishing trips to different places in Texas for me to study, experience, and photograph. We also share the love of fine dining, of which Mike is the expert.

Dr. Lloyd Wruble is a fly fisherman and an expert of the backwaters of the Everglades. Lloyd can go places in the Glades most anglers couldn't get out of with a GPS, literally. Through him I've seen the world of the redfish in areas so remote, I would never have been able to go by myself, let alone get back to the dock. Also, I want to thank both Lloyd and his wife, Rae, for the invaluable help with Marilyn's health issues during the writing of this book. I have no way to express the enormous gratitude I feel. Thank you guys.

Joan Wulff, a friend of many years, is one of the great fly fishers and casters. She is a true expert on the mechanics of fly casting, which she can do with ease, even at the young age of 87. Joan is an inspiration. She was a great help on the subject of pinpoint accuracy.

Other friends that had input in one way or another while teaching at the Florida Keys Fly Fishing School were Diana Rudolph, Captain Tim Klein, Captain Craig Brewer, Captain Paul Tejera, and Captain Drew Moret. Thank you.

A great fishing guide can offer a very insightful perspective on the character and behavior of a redfish and the tackle to use, mainly because their experience is based on thousands of days on the water. Most of the guides mentioned below are good friends.

Captain Richard Black, Islamorada, Florida, for great fishing trips, allowing for lots of photos taken, and good info on reds, on big seatrout, and on big shark, all within the redfish's world. Cool.

Captain William "Bou" Bosso, Islamorada, Florida, for great fishing trips where we took some nice reds, and for the information.

Captain John Bottko, Jacksonville, Florida, for the days fishing the surf with me after reds, and the info on that environment. Also for the trips wading the spartina grass after reds and sheepshead.

Captain Tad Burke, Islamorada, Florida, for the fishing trips, the long photo-shooting session, and the info on different salinities and water temperatures.

Captain Jon Cave, Orlando, Florida, for the great info on using a spoon-type fly, the Wobbler, in this case on redfish, and for the many Wobbler samples.

Captain Fuzzy Davis, Hilton Head, South Carolina, for exposing me to the redfish fishery in that area. It was under 40 degrees, but we caught redfish on fly, and I learned a lot about that area.

Captain Dave Denkert, Islamorada, Florida, for thirty years of friendship and fishing trips, the huge amount of information you've shared with me, and the great insight on the redfish's character. Also for info on tripletail. And to Deve's wife Linda, for being such a great host during the many overnight stays at your home.

Captain Greg Dini, New Orleans, Louisiana, for the insight on reds and their ways, in mid-Florida and Louisiana.

Captain Brian Esposito, Fort Lauderdale, Florida, for the redfish info in Chokoloskee and Florida Bay.

Captain Rob Fordyce, Homestead, Florida, for all the great and often different info on redfish, their ways, and how to find them. Also on ways to approach different flats. I've always enjoyed our technical discussions on sight-casting, tackle, and leader formulas. Looking forward to more. Thanks.

Captain Eric Herstedt, Homestead, Florida, for good insight on tailing reds and a different presentation to them.

Captain Steve Huff, Everglades City, Florida, for more than forty years of fishing and friendship. I've learned a ton of information from you in all those years, not just on redfish, but on snook, permit, and many other species. My son, Stephen, and I pole more now and run the boat less because of you. And we are catching more fish because of it. He also helped take lots of photos for this book. Thanks.

Captain Mark Krowka, Islamorada, Florida, for great and detailed information on the red's ways, and for all the great fly samples.

Captain Lance Ledet and the late Captain Leland Ledet, of Dulac Charters, Dulac, Louisiana, for the many trips out of your camp, for the great hospitality and friendship, and for teaching me about the ways of those exciting big reds.

Captain Chuck Naiser, of Rockport, Texas, for the great fishing trips we've had, often taking a few dozen reds in a day, and exposing me to the great variety of settings in the Rockport area.

Captain Dale Perez, Islamorada, Florida, for the fishing trips, the info on the redfish flats, and the patience to let me take all the photos I needed.

Captain Jared Raskob, Islamorada, Florida, for the great info on reds, but especially the highly specialized methods of sight-casting to sheepshead, which can be tougher than permit in South Florida, at least for me.

Captain C. A. Richardson, Tampa, Florida, for the redfish info on the Tampa area and your use of long leaders for tough redfish, but mostly for info on tackle and leader construction.

Captain Nick Sassic, Titusville, Florida, for the insight on red behavior in Mosquito Lagoon and the Indian River during the hot summer months. And the ways of the big seatrout with a fly rod.

Captain Gary Taylor, Slidell, Louisiana, for the great and detailed information on the big reds in Louisiana.

Captain Andy Thompson, Miami, Florida, for a great fishing trip to Flamingo and good insight on the reds in South Florida and Texas.

Captain John Turcot, Titusville, Florida, for the trips to Mosquito Lagoon and Indian River in the super shallow waters and the redfish info for the area.

Captain Scott Warner, Savannah, Georgia, for showing me the oceanside flats of Savannah, where we took some nice-size reds in a different and fun environment. And for the fly patterns of the area.

Taking great images of the redfish's world requires that you not only be an accomplished photographer and have a good eye for composition, but also that you understand the redfish and its environment. It's no wonder that the photographers mentioned below are all fly fishers.

Joel Arrington, photographer and outdoorsman, for facilitating the trip to North Carolina that produced my world-record redfish thirty years ago. And for taking the wonderful image of me with the big red. It was a memorable trip, so thanks, Joel.

George Contorakes, friend and professional photographer, for taking so much time to shoot the boat-to-boat images.

Angela Fernández, my mother and friend, for taking the photo of the first redfish I ever caught, in 1952, and for taking other fishing photos of me, always with her Rolleiflex. She was not a fly fisher, but she loved to see me fly cast.

Pat Ford, great photographer, fly fisherman, and friend, for the many images contributed, both above and underwater. And for the help during the many trips we've taken together.

Markus Haugg, a photographer with a great sense of composition, immensely knowledgeable in black and white images, a fly fisherman, and close friend. Thank you for the great images and for taking time to travel with me to gather more photos.

Woody Huband, professional photographer, for the photos in the spartina grass and especially for the tough photos on the beach with strong winds and giant waves. It was quite an adventure.

Brad Miller, a brilliant photographer, from view cameras to digital, a fly fisherman, and a friend. Thank you for the great images and the travel time.

Captain Scott Sommerlatte, Texas, for the fishing trips, redfish ways in Texas, and the great photography.

A great fly tier has to be, by necessity, a good fly fisherman. You can learn the mechanics of tying the fly, but you have to be an angler and have an understanding on how the fly will swim in the water to get the proportions right. That is why all the tiers mentioned below are also avid fly fishermen, and also friends, by the way.

Captain Steve Bailey, Fort Myers, Florida, for the many fly samples and how you fish them.

Captain Chris Dean, Miami, Florida, for years of fishing together, supplying the history of several flies, and tying many of the flies in this book and the flies I often fish.

Patrick L. Dorsy, Miami, Florida, for supplying samples of the Dorsy's Kwam pattern and the Dorsy's Red Slappa' pattern. Great fly patterns.

Frank Oblak, for contributing flies to this book and for years of tying many fly patterns that I currently fish. Thanks, Frank.

Enrico Puglisi, for the many samples he has sent me for this book, and for my personal fishing, especially the great Spawning Shrimp patterns. They're a personal favorite for reds, and for bonefish.

In the actual making of this book I want to thank:

Dr. Aaron Adams, marine biologist, and a fly-fishing friend, with whom I've fished many times, for writing the first four chapters of this book and for contributing many photographs. It was great working with you.

And Judith Schnell, my publisher, for her warm encouragement, help, and advice in organizing and producing this book.

Janice Goldklang, a very experienced publisher, for giving me publishing advice and encouragement in the making of this book.

Stephen Fernández, my son and favorite fishing partner, who started fishing with me at age 6, and fly-fishing at age 11, and is now husband to Kelly and father of my two granddaughters, Alyson and Avery. Thank you for taking the time of what is now a very busy and meaningful life to help me with this book. For traveling, poling my Waterman skiff and canoes, taking photos instead of fishing, and so much more. But mostly for the many weekly calls closely following the progress of the book, and my life in general. And, for simply being you. Thank you, son.

And a very special thanks to Chris and Wendi Peterson and the whole gang at Hell's Bay Boatworks, Titusville, Florida, and Chas MacDonald, Al Perkinson, Dave Bulthuis, and the whole gang at Costa Sunglasses for your constant support and encouragement, especially through the rough times, which has meant a world to me.

Finally, it occurs to me that after so many years in making this book, I am bound to forget someone important. No matter how hard I try, I'll miss someone special. If this happens, I want you to know that I am truly sorry, and want to thank you for your help.

—Chico Fernández

I thank Jon Lucy (Virginia) and Spud and Chris Woodward (Georgia) for information on redfish diets.

—Aaron J Adams, PhD

Bibliography

Adams AJ. *Fisherman's Coast: An Angler's Guide to Marine Warm-Water Gamefish and Their Habitats.* Mechanicsburg, PA: Stackpole Books; 2004.

Adams DH, Tremain DM. Association of large juvenile redfish, *Sciaenops ocellatus*, with an estuarine creek on the Atlantic coast of Florida. *Environmental Biology of Fishes*. 2000; 58: 183–194.

Baltz DM, Fleeger JW, Rakocinski CF, McCall JN. Food, density, and microhabitat: factors affecting growth and recruitment potential of juvenile salt marsh fishes. *Environmental Biology of Fishes*. 1998; 53: 89–103.

Bass RJ, Avault JWJ. Food habits, length-weight relationship, condition factor, and growth of juvenile redfish, *Sciaenops ocellata*, in Louisiana. *Transactions of the American Fisheries Society*. 1975; 104(1): 35–45.

Beckman DW, Wilson CA, Stanley AL. Age and growth of redfish, *Sciaenops ocellatus*, from offshore waters of the northern Gulf of Mexico. *Fishery Bulletin*. 1988; 87: 17–28.

Boothby RN, Avault JWJ. Food habits, length-weight relationship, and condition factor of the redfish (*Sciaenops ocellata*) in southeastern Louisiana. *Transactions of the American Fisheries Society*. 1971; 2: 290–295.

Collins MR, Smith TJI, Jenkins WE, Denson MR. Small marine reserves may increase escapement of red drum. *Fisheries*. 2002; 27(2): 20–24.

Denson MR, Jenkins WE, Woodward AG, Smith TJI. Tag-reporting levels for redfish (*Sciaenops ocellatus*) caught by anglers in South Carolina and Georgia estuaries. *Fishery Bulletin*. 2002; 100: 35–41.

Desfosse JCP, Merriner JPD, et al. 2002 Review of the fishery management plan for red drum (*Sciaenops ocellatus*). Atlantic States Marine Fisheries Commission; 2002: 12.

Doerzbacher JF, Green AW, Matlock GC, Osburn HR. A temperature compensated von Bertalanffy growth model for tagged red drum and black drum in Texas bays. *Fisheries Research*. 1988; 6: 135–152.

Geary BW, Rooker JR, et al. Utilization of salt marsh shorelines by newly settled Sciaenids in a Texas estuary. *Gulf and Caribbean Research*. 2001; 13: 37–49.

Herzka SZ, Holt SA, Holt GJ. Characterization of settlement patterns of redfish (*Sciaenops ocellatus*) larvae to estuarine nursery habitat: a stable isotope approach. *Marine Ecology Progress Series*. 2002; 226: 143–156.

Holt SA, Kitting CL, Arnold CR. Distribution of young red drums among different sea-grass meadows. *Transactions of the American Fisheries Society*. 1983; 112: 267–271.

Lassuy DR. Species profiles: life histories and environmental requirements (Gulf of Mexico): Gulf menhaden. U.S. Fish and Wildlife Service, Division of Biological Services, FWS/OBS-82/11.2. U.S. Army Corps of Engineers, TR EL-82-4; 1983: 22

Mercer LP. A biological and fisheries profile of redfish, *Sciaenops ocellatus*. North Carolina Department of Natural Resources and Community Development. Special Scientific Report No. 41; 1984.

Murphy MD, Taylor RG. Reproduction, growth, and mortality of red drum (*Sciaenops ocellatus*) in Florida waters. *Fishery Bulletin*. 1990; 88: 531–542.

———. Direct validation of ages determined for adult red drums from otolith sections. *Transactions of the American Fisheries Society*. 1991; 120: 267–269.

Music JL, Pafford JM. Population dynamics and life history aspects of major marine sportfishes in Georgia's coastal waters. Georgia Department of Natural Resources. Contribution Series Number 38; 1984.

Oh C, Ditton RB. Specialization differences in anglers' preferences for redfish (*Sciaenops ocellatus*) harvest regulations. Proceedings of the 57th Gulf and Caribbean Fisheries Institute. 2005; 57: 14.

Overstreet RM, Heard RW. Food of the redfish, *Sciaenops ocellata*, from Mississippi Sound. *Gulf Research Reports*. 1978; 6(2): 131–135.

Patterson HM, McBride RS, Julien N. Population structure of redfish (*Sciaenops ocellatus*) as determined by otolith chemistry. *Marine Biology*. 2004; 144: 855–862.

Perez-Dominguez R, Holt GJ. Effects of nursery environmental cycles on larval redfish (*Sciaenops ocellatus*) growth and survival. Marine Science Institute, University of Texas, Austin; 2002: 5.

Peters KM, McMichael RHJ. Early life history of the red drum, *Sciaenops ocellatus* (Pisces: Sciaenidae), in Tampa Bay, Florida. Estuarine Research Federation. 1987; 92–107.

Porch CE, Wilson CA, et al. A new growth model for redfish (*Sciaenops ocellatus*) that accommodates seasonal and ontogenic changes in growth rates. *Fishery Bulletin*. 2002; 100: 149–152.

Reagan RE. Species profiles: life histories and environmental requirements of coastal fishes and invertebrates (Gulf of Mexico)—redfish. U.S. Fish and Wildlife Service Biological Report 82(11.36). U.S. Army Corps of Engineers, TR EL-82-4; 1985: 16.

Rogers SG, Van Den Avyle, MJ. Species profiles: life histories and environmental requirements of coastal fishes and invertebrates (South Atlantic)—Atlantic menhaden. U.S. Fish and Wildlife Service, Division of Biological Services FWS/OBS-82/11.11. U.S. Army Corps of Engineers, TR EL-82-4; 1983: 20.

Rooker JR, Holt GJ, Holt SA. Vulnerability of newly settled red drum (*Sciaenops ocellatus*) to predatory fish: is early-life survival enhanced by seagrass meadows? *Marine Biology*. 1998; 131: 145–151.

Rooker JR, Holt SA, Holt GJ, Fuiman LA. Spatial and temporal variability in growth, mortality, and recruitment potential of postsettlement redfish, *Sciaenops ocellatus*, in a subtropical estuary. *Fishery Bulletin*. 1999; 97: 581–590.

Ross JL, Stevens TM. Life history and population dynamics of redfish (*Sciaenops ocellatus*) in North Carolina waters. Morehead City, NC, Division of Marine Fisheries; 1992: 129

Ross JL, Stevens TM, Vaughan DS. Age, growth, mortality, and reproductive biology of red drums in North Carolina waters. *Transactions of the American Fisheries Society*. 1995; 124: 37–54.

Scharf FS. Patterns in abundance, growth, and mortality of juvenile red drum across estuaries on the Texas coast with implications for recruitment and stock enhancement. *Transactions of the American Fisheries Society*. 2000; 129: 1207–1222.

Scharf FS, Schlicht KK. Feeding habits of redfish (*Sciaenops ocellatus*) in Galveston Bay, Texas: seasonal diet variation and predator-prey size relationships. *Estuaries*. 2000; 23(1): 128–139.

Seyoum S, Tringali MD, Bert TM, McElroy D, Stokes R. An analysis of genetic population structure in redfish, *Sciaenops ocellatus*, based on mtDNA control region sequences. *Fishery Bulletin*. 2000; 98: 127–138.

Sosin M, Clark J. *Through the Fish's Eye: An Angler's Guide to Gamefish Behavior*. New York: Harper & Row; 1973.

Stunz GW, Minello TJ. Habitat-related predation on juvenile wild-caught and hatchery-reared redfish *Sciaenops ocellatus* (Linnaeus). *Journal of Experimental Marine Biology and Ecology*. 2001; 260: 13–25.

Stunz GW, Minello TJ, Levin PS. Growth of newly settled red drum *Sciaenops ocellatus* in different estuarine habitat types. *Marine Ecology Progress Series*. 2002; 238: 227–236.

Thomas RG. Hook-release mortality of red drum (*Sciaenops ocellatus*) and spotted seatrout (*Cynoscion nebulosus*) caught with four hook/bait combinations. Grand Isle, LA, State of Louisiana Department of Wildlife and Fisheries; 1996: 3

Ward R, Blandon IR, et al. Comparisons of critical thermal maxima and minima of juvenile redfish (*Sciaenops ocellatus*) from Texas and North Carolina. *Northeast Gulf Science*. 1993; 13(1): 23–28.

Wenner CD. Red drum: natural history and fishing techniques in South Carolina. Charleston, SC, South Carolina Department of Natural Resources. 1992: 40.

Whitehurst A, Robinette HR. Tolerance of juvenile red drum (*Sciaenops ocellatus*) to rapidly decreasing water temperatures. *Journal of the World Aquaculture Society*. 1994; 25(2): 225–229.

Wulff J. *Joan Wulff's Fly-Casting Accuracy*. Guilford, CT: Lyons Press; 1997.

Index